# BLESSED ARE
# THE MEEK

# BLESSED ARE THE MEEK

*A Novel about St. Francis of Assisi*

BY

## ZOFIA KOSSAK

*Translated by Rulka Langer*

Roy Publishers, New York

1944

# CONTENTS

CONTENTS

## PART TWO

# BLESSED ARE
# THE MEEK

# PART ONE

---

# 1.

# A New Century Begins

ALTHOUGH TWO HUNDRED YEARS HAD PASSED SINCE AT THE TURN OF THE millennium the entire world trembling awaited its doom, every time a century came to a close mankind once more lived through that old pang of terror. The end of a century! The very words were fraught with vague forebodings; a day of eternity was banging the door behind it. Not even a day, for were not people wont to sing: "A thousand years shall pass before thine eyes even as yesterday!" A thousand years, mind you; what then did a century amount to? No more than one hour. But even an hour has its importance. An hour that goes by, never to return. An hour gone that brings closer the day of reckoning.

The last years of each expiring century and the first years of the new one were always full of vague premonitions and endless conjectures. Everything that happened was believed to hold prophetic import. Each event was interpreted to mean that the crops would be good or bad, the years to come, fortunate or unfortunate. People would call to mind what their grandfathers had told them of similar happenings and their influence upon the future. And as though all of nature itself shared in human apprehension, multiple signs would appear upon the earth and in the sky; the sun would grow dim or take the shape of a cross, after sunset red clouds would roll over the skies, the moon split asunder, and at times even the dead would rise from the graveyard and visit the dwelling places of the living.

The critical years which divided the Twelfth from the Thirteenth Centuries—from 1195 to 1205—were not free from similar fears. Indeed everything seemed to indicate that the times to come would be marked by disaster, conflagrations and horror.

To be sure at the threshold of the new century death had removed Henry IV, the terrible Hohenstaufen, that enemy of Italy and of the Holy See who had so heavily oppressed all of Central Europe. To be sure, his minor son had been put by a pious mother, Constance, under the tutelage of the Pope. But what good would that do since it was already whispered that according to prophecies this Frederick II, still in his nonage, was to become the future Antichrist foretold by the Revelation of St. John?

Even apart from that one might easily have assumed that the Antichrist had already been pacing the world and sowing the seeds of evil, such was the unrest in human hearts. The rich and the learned as well as the simple and the poor felt it alike. The old feudal order which had lasted practically unchanged since the fall of the Roman Empire suddenly had begun to totter and break down. People no longer believed that whatever was good for their forefathers was good enough for them, and such faith, as anyone knows, is the cornerstone of all well balanced order. Few were contented with their lot. People had torn themselves away from the soil from which once they used to grow like trees, and now wandered about, restlessly craving a better lot, better conditions, a better and more perfect faith. That faith they craved above all else. The Roman Church, never so far judged by anyone, ruling masterfully over all souls, putting her priests, monks and bishops above all other estates, suddenly found herself face to face with stern judges who accused her of betraying Christ the Lord. Those judges, strange to say, came for the most part from among the common people. When the nobles wrangled with the clergy it was over rights and revenues. The common people were concerned with principles. Sects calling for the return to early Christian simplicity sprang up like mushrooms after rain.

From the purely spiritual domain this unrest spread to learning and social customs. In learning people craved new horizons, in social customs new freedoms. The old order was doing its best to defend itself against these assaults. It fortified with strict regulations the learning dispensed at the universities: it mercilessly persecuted anything that could be classed as vice, heresy or witchcraft. Mankind thrust upward with an impetus never known theretofore or after. It shot skyward with the steeples of its cathedrals, it clamored for great deeds. The old order did not understand this urge. It crushed it and throttled it, until, abandoning its upward trend, humanity waited until it found once more the joy of living in the earthly glory of the Renaissance.

This, however, was to come much later. Now there was only restlessness, unconscious, yet throbbing. Restlessness and fear of what the coming century would bring.

It was these things that Pope Innocent III pondered during sleepless nights. Bitter were his thoughts. They gnawed at his strength, sapped his body to such an extent that the Holy Father, though still in his forties, often felt like an old man nearing the end of his days.

He was crushed by his responsibility for the fate of the Church, for the fate of the entire world which the Church was supposed to guide. He felt small and unequal to the task. In vain did friends and foes alike maintain that he had accomplished things that were great and seemingly impossible. He had restored the dignity and the power of the Papal authority in Rome and of the Church States. He was the master, while his predecessors had been forced time and again to flee, to hide in the castles of friendly barons or to bribe the Roman mob for permission to enter their own capital! He had expelled the loathsome Germans; he had set Italy free again. This he had done. But all this was nothing; he yearned to accomplish infinitely more. With the passion of a political genius he dreamed of converting the constantly warring European nations into one body of great Christian States living in peace, recognizing the successor of the Fisherman as their arbiter and the highest mediator on earth. He dreamed of abolishing all class differences and of securing prosperity to all Christians. To attain this aim he craved power, greedily, rapaciously. Power and strength. In his eyes secular independence was the indispensable basis for the spiritual freedom of the Church. He fought for it unceasingly. Had he only possessed it Jerusalem would not have fallen.

Jerusalem!

This was the most painful thorn, the running sore impossible to heal, the cause of sleepless nights and the secret, helpless tears absorbed by the cloth that covered his praying bench. Jerusalem! Recovered then lost again! Squandered, fallen Jerusalem!

Cursed be the century which allowed it to happen! Cursed be the year, the cursed year that brought the disaster! Let it be forgotten, wiped out, likened by history to the day of Abel's death, the day of the massacre of the Innocents, the year of the terrible plague that emptied Rome of its population! Let the men who allowed this disgrace to happen never know eternal rest! Let the elements rise against them, let evil spirits possess them—these men who let it come to pass!

Cursed be all of them who did not lay down their lives in the defense of the Holy Sepulchre! Cursed and cast away be the Christ's representative who was not able to drive them to it! Woe to them all on the Day of the Judgment!

Jerusalem was lost!

Staring blindly into the darkness of the night Innocent III lived for the hundredth time through the agony of shame and despair. He suffered for himself as well as for his predecessors. For the melancholy Gregory VIII who two months after his election died of despair at the news of Saladin's victory, and on his deathbed kept repeating: "Lord, Lord why has this befallen me?" For the patient Clement III who stubbornly prepared a new crusade and for that purpose reconciled the English with the French king, Pisa with Genoa. And last, and most bitterly —for himself.

From the moment he ascended the Pontiff's throne the recovery of the Holy Land had been his guiding star, his supreme goal. He had emptied the treasury to equip an army. He had stripped the Church of money. Holding his impetuous nature in check he had acted cautiously, deliberately. On the bench by his bedside still lay a large volume containing a detailed report on the cities, the people, the climate and other particulars of the Holy Land. It had been prepared at his request by the Patriarch of Jerusalem (in partibus infidelium) Aymar, nicknamed the Monk. After the untimely death of Aymar the unfinished report had been completed by his successor, Albert de Verceuil, and supplemented with notes concerning the strength, war tactics and character of the Saracens compiled by the Cardinals Soffredo and Pietro Capuano, who for many years had been Nuncios in the East. Everything had been foreseen, carefully prepared. This was not to be a blind venture into the unknown as once in Godfried's times, but a deliberately planned expedition. He had sent tidings from the Lateran summoning all Christians. And lo and behold the miracle had happened again, even as it had in Clermont a hundred years before. The old cry of "God wills it" had come to life again. Roads swarmed with men on foot and on horseback. A great army stood in readiness. Why, oh why, had he not personally taken its command? His heart had yearned for it but he could not, truly, he could not. Once he left Rome who could tell whether he would be allowed to return? And so he only gave the departing troops his blessing and stayed behind.

And on the way the Venetians had persuaded the Crusaders to strike at Byzantium instead of Jerusalem. . . .

They lured the greedy with tales of Greek riches, they convinced the honest, simple folks that the Greeks had always been the greatest obstacle to the recovery of the Holy Land and that once Byzantium was conquered Palestine would without fail be restored to Christendom. And so they had gone . . .

They scaled the until then unconquered walls of the "City guarded by God," they took possession of the town, they drove the Basileus away and proclaimed a Latin Empire. They gathered spoils richer than anything the world had ever seen. . . .

When the Holy Father Innocent III had heard of these doings he was beside himself with wrath and grief. He threatened the leaders with excommunication and ordered them to leave Byzantium at once and sail on to the Holy Land. He reminded them of their vows, he begged, he implored. All to no avail. Men had already tasted gold. . . .

That sly old man, Doge Dandolo, gathered and sent to Venice priceless treasures. He had removed from their pedestal the bronze horses of Alexander the Great, the work of artists from Chios which Nero had brought to Rome and Theodosius the Great had moved to Byzantium. He collected untold riches and made the Republic of St. Marc the mistress of the seas.

What the Venetians did not take was shared among the knights of Normandy, Italy and France. Almost overnight poor simple warriors found themselves richer than kings.

In the face of such fortunes, such dazzling possibilities, who could think of that poor, inhospitable, arid Holy Land? To Byzantium, to Byzantium! There lay treasures that were yours for the asking. There Emperor Baldwin of Flanders distributed free land and summoned all knights to come. The Greeks hated these new rulers; they hated them with a bitter passion. Surrounded with universal hatred the new Empire could have no future; it was an artificial creation, accidental, unnatural. Only a madman could believe that it would last. But people hurried there, heedless of everything. There was gold in Byzantium!

The Crusaders were not the only ones Byzantium attracted. The last defenders of the Holy Land, who hitherto had held on so heroically to that still free strip of shore, to those few coastal towns which were all that remained of the Kingdom of Jerusalem, these, too, left for Byzantium. Already before many had been lured away by Cyprus—now by this Latin Empire. Instead of gaining, the Holy Grave was losing defenders.

No wonder that the Holy Father's hair had turned white, and that his nights were sleepless and filled with bitterness. All the toil, all the pains gone to such a shameful end!

And what would happen next? For unperturbed, hindered by no one, al-Muzaan, the grandson of Saladin, was building a citadel on Mount Tabor, on the Holy Mountain of the Transfiguration. The torn walls of the old Basilica built by Helen would serve in the new construction. Less stone would have to be carried up the steep slopes by Christian captives who, under a ceaseless rain of whips, were painstakingly raising a citadel on the very spot where once the Apostles had said: "Lord, it is good for us to be here."

The Holy Father moaned in pain and beat his forehead against the rail of the praying bench. . . .

In such agony hour would drag after hour till dawn came. It was even worse when, mortally exhausted, Innocent fell asleep. Sleep would at once seize his soul in a whirlpool of mad dreams where, tangled in a weird dance, Doge Dandolo, Baldwin of Flanders, Sultan Malik al-Adil, Saracens, Crusaders and merchants circled unconcerned around the Holy Sepulchre while the Pope helplessly looked on. . . .

When daylight came this chief concern had to give way to lesser ones. Life had to go on, and regardless of what happened overseas each morn brought its own local cares and matters to be disposed of. Innocent III rose from his knees, rubbed his smarting eyes and sat to work. Thanks to a well-organized post he knew fairly accurately what was happening in the world. The Bishop of Paris informed him as to the latest moves of King Philip August. A clever Lord's Anointed that one; assiduous, never missing an opportunity to add new territories to his kingdom or enhance his authority. Withal, true to the tradition of all French kings, he had dismissed his lawful spouse who was virtuous but not comely and lived with a beautiful sinner, in this case Agnes of Meran, sister of the pious wife of the Silesian Prince, Henry the Bearded. And also according to tradition he was for that reason excommunicated from the Church. The Bishop of Paris was convinced, however, that the King, who so far had not seemed perturbed by the anathema, would probably now wish to reconcile himself with the Church in order to get his share of the Albigenses possessions. Who knows, he may even return to his wedded Ingelburg. . . .

The Holy Father made a wry face at the mention of Albigenses. This Crusade, no more than the other one, proceeded according to his wishes. Although he was in favor of using stern measures with heretics, as a fundamentally honest and just man he did not approve the high-handed manner in which Simon de Montort, a notoriously cruel and greedy man, led the Crusade against the Albigenses.

If only this severity had brought good results. But it did not. The number of heretics constantly increased. In addition to the Albigenses or, as they called themselves, "the clean ones," the Christian world was befouled by Beggars and Patarenes; Waldenses; the Poors from Lyon who demanded absolute poverty of the clergy; the Apostolic Brothers who considered themselves the sole followers of Christ; others who rejected the Holy Sacrament; Aymerites who denied the existence of reward and punishment, heaven and hell; loathsome sectarians headed by Carnonensis who maintained that the division of the sexes was the result of the original sin; Humiliants who, though still belonging to the Church, were already under suspicion, for, stern and proud, they vehemently attacked the clergy. It seemed as though only lately a half-wit had appeared in Assisi preaching life according to the teaching of Gospel. Those were dangerous precepts in the mouth of an irresponsible simpleton! Every day one heard of new sects. And what would become finally of the unity of the Church?

Innocent III, himself ascetic and by no means a fool, had realized long ago that often enough it was the Church herself who was to blame for these schisms. The accusations hurled at the monks and priests by the sectarians were for the most part more than justified. He fought this evil, he urged the clergy to completely reform their manner of living, he threatened with punishment—but the results were meager.

With a sigh he reached for other letters. He scanned the missive of the Archbishop of Gniezno, Kietlicz, containing some obscure complaints.

Bother, Poland! How hard it was to determine which one of these princes with their unpronounceable names and continual brawls was right: Leszek the White, Wladislaw the Spindle-legged, Mieszko of Ratibor, Odonic, Conrad or Henry the Bearded?

Each of these princes had an allied bishop who would present the claims of his master in a favorable light to the Holy See. And so the aspects of the Polish problem changed completely depending on who wrote about it; the vindictive, dour Kietlicz of Gniezno, the mild, learned Kadlubek of Cracow, Lawrence of Breslau or Arnold of Poznan.

As a result of their conflicting expostulations Innocent had lately issued a bull which reinstated the right of primogeniture. He did so moved by the memory of Wladislaw the Exiled who participated in the Second Crusade. As a result of this bull Mieszko of Ratibor, the oldest of the living Piasts, now sat on the Cracow throne. In no time, however, Kietlicz made it clear to the Pope that Mieszko was an old man with one foot in the grave and that his promotion was an intrigue of the Spindle-legged, the next in age, who thus worked for his own and not the Church's good. A dangerous man that Spindle-legged. He disregards Church orders, abuses the bishops, reserves for himself the right to grant beneficia and levy tributes from Church estates! No question but that the only one worth supporting is Leszek the White, meek, mild and manageable. One could at least expect that this prince would respect the rights of immunity, abolish the "ius spolii" and free the clergy from princely jurisdiction.

. . . Well, once the bull was issued it would be hard to retract it. . . .

The hotheaded and impulsive Innocent did not like the sight of his own mistakes, and at the mention of Poland he winced almost with the same distaste as at the mention of Albigenses.

Postponing his study of Kietlicz's griefs he turned to the report from England. There nothing new had happened lately. King John-Lackland continued his ineffective and treacherous rule. Since with his own hands he had strangled his youthful nephew Arthur of Brittany, his people had completely turned away from him. When he rode through the city his subjects did not look at his face. They only stared at his hands, at the fingers which had strangled Arthur's throat.

The Holy Father put the letter away and picked up another one. What was this? The Italian cities Pisa and Genoa, Florence and Milan,

Perugia and Assisi at war again! They fight mercilessly, blindly. They fight as though there was nothing more important in the world than their petty differences.

The Pope sighed and leaving his letters for the time, stepped into his chapel to pray. But praying brought him no peace. His heart was over-filled with bitter grief, distaste and contempt for people. The low worms! Gold, power, lust! Those are their gods; those are all they crave!

Thus appeared the beginning of the new century in the Christian world as seen through the eyes of Christ's vicar on earth. What of the same year, the 600th year of Hiddgra, in Mahomet's countries?

The great, the wise Sultan Saladin was dead. He had left behind seventeen children and as many nephews, cousins and kinsmen who pulled to pieces among themselves the vast inheritance of Islam's Unifier. One closely-knit country had fallen apart into ten small states engaged in unceasing warfare. The youngest brother of the dead Sultan, Malik al-Adil, a pliant, sly and self-controlled man, emerged unexpectedly on top of other heirs. He seized for himself the Damascus Sultanate and extended his protection over Egypt. Skillfully he took advantage of the discord among his nephews, imposed himself as their mediator, reconciling some, setting some against each other, according to whatever would serve his purpose best.

In his attitude towards the Christians Malik al-Adil did not share the hatred felt by his nephews and sons, al-Aldal, al-Muzaam or al-Kamil. Although he bore no likeness to the great Saladin he had acquired something of the latter's broad viewpoint. In fact, several years before he had toyed without distaste with the idea born in Richard Coeur de Lion's wild head that he should marry Joan, the English princess, and together with her rule over Jerusalem.

The plan miscarried—owing to Joan's refusal—and to this day Malik al-Adil, in spite of his cunning and his wide experience, could not understand the Franks. As had once been the case with Saladin they were a tantalizing riddle to him. Truly it would have been easier to fathom the nature of the desert wind than the nature of the Christians! They were unpredictable. With no apparent reason they would turn from indolence to heroism, from meanness to greatness, from cruelty to tenderness and kindness. One never knew what to expect of them. . . .

That was why although the Jerusalem Kingdom no longer existed—

those few coastal towns did not amount to anything—old Malik al-Adil could not help thinking that the struggle between the Crescent and the Cross had not yet come to an end, that the last word had not been said and that no one knew in what voice Allah would say it.

The Old Man of the Mountains, the ruler of the Ismailites, successor of the terrible Sinan and master of the inaccessible mountain nests Alamut, Kalat al-Kaf, Kadmus and Oleika which dominate the Syrian coast, wrathfully paced the rocky terrace of his abode. Like a vulture he stared down at the valley at his feet. Upon the walls and turrets of the castle leaning over a seemingly bottomless precipice, stood the motionless white-clad figures of his servants, his faithful "fidais," pliant tools ready to obey his slightest whim. Were he to point down there, they would without a moment's hesitation jump into the abyss. Were he to order them to go to Damascus and kill the Sultan they would do it at once; were he to change his mind and send them to Rome to murder the Holy Father instead they would do that, too. There was no protection against their sly, cruel daggers. That was why the Old Man of the Mountains was feared by all the world. That was why men who wanted to get rid of their foes, or of inconvenient witnesses, were ready to pay him fortunes. The Old Man of the Mountains would undertake any task. His disciples knew no distance, no impossibility. They were more cunning than serpents and had no fear of death. Certain to obtain paradise, the foretaste of which they found in the hemp brew called "hashish," they looked forward to death. Nothing could disturb their faith.

Thanks to them the Old Man of the Mountains was powerful and terrible. His mountain castles contained treasures greater than the Sultan's. There was no man in the world who would dare to cross him. . . .

Nevertheless he was downcast. Now he could no longer order his best men to jump into the abyss, as he once did to provoke Henry of Champagne's amazement. He had too few of them. And increasingly fewer. They were wearing out, like any perfect tools, and it was difficult to find new volunteers.

Besides to take grown men into the sect would serve no purpose; for it was well-nigh impossible to rid them completely of the instinct of self-preservation and the inborn fear of death. They ended by losing their minds—became useless. Those things had to be inoculated from childhood.

But how was one to procure children in a spot where women were not allowed? The Old Man of the Mountains, the dour lord of the Assassin's sect, recalled not without envy the fearless Saracen regiments of Mamelukes composed exclusively of the sons of Christian prisoners brought up from early childhood on Sultan's bread.

The Genoans, awed by the sudden prosperity of Venice, were determined to equal it at any price. Venice having taken possession of Byzantium, Genoa established close commercial contacts with Egypt and Moslem Syria. The podestas of Genoa were even ready to embrace Islam in secret provided Malik al-Kamil, the nephew of Saladin and ruler of Egypt, let them establish their own trading posts in Alexandria.

The huge golden reliquary containing the timber of the Holy Cross stood in the Sultan's dressing room among discarded odds and ends. Save for Innocent III hardly anyone ever thought of it. People had their own troubles.

And so the new century began.

# 2.

# The Inn of the Good Guardian

THE INN OF BAPTISTO VINO WAS USUALLY THE LAST STOP FOR TRAVELERS on their way to Rome. On clear days one could see the Eternal City from the hilltop and hear the ringing of its bells. The inn was named "The Good Guardian." Nearby stood a small roadside chapel, weather-beaten and black with age, and in it was a stone figure of the Madonna. From this chapel the inn of Vino took its name, for a great miracle had happened here once. An evildoer on his way to the gallows had stopped before the Madonna to say his last prayer, and lo and behold, before the eyes of everyone present the stone arm reached out to him, the stone hand grasped his fingers and held them till the wretch was pardoned. Ever since all the condemned had begged to be led this way, but the judges would not have it.

The inn was large and low, built of stone. In the littered courtyard hens ambled idly scratching in the horse dung. Two bony mules stood tied to the fence. Sabina, the landlady, round and squat, stepped out of the house, put her hands on her hips and looked around.

"Tina! Beppo!" she called in a shrill voice.

No one answered. Only the hens ran to her in the hope that she might throw them grain.

Sabina chased them away with an angry flap of her hand and continued to call: "Tina! Beppo!"

From the yard she stepped into the deserted road and walked as far as the chapel of the Good Mother. She peered into the moss-covered stone face as if she meant to complain and still calling "Tina! Beppo!" turned back in the direction of the house. Her voluminous double-chin sagged dejectedly upon her heavy bosom.

Inside, in the big, murky room, filled with the odor of onions and herbs, the host dozed under a wreath of garlic. In one corner the two owners of the bony mules left in the courtyard conversed over glasses of thin, sour wine. They had met only an hour or two before but were already friends. Folks soon get acquainted when traveling.

The older one of the two, Matteo Pesaro, was a learned man. He was well versed in Latin and even had a smattering of Greek. He could have led a quiet life in any monastery copying books and commanding general respect, but an itching foot was forever leading him about. He was too curious to stay peacefully within the circle of thoughts set for him by an abbot.

The younger one, Pietro Cani, had no education but was endowed with a remarkable memory and a large dose of cunning. He wandered around for the sheer fun of it and never stopped anywhere for any length of time. According to circumstances he gave his occupation as scholar, barber or songster. He had little knowledge but very definite opinions on everything. Now, too, it was he who was making conversation. The learned Matteo only listened with infinite patience and generously stood wine for both of them.

Pietro, after wiping his mouth with the back of his hand, was proceeding to prove the superiority of lay over monastic life.

"There were two brothers," he said. "One was brought up in a monastery, the other in the outside world. After a few years the first one knew every evil trick while the other remained innocent. . . ."

"Surely, life in the outside world is no paradise, either," remarked Matteo, who was impartial by nature.

"Indeed not, messer Matteo, indeed not. But anything's better than to rot in one spot. A man is not a plant to remain rooted in one place. Had Blondel been a home-loving man, King Richard would have perished miserably in his prison and never seen his country again. Nothing else saved him but the wanderings of his troubadour friend. And have I told you messer Matteo, that I know the song by which they recognized each other? Here is how it went: 'No one, fair lady, can behold thee with impunity; each shall be smothered with love. But I shall not let myself be captured by beauty which is accessible to many. Rather deign to look upon me with hate, if hated I can be alone.' "

"A proud song," admitted Pesaro with indifference. He was not sensible to the beauty of rhymes.

The door creaked. Heavily as though weighted down by a burden, the landlady entered the room. Without a glance at the drinking men she jostled her sleeping husband.

"The children are gone again!"

"Likely they are picking olives," he muttered rubbing his eyes.

"Nay, nay. The baskets hang on their pegs," she answered.

She clasped her hands and gazed at the ceiling with such pain in her eyes that Baptisto shrugged his shoulders annoyed.

"Don't stare like a cow. What can happen to them? They are no babes any more. They ran somewhere and will be back soon."

She made no answer. Pietro became interested in the conversation.

"Are there robbers here or wild beasts," he inquired, "that you should worry over the children?"

"There is nothing," snapped the husband. "The wife fusses over trifles as mothers will."

"Not trifles," she retorted angrily. "In the last few weeks a stranger loiters around here and lures children to him. They go after him like flies after honey. He gathers them in a clearing in the woods and there he does his tricks with them. No use to beat or to forbid, they run to him from everywhere."

"What is it he does with them?"

"Nothing much, and nothing sinful," assured Baptisto. "He tells them of the Holy Sepulchre, the lost city of Jerusalem. He sings hymns with them. I see no evil in it."

"Better keep your mouth shut," his wife snapped. "No evil, indeed! And why, pray, does he not gather them in church? Why doesn't he sing there? Would anyone object? Would anyone forbid? Why should they hide in the woods like heathens? Why does he tell the children not to heed the priest; not to mind their parents? For he has told them so. I know! A man will not notice things unless they lie under his very nose, but to me it's plain as daylight. The children are as though bewitched. So quiet, so good, somehow. Bawl at them, beat them, they won't say a word! Oh, Lord! If I only could lay my hands on him he would never show up again. But he won't come near, not he!"

"Who is he, anyway?"

She shrugged her shoulders.

"None of us grown people has seen him. All we know comes from the children. Some tramp, some rat-catcher like the one who led the children away from the town of Hamelin. There, too, it would seem, fathers were wont to say: what does it matter if he plays them a tune on his pipe. Let him play! And so he led the poor little wretches somewhere to their death."

She left, banging the door behind her. From the outside they could hear her shrill voice calling: "Tina! Beppo!"

The landlord sighed and significantly tapped his forehead with a finger.

"Must be a monk who wants to become a children's prior or lure novices to his monastery," laughed Pietro. "Those monks! I have no love for the breed. Did you ever hear, messer Matteo, the tale of the devil? He had seven daughters and he married them off: Simony to the priests, Hypocrisy to the monks, Rape to the soldiers, Luxury he destined to become a harlot. . . ."

"And what about the other ones? He still had three left."

"It has slipped my mind," said Pietro unabashed, "but behold and wonder! We talk of monks and here they come, jogging along."

Sure enough, a group of about twelve men all dressed alike in dingy gray was coming down the road.

"They are not monks," observed the innkeeper after one glance at them. "Too skinny. Every monk has a fat pouch. And tattered! Must be beggars."

"The landlady is already talking to them, so we shall learn presently."

The newcomers had stopped in front of the gate. Sabina, standing at the entrance, faced them, arms akimbo.

"There is no room in the inn," she shouted sternly.

"We need no room," they called back in a gay chorus. "What should we be doing in such a splendid inn?"

"The shed is full, too!"

"The shed is much too good for us!"

"Then . . . where do you want to spend the night?"

"Outdoors, under the stars if you will let us."

"There's plenty of room in the courtyard," she muttered, mollified, "but nights are cold now."

"Cold does not bite us; we are used to it."

"Beggars, beggars of course, not one of them has as much as a sack or a bundle," scornfully observed Baptisto, standing by the window. "And they come from afar. You can tell by their speech that they are not from these parts, and they are covered with dust."

"Maybe some sectarians?" suggested Matteo.

"Maybe so. Hey, Mother. Ask them who they might be?"

"Who are you?" she repeated.

They glanced around as if abashed and pushed to the front one who evidently was their leader. He seemed to be less than thirty, short, slight, with a small head set upon a thin aristocratic neck emerging from the loose collar of his ugly, coarse garb. Nothing much to look at, decided Sabina. Still she could not help liking his eyes. They were nice eyes, both kind and merry.

"May the Lord give you peace," he said. "We are Christians, though mean ones, unworthy of Our Lord."

"No heretics? All sorts of people loiter around here. . . ."

"Oh, no. We are faithful sons of Our Mother, the Church."

"And what do they call you?"

The man rubbed his cheek with an embarrassed smile.

"The fact is we are on our way to Rome to beg the Holy Father to confirm our Rule and give us a name. In the meantime you can call us any name you like. Best of all, little brothers, or brothers minor."

"Will the Holy Father send you then to some monastery?"

"Oh no, we are not monastics, we are free."

"What do you mean? Not monks?"

"Well, let us say God's jugglers, singers. . . ."

She shook her head in disbelief. Obviously the subject was exhausted but Sabina kept on.

"What shall you have for supper?" she inquired. Her keen eye had noticed that they had not brought along any provisions. Good God, what if they go after my hens, the thought flashed through her mind.

"If you give us some work to do, and reward us with food, then we shall eat."

"Work? We sell food for money here, not for work. I won't charge you much."

"But we have no money," replied the leader of the band and began to laugh as heartily as if he had been suspected of carrying the moon in his pocket. There was something infectious in his laughter and the others joined in his mirth.

Sabina, shocked, crossed her hands upon her ample stomach.

"There are so many of you and not a penny among you all?"

"Not one," they assured her with renewed peals of laughter. "We will gratefully accept food, though, if you'll let us work for it. What would you like us to do: cut wood, clean the courtyard, scrub the kitchen?"

"We have a wight to attend to such matters," she retorted, scornfully pursing her lips. "We need not wait for someone from the outside world to happen along."

"Still, perhaps you'll find something for us to do?"

"I already told you no!"

"Then we shall get along without supper. It is no good to sleep on a full stomach, anyway."

"Will you be able to sleep on an empty one?"

"Like logs."

Loath to leave them, she still stood, though shaking her head.

"If anybody tried to feed all tramps free of charge," she remarked as if speaking to herself, "one would soon find oneself tramping the roads carrying an alms sack. . . ."

"And what harm would that be? He would be rid of worry, and under the protection of Our Lord he would in turn benefit by human kindness."

At that she shook with indignation.

"Charity bread is bitter," she announced. Suddenly she was pleasantly conscious of her own settled prosperity.

"To us it seems sweet. We are happy."

"Surely, only lazy bones can find such idleness to their liking," she sputtered contemptuously.

He opened his eyes wide.

"We—lazy bones? We accept nothing free. But we also accept naught that is worthless. Poverty is a sacred thing, she is our Mistress."

He turned to his men. They sat down on the ground closely huddled together. The sun had already set and the cold was rising from the ground.

Sabina went into the kitchen.

"Night is coming and still no children!"

Her hands shook with anguish, but now she had come here for another reason. She stooped over to a low shelf and swept from there the stale crusts left over from the last week. She put a small vial of olive oil and a pitcher of green wine under her arm and quickly stepped out towards the wanderers. They were trying to build a fire with sticks they had gathered along the road. And as they blew on the flame their faces looked young and wan.

"You poor things," she thought, and said aloud: "Here, have some supper."

They exclaimed all together and with such hearty gratefulness that it embarrassed her.

"May Our Lord reward you, dear Lady and sister. . . ."

"Come, come, not sister. . . ."

"Why not? Have we not a Father in common?"

The older one came up to her.

"May Our Lord give you peace and all His blessings. We ourselves will find some work to do tomorrow. We shall not leave before we've done our share."

"To be sure the courtyard needs some cleaning," she admitted.

"We will sweep it as clean as if it were a chamber. But, Lady Sister, what is that worries you, for woe is written upon your face?"

He looked at her with such deep sympathy and his eyes were so kind and clear that she told him of her trouble. The children escape from home. Even now, 'tis night and still no children.

He listened greatly concerned.

"An evil man he must be to exhort the children to disobedience. Our Lord told us to leave everything, father, mother, and follow Him, but He spoke to grown men, not to children. As a child, He Himself was docile to His parents' will. But do not worry, Lady Sister. As soon as daylight returns we shall go and look for your children. Perhaps we will also come upon the man who lures them and we will ask him not to do it any more."

"Why ask?" she exploded. "Better kill him like a vile beast!"

Again he burst into that gay hearty laugh of his.

"Our Lord allows us not to kill. And a good word means more than . . ."

He did not finish for at that moment a clatter of hoofs came from the road. Torches glittered in the dark. Some belated and noble guests were arriving.

Sabina ran back to the house. In a minute the courtyard was swarming with horsemen and servants on foot. Stern voices were summoning the innkeeper who, humble and obsequious, promised excellent wine and a copious supper and, bent in two, begged the noble knight to step inside.

"Who is that? Who is that?" Pietro, always curious, inquired of one of the servants.

"No companion for you," the other retorted scornfully. "'Tis Sir Jean de Brienne, himself of the Champagne counts. On his way to Rome to become the King of Jerusalem."

"Whc-ew!" Pietro whistled his appreciation and nimbly dodged the fist of the indignant servant.

# 3.

# King Against His Will

S IR JEAN DE BRIENNE WAS SIXTY AND GREY. BUT BOTH HIS YEARS AND his greyness—those two proofs of advanced age—fitted ill his looks and temperament. He still was a comely man, and women looked upon him more gladly than upon a youth. His vitality seemed inexhaustible, his strength unimpaired, maybe because he had spared them in his youth. Younger son of one of the mightiest French families, he had been destined since childhood to become a priest. Unable to accept such a fate, he had fled the paternal house. He did not have enough money to become a knight; he would not go into anyone's service as squire. What else was there for him to do? He could either join a band of brigands or hide in a monastery and there bide his chance. He chose the latter. Under an assumed name he spent several hard years with the Cistercian Fathers. As a convert brother he performed the lowliest tasks; he swept the kitchen and cut wood. He did not betray his identity for he well knew that his parents were looking everywhere for him. At last in one way or another his whereabouts was discovered by his older brother who by that time was already a famous captain with many victories to his name. Walter pleaded with the Fathers to release the fugitive and promised to endow him so he need not become a priest.

Jean de Brienne left the monastery kitchen and stretched for joy. At last he was going to live. Live! A full glorious life! Indepedent of anyone, free to do as he pleased!

"I was not meant for a yoke," he said to his brother to whom he had vowed eternal gratitude.

He soon achieved fame as the foremost among knights. Probably out of jealousy for his hard won freedom he never married, although he did not shun women. His out-of-season, wry good looks attracted the weaker sex. Lately a deep passion had bound him to the wife of a near kinsman, Blanche of Champagne, the royal Princess of Navarre.

She was a superb woman, sole heiress of a family which claimed Merovingian descent and for over three hundred years had ruled the kingdom of Navarre. Great stock indeed. Each generation had fought the Moors, and Blanche's grandfather at the age of ninety-five had stopped and dispersed the victorious army of Calif Abderson III. Verily she was a woman in a thousand. Like Jean, she was no longer young, yet she was still beautiful, still desirable. They were madly in love with each other. Thibault, the Count of Champagne and Blanche's prematurely old and decrepit husband, noticed none of it or more likely pretended not to notice. Jean was kin, a fact which considerably lightened the guilt. And the stanzas which de Brienne, faithful to the custom of those days, composed for his beloved were ascribed to young Thibault, the son of Blanche, who was wont to emulate the bards.

Years passed. Valor and love filled the life of de Brienne, keeping his spirit in perfect equilibrium. This equilibrium was suddenly shattered by the arrival of envoys from Acre, the capital of the Kingdom of Jerusalem.

The Kingdom of Jerusalem, or rather the scrap that remained of it, was again kingless. The heiress, Marie de Montferrat, was a weak, sickly girl of fifteen. The Syrian barons had sent a legation to Rome to ask the Holy Father that he choose a proper knight for her to wed. Innocent III turned the matter over to Philip August; it was right that the King of the Franks should choose a king for Franks.

The arrival of the envoys caused a great stir. The news was on everybody's lips and everyone wondered upon whom the royal choice would fall. The names of the likely candidates were whispered about. The King summoned the flower of the knighthood to Paris for a council. He let them all have their say, then he announced that his choice had already been made: for husband the Princess de Montferrat should have Sir Jean de Brienne.

De Brienne's name had not been even considered; in dumb wonder the peers stared at him as he stood there, the color in turn rising and ebbing from his face, till at last he said in a voice which excitement made hoarse:

"Your Majesty deigns to make sport of me. I am grey, and sixty."

"Years seem not to weigh upon you," the King retorted. "Besides what they need out there is an experienced man, not a green youth. Upon Roland's sword Durandel! You shall go and none else!"

The last words were uttered with unwonted harshness, and the King's small eyes held a malevolent smile. Suddenly de Brienne understood: the King was doing it deliberately! For some time already he had been openly courting Blanche. Perhaps he was tired of the fair Agnes of Meran; perhaps he had some designs upon the Kingdom of Navarre? Whatever it was de Brienne stood in his way.

The knight was conscious of the blood rushing to his head. The world turned black before his eyes. Such wrath would never do at his age. With an effort he controlled himself, while the King continued in unctuous tones:

"We do not need to tell you, Your Honors, how important to the entire Christian world is the proper choice of the King of Jerusalem. Whomever this honor befall owes gratitude to our Creator and Lord. For is there anywhere in the world a cause as sacred and worthy as the liberation of the Holy Sepulchre from the hands of the unfaithful? We shall grieve to part with Sir Jean de Brienne, whom we hold particularly dear to our heart but we shall gladly make that sacrifice for the love of God."

He smiled the characteristic crooked smile of his and cast a sidelong glance upon the future king. Black circles were still spinning before de Brienne's eyes. There was a roar in his ears. It was all he could do not to shout: "You lie, Sire! Not for the love of Christ do you do this but to gain access to a woman!" But he held his tongue. Not because he was afraid for his head, but not to endanger Blanche's reputation. For a long while he remained silent, then he breathed deeply, wiped the perspiration from his forehead and said:

"I feel neither worthy nor equal to this honor, Your Majesty. Besides I am a poor man and they need money out there. Only a wealthy man can aspire to be king."

"Have no worry, brave knight," exclaimed the King with great amiability. "I shall give you forty thousand ducats out of my chest and methinks the Holy Father will do the same."

"Forty thousand ducats!" A murmur of envious admiration rose from the hall. Lucky fellow, that Brienne.

"I feel old," repeated de Brienne stubbornly.

"None will believe you."

"I won't know how to rule."

The King laughed with feigned good-nature.

"Invent no excuses, Sir Jean de Brienne. Better tell us in all frankness what is the reason that makes you decline such high honors?"

He stared provokingly into the knight's face. Deep in his heart Jean felt regicide.

"No wonder he's not fain to accept," remarked one of the older knights in a conciliatory manner. " 'Tis no easy post."

The veins stood out in Jean's temples. This was the last straw. That any one should suspect that he, de Brienne, was afraid to face danger, no matter what it might be. . . . There was no escape. He bowed low before the King who lifted and kissed him.

"Welcome, beloved brother-king."

The corners of Philip's mouth twitched as though to say: "See how I've disposed of you?" Once more Jean felt his rage getting the better of him. Only to lash out with his fist at those smiling eyes, that mocking face! And once more he mastered himself not for fear nor in respect for royal majesty, but for the sake of a lady's honor, Blanche's honor.

He received the royal kiss; he kissed the King's hand. The knights surrounded him, some with glee, others with envy and grief. A messenger was dispatched to Rome and de Brienne returned to his castle and there bit his knuckles in helpless rage. And though the Pope urged him to hurry to Rome because the envoys would not return home without a king, de Brienne dallied and delayed his departure from France for more than a year. Day after day he was held back by a senseless hope that something would happen; that the princess would not wait so long, or the envoys might take offense and leave. . . . But nothing happened and at last he was forced to set out for Rome, leaving his castle, his hounds and his falcons to his brother, and worst of all leaving behind his beloved Blanche!

If only he could have set out for that outlandish, weird kingdom with her, that superb woman who could mount the wildest horse, lead a hunt and wield a sword no worse than a man! If he could only take her along! What could they not have accomplished together! But no! He had to abandon Blanche, *his* Blanche, for the sake of that wretched maiden!

Like his contemporaries Sir Jean de Brienne held unwedded girls in small esteem. According to the generally accepted precepts of troubadours only a married woman understood and was worthy of love. Only she knew the taste of life and passion. A maiden—what was a maiden? A tasteless fruit, a flavorless herb, the must of unripened wine. . . .

The delegates who were awaiting him in Rome, Walter the Bishop of Acre and Aymar de Layron, the Lord of Cesarea had sent Jean a likeness of the Princess, his betrothed. It would have been better if they had not. The very sight of the painting made the knight's stomach turn. Skinny she was, unsightly, with an elongated ferret-like face, in nowise like her parents who both had been sightly and fair. And it was he, de Brienne, whose hunger of life was still unappeased, who so wistfully watched each day go by, it was he who must renounce the last years of his youth and his beloved mistress in order to share to the end of his days the bed of that skinny ferret. It was enough to drive anyone mad! Stark mad!

Whatever curse hung upon the Jerusalem crown that it always was passed on to daughters? That there was never a male heir to inherit it? This must have been the fourth or fifth time in the last twenty-five years that they were looking for a husband and king. First there was that handsome and stupid Guy de Lusitan of whom Princess Sybille had become enamored. . . . God rest his soul, what a fool the man was. Later during the Third Crusade, Sybille so persistently pleaded with Richard Coeur de Lion, who was sensitive to feminine allures that he gave her and her husband the rule over the newly conquered Cyprus. Not for long did she enjoy that gift; the stench of dead bodies brought a plague to the camp and of that plague she had died. If there was one thing she could have told herself upon her deathbed it was that she had wrought an uncommon amount of trouble and grief in the world. In spite of her death Richard did not withdraw his gift and Lusitan continued to rule there—though not for long. He, too, died soon after. Young though he was, grief got the better of him. People looked at him askance because he had forfeited the Holy Sepulchre. Remorse gnawed at his heart. . . . His brother, Amalric, took over the island after his death.

Meanwhile, the Syrian barons must have a king. After Sybille's death the throne fell by right to her step-sister Isabelle. The latter, still as a young maiden, had wed Humphrey de Thoron, a handsome milksop, inept in war, inept in council, even worse than Guy de Lusitan. So they ordered her to divorce him and wed Conrad de Montferrat, the defender of Tyre, a great lord and a mighty warrior. The Patriarch himself agreed to the divorce for the good of the kingdom and no doubt Conrad would have reconquered Jerusalem if two weeks after his wedding he had not been murdered by Ismailites sent by the Old Man of the Mountains.

They had come pretending they were fugitives in search of true Faith. Conrad himself was their godfather. Once baptized they stayed on at his court. De Montferrat trusted them and willingly used them as servants. "They know not our language," he said. "They will repeat outside nothing of what we say."

But they were only biding their chance. . . .

Afterwards they were torn to shreds but that did not bring de Montferrat back to life. Nor did anyone learn at whose wish the Old Man of the Mountains had sent the assassins. Some mentioned Saladin, others Richard and Humphrey, but even a child would not believe such tales. And so it remained. The truth was never known.

Thereupon Isabelle was wedded to Henry of Champagne. Though neither as mighty nor as keen minded as Conrad he too was a brave, sensible, trustworthy knight. But what of it, when he likewise was not fated to live long! About a year after the coronation he was found dead at the foot of the tower. During the night he had fallen out of the chamber window. His dwarf lay by him smashed to pulp. Again no one knew what had happened. There were endless conjectures: that the king could not sleep, that he wanted to take a breath of fresh air, that he was subject to vertigo, that he had leaned too far and lost his balance. That the dwarf had tried at the last moment to hold him by his jerkin and had also fallen out. . . . So people said but the truth was never known. No, there could be no doubt but that the Kingdom of Jerusalem was luckless. And so was poor Isabelle. When with her fourth husband, Amalric Lusinian, she stood before the altar, she was not even twenty-six and still beautiful to look at. Amalric had come into his own. Cool, secretive and ambitious he had at last become king of two kingdoms. He sat tight and never opened his mouth, yet events seemed to play right into his hands. He knew how to bide his time.

Neither did any strange accident befall him. He was not buried under a rock, nor stabbed by a godson, nor did he fall with his dwarf out of the window. He died a natural death in due course. He left a son who ruled over Cyprus.

But for the Jerusalem throne the barons would no more have a Lusinian, and so they proclaimed as heiress Marie, whom Isabelle had conceived during her two weeks of wedlock with Conrad. It was that Marie whom Jean de Brienne was to wed, now in Anno Domini 1210, at the wish of Philip August.

"No," de Brienne repeated to himself, already on his way to Rome, "no, I will not, I will not!"

He was now pacing the floor of The Good Guardian inn, repeating his stubborn and useless "No, I will not," though he well knew how foolish and fruitless this protest was. For all his reluctance, for all his deliberate delay, this was his last stop. Tomorrow, irrevocably, he would be in Rome. He was already awaited there. It would be pure madness to think that tonight a miracle could happen which would free him from that unwanted kingdom.

. . . Should he confide in the Holy Father? Ask his assistance? What folly! If the Holy Father but knew what it was that held the knight back he would dispatch him to Jerusalem all the quicker in order to break the sinful tie.

"No, I will not! I will not go! I was and I am a free man. I am a free man and I will remain free!" de Brienne told himself.

What irked him even more than the loss of his love was the fact that he had been forced into this situation which was driving him like a sheep toward an unknown and unwanted fate.

"By the might of Heaven and Hell! I won't go!"

He paced to and fro, stamping his feet upon the earthen floor. He encountered a bench and kicked it over. He was seized with the desire to smash something, bash in someone's head, scream out his rage. But there was no one around.

Sometimes he stopped in front of the window. Though the night was chilly, he had ordered it left open because the air of the room was heavy with the mixed stench of onions, garlic, sour wine and tallow. Through the cool, dark-blue opening he could see on the left the unsaddled horses of his retinue, and his servants asleep near-by. To his right a fire built of sticks smouldered and smoked and around it a score of men sat in a circle. They looked ragged and unkempt. They were not asleep, they talked. The hum of carefree voices came to his ears.

This enraged the knight. Here he was torn by passion and there that rabble engaged in useless prattle. He stuck his head out of the window and was about to shout to them to stop their noise, but at the last moment he checked himself. They seemed to be monks. Better not enter into an argument with monks in such close vicinity to the Holy Father whose indulgence he might still need. Let their laughter choke them!

With loathing he glared at the men by the fire. What could that herd have to laugh about or talk of? What did they know? What did they feel? Not more than a mule! Likely they had gorged themselves and now the fire warmed them and so they were well content. What else did they need? What could they know of the wild passions which tear at a nobleman's heart?

He spat his wrath and disgust. "Common herd! Obscure slaves!"

Unaware of the nobleman's displeasure the lowborn talked of this and that. Matteo Pesaro and Pietro Cani whom de Brienne's men had ejected from the inn had joined their company. Matteo dozed, Pietro complained and grumbled against the lords.

"Anyone who comes to an inn and pays is as good as another," he insisted.

"Only before Our Lord, not among men," one of the brothers named Sylvester corrected him; he was an elderly man of serious mien.

"Inasmuch as he is a knight he can sprawl in the room all by himself, whereas we have to freeze outdoors!"

"It is better outdoors than in. One can behold the stars."

"Truly better," agreed brother Francis, the leader of the group. "The trees listen to our conversation and brother fire warms us nicely. The air is sweet. It is stifling inside. Just look; you can see the knight from here. See you how he restlessly paces the room and throws his head and arms about? No doubt he is suffering. It fairly wrings one's heart to see him struggle and bridle so. May God grant him peace!"

"For my part I wish him nought but ill." Pietro shrugged his shoulders. " 'Tis so cold a body is fair numb!"

"Come closer to the fire, messer brother! 'Tis not so bad to freeze when one can gaze upon our sisters the stars."

"Is all a brother and a sister to you, be it the stars and the fire?" Pietro asked mockingly.

"Aye, all," agreed Francis cheerfully, "for has it all not come from the same hand?"

"I wonder if the bishops won't deem your talk heathenish?"

"Methinks not. We are just on our way to obtain the approval of the Holy Father."

"What if he refuses to grant it?"

"We shall do whatever he bids."

"Oh, what obedience!"

"What will you, brother? Obedience is a great thing. 'Tis the confirmation of one's own freedom."

"The negation, you mean."

"Oh no! If you can obey or not obey it means that you are free to do as you please. And the greatest things in this world have come about through voluntary obedience."

"Nonsense. I would like to hear of a single one."

"The birth of Our Lord," replied Francis calmly.

"What's that? What are you talking about. I don't understand."

"Had the Virgin not agreed, had she not said 'I am Thy servant' would the Lord have acted against her will? That is why we should love that sacred Mother of ours, inasmuch as if it were not for her what would have become of mankind?"

"I must say those precepts of yours look pretty suspicious to me," said Pietro. "Heresy drips from them like water from a pierced bag. They will not welcome you in Rome."

"They will receive us just as Our Lord will deem fit."

"That obedience should mean freedom," Pietro continued to ponder. "Never. It is just the free who need obey no one. But none save the nobles have such freedom. 'Tis not for us paupers."

"Oh, brother. The nobles and freedom. Why they, more than anyone else are bound by their wealth, their posts, their honors. Only that man is free who owes naught and cares for none but God."

Pietro yawned loudly.

"Every pauper tries to comfort himself thus but in truth only money gives freedom. I'd gladly accept the servitude of the rich. When you have money people bow low wherever you go."

"Brother, would you like them to bow and hate you at heart? Because anyone who bows to a man must hate him for that very reason."

"Let them hate! What does it matter? How much, think you, the nobles care that anyone would drown them in a spoon of water? Just take that knight over there. He has chased us out of the inn, me and the learned Matteo who snores right here. . . ."

"I am not asleep and I do listen," objected Pesaro. "You have strange thoughts, brother Francis. I know not whether they be heretic, but strange indeed. . . . I would fain talk of these matters at length with you someday. And I am no longer sorry that Sir Jean de Brienne has chased us out into the courtyard."

"De Brienne?" Francis exclaimed. "Surely the brother of Sir Walther, the great hero who fought with the Germans for Italy. I remember; I once joined his colors. . . ."

"You," chuckled Pietro, casting a mocking glance upon the common garb of the speaker.

"Aye, so I did . . . I was a fool then . . . a youth."

"Did they take you to clean the horses' hoofs?"

"I never got there, for I was taken ill on the way."

"I likewise would have been elected Pope after the death of the last Holy Father had I been in time for the election."

A young, slender brother sitting at Francis' side got up without a word and began to wander around as though to keep warm. His movements were quick and restless, like a moth.

"Brother Angel," Francis said in a low voice. "Brother Angel!"

The man moth did not reply. He walked quickly straight ahead in the direction of the woods as if he were fleeing.

Brother Francis's eyes followed him with tender, motherly concern. Most of the other brothers were dozing. Pesaro propped himself up on his elbow and said musingly:

"If I understand rightly, wealth in your opinion hampers man's life and salvation?"

"'Tis not I, an unworthy servant, but Christ Himself who said so. . . ."

"Aye, I know, but the Gospel after all cannot be taken literally. . . ."

Francis turned to him a face full of surprise and indignation.

"Why not? Our Lord has told us to be like children, which means that we should take His words simply and literally. What He said He said openly, not figuratively as in the Old Testament."

"Such things are impossible for human nature," declared Pesaro. Pleased that they had at last entered the field of dialectics at which he was past master he spread out his fingers to enumerate the successive points of his reasoning. Francis, however, was gazing in the direction of the forest from which brother Angel was returning once more calm and serene.

"Oh, brother Francis," he called out, "close near-by, only a few hundred steps from here there is a chapel of the Holy Virgin."

"Let's move over there," exclaimed Francis with glee. "We shall be better off so close to Our Mother."

"What? Will you move the fire, too?" protested Pietro.

"No, we shall leave the fire here. Dawn is not far off, we can get along without it."

The brothers got up with zest and followed Francis and brother Angel. Pietro Cani stretched comfortably close to the embers.

"Did you ever see such queer birds?" he asked Matteo. "Such half-wits?"

"I can't say I have," admitted the learned Pesaro.

# 4.

## Pilgrims and Visitors

THE BIRDS HAD BEGUN TO TWITTER IN THE THICKETS AND BROTHER FRANCIS rubbed his eyes, red from sleep and morning dew. A pearly twilight was filling the world with its clear coldness, the freshness of the awakening day. Francis smiled in greeting at the surrounding trees. His head rested upon the stone feet of the statute of the Madonna. He had prayed to her long into the night and had fallen asleep in the midst of his prayers. Now with a gesture of tender courtliness he hugged the clumsy shape of feet, blew off the dust and wiped off the moss with his sleeve. Then, with the smile of a knight saluting the lady of his heart, he lifted his eyes to the face. Though many years had passed since the day of the miracle which had saved the condemned man, the reflection of that occurrence still seemed to linger upon the face of the statute giving it a softness and a look of tender solicitude strange to behold in stone. Though Francis knew naught of the legend he, more than anyone else, was able to see in that hard stone the traces of supernatural life. Overcome with sudden emotion he once more embraced the feet of stone.

"It is good to be here," he whispered, "as good as in Portiuncula where angels sing at night.

"It is good," he repeated and looked around him. His companions were still asleep, wrapped in their ash-brown cloaks, pressed close to each other for warmth, like a flock of sheep. . . . He did not wake them up. Let them sleep till the sun rises to warm the world. They had been up so late last night! Tenderly he surveyed their heads steeped in slumber. His brethren . . . his children. . . . He was responsible for them before the Lord. They had left everything in answer to his summons. They considered him their leader, their father, they trusted that the path to which he pointed was the most sure to lead them to eternal salvation and most pleasing to God. Each had come from a different household.

There were not two among them that were alike save for the same love of God in their hearts. Here now was his beloved brother Gilles, one of his first and most faithful companions. The son of a farmer he was also a good farmer himself, strong, patient, gentle, like an ox, deliberate and reliable. Francis liked to consult him, for in his judgments he was honest and simple, like the earth. Brother Gilles' soul was extremely sensitive to music. Not that he could play himself. No! His clumsy fingers were not meant to pluck at the strings of a harp or a viola, but all around him he was forever hearing music. The woods would play to him, the water, the air. . . . At times, he wondered why others did not hear the tunes. Again he would snatch at two long sticks and, resting one against his chin like a violin, he would fiddle away with the other upon invisible strings and play a tune to himself which none but he could hear. He could play thus for hours. Francis was sure that the angels heard the music of brother Gilles which no human ear could catch.

Side by side with Gilles, his head resting upon the farmer's shoulder, slept another old and steadfast companion, brother Bernard de Quintavalle. Once a learned, wealthy lawyer, he had distributed all his possessions among the poor and followed Francis. Above all else he was fond of solitude and would be perfectly happy to become a hermit in some inaccessible mountain cave. In this he resembled brother Rufin Sciffio who also disliked tumult and felt lost among people. In both there was that unconscious dignity of solitude which craves the silence of a hermitage. But Francis, though deep within his heart he yearned for the same thing, would not allow his brothers to escape from their fellow-men. "God has bid us to think not only of our own salvation," he would say, "but likewise of the salvation of others. How are we to accomplish this if we hold the world in contempt?"

Francis loved brother Rufin. It was with a strange emotion that he always gazed upon him. This young aristocrat, the scion of the lords of Assisi, bore a likeness to his kinswoman, Clara Sciffio the fairest and most pious of all Assisi maidens. And looking at him Francis could not help thinking of her. He adored her and prayed from the bottom of his heart that God would keep that marvelous human flower, that perfect work of His hand, as clear and pure as the maiden's name itself. May she not stoop to the wretchedness of a normal earthly life. May she choose the hardest path but the most beautiful one, the only one worthy of her.

Next to brother Rufin rested his complete contrast, the rubicund, jolly, invaluable brother Masseo. The hardships of a vagrant life had not robbed his cheeks of their ruddy glow nor subdued his hearty laughter and glib tongue. He had a special gift to soften the hearts of the most tight-fisted among housewives and would receive for his work better and more generous treats. And so the brethren were forever begging that brother Masseo be the one to go forth and collect the food.

Next came brother Angel and brother Leo, great chums these two. Francis was used to dub brother Leo "Lamb" because he was so meek and modest. The only anxiety that would at times assail brother Leo's heart concerned Francis himself. Did good father Francis still love him as much as of yore? Had he, Leo, perchance offended him by disobedience or lack of understanding? Although among the brethren there were several more versed in the art of writing, it was him that Francis had appointed his secretary. It was brother Leo who carried a roll of parchment and a quill as well as the precious Rule of the congregation which the Holy Father would or would not confirm. This mark of confidence filled brother Leo with pride. Francis knew that such souls as his needed to feel useful.

Brother Angel was a knight of great lineage. His name was di Tancredi. It so befell that, barefoot and bedraggled, Francis had been passing through the valley of Rieti and met there a knightly train on its way to a tourney. A young knight, fair as a maiden, cast a glance full of curiosity at Francis and the latter shouted: "You have carried long enough the sword and spurs of your worldly master. 'Tis time to exchange the girdle for a cord, the sword for a cross and the spurs for the dust of the road. Come with me! I shall dub thee the Knight of our Lord!"

Others had guffawed with laughter but the youth had dismounted, handed over to his squire reins, sword and armor and followed Francis. This was brother Angel, Angelo di Tancredi. Francis held him particularly dear; he called him his knight of the Round Table.

Brother Elias Bombarone was not Francis' favorite. The fact distressed Francis who reproached himself for it, but try as he may could not help feeling that brother Elias was somehow alien to the little group. Brother Elias was clever, reserved and ambitious; he had cold and penetrating eyes. He never revealed what lay at the bottom of his thought. Still his piety and honesty were beyond reproach.

Brother Sylvester, the oldest among them, was also the only ordained priest in this group of laymen and for that reason was looked upon with great respect by the others. And indeed he fully deserved it. Once he had been the parson of Assisi and over-fond of worldly goods he was then. But under Francis' influence a great change had come over his soul.

Brother John Parenti, the learned professor of the University of Bologna and a judge, had only recently joined the brethren. Who knows whether he would have joined them at all were it not that once while he was taking a stroll he overheard a farmer calling to his herd: "Whoa, get ye into that stable like judges into hell!"

"Why should judges sooner than anyone else go to hell," inquired the professor smiling.

"Oh, Your Highness, 'tis common knowledge: a good lawyer, a bad Christian. Never yet has a judge achieved salvation. Aye, aye, surely. There is a special spot in hell reserved for them. They all sit there."

The learned professor laughed at the bumpkin's arguments but that very evening he began to ponder over them and to wonder whether indeed he himself would achieve salvation. And the longer he thought the greater grew his doubts till the next morning, taking off his gown, he set forth in search of Francis.

Another brother, John, had even more recently joined them and so far it was hard to tell anything definite about him. He easily succumbed to sunstroke and for that reason had asked leave to retain his hat. The other brethren went about bareheaded; when it rained, or in wintertime, they would pull their hoods over their heads. Because of this hat the brothers had dubbed their new companion John a Capello.

Last of all was winsome, dearly beloved brother Juniper. Drawn up in a tight dark ball he really looked from a distance like a juniper bush. His was a simple cheerful soul who cared for naught save the glory of God. He went through life singing to God, like a bird. His heart was invariably overflowing with joy just because he was alive and could love and praise the Lord. He feared neither sin nor the devil for would not God protect him from both? Indeed he feared naught in the world. Why should he; God watched over him.

"Had I only a whole forest of such junipers," sighed Francis.

Again his eyes made the round of these slumbering heads so dear to his heart. He committed them to the care of the Madonna of the Compassionate Face. May she give them strength, may she dispel worldly temptations.

Of all temptations the hardest to conquer were those which threatened their absolute poverty, so dear to Francis because he deemed it essential. Had not Christ said to leave all and follow Him? That was precisely what they had done. They possessed nothing, literally nothing. They were independent and free, like birds. Nothing bound them. Like pilgrims and visitors from strange lands they looked with kindness upon all that surrounded them but they themselves belonged to a different, a distant world. They were ready for whatever their Lord might bid them to do. Free! Aye! Free! . . .

O wondrous, God-given word! Up to now it had seemed as though upon this earth doomed to bondage there was no room for freedom, the exclusive attribute of God. And now it appeared that it also belonged to those who for the sake of God had renounced everything.

The coolness of the air was growing tense, more penetrating; it drew closer to the ground as always before sunrise. Golden rays shot from behind the mountain followed by the sun itself. No sooner had the sun appeared in the sky than it began to warm the world. Its beams, like warm fingers, gently touched the cold faces of the sleeping men. The brethren began to lift their heads and rub their eyes. From where he sat at the feet of the statue of the Madonna Francis smiled upon them and stretched his hands, numb with cold, to the warm glow of the sunshine.

"Now we will separate," Francis decided as soon as they had recited their morning prayers. "Some will return to the inn and tend to the chores for which we were given our supper last night . . ."

"And this morning breakfast, I trust," remarked brother Masseo, who was not likely to rest contented with only the memory of food.

" 'Tis for them to decide. Mind though you take not more than be your due."

"More? Brother Francis, I took a peek last night: such filth as there is in that courtyard and stables I never beheld. 'Tis shameful! Dungwater overflows to the very house. Were we to put all that aright— although I doubt one day will suffice—they ought to feed us for at least a week."

"A costly laborer you are, brother Masseo. Besides we will be off today. So, as I said, half of us will go to sweep the courtyard and the rest must set forth in search of youngsters who it seems from what the landlady said last night, have run away. It is not as though the children were in any immediate danger else we would have sought them at once yesternight. But it seems some stranger is luring them away from home. He is doing ill, for the children's place is by their elders' side. Hence, it matters not so much to find the children, who by now have probably returned of their own accord, as to encounter that tempter of babes. Mayhap he does not know the wrong he does. We must beseech him in the name of Our Lord to do it no more. After our work is done we shall meet here and set out straight for Rome."

"But we shall never get there today," exclaimed John a Capello.

"Indeed not. We will sleep by the roadside even as yesternight."

"And what are we to eat tomorrow?"

"Whatever the Lord provides."

"Should we again be forced to waste more than half a day to earn our food we will never get to Rome."

"And how would you have it otherwise?"

"I thought . . . well . . . I thought brother Masseo might ask for more so 'twould suffice for two days . . ."

Francis shook his head angrily.

"No provisions," he snapped. "If for two days then why not for a week, a month, perhaps even a year? 'Twould be even more convenient! Let us not talk of the matter any more, but be on our way, rejoicing in Our Lord. . . ."

"Why should we rejoice?" mumbled John a Capello, peevishly.

"If for no other reason, then because we are alive, because the sun shines, the sky is blue, the grass is green. . . ."

"If the sun always shone, if there were always summer, aye, indeed we might. . . . But as it is, whenever it rains in that dog-house of ours in Rivotorto, water pours on our heads . . ."

"Only so that we might better appreciate our dear brother Sun!" laughed Francis, but it was plain that John's words had pained him.

Although but a minute before he had urged them to be on their way, now once more he seated himself upon the grass and thoughtfully gazed at the grumbler. John bit his lips and scowled. Not in truth for the first time he felt that he must have joined the congregation in a moment of incomprehensible folly. Whatever made him do it? Had he not his own home, his workshop, a secure existence and human respect to boot? Why had he abandoned it all to wander about dressed like a beggar and hungry? He had been attracted by rumors that Francis wrought miracles. Now ever since his childhood days miracles had fascinated him. And for the sake of miracles he had followed Francis. But miracles there were none. Weariness there was and hard work aplenty and a dog's life. Nothing more. Aye, and prayer of course, but then one could pray at home, too. And people used to tell such wonders! Stuff and nonsense. Although who knew? Maybe after all Francis could perform miracles, only kept it a secret. To be sure he looked common enough, slight, thin, undistinguished, always smiling, but who knew? If Francis only could John would not mind the suffering and hardship. . . .

He lifted his gaze and encouraged by the kind, deeply concerned look of the other's eyes he asked Francis shyly whether he had ever performed a miracle?

"Of all silly questions," muttered brother Leo, and brother John flushed a deep red because Francis burst into peals of uncontrollable laughter.

"I and a miracle," he stammered, wiping tears from his eyes. "I and a miracle! Oh, brother John, saints perform miracles, not such a miserable, unworthy creature as myself! Miracles, indeed."

Again he laughed. Brother Masseo shook his big head.

"Tut, tut, brother Francis, talk as you please, but for all you talk one thing is certain. All of us are not such bad Christians either and yet the world talks only of you. It is after you people run, and it is to you we all came, not you to us . . . Why? There must be something in it."

Francis sprang from where he sat with unwonted vehemence.

"Ah! And don't you know why? No? Don't you understand what is simple and clear? What any child would understand? Then I shall explain to you and to brother John and to you all. And let brother Leo write it down because it is important and you must all remember it! You must know that all over the world the Lord found no creature more contemptible, more miserable, more stupid than myself. And that is why He chose me! Me, the worst of all; to use me to perform His great deeds! And He did so in order to put to shame nobility and learning and beauty and reason and wisdom and cleverness, and to show that all strength and virtue come from Him alone and that through Him even a rag, a stinking sinner filthier than dung, a plague such as myself can become a tool of great and sacred things! And He left me with my sins, though at times He deigns to speak through me. And this He does only so that the entire world would know that He alone deserves all glory! I know it—I know it from His own lips!"

He sat down, breathing hard. His companions gazed upon him respectfully. Whenever he spoke thus in exaltation he would become as though transfigured. At such times he, always so gentle and merry, would resemble St. John the Baptist or some other threatening prophet. His hair and scanty beard stood on end, his eyes flamed. Now with an effort he controlled himself. The silence was such that one could hear the scratching of the quill which brother Leo painstakingly drew over the paper.

"Let's be off," said Francis after a while. "Have you finished, brother Leo?"

"No, no, not yet," the secretary stammered out in despair. He was not very proficient in the art of writing.

Francis smiled at his lamb; once more it was his old smile.

"Then we shall bide a while. Do not hurry overmuch lest you make an error."

Silence fell once more. Francis was stroking the grass.

"I wonder how we shall be received in Rome?" mused brother Sylvester.

"We'll be there tomorrow," added brother John Parenti.

All were glad to talk now to cover up the shiver they had felt at Francis' discourse.

"Do we visit our Bishop Guido?"

"Indeed, yes! He gave us leave to stay in his courtyard and has promised his assistance."

"In that case 'tis even better we shall not arrive by nightfall. It would be unseemly to come at night a-knocking at his door."

"The more so as before we call on the Bishop we must surely visit the Apostle's grave?"

"They would not let us in there at night, either . . ."

"How will the Holy Father receive us? . . . I am fearful."

"What are we to do should he not approve our Rule?"

"It seems to me," said brother Elias, "it would not be amiss for us while brother Leo is still writing to read our Rule aloud. Maybe we can modify and temper it somewhat to make it more readily acceptable . . ."

"Not a single word," exclaimed Francis. "But by all means let us read it. Give us our Rule, Lamb."

Brother Leo hastened to produce from his bosom a parchment folded in four.

Brother Elias took it, unfolded it and read: "In the name of the Father, the Son and the Holy Ghost! The Rule of Brethren Minor derived from the Gospel of Jesus Christ our Lord: the Master said to them: Take nothing for your journey, neither staff nor wallet nor bread nor money, neither have two tunics. And whatever home you enter salute it saying Peace to this home. If then that home be worthy, your peace will come upon it but if it is not worthy let your peace return to you. And whatever home you enter and they will receive you eat whatever they lay before you. And as you go, preach the message The Kingdom of Heaven is at hand. Cure the sick, raise the dead, cleanse the lepers, cast out devils. Freely you have received, freely give. . . ."

Brother Elias interrupted the reading.

"This point ought to be changed or altogether omitted," he said in his cool, deliberate voice, "lest the Holy Father be wrath and justly so. What about fasts? 'Eat whatever they lay before you.' What if during the quadragesima they should lay a capon or a pig? Ought we to eat them?"

"These are the words of Our Lord, brother Elias! Our Lord has not ordered His disciples to fast. Fasts are for the very replete and the very mighty, not for bare bones like ourselves. . . ."

"Who are forever fasting, anyhow," muttered brother Masseo.

"Do as you like, but mind my word, this will cause a lot of trouble . . ."

"What trouble can Our Lord's own words cause?"

"I know they are Our Lord's. I know that they are from the Gospel. But you will not close anybody's mouth with that argument. 'Twould be better to prepare in advance what we are to reply, how to motivate our point. There will be learned men there. They will find a hundred arguments. That this behest was given to Our Lord's disciples, not to us; that times were different then . . ."

"The words of Our Lord are binding for all times. And deliberating will avail us naught. With our poor reason we shan't find anything. Besides, is it not said in the Gospel: 'But when they deliver you up, do not be anxious how or what you are to speak; for what you are to speak will be given you in that hour. For it is not you who are speaking but the Spirit of your Father who speaks through you.'"

With an imperceptible shrug brother Elias continued to read:

"And the most important commandment given to the brethren is that they shall love each other. By that sign they will know you for the true disciple of Our Lord, that you shall have love for each other. And every man who shall come to the brethren, be he a thief or a robber, must be welcomed gladly even as he were one of them."

Brother Elias once more put the parchment down:

"And to this, too, the Holy Father will never agree," he remarked. "Why, 'tis pure folly! So if a notorious murderer came to us we should take him in and perhaps even offer him hospitality."

"Aye," nodded Francis with conviction. "Because who knows whether we can't bring him to repent?"

"And he, in the meantime, will rob the brothers and . . ."

"What will he rob them of? What can he do to us? None of us fears death. She is our sister. Only those who possess aught can be robbed. We have naught. Neither will he hurt our souls, for I reckon a brother will more readily convert a robber to the love of Christ than a robber induce a brother to take up the robber's craft. And of what use will we be should we associate with none but the good?"

"I have finished writing," announced brother Leo with a sigh of relief.

"Then let's go. We shall finish the reading of our little Rule at our evening halt."

They rose with alacrity. Some followed brother Masseo back to the inn which they had left the night before, the others started for the woods in search of the man whom Francis had called the tempter of babes. They broke up into pairs. Brother Leo mournfully noticed that brother Francis had taken brother Angel with him. And so he went with brother John Parenti, sighing as he walked.

"What ails you, brother Leo?" inquired the ex-professor.

"I am no good," confessed brother Leo dejectedly. "I wonder how Father Francis allows me to be his secretary. I am so ignorant, so clumsy! I am sure you could have written the same thing so much faster. . . . Besides I have a great sin on my conscience."

Brother John could not restrain a smile.

"What sin, Lamb?"

"I dislike brother Elias."

Meanwhile Francis was saying to brother Angel: "I saw your disquiet last night, little brother, when the guest from the inn scoffed at knighthood or rather me as a knight. 'Twas nothing to take to heart. And you jumped up like a goaded horse. Do those matters still hold you fast?"

"They do," admitted di Tancredi, blushing like a girl, and he began to talk very fast.

"Aye, well I know I am a better, braver knight now than of yore and yet . . . particularly when I see . . ."

"It hurts?" asked Francis in a low gentle voice.

Brother Angel did not reply. Tears welled up in his eyes.

"Would you return to the world, little brother?"

Brother Angel jumped up, this time really like a horse touched by a spur.

"No!" he shouted with conviction. "No! Never!"

Francis breathed with relief.

"Aye," he said slowly, " 'tis hard sometimes and yet none of us would go back now. Or if he did he wouldn't be able to stand it even for a day, so empty, so arid his old life would seem to him. . . . Let us thank merciful God that He has called us and fight bravely the grief which comes upon us. . . ."

He broke off, for not far from the road came voices and the sounds of dry branches snapping under someone's feet. The face of Francis lit up.

"Luck would be with us, brother. Here are the children and no mistake . . ."

"Maybe other children."

"We will see."

They cut across the wood in the direction of the voices and presently beheld a group of youngsters, three boys and two girls. At the sight of the two brothers the little flock stopped abruptly and eyed them with suspicion.

Francis smiled at them.

"Peace with you. Are Tina and Beppo from The Good Guardian inn among you?"

A pretty, slim girl no more than eleven and a slightly older boy stepped forward.

"What do you want?"

"Your mother frets over you. 'Tis not right to leave her so, without telling . . ."

They shrugged their shoulders with complete indifference.

"Our Lord allows us not to grieve our parents," continued Francis.

"Our Lord has ordered us to leave everything and follow Him," shouted Tina.

"He told it to grown people, my little sister—to grown people, mind you. A grown man knows whither the Lord calls him. A child must trust its elders."

Thus talking they proceeded along the road. A few steps in front of them brother a Capello and brother Sylvester had emerged from the woods and, glad to discover there was no need of further search, now joined the little group.

"The elders have no thought for Our Lord," declared Beppo gloomily. "They live as though they were asleep. They care for nothing. The Lord's Sepulchre is in the hands of the heathen and it is all one to them. They think only of themselves. It is up to us to take their place . . ."

"It would be better if you tried to arouse them to serve Our Lord. Beg them to mend their ways for the sake of God, and your own, instead of running away and rousing their just wrath."

"There's no use. Nothing can change old folks."

"Who told you so?"

"Nicholas," exclaimed Tina and blushed under her brother's chastising glare.

"And who might Nicholas be?"

Beppo's frown deepened.

"A saintly man," he replied slowly, weighing every word as though afraid to say too much. "He has just returned from the Holy Land. He tells us of the plight of the Holy Sepulchre. We weep with him and then we pray for God's mercy upon Jerusalem."

"Why will he not tell of it in the village where elders could likewise gather and listen?"

"He does not want to. He says old folks' hearts are hard and set and it is no use talking to them. It was they who allowed the Holy Sepulchre to be lost."

"Nicholas is wrong. No man's heart is set as long as he lives."

"He asked us, too, whether we hear voices? Before none of us heard them but now we hear them quite plainly in the woods after he has talked to us. Those voices say: Free the Holy Sepulchre!" Tina said hurriedly.

"Wherever the voice might be coming from, do not forget it when you grow up and it is your turn to fight for the Holy Sepulchre."

"We cannot wait till we grow up. We want to do it now!"

"Now, my dear children? What can you accomplish now? How will you get to the Holy Land? How will you fight?"

"Nicholas told us great miracles will happen if only a great crowd of us gathers together."

"Miracles?" exclaimed brother John a Capello. He had so far kept silent. "What miracles?"

Tina turned to him, her eyes wide with rapture.

"Oh, great miracles!" she said with conviction. "The sun will drink the sea and we shall cross dryshod. The walls of Saracen fortresses will tumble down. Nicholas knows it for certain."

"It is a sin to expect such miracles from Our Lord," exclaimed Francis with warmth. "Where might Nicholas abide? I would meet him."

The children exchanged sly glances.

"Oh, no! You shall not see him. None will, lest Nicholas will have it. For he can make himself invisible or ascend to heaven . . ."

"Tina," Beppo reprimanded her sharply. "Nicholas bid us not to talk of it and you babble."

Francis looked at them with growing concern.

"And did you see how he rises aloft or becomes invisible?"

"No, but we know. He himself told us of it. And he took his leave from us as he will not be back for a month. That's why we stayed longer."

They were approaching the inn. The other children had left earlier and scurried to the village. Sabina now sighted the approaching group and came running into the road. In turn screaming, laughing and crying she hugged the youngsters, chided them, threatened them with harsh punishment, then once more gathered them in her arms. Beppo and Tina bore the maternal effusions with complete indifference as though they were strangers. When at last Sabina had quieted down a little, Francis drew her aside.

"Sister,"'he said gravely, "that man to whom the children run is worse than we both reckoned. He is a tempter."

"I knew it! I knew it from the first," she cried. "But never fear, I will get him yet. Wait until I rouse the village! It is with sticks we'll be after him."

"It will avail you naught. Even were you to kill him it would be of no avail. You would lose your children forever. They have faith in him."

"Then what am I to do?" she moaned, hiding her face in her apron.

"Revert to Our Lord with all your heart so that the wrongs done to Him may mean as much to you as they mean to your children. The young ones complain that their elders are heedless of the plight of the Holy Sepulchre. An evil man avails himself of that heedlessness of yours . . ."

"What am I to do? Go to the Holy Land? Enough folks have perished there already!"

"There is no need to go to the Holy Land. Only to love Our Lord as much as your children do."

She listened with growing annoyance.

"What do you deem me to be, a heathen? Think you I do not believe in God?"

"Aye, believe in Him you do, but you do not love Him enough. It is a warm, ever watchful love that's needed . . . like the love of children. It is of Him more than of anything else you ought to think. Then Tina and Beppo will return to you and together you shall yet bless that tempter . . ."

"May a plague smite him!" she screamed in sudden wrath. "And you too! Look at him! A beggar, a tramp, without even a shirt to his name and he will tell me what to do! Sister, indeed! I am no sister to you! I do not need your counsel."

She went her way, angrily muttering to herself. The four brothers turned toward the chapel.

"What a weird story," remarked brother Angel. "What do you make of it, brother Francis?"

" 'Tis wonderful," exclaimed John a Capello. "Those miracles!"

"Beware, brother John! All that surrounds us is a great miracle indeed, but I set no faith by miracles of which a man boasts. Simon the Magus once boasted that he would ascend into the sky. I fear this Nicholas may be of the same sort."

All were already gathered in front of the chapel. Brother Masseo had laid out upon a flat stone a fair quantity of bread, a handful of olives and some cheese received from Sabina.

"What a banquet," exclaimed Francis, once more cheerful and serene. "She feeds us well, our Lady Poverty. Make haste, brethren, let us eat and be on our way to Rome. To Rome!"

# 5.

## King of the Troubadours

THE ENVIOUS INSISTED THAT WILLIAM DIVINI NO LONGER SANG AS beautifully as of yore; he, however, did not seem to notice it. Self-satisfaction adorned the slightly wrinkled countenance and portly figure of the aging troubadour with unperturbed serenity. On his head he wore a black velvet cap, surmounted by a golden wreath of laurel leaves with which once many years ago, Rome had crowned him on the Capitol as king of singers. Youthful locks of hair carefully curled and dyed fell upon his shoulders, although the top of his skull under the velvet cap was bald. Nevertheless, the aura of the conqueror of feminine hearts had not ceased to surround William. The endless chain of his mistresses ran the whole gamut of womanhood from buxom peasant girls to the most distinguished ladies and authentic queens. In fact, the majority of women had come to believe that to live in the same age with Divini and not win his favor would be tantamount to dishonor.

At today's banquet, however, the king of singers paid no heed to any particular woman. The banquet was given by His Honor Sir Graciani Frangipani in honor of Sir Jean de Brienne, and the hostess, Donna Giacobbe Setteoli, the spouse of Graciani, was so unbearably, so annoyingly honest! Or was she simply dull witted? Young, comely, she was; and yet she understood naught of the subtle game of love, that pride and privilege of all troubadours. The participation of a noble lady in that game did not in the least slight the honor of her spouse. On the contrary, a husband could but rejoice when a singer of world fame dedicated charming stanzas to his wife and boasted of her colors pinned to his viola. But this Giacobbe seemed not to comprehend. Truly, despite her high birth she comported herself like a bumpkin. There was nothing feminine in her manner. Her transparent, hazel eyes looked upon the world more like a man's gaze, frank, daring, even a little brusque. In her stiff, formal gown

45

she seemed rather like a young lad disguised in women's clothes. Her speech was as reticent as her demeanor. She would not have in her chamber either dwarfs or Turkish slaves as was customary among the ladies of the day, and as for the duty of signing her name in the book of the divine William, this never even seemed to enter Donna Giacobbe's mind.

As it would have been unseemly to woo another woman in the presence of his hostess, the attention of the troubadour had nowhere to rest. The hero of tonight's banquet, Jean de Brienne, kept silent and did not invite conversation. He was seated upon a carved arm-chair with his host at his left and the Bishop of Acre, Walter of Florence, who had come to fetch him and had been waiting patiently for over a year, at his right. Across the table from Sire de Brienne the other envoy, Sir Aymar de Layron of Cesarea, a merry and adroit knight, held forth on the ease and charm of life in Syria.

"I shall not weary Your Honor," he was saying, "with a description of those wondrous temples and palaces which have no equal here, of those walls incrusted with mosaics, those courtyards where fountains play and waft a pleasant coolness even during the hottest days. Neither shall I tell you about the gallantry of the knights whose deeds are famous the world over. Nor of the comeliness of the ladies. Nor of the riches that flow through our cities. Half of the world's trade goes through our ports."

Jean de Brienne interrupted him with an impatient gesture of his hand. "I am amazed, Sir, to hear you speak thus! One might think the kingdom still lived in its happy might of bygone days. As though things were as they were wont to be at the time of Baldwin and Fulk. And yet well I know how those splendors look today; a strip of shore left by the Sultan's grace in your hands, a king at the mercy of all European lords, awaiting humbly whether they shall give him assistance or not."

De Layron blushed deeply.

"Over-bitter are Your Honor's words. Over-bitter, indeed. The situation you describe in such black colors may change at any time. In fact, not in many years have the horoscopes of the Kingdom of Jerusalem been as favorable as they are today. The might of Saladin no longer exists. Islam has crumbled. If six years ago instead of attacking Byzantium the knights had proceeded as was but right to Jerusalem, I vow upon my shield the Holy Sepulchre would have been in our hands today! The great war experience of Your Honor, your fervor combined with the Holy Father's help will surely bring about a new, this time properly directed, expedition."

De Brienne shook his head incredulously.

"I doubt whether it will be possible to assemble such strength as six years ago. . . . People's zeal has cooled down. They are no longer eager to fight."

"Oh, Your Honor," plaintively moaned the Bishop of Acre. "Can it be that Christians have become so indifferent to the plight of the Holy Sepulchre?"

Jean de Brienne did not reply. He drained his goblet and noisily replaced it on the board. He kept silent because were he to be frank he would have to answer: "Could it be? Just look at me!" Instead of rejoicing that God had given him an opportunity to fight for the Holy Sepulchre he— a knight—delayed, resisted, and instead of thinking of Jerusalem thought of a beloved woman who made that other goal seem remote. Blanche was close to his heart, indispensable. Tenderness and passion, increased by the bitter awareness of overripe years, held him fast. Under their spell he continued to rebel against the fate that had made him king. Almost angrily he glared now at the Bishop of Acre. The peaceful old man felt the displeasure of his future master, and not knowing what had brought it upon his head quickly changed the subject and began to praise the virtues of Princess Marie and to describe how impatiently she was awaiting the arrival of her betrothed. De Brienne drained another goblet. "May she perish ere I ever set eyes upon her," he thought in a sudden fit of wrath. Although the thought never found its way into words, his face betrayed it.

The Bishop stopped short, confused. For a moment silence fell over the table, a most unwelcome occurrence during any banquet. Graciani Frangipani glanced pleadingly at the king of troubadours. Would he not glorify the occasion by his divine singing? Divini, a seasoned courtier, understood and had not to be asked twice. He rose to his feet, thrust out his powerful chest, molded in crimson silk, and benignly nodded his head. He bowed in the direction of Giacobbe. The musicians who sat upon the balcony at the farther end of the banquet hall caught up their violas to accompany him. The maestro turned to Jean.

"In your honor, Your Highness—soon 'twill be Your Majesty—I shall sing a song in your language."

And in the melodious Provençal tongue he began to sing a popular canzona:

> When grapes grow sweet and heavy on the vine
> And grieves my heart for the departed Spring,
> Enchanting lips of my beloved bring
> To love's rich banquet spiced and perfumed wine
> That sets my heart afire, and her embrace
> Hides me from Autumn's melancholy face.

Although connoisseurs maintained that the voice of the divine William was far from what it used to be, it still held incomparable beauty. His great skill chiseled every stanza, every note to perfection. And it was not alone a matter of skill that the voice of the no longer young singer vibrated with longing for that life which passes all too soon . . . The world turns away from the old, 'tis in vain they hasten after it . . . Smiles, glances, the embraces of women are for others. . . .

De Brienne lowered his head, overcome with the same sense of longing, the same gnawing pain. Could it be that the singer had divined his sorrow?

> Then do not dim thy light, oh day,
> Enchanting day; and dusk delay.
> Invincible lust of love! Breathes one
> Who would not pray to stay the sun.

Invincible lust. . . . Aye! Were he but free to enjoy those last days of his belated youth cruelly clipped by the years spent in the monastery. . . If only he need not waste a particle, an hour, a minute of what remained of it. . . . Invincible lust . . . Aye, indeed! It was that lust which held sway over him . . . he had no control over it . . . And no, he would not try to conquer it . . .

Divini had finished. Noisily rising to their feet the feasters clapped their hands. The king of troubadours stood smiling and wiped the perspiration from his brow. Jean de Brienne leaned toward him:

"Words are clumsy, indeed, when the soul is full to the brim. As long as I live I shall not forget your singing. Please accept this from me."

He slipped on the troubadour's finger a ring which King Philip, urbane to the last, had given him before he left France. A handsome, royal ring. Divini who, like every Italian, was enamored of jewelry, blushed with pleasure. And inasmuch as he was an experienced judge in matters of love he immediately thought: "I'll wager my head this oldster is still blazing with passion for some lady."

The silence amidst which they all had listened to Divini's singing ended. The big hall was now filled with a lively hubbub of conversation welcome to the host's ears. The banquet was drawing to its close and all present spoke at once as if fearful they might not get a chance to speak out what they had to say. Up in the gallery the musicians lightly plucked their violas. Dogs growled, fighting for bones under the table. Only Jean de Brienne drained goblet after goblet in complete silence.

"Not a great talker, that king of ours," thought the Lord of Cesarea resentfully. "We were told he was such a fine knight, and look at him— the gloomy owl! Still he is generous. Such a fine ring for a song . . ."

Casting delighted glances at the ring William Divini tried to entertain Giacobbe with conversation.

"I was just on my way here, grateful for the remembrance and honor," he was telling her, "when my progress was obstructed by a throng. A dense throng, like at an execution. My mount could not push through. The servants would have us by-pass it but I thought maybe the executioner was scorching a witch and I was curious. I pushed my way into the square. . . ."

"And what was there?"

"That's just it. . . . There really was scarcely aught to see. A slip of a man, bedraggled, skinny, stood there and spoke to the people. And they listened . . . Madonna! A while ago it was your pleasure to lend ear to my song but by the Immaculate Virgin that was nothing compared with the manner in which the crowd listened! I never saw aught to compare with it. Unfortunately, I could not catch his words. I might have were it not that the rabble produced so hideous a stench . . . I could not bear it. Tallow and garlic. And unwashed heads."

"What a pity, indeed. Were you not curious, Messire, to learn what he was saying?"

"I shook one of the mob by the scruff of his neck: 'What is it he says?' The villain stared at me as though out of his wits. 'About the love of God,' he muttered and went on listening . . ."

"Surely some new schismatist," suggested Graciani Frangipani. "A real calamity those heretics. . . . They spring up everywhere. . . . No sooner are they executed than new ones appear. . . . And that speaker of yours likely spoke not of love of God but only that church property be taken away and distributed among the mob. . . . Only to that people listen with such rapture."

Divini smiled.

"I confess it was not so much what he had to say that interested me as his manner of saying it. He was an artist, that man. A great artist. He gesticulated with such fervor and withal such sincerity that the very sight of him convinced one of the truth of his words. . . . At times he stretched upward as though he were about to ascend into the sky. . . . And the general rapture . . . ! It seemed as though the whole world was listening to him. The breeze stopped whispering. Swallows sat in a row at the edge of roofs and not even one twittered. . . ."

Frangipani guffawed with laughter.

"Listen to the minstrel, Your Honor. The swallows listened! What about the chickens and the pigs? Did they listen too?"

Giacobbe became pensive.

"I wish I could know what the man said, whence he came!" she sighed.

Frangipani's steward who sat at the foot of the board lifted his head. "I think, Madonna, it was one of those half-mad beggars whom Bishop Guido of Assisi has given abode in his palace for over a week now. There is a whole mob of them. They tend to all lowly chores around the Bishop's kitchen and in their spare time wander around the city and preach to the people . . ."

"They are no heretics. Maybe we ought to send a servant to fetch that speaker whom you heard, Messire. He might repeat to us what he was telling to the rabble."

Divini shook his head.

"I fear, Madonna, the effect will be spoiled. The poor wretch will be surely confused, awed, lost. Fear will make him tongue-tied. It would be better to hear him there, out in the square."

"With the swallows which will wait in silence till he finishes . . . Yes . . . But then the crowd will gather again, and, as you said, contact with them is not pleasant."

The sun beat upon the world. Particles of dust trembled in the air. The narrow stifling streets of Rome and its squares flooded with sunlight were swarming with people. The aspect and prosperity of the town revealed long years of peace—for over forty years the Eternal City had seen no invaders. Although not all of the burned buildings had been rebuilt rains had washed the char from their ruined walls and restored their serenity. New hovels and shacks which each fire erased, each invasion wiped out, grew once more thick upon the slopes of great pagan buildings. Life swarmed noisy and idle. A donkey loaded with vegetables climbed slowly up the steep narrow street. An old crone, not unlike a witch, ran out of a house in pursuit of a cat which she was trying in vain to reach with a poker. A group of half-nude urchins made faces at her and shouted: "What did she grab, Donna Sylvia? What did she grab?" Others screamed, "Why, she was going to eat that rat tomorrow for a roast." The cat was by now safe on the roof top and the lads in their turn were scurrying before the old crone's wrath. In the middle of the square lay a great block of timber. Several children had dragged a long board from somewhere, placed it across the block and were now playing seesaw so that tanned heels flashed in the air. Dogs nosed about through a pile of rubbish. Goats walked solemnly amidst people. Francis and his companion, brother Juniper, sat under a fence, resting before again starting on their way. It was there that the servant sent from the palace of Frangipani found them.

"Hey there," he shouted, "are you he who spoke in this square today, before noon?"

"I spoke," said Francis.

"You're lucky, fellow. Sire William Divini, the king of minstrels, has noticed you and all their honors are coming this way. You are to repeat to them what you said this morning. And in the same way. And mind that you stay here or else they will curse me for not finding you."

"I wouldn't have you cursed, brother, so I shall not go away," Francis promised.

Reassured, the servant turned to the problem of cleaning the square.

"Out of here, rascals!" he screamed. "The high-born, the nobles are coming! They have no need to breathe your stench! Clear out!"

He dealt with them effectively, not sparing his short whip. The rabble dispersed, the children climbed on the fence to see what would happen. The board they had just deserted still swayed on the block. There was no one in the square save Francis and brother Juniper.

"Mind you stay here! They are coming," the servant shouted once more and disappeared.

And indeed the beating of horses' hoofs could be heard. Brother

Juniper looked expectantly at Francis. Francis smiled at him in his usual manner.

"Brother," he said suddenly, "not since I was a child have I sat on such a seesaw . . ."

"Neither have I," agreed brother Juniper.

"What if we took a swing? There is nothing in it that might offend Our Lord."

"Surely not," exclaimed brother Juniper, eagerly skipping like a child for joy. They took their places at the two ends of the board.

Up! Francis with a kick of his heels shoved himself up in the air. The board lifted. "Now this is your turn, brother! Push hard, for you are heavier than I am. Up you go!"

Brother Juniper roared with delight. Now Francis crouched on the ground, squatted small like a sparrow. Juniper swung his feet delightedly. Up! Now Francis was on top again.

The noble retinue was already emerging on to the small square. Jean de Brienne and Madonna Giacobbe, William Divini with the laurel leaves upon his cap, and the noble knight Graciani Frangipani.

"That one, Your Honor! That one!" the servant pointed to the bouncing Francis.

Sir Frangipani drew the reins of his mount.

"What?" he asked amazed. "This fool on the seesaw? Are we supposed to listen to him?"

"He seems to be the same man," admitted Divini shamefacedly.

"I have better buffoons at my court. They can amuse us in a more seemly way. A preacher indeed! Let us turn back, Your Honors."

They agreed without a word. In truth, how could one pay attention to a half-wit swinging on a board? They rode away. Divini was morose, Donna Giacobbe disappointed, de Brienne indifferent. What was it all to him?

Francis climbed down from the board although brother Juniper would have liked to continue the fun. The dispersed crowds returned to the square. The cat on the roof arched her back.

The two brothers were returning to the palace of the Bishop of Assisi. Francis sighed disconsolately.

"I have done wrong," he confessed. "I have offended those great folks. It may be they really wanted to hear the words of Our Lord."

"Oh, no," replied brother Juniper with conviction. "I looked them over carefully. . . . They were all rich folks."

"And what if they were, brother? Must a rich man be worse than a poor one? It would be too bad if we started to think ourselves better than they. We should hate riches, but love equally all men, even though burdened with wealth. Each of them can get rid of his possessions by distributing them to the poor and become dear to Christ Our Lord, more precious than any of us. Aye, brother. I've sinned grievously."

"I am certain," insisted Juniper, "that they came out of sheer curiosity."

"How many come because of curiosity, and leave with their souls aflame? Pride, pride. . . . Dear brother, I've committed a great sin . . . I command you to tell of it to all our brethren and to all men with whom I shall speak and who may deem me better than I am. Tell them: 'Francis thinks himself a wise leader but in truth he is a vainglorious fool . . .'"

"I don't know whether I can say so," confessed Juniper, embarrassed. Francis turned to him indignantly.

"But I command you to say so in the name of monastic obedience. You must tell what I bid you to tell! Do you understand?"

"Well then, I will."

"And now let us hurry. I must confess before brother Sylvester and ask him for absolution."

But brother Sylvester was not there and no one knew where he had gone. Instead Francis found awaiting him his chance acquaintance from the inn of The Good Guardian, the learned scholar Matteo Pesaro.

"I met one of your brethren in town," he said, "and he told me I would find you here. . . . I would have you meet a certain man whom I have just come across and who thinks a great deal about the salvation of his soul."

"Thank God for it. Where is that man?"

"Not here," Matteo leaned towards Francis' ear and whispered mysteriously: "He is hiding. . . . A Cathari. . . . Perhaps you'll not want to come now that you know?"

"Why not? It is not the well but the sick who need a healer. . . . Save that what kind of a healer am I! The worst among sinners . . . If you only knew what I committed not a moment ago."

"Let's go," interrupted Pesaro.

# 6.

# Dilemma

FRANCIS HAD NOT FOUND BROTHER SYLVESTER BECAUSE BISHOP GUIDO HAD summoned the latter to a private conference. The Bishop had known him in the days when the present companion of that "madman" Francis was a prosperous, rotund, somewhat greedy parson with no compunctions about shearing his flock. The change was strange, indeed, and the Bishop with unhidden curiosity watched the man who was once his subordinate. The ex-vicar had lost weight, but in spite of that and though dressed in a heavy cloak of cheap woolen, a veritable hooded bag, he looked younger than of yore. His countenance was clear, serene.

"Be seated, brother," the Bishop said. "I am expecting His Grace, Cardinal John Colonna. We want to talk over with you the matter of the confirmation of your Rule. The Holy Father will receive Francis shortly and give his opinion. You know I am your friend and would like to help Francis. . . ."

"So help is needed?" inquired Sylvester perturbed.

The Bishop smiled indulgently.

"Is it needed? Let me tell you in all frankness: unless you change the Rule, the Holy Father will never confirm it. So much is certain. Yet knowing as I do how touchy Francis is upon certain points we wanted first to talk them over with you. You are a priest; you will more readily understand our objections. Francis I love and admire but I have always suspected him of being not quite sane."

"On the contrary!" protested Sylvester warmly. "Your Grace! He . . ."

He had no time to say any more, for in came John Colonna, the Cardinal of Ostia and Velletria, next to the Holy Father the highest among church dignitaries and a future pope himself. He was imposing of stature with a handsome and wise face. He cast a keen glance at

54

Sylvester, whom his very presence had thrown into confusion, and sinking into a deep aim-chair, asked curtly:

"So this is one of those half-wits? How many are you?"

"So far only twelve," Sylvester hastened to answer.

"How long have you been together?"

"That depends. Some have joined us but lately, but we, the older ones, already for three years . . ."

"Are there any amongst you who know how to read and write—with the most rudimentary education?"

"Yes, Your Grace. Brother Parenti, professor of the Bologna University, brother Bernard de Quintevalle, a lawyer, brother Rufin Sciffio. . . ."

"And brother Sylvester here was parson in my diocese," added Bishop Guido.

The Cardinal did not hide his surprise.

"I would have thought that the idea of such a Rule could have sprung only from the heads of complete illiterates. Do you actually live by it?"

"Indeed we do, Your Grace. We try not to deviate from the precepts of the Holy Gospel."

"And none of you has left, none of you regretted . . . ?"

"If any of us were to regret, we could leave at any time. We are free."

"It is but a manner of speaking. One might often be ashamed to leave, even though he sees the task he has assumed exceeds his strength. Have you no malcontents among you?"

Sylvester faltered. He knew the thoughts which beset John a Capello, for instance, and was aware that at times—no denying it—others shared them, too.

Colonna watched him closely.

"So there are? That's understandable enough. . . . I can guess what irks you most: this vagrant existence, living from alms, an uncertain tomorrow, so contrary to human nature. . . ."

"Yes," admitted Sylvester wistfully. "Sometimes a body longs for a fixed abode, for the slightest comfort. Particularly when a body sees smoke . . ."

"What smoke?"

"At night," mumbled Sylvester confused.

He was no poet and therefore unable to express his thought. The most poignant longing assailed them when, wandering at dusk over the hills, they would gaze down in the valley and see smoke rising from chimneys in white, straight plumes. Then they would often feel faint at heart. For each stack represented a family-hearth and as one looked from afar he could readily imagine it was a happy, God-fearing and a safe one. . . . In those distant houses men were warming themselves, seated comfortably around the fire, while they, the brethren, would spend the night on the bare ground with nothing more than hard stones to put under their heads. . . . At such times it was hard, indeed. . . .

"I also know," he continued, "that brother Angel who wanted to be a dubbed knight is torn with yearning whenever knightly exploits are mentioned. But those are short moments of temptation, inevitable in any order, after which we feel the grace of Our Lord more strongly. And there is none among us, I think, who is not happy. . . ."

"And is it true you possess nothing of your own?"

"We do not, Your Grace. This cloak, a cord for a belt, and breeches. Neither staff nor wallet, for so it is said in the Gospel. . . . And we must give even from these garments should the poor ask."

"And what then? Go about naked and scandalize people?"

"It has happened more than once that the brethren would first give away their hoods, then the cord, then the cloak . . . for there are some so poor that they will covet even such things. . . . Once two of our brethren were left with nothing but their breeches and thus they walked about for several days. And fearing that someone might want even those they smeared them with dung so none would ask."

"Revolting," shuddered the Cardinal.

"I recall that incident," broke in Bishop Guido. "I provided those brethren with new cloaks and had it proclaimed throughout the diocese that none should take your clothes . . ."

"Just so, Your Grace."

"Are you not tormented by the desire, so proper to human beings, to possess something?" the Cardinal inquired.

"Yes, indeed, but we fight it."

"That is precisely the point in your Rule to which the Apostolic See will never consent. Absolute poverty! It is pure folly, and none but a fool could think of it! It is contrary to life, contrary to social order, harmful. It can be maintained at great pain but little harm as long as there is only a handful of you but what would happen if your number should grow into hundreds and thousands? Of course it is not as though it can be presumed that your number may ever increase, but the Holy Father when confirming an order must reckon with its growth. How dangerous in such a case would it be for a host of men, well-meaning though they may be, without means of support, to become a burden to the region and scandalize people by their idleness and witless charity!"

"Idleness, Your Honor? Francis always says a body who does not work is not worthy of being alive or eating. He will not allow any of us to idle. . . . We may not accept food unless we have first earned it."

"He is right in this, nonetheless absolute poverty is but a fancy. Impossible to achieve, in fact even undesirable . . . Take away from men their instinct of possession and all will crumble down; art, civilization . . . all. You must persuade your leader to concede this point before I submit your Rule to the Holy Father."

"Francis will not yield," said Sylvester, crestfallen, "inasmuch as to him poverty is the most important thing. It matters more than anything else. A few months ago we stopped in a deserted and uninhabited region. Merchants were riding by. They gave us more food than we needed for one day. We could not but take it for they out of sheer kindness left the victuals and rode off. Francis was disconsolate. 'What shall we do? What shall we do with it?' he kept repeating, because there were no people around to whom we might have given the food. He wanted it thrown into the stream but I told him it would be sin to destroy God's gifts to no good purpose. Brother Gilles offered to spread them over stones for the night . . . Mayhap a fox would come or an owl and feed upon them, he said, and so, we, in our turn, shall have set the board for our little brethren from the woods. That calmed Francis. But the countryside was so deserted no beast, not even ants, came and the next morning we found the provisions untouched. Other brethren rejoiced, particularly brother Masseo, who is fond of good cheer, but Francis mourned and grieved. 'And so we are rich,' he wailed, 'with a larder and provisions!' "

"Incredible!"

"Then another time one of the brethren wanted to keep his psalter. He pleaded and begged so piteously that at last we all felt sorry for him and interceded with Francis. Let the lad keep his book. . . . But it is no easy matter with Francis. He became angry, as only he can. . . . He flared up. He shook with passion. The brother stood petrified while Francis screamed: 'You shall not have your psalter! You shall not have your psalter! Soon you would want a breviary and after the breviary still another book! And you would sit in the stalls like some great prelate and say to the brethren: Fetch me my psalter!' And then he grabbed a handful of ashes from the grate and rubbed them hard over the brother's head repeating: 'Here is your psalter.' The brother wept half the night, not because of the book, but because he had angered brother Francis so."

"Incredible," repeated the Cardinal. "I myself am not a greedy man, I care nothing for money, this white and yellow metal which owes its importance only to human folly. But I see no harm in owning a house and furnishings . . . To be sure Christ our Lord praised Mary but He did not condemn Martha who cared for the house. He gave His blessing to the wedding feast at Cana. . . ."

"Francis wants to live like the Apostles. 'Were I to possess anything,' he says, 'I must likewise possess weapons to defend it. Had I a house, I would have to surround it with a fence and cut myself off from my neighbors lest one of them might want to take my house from me. And I would have to keep a watchman or a dog which I would feed poorly and bait, so that his honest dog's heart turn wicked and he may bite and growl. And by and by I might perchance gather money and become a wealthy man. Whoever has money thinks he is entitled to everything, and thus thinking he commits a great sin, inasmuch as the whole world belongs to no one but to God. And I would have strifes and litigations and I would curse my brother and maybe even throw him in gaol. Befouled with so many sins how would I dare to face Our Lord? And the cause of all that would be wealth, nothing else.' So Francis always says. . . ."

There was a moment of silence. Bishop Guido became lost in thought. He just remembered the interminable law suit over a certain field which his neighbors the Benedictine brethren claimed as belonging to the Abbey while he himself considered it the property of the Bishopric. A bothersome law suit. How much time and pains it had cost him! Yes, yes, were one but free of the burden of possessions—of the duty to watch over anybody's property!

But the Cardinal would not accept Sylvester's arguments.

"Wealth can likewise be used to good purpose," he said. "Besides of the two, it is a lesser evil to take care of what one owns than to lead an adventurous, vagrant life deprived of any security. The first certainty is fraught with fewer opportunities to sin than the latter. Poverty which you have in mind can be adhered to, but only if one lives in hermit-like seclusion as the Lord's saints were wont to do. . . . The idea of living everywhere and nowhere, like birds, is barbarous and absurd."

"If we settled in one spot we no longer could preach the Gospel to people, and that is our chief aim."

The Cardinal shook his head inexorably.

"Warn your leader," he said drily, "that unless he introduces changes in his Rule, he cannot even dream of obtaining the approval of the Holy Father. Sensible changes. . . . First of all that ridiculous interdiction of possessions. Certainly the individual may have no possessions—this is the basis of every monastic order. . . . But the order as a collective whole must have some support! Must have something to live on! Otherwise, it will soon turn into a band of parasites and thieves. And another important matter—fasts! It would seem you don't observe them. 'Eat whatever they place before you,' that's how the paragraph in point reads, if I recall rightly. How can this be reconciled with the teaching of the Church? By and large, I see no need of a new Rule. Monasteries already in existence have already tried out every means of perfection accessible to men and it suffices to take a ready pattern from any of the existing ones. If you crave a strict Rule, take the Camaldulians!"

Sylvester was on the verge of tears.

"Camaldulians keep silence and think only of their own salvation! Francis does not want to seclude himself from people. He wants to tell everyone how Our Lord should be loved and thanked and praised. He wants to reach those whom the Word of God never reaches; the va-grants, thieves and such miserable wretches one might deem God had forsaken."

"What can be gained by playing apostle to thieves?"

"Oh, he has gained more than once, Your Grace! We once en-countered in the mountains fierce robbers, stained with many an inno-cent victim's blood, who hid there from God and human justice. And at Francis' order for three days we handed to them all the food we had gathered for ourselves, until some brethren found it odd, and they grumbled. And on the third day, after fetching food to the robbers, Francis began to tell them about Our Lord's kindness and love. And tears began to flow from those fierce men's eyes and repentance descended upon them and they confessed to me and made a solemn vow never to rob again."

"That was once," murmured John Colonna.

"Yes, Your Grace," admitted Sylvester with candor, "inasmuch as another time, other robbers caught two of our brethren who tried to speak to them, drubbed them and flung them from a great height into the stream. It was a wonder the poor things were not killed. It must have been that the time of penitence had not yet come for them. No, one does not always succeed in reaching a man's heart but one must always try. That is the reason why Francis will have none of the existing Rules. He wants to teach according to the Gospel. Each precept founded upon the words of Our Lord . . ."

"I told you already it is impossible. No use talking about it any more," said the Cardinal with finality, rising from the chair to show that the conversation was ended. But Sylvester, though terrified by his own audacity, still would not yield.

"Your Grace," he whispered pleadingly. "Should the Holy Father reject our humble plea—when all we ask is to live according to the Gospel—will it not imply that the teachings of Our Lord are impossible to follow?"

Silence fell after these words, a long unbroken, tormenting silence.

"His Holiness will do whatever he considers best for the good of the Church," said the Cardinal at last, and left with a rustle of his mantle.

"I expected more sense from you, brother Sylvester," sighed the Bishop. "Your case is lost."

Meanwhile Francis, Matteo Pesaro, and his new acquaintance, member of the sect of Cathari, alias Clean Ones, alias Albigenses, the most powerful of the Church's foes, against whom Sir Simon de Montford conducted a cruel and fierce crusade, sat in the corner of a quiet inn. Francis asked Matteo what had become of his one time companion Pietro Cani.

The scholar made a vague gesture with his hand.

"I do not know for sure, but probably nothing good. Although he himself always warned me to beware of two things, a red-headed man and an inn where the innkeeper is old and his wife young, as fate would have it we stopped at an inn where the innkeeper was red-headed and much older than his wife. What a coincidence—was it not? Well I do not know whether because of that or for some other reason the lad had no luck. One day town-guards came for him and took him away. They must have locked him in the dungeons for he did not return."

"Whatever had he done, the poor thing?" exclaimed Francis compassionately.

"That I do not know either, for I was out at the time and I did not care to ask too much lest I attract suspicion. . . . A body must be cautious these days, particularly in Rome . . ."

"We must discover where he is and see how we can help him."

"Oh, well! He will extricate himself somehow, I trust. . . . It is not as though he were a child. Besides, he is neither friend nor kin of mine, that I should trouble myself over him."

While expressing this sensible view Matteo made himself comfortable on the bench. From where he sat he looked down upon his companions, for they both had seated themselves upon the floor. Francis did so instinctively, first because he was no longer used to furniture and next because sitting upon the ground he felt more like himself—a small creature of God, than when perched on a stool. Noticing Francis' gesture the Catharus quickly did likewise, for he would not have anyone excel him in showing humility. Too portly and heavy to follow their example Matteo observed them with curiosity. Surely it was not so much care for the salvation of the heretic soul that had made him bring Francis here. Above all also he was fond of dogmatic disputes and he was looking forward to the argument between these two men. What could be more pleasant than to listen to the dispute of two representatives of two different viewpoints upon the nature of God? Which one of the two would advance more convincing arguments? So far, they were both silent, therefore, to warm them up he ordered some wine. The Albigens refused it scornfully. Francis took the goblet in his hand and smiled.

"It is long since I saw you last, brother wine," he said gaily, "and yet we used to know each other well."

He peered at the sunlight which was reflected in the golden liquid. Slowly his face assumed an expression of gravity, respectfully he set the untouched wine on the edge of the table. The Albigens watched him curiously.

"What is there of such interest in this goblet, brother . . . I know not yet how I am to call you?"

"Brother Francis, or brother minor."

"And what is it you see in that glass?"

"What is it I see?" Francis turned his trusting, serene gaze upon the heretic. "I likewise do not know how I am to address you, brother?"

"Oh, simply brother Perfect."

"I just recalled, brother Perfect, how Our Lord has honored the wine among all other things in the world. Wine and white flour. The grape and the wheat. They are the only things subject to transfiguration during the Sacrifice. What a miracle! And the wine in this goblet might be transfigured likewise were it a priest and not a sinner like myself who took it and used it during the Holy Mass."

"Do you believe this, brother?" the Perfect puckered his lips in disdain.

Francis did not reply. He continued to gaze at the wine with a rapt expression as though the gold of the liquid had turned before his eyes into the ruby-red of blood.

"You love poverty," the Catharus went on, "therefore, it would seem you belong to us."

Francis lifted his eyes from the wine. The sun had hidden behind the vine which grew over the wooden lattice of the window and the flame had gone out of the liquid.

"No mortal man can be perfect, let alone myself," he remarked with a smile.

"Oh, it is only a matter of comparison with other people, particularly the priests and the monks, those worshipers of Mammon . . ."

Francis puckered his expressive brows.

"Monks? Priests?" he repeated. "What right have we to pass judgment upon them? Even if they commit sins, what is it to us? Let us watch our own conscience. They are, by Our Lord's will, our intermediaries between Him and us and we must respect and honor them . . ."

The Perfect laughed, clearly displeased.

"Truly, you don't belong to us! We fight with the clergy to the death! We shall teach them yet how to understand true faith. And to which do you belong? The Popelicans? The Humiliants?"

"I am the most humble servant of the Christ's Church."

"Which one?"

"There is but one. The Roman Church. Subject to the Holy Father."

"Don't try to deceive me, brother Minor. Surely, you don't need to beware of me. If the Popish bloodhounds but got wind of me. . . . Ho! Ho! So speak openly. It is enough to look at you to see that you have nothing in common with those ones. . . ."

He pointed to the street where, through the wooden lattice, one could see mounted upon a white she-mule, surrounded with servants in liveries and clerics in white surplices, some high church dignitary riding by.

"How could I have anything in common with such a high and noble lord? But I shall always obey their orders. Let them advise and rule For me it is enough to obey, to believe and to love."

The Perfect one shrugged his shoulders disdainfully.

"So you are a Papist . . . A great pity! But explain to me then, how evil has come upon this world and why God, who is goodness itself, allows it to exist and does not destroy the devil?"

"At last!" Matteo shifted upon his seat with delighted anticipation. "Here comes the debate. The nature of evil. The corner stone of the heresy of the Catharists . . . We shall see how the poor little brother defends himself. . . ."

But the poor little brother was not thinking of defending himself.

"Why do you ask me, brother?" he inquired with a smile. "Go to the Church and hear what the priest says."

"I want to hear from you."

"I shall tell you nothing but the mysteries of the Holy Faith just as Our Lord has tendered them through the intermediary of His Church . . ."

"But the Church has perverted, misinterpreted this teaching."

"What assurance have you that it is not you who misinterprets it?"

"Oh, no. We possess the truth. We have discarded the felonious book of Genesis and discovered its true meaning falsified by Moses. . . . We know that Satan, the god of evil, is the master of the earth, as omnipotent on earth as God is in heaven. God's will is carried out by Eons, pure spirits which constitute the Pleoron, the Circle of Perfection. Christ the Lord was one of the oldest among Eons, Peter de Bruys another.

"Thanks to the Eons humanity can escape Satan and achieve salvation. The Holy Scripture confirms our teaching. When it speaks of the one who shall rise above God, it is Lucifer it means. Likewise did Christ in the parable of the unworthy steward . . ."

Francis listened absent-mindedly, Matteo with great interest.

"And the creation of man, according to you whose act was that?" he inquired.

"Not God's indeed, not God's! Had God created man he would have made him perfect. It would be sacrilege to believe that out of God's hands anything but perfection could come forth. It was thus it happened: Satan ruled over the earth absolutely and God knew naught of him. But Satan could not create a being with an immortal soul and for that he envied God. And for thirty-two years he lay in wait at heaven's gates biding his chance to address the pure, immortal spirits which abided there. And when this happened he promised them untold delights and power and the awareness of good and evil, and so the spirits commenced to escape to the kingdom which was promised them. They slipped through the crack in the door left ajar like a swarm of falling stars, until God beheld the light of the starlike nebula and inquired what it might be? Whereupon He was wroth and ordered the door slammed to so none should escape from heaven to earth. And thus Satan gained possession of immortal souls. And God in His wrath cursed him with all his domains—that is the earth and all products thereof. And this curse still lasts. That's why a pure and perfect man holds the earth in contempt and loathing. . . ."

"What you say is dreadful, brother. The earth accursed? That most wonderful masterpiece of God's hands?"

"Not God's, mind you, but Satan's. Each of us attempts to free his spirit by the destruction of the flesh, and the most noble hasten their death of their own will. . . ."

"Suicide?" inquired Matteo with curiosity.

"Yes, many of us commit it, usually by means of starvation. We, the leaders, are not allowed to, for who would preserve the true teaching and lead the fight against the Papists? But we encourage the younger ones. Liberation through death we call 'endura.' It is a great honor to go through endura and the name of a brother or sister who does so is held in great esteem. It is a hard test indeed, for some suffer for several weeks before they achieve liberation."

"And while it lasts, are they not tempted to resign from untimely liberation by accepting food?" asked Matteo suspiciously.

"Never. Besides, whoever determines to pass endura cannot draw back lest he scandalize the whole community."

"So even were he to yell for food, he may not be given any," guessed

Matteo. And he shuddered at the gruesome image of those tortures of hunger which were not always voluntary.

Francis paid no heed to what they were saying. The previous remark of the Albigens to the effect that nature was accursed completely absorbed his mind.

"To hate nature," he now said in a voice muffled by excitement, "to hate plants, beasts, all that the Lord has created with such miraculous love and care? Oh, brother, how dreadful! How can one loath water, so cool, so soothing, so clear? Water that washes one's body as the sacrament of penitence washes one's soul, and which serves for the sacrament of baptism? Or the trees? Stout, strong, widespread, so kindly, who would not bless them? It was wood that the Cross of Our Lord was made of! Or the fire; warm, glowing, sparkling? I love the water and the fire.

"Whenever a fire is dying, my heart yearns as though some beloved being was departing. I would never blow out a lantern or a candle for I would grieve for the flame! And the flowers, those fairest of all our brethren and sisters. The rose, the bloom of blooms, the symbol of martyrdom and divine love. None but the lily can compare with it, the lily whose beauty Our Lord Himself praised. And take but those smallest ones, the humble servants—herbs; the sage, sweet of scent, potent, useful. Agrimony, good for wounds . . . the pumpkin which, though it springs from a miserable seed, gives deep shade, climbs high upon trees. The mint, the house-leek, the thyme . . . there are so many of them and each has its own need and use. How can one hate the bee, that diligent, divine servant, the dog or the deer, the ox or the donkey which were first to behold Our Lord? And the birds? Truly, they are the best image of a good Christian. They soar in the sky, away from the bustle, care not overmuch for what tomorrow may bring. They pray while singing. Who dares assert that they came from the hands of Satan?"

His face darkened at such blasphemy. Matteo smiled superciliously. He had anticipated and looked forward to a learned debate; he had wondered whether Francis knew and could refute the theory of Eons, and instead Francis raved of flowers. The Catharus was openly annoyed.

"Go and tell such tales to the birds," he interrupted sharply. "We shall not be fooled and lured by sinful matter."

"Nevertheless you kill no animal, it seems? Is this true?" inquired Matteo.

"We do not kill animals because it is in the bodies of beasts that the souls condemned to purgatory enter. Nothing but fish and reptiles may we kill and partake of, inasmuch as their blood is cold and they are not fit to be the refuge of the human soul who is used to warm blood."

He rose and with relief stretched his frame, weary of sitting upon the hard ground.

"It is time I was on my way. As it is I stayed too long. I ought not to show myself in daytime nor speak so openly. . . ."

"The possibility of freeing yourself of your body likely holds no fear for you," remarked Matteo, not without malice.

"I yearn for liberation," assured the Perfect one proudly, "yet I have certain important matters to attend to. So I have to protect my miserable earthly cover."

"What matters?" Matteo's curiosity was aroused once more.

But the Perfect one was not eager to reply. Instead he began to lament about Rome.

"That loathsome city of Antichrist! When shall we at last demolish those temples and crosses?"

"Demolish the crosses?" asked Francis with an effort.

The eyes of the Perfect one shone red. "We loath the very sight of the Cross," he said in a hoarse whisper. "This shameful reminder of the degradation and death of Christ! Not of His divinity but of His bodily nature which he offered to Satan for us. Our God is in Heaven surrounded by glory. Our God cannot be humiliated."

Francis covered his face with his hands.

"God! God! The greatest sign of Thy Love!"

The Albigens cast him a scornful glance.

"Seeing that I have offended you, why not denounce me? Do! But remember that my own kind shall avenge me."

Francis lifted to him eyes full of tears. "Denounce you, my luckless brother?" he stammered amazed. "Denounce you? I should gladly lay down my life so that you may live a long while yet and have time here, still on earth, to correct your errors."

Through his tears he gave the dour heretic such a radiant smile that the latter, despite himself, lowered his eyes.

"And don't you fear," he asked after a while, "that instead of making 'penance' as you call it, I would use this long life to demolish all churches and crosses?"

"I fear not," exclaimed Francis, and added with a merry laugh, "No, no one will demolish the Cross."

He looked at the ground. At his feet two twigs had fallen one upon the other in the likeness of a cross. He picked them up carefully, holding them in the center so that the holy form might not be destroyed, and warmly, respectfully, he pressed them to his lips.

# 7.

# The Dream

Renzo, the page, was affixing long, silver spurs to his master's boots, while the squire Wilfred arranged upon the knight's shoulders a long gold-cloth mantle so it would fall in straight, even folds. Sir Jean de Brienne was about to start on his way to an audience with the Holy Father. The mirror before which he stood reflected his sullen, avid face surmounted by a crown of white hair. Displeased, he drew a hand over it, thinking how much younger he would look could he but shave it off as he did his mustache. Indeed his face was still youthful and smooth. Were it not for that accursed greyness . . . but shear it he could not. It would be unseemly for a knight to go with his head shaved like a slave.

The door creaked. A servant announced the arrival of His Honor, William Divini, the bard. De Brienne nodded. Since the feast at the Frangipani's he had met the "divine" William more than once. He had even grown fond of the man. On his part the singer had developed a deep affection for the future king of Jerusalem and did not conceal that he would like to join his court.

To those overtures Jean de Brienne made no definite reply. Indeed, he would have been glad to keep by his side the famous bard, a confidant if need be, but he feared the expense. William Divini was used to a high fee and the chest of Jean de Brienne, for all the help Philip and the Holy Father had given him, still remained empty. The fact filled the knight with bitterness.

"A man is but a slave," he mused. "Forever living in bonds. In no wise can he act according to his will. All goes against him. Never does he feel free and independent. Of what good is it to me to be king? I am more bound than ever. . . ."

Divini entered the room dapper and important as was his custom.

68

With a somewhat embarrassed smile he was leading a maiden of extreme youth and wonderful beauty. She had thick black locks, great humid eyes, a tight-fitting dress and lips that were redder than the dress. She advanced confused and shy and yet slyly coy. Though childlike in appearance she knew well why she had been brought here.

"The Italian spring brings homage to His Majesty," announced Divini pompously, drawing the girl forward. "Her name is Julia. I took her from a witch of a stepmother."

"Comely she may be but what is it to me?" mumbled de Brienne crossly. He glanced at the wench. She was casting beguiling glances at his squire Wilfred.

"What is it to me?" he repeated. "Truly she is spring, and what is spring to autumn?"

"Who dares speak of autumn?" denied the gallant Divini.

"Do you think, sir, it would be more fitting to speak of winter."

"God forbid," exclaimed the bard. "Our ripe age—forgive me, Your Majesty, for likening myself to you—is summer, the height of summer!"

"Tut, tut," shrugged de Brienne, "let us not fool ourselves."

Once more his face darkened. If he could but fool himself! If he could but believe he was still young. . . . Did every old or aging man feel the same way? Was everyone tortured by a similar helplessness in the face of passing years? He cast an inquiring glance at Divini but the troubadour did not notice his gaze. He was staring at the beautiful maiden with such melancholy that de Brienne burst into laughter.

"Spring, it seems, lures you more than me?"

"Youth is fair," sighed Divini sententiously.

They both fell silent. The wench, not in the least embarrassed, peeped coyly in turn at the page and the squire. All three exchanged conspiring smiles, and seemed to have completely forgotten the presence of two kings, the King of Jerusalem and the King of Song.

"Does Your Majesty wish to keep her?" asked the troubadour.

"It would be wronging you."

"By no means," denied Divini warmly. "Indeed, it happened once that the troubadour de Miravel sang the allures of Adelaide de Boisson with such eloquence that King Peter of Aragon fell in love with her sight unseen and took her away from the troubadour. After that Miravel was called a beacon lighting the path of lovers. I, however, shall not be so dubbed for it was I who brought this marvel to your Majesty."

De Brienne did not reply. The mention of Peter of Aragon and Adelaide reminded him of Philip and Blanche. This was enough to silence him. Courteously he bid the bard good-bye. It was time to set off for the Lateran. "I am very late," he remarked. "His Holiness may grow impatient."

"What of the wench, shall I leave her here?" insisted Divini.

"Do as you please," de Brienne called back over his shoulder. His mount had already been brought. He leaped to the saddle with the sprightliness of a youth and set out at a rapid pace. Four squires and as many servants followed him. Divini remained at the door, greatly disappointed.

"Do as you please. What does he mean? What am I to do now?"

Jean de Brienne was not late for the audience. On the contrary, he had to wait for over an hour. Innocent III felt ill that day and had risen later than was his custom. At night he had long lain wakeful and when at last he fell asleep he was tormented by persistent and evil dreams. It seemed to the Holy Father that he stood in front of the Lateran church, that most venerable of all temples, called the mother and the heart of churches, and suddenly beheld with horror a deep crevice upon the gable wall. The wall was splitting asunder. Innocent lifted his arms in despair for he saw that close to the first one appeared other crevices and cracks. Lengthwise and crosswise they blackened the walls covering them with a net-like design. The walls were already cracking and bending. . . .

"Help, help!" called the Pope, but his voice would not come out of his throat. It was in vain that he tried to scream, his numb lips would not move. He tried to rouse himself, run to the rescue, support the crumbling walls, save them . . . but his feet were rooted to the ground, he could not move. . . . It did no good to strain and struggle, he could not take a step. . . . Helpless, voiceless, he could only stare. . . . And the cracks were growing deeper with every second. The whole building was already split, cracked to its very foundations. It tottered, it was about to collapse. . . .

Perspiration dripped from the Holy Father's face. His teeth chattered as though in a chill, his cheeks had grown pale, there was despair in his soul, horror in his heart. . . . The Lateran, the mother of churches, was crumbling. . . .

The sound of approaching steps reached his tormented ears. Someone was coming . . . someone was coming. . . . A patter of bare feet. . . . Here! A man short of stature, miserably clad, slight. . . . An ash-brown ordinary beggar's cloak, a rope for a belt, a hood, a bare head. . . . He advanced quickly toward the cracked walls, stretched his arms as though he meant to embrace the church and hold it up. . . . And in the stupefied eyes of Innocent he began to grow, grow . . . he was no longer short and slight . . . he was as tall as the trees, as a mountain, his head reached the cornice of the roof . . . his arms stretched from corner to corner. With one strong heave of his back he straightened the leaning walls. He drew his palms over the cracks and wherever his hand touched the crevices disappeared, the walls grew smooth. The great, venerable building stood strong, straight and sound as before.

With voiceless lips the Pope prayed his thanks. Tears of joy flew from his eyes; and the giant began to shrink, grow small, once more he was slight and unsightly. . . . He turned away from the wall and for the first time the Pope caught a glimpse of his face. He stared at him avidly, blessed him with his eyes. . . . A common face, this was, with a scanty beard, a thin neck, a clear gaze. Innocent noticed a peculiar trick he had of throwing his head back and lifting his chin as though peering into the sky. The little man smiled at Innocent and turned away, skipping merrily as he went. There was not a grain of dignity in him. And the Lateran stood haughty, undaunted, unimpaired. . . .

Daylight dispelled the murk of the chamber. The Pope awoke. He drew a breath at the recollection of the nightmare. A strange, evil dream! The Cardinals Pelagius, Colonna, Ugolini entered the chamber to inquire as to his Holiness' health. Innocent related his dream. "I fear," he concluded, "this bodes new dangers for the Church."

"Dangers are already here," sighed John Colonna. "Those unending heresies. The devil himself sends them."

"Heresies are as old as the Church itself," corrected the Pope. "Even St. Paul the Apostle said, 'Haereses opportet esse.' Heresy oftentimes springs from ardent faith, from excessive zeal to surge onward. The misfortune and the danger for the Church lies in the fact that heresies find so many adherents."

"It is for that reason I call heresies the sowing of the devil," insisted Cardinal Colonna. "It is not so much ardent faith that causes them as pride. Pride! Men are fain to enforce their own explanation of mysteries to show themselves more righteous, wiser than the Church! It is the most frequent reason of heresy. It is why heresies grow in number."

"The chief cause," retorted the Pope sternly, "lies in ourselves. None else. Were it not for evil priests, no Christian would follow heretics! Unfaithful, greedy, guardians who sell the truth, absolve the rich and condemn the poor! Those are responsible for heresies!"

To Cardinal Pelagius the Pope's judgment seemed over-harsh.

"There are many heretics," he asserted, "but only a few priests unworthy of their calling. Therefore it cannot be priests who are guilty of the criminal tendency to cast doubt upon the teaching of the Church."

"Unfortunately, one evil representative of Christ can bring about the schism of scores of souls!"

"For my part," said Cardinal Colonna, "I still insist the chief reason of heresy is pride. Heretics advocate poverty, the return to life according to the Gospel, only to point out to the clergy their own failing and to set themselves above them in the eyes of the multitude."

Innocent smiled wryly. "Aye, this bears out my words. The clergy have shortcomings easy to point out."

"I believe," remarked Ugolino, the Cardinal-Chancellor, "that Your Holiness is to receive today one of these prophets who proclaim humility and absolute poverty."

"Just so. Today after Vespers."

"Probably some new Arnold of Brescia?" scoffed Pelagius. "Why does Your Holiness receive him, instead of driving him away or better still locking him up?"

Cardinal Pelagius was a man of great stature, with a masterful face and quick abrupt movements. The crimson which his colleagues wore only on state occasions, he wore every day from morning till night. Hence the rabble had dubbed him "the Red Cardinal." Harsh and unyielding, he had few friends.

"We cannot lock him up," expostulated Colonna, "for the Bishop of Assisi holds him particularly dear. I even went to see him in this matter. I did not see the reformer himself, but I talked with one of his followers whom Bishop Guido considers the most sensible of the lot."

"What manner of man is he?"

"Mad—though he looks placid enough. To maintain absolute poverty seems the most essential thing to him. According to them one ought to possess nothing—not even a prayer book, or clothes. . . . Nor should one set aside provisions, not even for a single day. Every man, even a brigand, ought to be treated like a brother."

"Dangerous precepts are these. . . . Very dangerous indeed. Exactly like Arnold of Brescia!"

"Forgive me, Your Honor, but there is a difference. While Arnold and his likes proclaimed their teaching wilfully, this one came to Rome to beg the Holy See's approval. . . ."

"He shall not get it, I trust. The renunciation of all possessions! What a fancy!" Cardinal Pelagius was a man of great wealth. "Christ the Lord did not condemn rightful possessions. . . ."

"But He ordered His disciples to renounce all worldly goods," Innocent said quietly. "Besides I never saw it mentioned anywhere that He Himself possessed anything."

"Where would the Church be were she to act on this principle! In the world nothing but force avails, and in order to be mighty one must be rich."

"There is spiritual force, independent of wealth."

"It seems Your Honor shares the view of this new sectarian!"

"By no means. I told his disciple frankly they will surely not obtain approval. But then he told me something I shall remember . . . grievous words, indeed."

"What words?"

"He told me; were the Holy Father to forbid us to live according to the Gospel won't it be a proof that the Gospel is impracticable. . . ."
Silence fell.

"And in truth, is it practicable?" sighed Ugolino.

"Is it practicable? You blaspheme! Christ the Lord knew our strength. . . . He would not impose a task that exceeded them. . . . It is only we . . . we . . ." Innocent clasped his weary, tormented head. "It is we who break faith at every turn. . . . We. . . . I feel it. . . . And I cannot help it. . . . I am helpless. . . . Now this dream. . . . That awesome dream. . . . It contains some warning which I cannot fathom. . . . It is in vain I think. . . . O Lord! have mercy upon me!"

"Not all dreams are prophetic," Cardinal Colonna tried to comfort him.

"Nay, indeed! Yet this dream had a meaning. . . . Like the dreams which Joseph interpreted in Egypt, like the dream of Joseph, husband of Mary. . . . This dream was not a common nightmare that vanishes

with daylight. . . . I remember it as if it were reality. . . . I would recognize the man who supported the Church with his arms if I were to
meet him at the world's end."

"Was it not one of us, members of the Holy Collegium?" inquired
Pelagius.

"No! He was not a church dignitary."

"A monk, perhaps. . . ."

"Neither. He had the appearance of a common beggar."

"I shall never believe a beggar could save the Church," said Pelagius
with deep conviction. "There are dreams sent by God, but there are likewise dreams sent by the devil. The devil could have tormented Your
Holiness with an evil fancy in order to deprive you of peace and impair
your weak health."

"No," the Pope warmly protested, "this dream was not of the devil."

"So many strange things befall nowadays," added Ugolino in a conciliatory manner, "anything seems likely! The world is running in reverse. Bishops advise us that in France, Germany and even here in Italy,
children collect in groups and weep over the plight of the Holy Sepulchre and vow to set forth and fight for its liberation. Has anything like
it ever happened before?"

"God bless them!" said Innocent fervently.

The Cardinal-Chancellor did not share his enthusiasm.

"Does not Your Holiness think," he inquired, "that such ardor, even
though beautiful, is fraught with danger? Such an expedition of infants
—expeditione nugatoria, expeditione derisoria—must end in a grievous
defeat which would deride the Christians in Saracen eyes."

Pope Innocent looked at the speaker with surprise.

"An expedition? A defeat? You speak in jest, my son! The children
are gathering but they shall not start. Who would lead them? Who
would ferry them across the sea? Or give them vessels? Who would let
them out of the ports? No, no, these are vain fears. Their holy enthusiasm can accomplish but one thing: wake up their elders, put to shame
the sluggish conscience of grown men. For note, beloved, that whenever
children undertake a task which exceeds their strength, it means that the
world is ailing and forgets its duties. The new generation which ought
to act tomorrow applies for its job today, seeing that the elders are dozing and none attends to the task. . . . It is an evil sign. . . . Woe to the
world should it not rouse at the children's voice!"

"Do not the bishops write," inquired Cardinal Colonna, "under whose influence the children gather? Who collects them, who rouses them, and to what purpose?"

"They do not say. Perhaps of their own accord?"

"Impossible. Numbers do not gather without being summoned. . . ."

He broke short at the entrance of the chaplain of the Holy Father, who timidly inquired whether His Holiness would be pleased to receive Sir Jean de Brienne who had been waiting for a long time. . . .

"By the net of the Fishermen," exclaimed Innocent, frankly grieved, "I forgot! It is the dream's fault. . . . The noble knight must be surely angry. Bid him at once into the hall!"

Jean de Brienne was annoyed indeed and on the point of leaving when he was informed that His Holiness was awaiting him. After a few moments of conversation, however, his irritation abated. Innocent, although much younger in years than Jean, gave the impression of an old and ailing man. He seemed to bend under the burden of the whole world. Grey before his time, worn and weary he gazed at his guest with such friendly and wise eyes that de Brienne for all his hot-headedness realized that there was no intentional offense in the delay. They conversed in a friendly manner. The Pope rejoiced that the Kingdom of Jerusalem would once more have a knightly king who, God willing, should be able to recover the Holy Sepulchre and put to right the most horrible mishap which had befallen in the last century.

"This shall be my chief concern," de Brienne assured him.

Innocent did not notice the politely casual tone of the knight's reply. Once started on the subject of the loss of Jerusalem he was unable to think of anything else.

"The loss of the Sepulchre!" he repeated, shaking his head. "The loss of the fount of Christendom! Men do not speak enough of it, do not think enough of it. People become accustomed to it. That is the worst. Where are Christians? Are they all asleep? Where are the faithful ready to shed their blood for the glory of Christ the Lord? I have just been told that in Germany, France and even in here flocks of children gather, eager to save the Holy Sepulchre. . . . What a grievous lesson for the world! What a shame for the sleepy heads who care for nothing save their own gain. Will it bring them back to their senses? Innocent children suffer over the disgrace of Christ and the indifference of their

elders. But you, Sir, shall arouse the slumbering ones. You shall inflame
them by your example. Your fame, the noble readiness with which you
accepted an honor which is not easy, are a guarantee that you will succeed. I have put in you my last hope. . . . You must lead a new, mighty
crusade which will bring the task of liberation to its conclusion without
deviating from its course—as the previous one did."

"I fear Your Holiness overestimates my humble possibilities. Who
will listen to my voice?"

"I shall call them and you will lead."

Cardinal Pelagius, who had listened in silence, now stirred impatiently.

"Does Your Holiness not think that the crusade should be led by a
churchman? Under lay leadership none seems to succeed. The first crusade was the only one which achieved success, and it was led by Adhemar the Bishop of Puy. . . ."

"The Bishop of Puy died in the middle of the expedition," interrupted de Brienne.

"It was so," the Cardinal admitted grudgingly. "He died at the siege
of Antioch but he was replaced by Arnold de Rhodes."

"Arnold de Rhodes dubbed Malecome?" exclaimed Jean indignantly.
"He—the leader? Who said so? Who wrote so?"

"Was he not elected Patriarch in recognition of his merits?" replied
the Cardinal evasively.

"According to the witness of chroniclers he so proclaimed himself,
but the Holy See quickly removed him from the post!"

"That is beside the point. It seems to me he contributed to the taking
of Jerusalem. Without him lay captains would have thought of their
own gain, not of the cause."

De Brienne's face darkened at the insult flung at his estate.

"Your honor offends the entire knighthood," he growled.

"I only state what is true."

They glared at each other, conscious of a growing mutual animosity.
Displeased at the turn the conversation had taken, Innocent tried to
soothe the impression left by Pelagius' words.

"The Cardinal did not mean to offend the knightly estate, my son.
He only pointed that among lay lords strifes over priority are frequent,
while our men should have nothing but the purpose in mind. . . ."

"I have seen Bishops aplenty who fought each other tooth and nail," de Brienne retorted sullenly. Out of respect for the Holy Father he refrained from adding that not so long ago he had seen two popes engaged in bitter strife. The conversation lagged in spite of Innocent's efforts.

De Brienne rose to take his leave. The Pope pleaded with him not to delay his departure for the Holy Land. "It is high time the battered kingdom had a king. For the love of Our Lord set out without delay!"

He gazed upon the knight so pleadingly that Jean was moved. Quickly he enumerated all the important and sensible reasons which had detained him so far and promised to do his best to hasten his departure. In two, three weeks he would sail. . . .

"But not later, not later, my son," pleaded Innocent, and he bid him farewell.

It was with a sense of relief that de Brienne left the palace. In the face of such ardor, such certainty, he felt small and inadequate. But what was he to do? Nonetheless, being an honest man he promised himself to keep the date of departure he had pledged to the Pope.

For Jean de Brienne was a trustworthy man, there could be no doubt of that. He held heresy and paganism in loathing and loved God. It was only that his love was not the chief of his emotions. God seemed remote to Jean, taking no direct part in his life. A brave knight, de Brienne would prefer to die for a godly cause rather than force himself to an unwanted departure for the sake of the same cause.

The sun's heat was unbearable. The cattle driven along the road stirred up clouds of dust. The knight while riding looked around, observing this strange city where houses grew upon ruins, where in spite of everything the ghost of the Caesars overshadowed the Fisherman. While he was staring at old, ruined and yet still beautiful buildings two men, advancing quickly, passed him by. The first one seemed to be a beggar, slight and bedraggled. The other, stout and well dressed, was the chaplain of Bishop Guido. He was breathing hard and wiping the perspiration from his forehead. As he passed he cast the knight a doleful glance as though to say: 'It is not of my own will that I follow this fool.' The first was smiling to himself, heedless of anyone. His face seemed familiar to Jean. Oh, yes, it was that street preacher, that jester of the seesaw whom once, upon William's advice, they had gone to hear with Frangipani. Graciani could not to this day forget that occurrence.

A droll man, Divini. Moved by a preacher yet this morning he had brought Jean a wench! Eager to join the court of Jerusalem and to that purpose evidently willing to serve as best he could . . . He procured a wench for another yet stared at her as a cat might stare at a mouse. . . . The pander! But he had overreached himself. De Brienne cared nothing for the wench. If only it were Blanche! Could he but see Blanche, could he but know what she thought about, talked of. . . . Divini could not tell him that . . . !

Suddenly he struck his forehead. Strange he had not thought of it before! He pressed the flanks of his mount and started to gallop towards his house, while he sent one of his squires for the troubadour.

Divini arrived promptly, a little annoyed, a little morose after the morning's disappointment. But de Brienne greeted him cordially, bid him take a seat and ordered wine to be brought.

"He will order me to fetch Julia," guessed the troubadour.

But de Brienne was not thinking of Julia. He paced the chamber restlessly not knowing how to broach the matter. He was loath to confide his deepest feelings to a stranger who was aging, vain and greedy to boot but there was no other way. . . .

"You are the bard of love, messer," he began, still pacing the floor. "You must be aware, therefore, of the existence of passions that are very unwise indeed."

"Love is true only when it conquers wisdom," replied Divini and pricked his ears.

"I have never told anybody what I shall tell you now. Listen. I love a noble lady."

"Wedded?" guessed the bard.

"Yes, wedded. She has sons, daughters. I must protect her name. . . . And it is hard for me to live without her."

"Love harms none, disgraces none."

De Brienne shrugged his shoulders.

"This is not your troubadour, songster's love, standing under the windows of the beloved, composing rhymes and taking vows. . . . Such love is not sufficient for me. . . . I am a man, not a poet. . . . I was her lover not only in singing. I shared her bed . . . She got into my blood. . . . All my body yearns for her. No other can take her place, no matter how fair she might be. I am old. I cannot wait till her husband dies. . . . Passion gnaws at me. The last mortal passion. I care nothing for the kingdom which has been thrust upon my shoulders; I care nothing even for fame. . . . It is an infamy for a knight even to admit it, but I feel I can confide in you. Let me express it for once, for unsaid it torments and well-nigh chokes me!"

"A man who does not know of the power of love is not a complete man," interjected Divini.

"I have known it. Maybe because I did not begin to live till late. I spent my youth in bondage, working in a monastery. . . . Little time remained for love—perhaps that is why it came upon me so strongly. . . . I think sometimes that the passion of Tristan and Isolde was nothing compared with mine. . . ."

"Love without suffering and obstacles is worthless. Should fate interpose no obstacles, a wise lover would create them for himself so he would not lose the proper taste of passion. . . . I admire you and worship you, Your Majesty . . . Can you trust me? By the honor of the Saint Virgins! Who is it that fears to confide in his confessor? And what is a troubadour if not the priest of love, the confidant of lovers. . . . Tell me more. Can I be of any assistance to you? Shall I compose a song for the noble lady? Hectametre with mixed rhymes are of particular beauty."

"No, I need no song. I myself was wont to compose no ordinary songs, which are still sung in Champagne, though none knows whose they may be. It is news from her I want. . . ."

"Shall I write a letter?"

"No, no! It would be dangerous to send a letter. The servant may make a mistake, or hand it to someone else, or he may be caught and the letter intercepted."

"But a letter can be written so that no one can guess its meaning. . . ."

"Under a figure of speech, you mean? But in that case the lady would not understand it, either. No, writing will not do. I think of the matter constantly. The only way would be to send a trusted man, a friend who can be relied upon not to do anything rash and repeat to her properly. . . ."

"Well, in this case. . . ."

"I know what you are about to say; one of my companions, a knight or a squire. But it is not possible. The arrival of a strange knight would attract attention, arouse curiosity. He will be asked what he came for. The envoy must be a man whose arrival would seem natural, a man whom any court would welcome, a man like . . ." He stopped in front of the bard and said with effort, "Like you!"

"Like me?" repeated Divini slowly.

"Take no offense that I beg you to be my envoy. You are a bard of great fame, welcome everywhere with joy. . . . Troubadours are known to travel. None will be surprised at your coming from Rome to Champagne. . . . For she is the mistress of Champagne, my beloved is. And the sister of the King of Navarre. . . ."

The bard gasped. In his heart he decided to go.

"My lady is of great stock," continued de Brienne, not without pride, "but though high born she excels her birth by many other virtues. . . . Fair, brave, stately. . . . There is none to equal her. . . ."

He broke off. He suddenly remembered his skinny, ferret-like betrothed. What ill fate forced him to exchange one for the other!

"Anyway, you shall see for yourself," he continued in a low voice. "Tell her I live in torment for well-nigh a year, and each day it is worse. . . . They say a man forgets, gets accustomed to absence, but my yearning for her grows and grows. Like a spell . . . maybe it is a spell? At the court they have a witch, the cross-eyed Margot; maybe she has cast a spell upon me. No telling. But no matter. Whether it is a spell or my obdurate nature, I cannot forget, I cannot vanquish my love. So be it. Let her leave her husband and come to me! Let her cast all away! I shall make her queen. . . . What nonsense am I saying? As though I had drunk henbane. . . . She will not do that. . . . She will not come to be a paramour. . . . And it will be that Marie, to whom they have betrothed me, who will be queen. . . . Soon my wedded wife. . . . None of us is free: neither Blanche nor I! But something else she can do: let her come in pilgrimage to Jerusalem! No one can forbid her that. . . . Nor will anyone suspect. How many noble ladies have made a pilgrimage upon taking a vow! Let her do likewise. . . . She can bring her son, Thibault, along. . . ."

"Jerusalem is in the hands of heathens," Divini reminded him.

"So it is! I am talking nonsense! But never mind. Let her only come to Acre. . . ."

"It would be hard to make the pretense of a pilgrimage when the Sepulchre is in heathens' hands."

"The heathens will let the pilgrims in, though with great difficulties and at great cost. Anyway, I will arrange all. I will conclude a pact with the Sultan. . . . I will do anything so that she will have no hindrance. . . . Only so I may see her. . . . Only so I know she is coming. . . . You will persuade her. . . . You will convince her. . . . I shall be grateful to you as long as I live. . . . I will make it up to you. . . . Poor as I am I will find a way to reward you. Fighting the Saracens, knights soon grow rich. . . . All the spoils of my first expedition I will turn over to you, and later I will add more. . . . You will not regret. . . ."

"I am willing to travel to the end of the world, not for the sake of reward, for which I care naught, but to rejoice your Majesty's heart," Divini replied.

"Thank you, thank you! Start as soon as you can."

Proud of the mission entrusted to him the king of troubadours took his leave and departed. Left alone, Jean de Brienne brooded on the folly to which love could drive a man. Here he was, no longer young, stern, reserved, a king, to be confiding his innermost thoughts to a man whom only a few hours ago he had called a pander. He had conversed with him as with a friend; left his fate in his hands; beseeched him to give him his precious assistance. . . . Oh, the drollness, the awesome drollness of it! What if the envoys, the Bishop of Acre or the Lord of Cesarea were to get wind of it? The king . . . the king . . . enamored like a silly page . . . sending a troubadour . . . Maybe it would be better to send a servant to call William back. He could tell him it was only a jest, a droll tale, that there was no Blanche?

No, no, no! Let the people think what they may. . . . Let the world scoff! William must go!

Matteo Pesaro might have forgotten his chance companion, Pietro Cani, flung into jail without good reason, but not so Francis. Immediately after his conversation with the Catharus he ran to the prison to find out what had befallen his acquaintance.

The law, though stern, permitted prisoners to be visited. It was only that no one was eager to do so. To admit that he knew a man suspected of heresy—and heresy was the most frequent charge—was to draw suspicion upon oneself. Therefore a prisoner was deprived of any means to defend himself. A trial, if it ever took place, invariably ended in torture and death.

The regular prisons of Rome were overflowing. Indiscriminately huddled together, those whose interpretation of Christ's divinity differed from the teaching of the Church, brigands perennially devastating the Roman Campania, all those who had assisted the previous anti-pope, those suspected of conniving with the German invaders of Sicily, those who had once been in favor of the French troops of Walter de Brienne, crowded the narrow cells, shackled, clattering the chains that held them to the walls, cursing the world, life, God and themselves. There were so many that in spite of all the efforts of the gaolers there was no room for more. The newly arrived prisoners, therefore, were crammed everywhere: in the old thermae, in antique pagan temples, in dungeons which either on purpose or because of land slides were buried underground. In this chaos it was no easy matter to find someone who was not generally known, and for two days Francis roved through the prison in an obstinate and vain search of Pietro. The soul within him withered from these wanderings. The humid dungeons, the livid ghosts who dwelt there oftentimes for many years, seemed to him more horrible than hell itself.

Among the prisoners some were rebellious, strong, seething with an inner, smoldering rage. Never did they stop thinking of revenge; of the moment when they would get a chance to attack the gaoler unexpectedly, choke him, fling his body to the ground. . . . Like salvation they awaited a foreign invasion or some other calamity—the plague or an earthquake—one of those moments when prison gates fly open and gaolers flee. It would be their chance to escape, to hide from human eyes, recover their strength and then return to avenge themselves. Vengeance! The very thought kept them alive, lent them strength and determination. They dreamed of it, they summoned up pictures more horrible, more cruel every day; they fed upon them, exulted in them. Others, less rancorous or weaker or kept in prison too long, dreamed of nothing. Wan shadows, devoid of thoughts, memory and feeling, they no longer knew why they had been cast here or how many years ago. No word of sympathy or comfort could reach them, just as no threat could arouse fear in their hearts, and looking upon them Francis wept bitterly. . . . If one could but lead them out into the bright daylight, out into the sunshine and wind, and shout "Brethren! You're free!" Maybe they would come back to life! But this he could not do. The Pope himself could not. The Church State, just as any other state, must have its stern laws and jails, to punish and imprison those who oppose it.

Overcome with horror Francis would walk out of the dungeons staggering as though he were drunk. Oh! if only it were possible to destroy and tear down all prisons, raze all implements of torture and punishment from the surface of the world. Punishment! What a terrible word! None but God had the right to use it. A man should not punish his brother in any way save by saying, "Brother, go and sin no more!"

If all men loved each other as Christians should, such punishment would suffice; if men loved each other there would be no criminals. And again the whole matter resolved itself to the thing that seemed so simple: to rouse Christian feelings in men.

At last he found Pietro. He was not chained to the wall and the decay of prison had had no time to weaken his muscles and drain his cheeks of color. But he was down-hearted and overcome with despair. He beat against the walls like a captured bird. At the sight of Francis he laughed with wry pleasure.

"You, too? We are meeting again! Did I not tell you that 'brother fire' and 'sister water' were pure heresy?"

"It would not surprise me were I to be cast in here," Francis replied unperturbed. "For I deserve it more than all those who are here. But for the present that is not what happened. I came here of my own accord to find out about you."

"About me?" exclaimed Pietro, astonished. "About me? How can that be—we scarce knew each other. No more than the while when I sat by your fire!"

"Is that so little, brother?"

"Matteo and I wandered together for weeks and if he only as much as asked. . . ." Pietro turned his face to the wall and burst into tears.

"Fret not at Matteo," Francis expostulated, "for it was he who told me you were jailed."

"He told another, but he himself would not come; he feared for his own skin!"

"Knowing I would go, he had no need to come."

"Do not defend him. . . . I know now what manner of friend he is . . . All those learned scholars are the same. . . ."

Francis crouched upon the floor as was his custom.

"Why have they cast you in here?" he asked.

"If I only knew! If I only knew!" shouted Pietro, striking out with his fist at the wall in helpless wrath. "I ponder and ponder whom I might have offended and I can think of none. I had no quarrel with anyone, I wooed not another man's wench. . . . True, I once hugged an innkeeper's wife but the innkeeper did not see . . . Besides, he was old. He should have known that the owner of a hostelry keeps a wife for guests . . ."

"Tell me from the beginning how it happened. . . ."

"I will. We came, Matteo and I, to that hostelry, and though the host was red like a ram, we stayed on because the wine was cheap and good. Then too the woman was comely. . . . The day they grabbed me I had seated myself in the morning in a corner where it was cool. I sipped my wine and winked at the hostess, meaning for her to come. . . . I had deliberately picked that corner so no one could see me. . . . But in came four men: two were sumptuously attired, like Venetian merchants, the third something like a monk, and the fourth, one of your brethren, the one with a hat."

"John a Capello!" exclaimed Francis, surprised.

"How would I know what you call him? He seemed restless, wandered around the room, saw me. He must have recognized me for he looked a trifle confused, quickly took leave from the others, and departed . . . The rest ordered wine and began to talk. . . . And for want of something better to do I began to listen. For the hostess would not come to me till they had left, anyway.

"One of these Venetians says: 'It takes too long. Much too long! We cannot wait any more.' The one who looked like a monk cowers and whimpers: 'Have patience, messer, have patience! Such a net can be drawn but once . . . and the longer one draws it the better the catch . . . and it will be a handsome catch, indeed . . .' 'Too long,' the Venetian repeats, 'if it is too much for you take a helper.'

" 'I already have one, the man who left a moment ago.'

" 'Take more.'

" 'Believe me, messer, I will better manage alone.'

" 'You will not share your gains with anyone, you rascal! When do you promise?'

" 'In the spring, messer, for certain.'

" 'The vessels will be ready, but woe to you, Nicholas, if you should fail us.'

"This Nicholas cowers and vows even more that fail he shall not. By then I was mighty curious to learn what they were talking about for I was not such a fool as to believe it was real fish they meant. So playing the simpleton I get out of my corner, bow handsomely to them and ask: 'I heard you speak of fishing and I am particularly fond of fish. Perhaps I could be of use . . . I am right handy at any task . . .'

"They turned red in the face when they saw me, thus unexpectedly, but they betrayed nothing. They slapped me on the back. 'That's the sort of braves we need,' they said. 'Today we are pressed for time but be here tomorrow at this hour and we shall take you along.' And they left at once.

"'Hey! I scared the birds,' I said to myself. Had I any sense I would have left that hostelry then and there. But as luck would have it the hostess came in. And she began to cling to me and wonder who the visitors might be. 'They are strangers,' she said. 'They never were here before, likely some mighty lords.' And I say that they surely were thieves and so we argued till all of a sudden the door flung open and in rushed the town guards. They fell right on me. Grabbed me by the collar, they did.

"'Here you are!' they shout. 'You heretic dog!' I yelled it must be some mistake, that I was a peace-loving man and a good Christian, but they hit me with their fists in the stomach, kick me in the seat and drag me out! 'What is it you want?' I scream. 'I have never set eyes upon you before, nor you upon me!'

"One of them hits me in the face till I saw black and says, 'You don't know us but we know you. Only a moment ago three good Christians told me where you were, you foul heretic, plague, Antichrist!'

"'I am no heretic! Let go of my hands and I shall make the sign of the Cross . . . Take me to a priest . . .'

"'No, indeed! Didn't you tell those good lords that you eat nothing but fish? Remember? Ah!'

"I said I was fond of catching fish not of eating it! Give me pork, give me mutton, a chicken, anything! You shall see how I gorge myself. Me a heretic? Good God!

"They would not listen, only dragged me out and flung me in here . . . It is a week I am jailed . . . I beseech, I weep, I plead: let me explain, let a priest hear my confession; all to no avail. . . . As though I spoke to a stone. They keep me here and will keep me till I die; maybe put me to the stake . . . ! O Lord Jesus! Most Holy Virgin!"

Sobbing he threw himself upon the pallet . . .

Francis rose to his feet.

"I shall go at once to the Bishop. He is sure to help."

"God bless you! God bless you! A stranger, yet you showed concern. You came to inquire. . . . Matteo gave no heed. . . . That's the sort of companion he is. . . . And do you think there are no others like myself here? I talked with many. . . . They were incarcerated as heretics though it never occurred to them to befoul their souls with heresy. . . . One was accused by his kinsmen who wanted his land; another by a man who had seduced his wife. . . . They are good Christians. But what of it? No one will ever as much as ask about them. Stay here till you rot, and don't scream too loud lest they remember you and burn you at the stake . . . O Lord!"

But Francis listened no more. He ran straight to the Bishop and implored him to send his chaplain to the prison in order to ascertain the spiritual condition of the prisoner and, by bearing witness to his orthodox belief, cause him to be released. The Bishop readily agreed but not so the chaplain. He would not consort with a heretic. "Where there is smoke, there's fire," he insisted. "He was not locked up without reason. Any blasphemer turns a saint when he feels the hand of justice upon him."

At last, however, he gave in and set out for the prison accompanied by Francis. It was then that Jean de Brienne, returning from his audience with the Pope, had met them.

Pietro Cani awaited Francis' return with mixed feeling of trepidation and incredulity, torn between despair and hope. Falling at the chaplain's feet he made his confession with such fervor as he had never known in his life; he swore that he believed all that the Church told him to believe; that he humbly respected the Holy Father and the entire Holy College as well as all bishops, prelates, priests and monks. "In proof of my sincerity," he concluded, "I am ready to spend the rest of my days in a monastery." Moved by this assurance, the chaplain agreed to vouch for Pietro Cani's good faith.

Late that afternoon the lad was released . . . He was out of his mind with joy; he could scarce believe it was not a dream. In a burst of wild gratitude he threw himself at the neck of Francis who walked by his side, unusually silent and pensive.

"I am free! Free!" repeated Pietro, skipping as he walked. "I am free!

And thanks to you! But . . . does anything ail you? You seem grieved."

"I was thinking of those who remained there," Francis confessed. "And also . . . are you sure the man whom you saw in the hostelry was our companion?"

"How else? Did I not tell you I recognized him? I remembered him because all the others were bareheaded and he wore a hat."

"And that Nicholas said he was his assistant?"

"He did."

"O Lord! Merciful Lord! Our poor brother . . . Nicholas . . . I have heard that name but a while ago. . . ."

"There are many Nicholases."

"I think it is the same one."

They had arrived in front of the Bishop's palace where, in the courtyard, camped the brethren, for they would not accept the hospitality of a chamber.

Francis stopped to bid farewell to Pietro.

"Do you think I shall go away?" the lad protested. "Have I not told you I shall take orders? Only I will not go among fat monks! Not me! I shall remain with you till my dying day!"

Francis' face lit up.

"Welcome among us, dear little brother, welcome! May the Lord give you peace."

He put his arm around Pietro's waist and led him to the brothers. Gathered in a circle in the corner of the Bishop's courtyard they were engaged in a lively discussion.

"Here you come at last." Brother Elias turned to Francis, a note of reproach in his voice. "Any minute now you are to be called to appear before the Holy Father."

"At last! Thank God."

"No telling whether there will be anything to thank God for," mumbled brother Sylvester mournfully.

"I bring you glad tidings," continued Francis. "A new, good, dear brother has come unto us. I grieved because one of our flock had left us. . . . And here God sends us in his place a new one."

Pietro Cani, still grimy with prison dust, his hair all tangled, greeted them with a friendly but slightly foolish grin.

"Welcome, brother!" they called out in unison.

He sat down by Francis' side and in silence listened to the debate that followed. With infinite joy he inhaled the fresh gusts of wind; with delight he gazed into the flaming sky overhead.

"Brother Francis," Elias returned to the subject, "the Bishop said you will appear before the Holy Father in a moment. What will you say? You ought to prepare an oration . . ."

"An oration?" repeated Francis aghast.

"What else? Did you think that one can come to the Holy Father and speak whatever comes to mind?"

"In all truth I never gave it a thought . . ."

"Brother Elias," continued brother Gilles, "whatever Francis will say will be perfect. Have you not seen how people hearken to him?"

"It is not all one, the rabble and the Holy Father," Elias insisted. "Am I not right, brother Sylvester?"

The ex-vicar made a vague gesture with his hand.

"True, true," he muttered. "When one speaks to the Holy Father one ought to use more elaborate speech."

"Well then, if you both say so, it must indeed be true. Who will compose the oration?"

"Who else but yourself, brother Francis?"

"I? The most dull-witted of you all? How could I?"

"It is you who will deliver it."

"No matter. I cannot. The oration ought to be a learned one and what learning have I? You compose it, brother Bernard."

Bernard gazed upon Francis with boundless love.

"Simply say what God inspires you to say."

"But the other brethren say it is not enough. Would you, brother Elias?"

"No, no, none of us."

"In that case, be it so. I shall try. . . . Maybe I could begin thus: 'Our most venerable Holy Father. There lived once in the desert a woman very poor but comely. A king beheld her, took her for wife and had beautiful children by her. When the children grew up their mother told them: Be not ashamed of your want. Go fearlessly to the King's court and ask him whatever you may need and he shall not refuse you, for you are his sons! The children rejoiced and not only were they not ashamed of their poverty but deemed it to be great wealth. And they said: We are the children of a mighty king. And when the time came they went to the royal court and their father recognized them, embraced them and told his courtiers: All I possess belongs to them for those are my beloved children. And then I will say, Most venerable, most kind Holy Father: I am that poor woman whom God has chosen and these my brethren are His children.' "

"Marvelous," exclaimed brother Angel enthusiastically.

But brother Elias thought otherwise. "Whatever you say, Francis, you must forever add those lay tales of yours! It is unseemly. We are not jugglers or troubadours . . ."

"Oh, but we are!" exclaimed Francis. "It is the most beautiful thing in the world! Indeed, we are jugglers and troubadours, God's own!"

He looked around at the brothers and under his luminous gaze and merry smile their souls melted. Oftentimes they thought that were it not for Francis, for that smile of his, they would not be able to carry their heavy load. When he was not around each was besieged by doubts and evil thoughts. Brother Bernard trembled lest he would not endure. Brother Sylvester feared lest, tempted by common sense, he should abandon the chosen path. Even brother Gilles often felt worldly temptations and lures. But all these weaknesses vanished when Francis smiled with that radiant confidence, as he did now.

A young cleric came running down the stairs toward them. "Quick, quick," he called out, "to the Pope, to the Pope!"

They all sprang to their feet and crossed themselves. "I am coming," Francis said gravely. "Brother Bernard, Brother Gilles, come with me."

All three started hurriedly.

"I was loath to sadden Francis," Elias said to those who remained, "but there is grievous disappointment in store for him. The Holy Father will surely not approve the Rule as it stands now. We will have to depart from absolute poverty." And his voice betrayed no grief.

"Brother," whispered Gilles, hardly able to keep pace with Francis, "was it John you had in mind when you said one of us had left? He has not been back for several days, now . . ."

"Yes, it was of him I thought, brother. We must pray for him. I fear he has fallen into bad company . . ."

"When I saw him last, he was telling with rapture that some one had promised to show him miracles . . ."

"He will be bitterly disappointed. . . . None but God may foretell miracles. God or . . . the devil . . . !"

"Maybe he will discover it in good time and come back."

"Maybe. May God grant it! Our first backslider."

"I thought, brother Francis, you would take it more to heart . . . The arrival of Pierto has consoled you at once . . ." Something like reproach showed in Bernard's eyes.

"Not that alone, brother. It ocurred to me our order was like a net which draws a great many; the smaller fish fall back into the sea; the bigger fish remain. Among multitudes."

Gilles and Bernard could not help laughing. "Great many? Multitudes? Beyond computing, indeed. We are twelve, even as we were!"

Francis looked at them as though aroused from a dream.

"It is true, beloved. Twelve . . . and it seemed to me for some reason that we were a thousand and more than a thousand . . . And that from every side people came to us . . . That's how it seemed to me, somehow . . . How droll. Could it be I was dreaming of miracles like that poor John a Capello of ours?" He laughed at himself and added firmly: "Let us think of nothing but that in a little while we shall stand before the Holy Father . . ."

As it turned out, however, they were not to see him that night, for Innocent III suddenly felt ill and postponed the audience till the next morning. The little lout from Assisi could wait. No matter whether tonight or tomorrow he would have no for an answer. The foolish Rule which was to be the base of a new Order had already been read by the Pope and all the Cardinals. It was one of those infrequent cases when the entire Holy College had been unanimous. True, Cardinal Colonna had wavered a little, and even advised a year's trial, but soon he gave in. The case should be cut short. The Rule of Francis, son of Peter Bernardone, impracticable in life, harmful in execution. . . .

Francis, son of Peter Bernardone, and his companions if they want to devote themselves to God, shall enter one of the existing Orders. This they shall be ordered to do by the obedience due to the Vicar of Christ.

"That is what I shall tell him," decided Innocent, and rose from the chair to retire.

The Cardinals respectfully accompanied him to his chambers.

"Rest in peace, dearly beloved," he said, bidding them good-night on the threshold, "and wish me peaceful slumber. For I am tormented by evil dreams and horrible images. I see the world perish, I see it drown in sin and madness. . . . The wolf, the lion and the panther, greed, pride and lust rule where humility, love of the Cross and humanity should rule . . . The entire world is but a magna meretrix, a great harlot . . . Naught but cruelty and abuse of the weaker by the strong ones . . ."

"This will cease as soon as we exterminate heresy," Cardinal Pelagius said with conviction.

"Shall we ever exterminate it if we continue to act as we do now?" sighed Innocent.

"How so? The last news from Alba."

"Oh! That is not what I had in mind . . ." With a despondent gesture, he dismissed his companions and entered the chamber.

"Amazing how quickly that man grows old," remarked Cardinal Pelagius with supercilious pity, pointing with his head in the direction of the door.

Though unaware of the Pope's decision, Francis could not get to sleep for a long while that night. He tossed and turned restlessly till at last he nudged brother Bernard who slept by his side.

"Forgive me, brother, for waking you . . . But it has just occurred to me the parable of that woman is too long. . . . Before I finish, the Holy Father may lose patience and interrupt: What, are you babbling of paramours? Maybe it would be better if I started thus: 'Most venerable Holy Father! Our Lord has revealed to us His will that we should live . . .' No, that will not do . . . The Holy Father may think we boast of a particular grace of Christ the Lord. Maybe thus: 'Loving Our Lord most warmly!' No, wrong again . . . for there are surely others who love Our Lord better than we do and don't brag of it. . . . Truly, I can think of nothing else. . . . Indeed, I am sorry brother Elias and brother Sylvester bid me to prepare an oration and I know not how. . . . I am all mixed up. . . . Brother Juniper could talk better than I. . . ."

Brother Juniper was snoring noisily close by and brother Bernard laughed silently at the thought of the oration he would deliver. . . .

"Perhaps brother Masseo could do it," continued Francis. "He is such a splendid speaker; he has such a loud voice. Maybe he could go instead of me?"

"Francis," said Bernard sternly, "you should be ashamed to speak such nonsense. It was you who summoned us, it is you who are our leader, our head, it is you who must go to the Holy Father! He expects you—not us. You would not deceive him?"

"I?" exclaimed Francis in despair, "I deceive him? But what am I to do when I know not how?"

"Do not fret about it! In harder times than this one Our Lord has shown you what to do. Why should He not show you now?"

"You are right!" exclaimed Francis. "You are right! You are always wise, Bernard . . . Why should I worry? Surely the Lord will help me. . . ."

He stretched out his arms in the dark, hugged his companion with feeling and fell asleep, peaceful and trusting as a child.

The next morning when he was advancing toward the Papal throne, small, inconspicuous, tattered, gazing as though surprised at his own reflection in the shining floor of the palace, he looked like a small grey bird, a sparrow, which might have strayed there by mistake. His brothers had remained by the door and followed his progress with anxious eyes. They were aghast at the abyss which seemed to separate Peter's majesty from the beggar who advanced toward it. . . . It took him long to cross the vast reception hall and as he advanced his awkwardness and shyness increased. He blinked at the crimson of the Cardinals' robes as they surrounded the throne and surveyed him with a mixture of curiosity, pity and supercilious indulgence. What did that poor fellow want here? As for him, all thought had fled from his brains, he was not even able to pray. Completely awed and filled with the sense of his own worthlessness, he approached the throne, humbly kissed the foot of His Holiness, looked up imploringly into Innocent's face and . . . found no word to say. God upon whom he had relied, had sent him no inspiration.

"What a lout! He does not even know how to address a plea," muttered one of the Cardinals.

"Hush! Look at the Holy Father!"

And indeed, all eyes had turned to the Holy Father, staring in wonder. The Pope's dilated pupils were fastened upon the grey little figure with something akin to terror. Where had he seen him? When? Surely he knew that beggar! It was he! It was he who had supported the Lateran!

With a moan Innocent covered his face.

"By the wounds of Christ Our Lord!"

They all saw the gesture, they all heard the moan. And the Majesty of Peter and the mendicant in the coarse cloak continued to face each other without a word.

The heart of Innocent was flooded with such joy that it choked him just as Francis was choked by shyness. So God was still with him! In spite of sins and faults committed by His servants, Christ continued to watch over the Roman Church! He was giving a manifest, miraculous sign. . . . Oh the inexpressible, unutterable comfort!

And they all saw how the Pope, taking his hands away from his face, held them to Francis. And when the latter, confused but radiant, climbed the steps of the throne, Innocent pressed his head to his breast.

"My son, my son," he whispered almost beside himself, "I bless thee and all thou doeth . . ."

Francis sobbed for joy, the brothers by the door fell to their knees, the Cardinals stared in shocked amazement. They understood nothing of what went on.

"Fetch me that paper, ink and a quill," ordered Innocent. All knew it was the Rule he meant. He was to tear it in two and hand it back to Francis Bernardone.

His eyes still on the poor little man, as in a trance the Pope reached out for the quill and at the bottom of the parchment, with a hand that trembled, he wrote: We bless and approve, Innocent III, the servant of God's servants . . .

He handed the document to Cardinal Ugolino, the chancellor. The latter knew well what was expected of him. Without concealing his astonishment but also without protest he added: Dated in Rome under the Fisherman's seal.

Francis fell at the Pope's feet. At the door brother Elias sharply nudged his companions:

"Has he confirmed? Is it sure? How? What has happened? Why has he confirmed? Yet all said . . ."

"Our Lord must have told him," suggested Juniper.

Irritably, brother Elias shrugged his shoulders.

# 8.

## The Tempter

YOU ARE TOO LATE, YOUR HONOR," SAID BISHOP GUIDO.
It was hard to tell from his manner whether he was sorry or glad.
The man whom he addressed scowled with ill-concealed wrath. He was
a tall elderly knight, with a thin face and aquiline nose and proud eyes.
Sir Sciffio, lord of Assisi and Sasso Rossi, came of proud stock. His an-
cestors never bowed to anyone; others bowed to them. They feared no
one, though they wrought fear in other people's hearts. They settled—
or slashed—all matters by the sword. And so the sense of frustration
which filled Bishop Guido's guest now was something new and well-
nigh unbearable to him.

"Too late?" he repeated slowly. "Can it be this nincompoop has already found his way to the Holy Father?"

"So he has, and obtained the Holy Father's approval to boot!"

"What? The approval? Is this a jest, Your Honor? Could the approval be granted without deliberation, without consideration, without
hearing the opinion of others?"

"The Holy Father never does anything without deliberation. Day before yesterday he received Francis, son of Bernardone, and confirmed
his Rule, and yesterday the Brethren Minors, as we are to call them now,
left in a band."

"I might have crossed them on my way . . . They left by one gate, I
entered by another. What a pity! It would have pleased me to belabor
them a trifle so they would not go back so soon."

"Their Rule has been confirmed," the Bishop repeated emphatically,
"therefore anyone offending them, offends the Church . . ."

Sir Sciffio shrugged his shoulders. "True, true. . . . But amongst ourselves we can speak openly, I trust. Were I to be threatened with anathema I shall never praise the son of Bernardone or call him anything but

an accursed idler! The fellow is a half-wit and yet the Holy Father . . ."

The Bishop interrupted him sternly. "I myself love Francis as though he were my own son and rejoice that the Holy Father shares this feeling. Like a midwife I once took him naked unto me when, fleeing paternal wrath, he hid under my cloak . . ."

"Yes, I have heard that story . . . Nevertheless the weakness which Your Grace feels for that fool ought not to blind you to the danger of his teaching . . . Never did I expect the Holy Father should lend ear to the nonsense he preaches. Or could it be that the Holy Father considers that such foolishness will lure no one and the whole matter will rest there? It is not so, Your Grace. No, indeed. That is why I hastened here to warn the Holy Father that in Assisi new adepts are already awaiting Francis' return. . . . Droll, is it not? Your Grace does not believe me? It is true. At least thirty men await that nitwit. In the meantime they have set up camps in front of the church and pray aloud . . . And as many crazy females can hardly wait to beg Francis to accept them, likewise. . . . That's where the merriment will begin, Your Grace! Everyone laughed when that fool, naked, left his father. . . ."

"I did not laugh," remarked the Bishop drily.

". . . or when the sensible, learned Bernard de Quintevalle distributed in the market place a truly great wealth among the poor. After all it matters little when three or four fools want to play saints. To be sure their families justly complain they have been wronged, but three or four families is not a town. But when their number grows! By St. Rufin, my good patron! It is a menace! Those madmen turn men away from their occupations, upset peace and order; indeed, they even forbid family feuds. I heard myself of men who under Francis' influence shamefully forgot the blood shed by their own kin and made peace with the family of their slayers! Where will this lead to? Your Grace knows as well as I do that the family feud is the very keystone of justice . . . It fills with salutary terror not only the murderer himself but his entire kinsfolk who for their own sake will tend to prevent murder. . . . If we abolish the feud, what will be the outcome? Homicides will become rampant. . . ."

"Those who abandoned vengeance under Francis' influence will surely not turn slayers?"

"Will your Grace deny that this lunatic turns people away from their proper estate and duties? That those he lures he flings penniless and homeless into the world, first instructing them to squander their patrimony? They must distribute all their possessions amongst the poor and later live on alms, thus becoming a burden to the community? What would become of a community where such nitwits would predominate? What would become of us all? Of the whole world?"

"Steady, Your Honor, steady," the Bishop tried to calm the vehemence of his guest. He sought words with which to refute the other's charges but found none. And so again he repeated "Steady" and fell silent. He knew those objections seemingly so just, so human, so very human indeed. He knew them well and to some extent . . . shared them. "The Holy Father has confirmed their Rule, thus doubtless he considers it good," he said, at last, shielding himself behind the authority of those words.

"Forgive me, Your Grace, but there surely must have been some fraud in that confirmation. I shall never believe the Holy Father, who is a sensible man . . ."

"There was no fraud but a manifest sign of divine will!"

"Tut! Tut! Has the nitwit turned to performing miracles now? I would never have suspected him of such cunning!"

"I shall tell you frankly how it came about, although the Holy Father would not have it spread abroad. It is a fact that the entire Holy College was opposed to Francis. They raised objections well-nigh the same as yours. And the Holy Father whole-heartedly shared their opinion. But he had a dream. A very strange dream, indeed. The Lateran Church was tumbling down and a strange little man was holding it up. . . . The Holy Father was much impressed with that dream, and when Francis came to him, he recognized him to be the very man of the dream, and after embracing him he confirmed the Rule. That is the plain truth of the matter."

Such was the credence accorded to dreams that Sir Sciffio accepted the Pope's action as completely natural. He answered, however, that the dream might have been a deceit sent by the devil.

"Your Honor," the Bishop retorted indignantly, "you may call Francis a madman, but even a child will not believe he connives with the devil."

"I did not mean it that way," retracted Sir Sciffio. They both fell silent. Bishop Guido stared into the quadrangle which the window-frame cut in the blue sky. From whose hands, he wondered, came that por-

tentous dream which made Innocent bless Francis instead of repri-
manding him severely as mundane wisdom would have him do? Mundane wisdom? Mighty, insistent, seemingly irrefutable, understandable
to all, beloved by all! How many people held the same opinion as that
of the Lord of Sasso Rossi? How many would condemn the weakness,
presumable short-sightedness of the Holy Father? How many would
consider Francis a dangerous lunatic? Ah! What was the use of asking
how many? The whole world, indeed!

And suddenly it occurred to him that twelve hundred years ago it
was the same . . . ! When Christ, that terrible, undaunted reformer,
came to call away fishermen from their nets, had not the prosperous
dwellers who lived around the lake scoffed even as Sciffio scoffed today?
And when Paul stood upon the Areopagus and Peter in Rome? In the
face of that established wise, rich, perfectly organized world they flung
ideas that completely overturned the social order! How could one wonder that the Caesars persecuted those mad innovators? Any government
would have done the same. And what madness took hold of those privi-
leged, well-fed, powerful men that they should cast aside their happy
existence to follow that astounding call, ready to face poverty, contempt
and death?

Aye . . . that was how it was . . . once. . . .

It was so once . . . but no more. Like water that had been stirred to
its very bottom, things had settled down. . . . The Roman Church in
turn had become powerful and mighty. She had established an earthly
rule, a temporal rule, equal to that of the Roman Emperors . . . ! She
had followed that overturned rule, she had patterned herself upon
it. Then she had forgotten her own mad, revolutionary beginnings.
The beggar from Assisi was arising now to remind her of it. . . .

The Bishop gave a start and awakened from his thoughts for Sir
Sciffio once more spoke with bitterness.

"The Holy Father will yet regret his decision, indeed he will. Nov-
elties lure, freedom lures, and in no time we shall see swarms of disciples of that barefooted prophet. Women, in particular, easily swallow
the bait of lofty words. I told you already, Your Grace, a fair crowd of
them awaits Francis' return. When he takes them into his Order, what
then? What offense it is going to give! Shall we look on and do nothing
about it?"

"Indeed, Francis will not take them in together with his brethren," the Bishop answered. "I know Francis, he will give offense to no one. Besides, the Rule contains not a single word concerning women. Should they want to join the Order, the Holy Father will set a separate Rule for them. There is no reason for worry, Your Honor. What woman would care to share that harsh, dour life, harder than anything found in any convent?"

"Those devils will lure any woman!" exclaimed Sciffio with such venom that Guido cast him a curious glance.

"One might be led to believe you had a personal grudge against the Minor Brethren?"

"Indeed, I have," retorted Sciffio defiantly, "they've abducted my kinsman. He abandoned his castle and now tramps around with them, bringing disgrace upon the family."

"Why disgrace? Some might call it otherwise. But I thought that Rufin's parents—for it is surely Rufin you have in mind—and Your Honor have been at odds for many years."

"We have our differences, still the blood is the same. . . . It is my duty to care about it . . . and it is not Rufin alone!"

He clasped his head in his hands and broke off as though he had already said too much.

"Is there someone else amongst your kin partial to Francis?" cautiously inquired the Bishop.

Sciffio nodded.

"Who might it be? I can think of none."

"Don't you know? Can't you guess? It is hard to tell . . . she . . ."

"Clara?"

"Yes, Clara! Clara, my well-beloved Clara!"

Again they lapsed into silence. Before their eyes rose vividly the image of the fair maiden. The comeliest of Italy's maids, troubadours called her. Tall, and slim she was, with a clear face and grave eyes, her father's favorite daughter. And for that matter everyone who knew her loved and admired Clara.

"Ever since she was a child it seemed to me that maiden was destined to God," said Guido by way of consolation.

"Indeed my wife often told me it was not for the world we were rearing Clara. And I've reconciled myself to the thought. Much as I would like to keep her in the world I would not forbid her to enter the Benedictines or Norbertines Order . . . or any other convent where the deportment is seemly and the endowment proper. . . . Let her be an abbess if she loves God more than the world. But that my child should join those beggars, those vagrants, and bring misery and contempt upon herself! I would rather see her dead!"

His whole body shook with passion and grief.

"Has she told you already that this is her decision?" asked the Bishop, sincerely perturbed. (Should the girl commit some folly the new Order would acquire a deadly foe. Sciffio would, no doubt, arouse the entire knighthood against it. This might well lead to trouble for the Holy See.)

"No! that she would not dare! But I have eyes . . . I see. . . . The girl is bewitched. . . . Dreadful to say. . . . She . . . by God, Your Honor, to no one but yourself would I tell this! She . . . is enamored of that nitwit. . . . She, who has disdained so many gallant knights . . . ! She, my daughter! Enamored of that lout, that wool merchant's son! Clara? How can one understand such a thing? How is one to bear it? It exceeds all comprehension. Could it be witchcraft? He has beguiled her, as he has beguiled the Holy Father. . . . For, consider, Your Grace, that had she taken a fancy to him before it would have been sinful, shameful, but understandable enough. Blood is thicker than water and once he was comely enough, that Francis . . . ! Remember how people would make fun of the old Pica Bernardone because the child looked like a nobleman's son? Handy with the sword and handy with the goblet. Not bad, indeed. But she would not even look at him then. Only now . . . When he has not even a shirt, sleeps upon the ground, eats grass like a beast, and is the laughing stock of the countryside. And my daughter—my own daughter—blushes whenever his name is mentioned. . . . When he does the craziest things, she approves, yes, she approves of him, she says he is but doing right, that Christ our Lord has ordered so! She holds him to be a saint and a hero . . ."

He broke off, unable to continue, for grief choked him. His pride and parental love suffered. It was in vain that the Bishop tried to comfort him.

"Surely without your consent she will undertake nothing, and as long as you do not consent, she will shed some tears and forget, as women will . . ."

"Of course, I shall never give my leave! I will not let her step out of the castle as soon as I hear he has returned!"

"And he . . . does he love her too?" inquired Bishop Guido cautiously.

The old knight stared at him amazed.

"Does he love her? How can you even ask? A ragamuffin like that . . . A noble maiden comes to his very hands and he would not love her?"

"They have an understanding?" the Bishop was aghast.

"That I don't know. They never talked with each other alone. Clara is always accompanied by her duenna."

"Ah!" sighed the Bishop relieved, "you had me frightened! It is nothing but a father's fancy. They never bespoke each other, so what is there to it? Francis always says he knows but one mistress, Holy Poverty, and he will never know another . . ."

"You will see, you will see. I have eyes. . . . I am old. . . ." He broke off and after a while added: "We saw once from the castle how this ragamuffin walked down the street and urchins flung horse dung and mud at him. And he, instead of driving them away, only called out, 'Right you are, right you are, for no worse rascal than I has ever trodden the earth.' And thus he walked all besmeared and muddy, the urchins after him like sparrows after a crow. So I quickly called Clara. 'Look,' said I. She stared, she turned white and tears streamed down her cheeks. Do you think, Your Grace, it was for disgust and shame? No, it was for admiration. She would have not looked more gladly upon a tourney victor. . . . How am I ever to endure it . . . !"

Unable to control his rage he sprang to his feet and ran out of the hall.

Unaware of the grief of the noble lord, Francis and his companions gaily proceeded on their way. Francis felt happy and free beyond words. It was early morning, the air was clear and scented, shrubs glittered with dew. Birds sang in the thickets. He joined them. Disconnected words, bits of tunes, weird notes that were neither human nor birdlike but sputters of rapture, exclamations of delight and adoration for the beauty of the world and the wisdom of its Creator, an unwritten hymn to the beauty of the earth which is the mirror of God, flew almost unconsciously from his lips. He wanted everything to rejoice with him, everything, even his shadow—that faithful companion of the temporal steps of men. He stretched his arms to it and laughed like a child because brother shadow responded to his advances. He lifted his unburdened arms high, like wings.

"Hi, brother pheasant," he called, "leave feeding alone for a while! Sing with us the glory of God!"

And the pheasant turned his metallic neck to and fro, glittered with color, and followed for a while that strange man who continued to sing and step as though he were dancing and was about to soar into the sky.

Walking behind him his brethren followed his every gesture, some with rapture, others with frank displeasure. Brother Elias and brother Sylvester were among the latter. Moved by the same impulse they caught up with the singer. He greeted them with gay peals of laughter.

"Why are you all so silent?" he asked. "I am the only one to bellow. Let us sing together."

"Some seemly song we might sing," admitted Sylvester, "but how can you expect us to imitate your weird cackle?"

"Cackle! Right you are, brother. Trouble is it is more pleasant thus. I must sing out what well-nigh makes me burst with joy. . . . Wait though . . . I will try to write down the words and we shall all sing together. Our own hymn. . . . The praise of Our Lord in all His creation. And we shall start with brother sun who gives us heat and light. . . ."

"It would be more seemly if we sang some church hymn. Do step quietly . . . What would the Holy Father say should he see you now, skipping like a puppet on a string. . . ."

"And after the sun, a praise of brother moon and our sisters, the stars. They are so precious and bright. . . . They twinkle up above so mercifully. . . . What was it you said? That the Holy Father. . . ."

"Would be scandalized by your deportment!"

"Why? He would rejoice with us. It is such a glorious day. Can anyone help rejoicing? Beloved brethren! We have his consent. We are off to conquer the world!"

"May it please God," sighed Sylvester, "to let us conquer the world. Though we never will unless you change your ways."

Francis, perplexed, let his arms fall, and from his dancing step changed to a normal gait.

"How would you have me act?" he asked in a puzzled voice.

"You are our leader and head, therefore you should deport yourself with seemliness. You cannot allow simple-minded men like brother Pietro or brother Juniper to treat you with unbecoming familiarity or even upbraid you whenever they dislike this or that. . . ."

"But brethren, you, likewise, are upbraiding me, right now!"

The ex-parson of Assisi and Elias Bombardone exchanged scandalized glances.

"Forgive us, Francis, but surely you must see a difference between our minds and experience and the minds of those others. Particularly brother Juniper, who is so coarse. Apart from that they express their opinions openly in the presence of all, while we remonstrate with you in private with none to witness it."

"But I much prefer you did it in front of everyone! So that's why you . . . I shall call them all at once. And as for brother Juniper, he is surely more dear to the Lord than I, therefore. . . ."

"Call no one and listen to us. We do not deny brother Juniper's worth, all we say is that a leader must possess dignity. . . . Don't you understand, Francis? Dignity!"

"If dignity means setting oneself up above others, I shall never be a leader, for any feeling of superiority is sin to my mind."

"Dear brother! The Church is based on hierarchy, which is nothing else but the superiority of some over others . . ."

"Oh, no! The Church is based upon obedience. That's quite another thing. Hierarchy is only the mark of greater responsibility . . . ! Brother Leo! How was it the Holy Father signed himself upon our Rule?"

"Innocent III, the servant of God's servants!" shouted brother Leo from the distance.

Brother Sylvester, defeated but not convinced, gave up. He fell back and walked among the others. Francis' bliss, disturbed for a while, returned once more. He began to sing and march at a rhythmic pace.

"Be thou praised, O Lord, for our brother the wind and for the clouds and for the sky and for fair weather and likewise for rain. . . . For snow in wintertime and for grass in the summer. . . . For the heat and the cold . . ."

Walking at the edge of the road brother Elias watched him from the corner of his eyes. His feelings towards Francis were hard to define. Indeed he loved him. He admired him, too, but with many reservations. Personally he had a passionate fondness for order, system, organization.

There was nothing of the poet in him, therefore the greatness of the Creator revealed itself to him in logic, not in beauty. True, he could not deny that Francis in every impulse was perfectly logical, but his was not the kind of logic Elias could understand. "The eternal dreamer," that was how he defined his friend. He looked upon him as one looks upon a child in need of protection and guidance. Unlike Francis, he himself was endowed with the gift of leadership. And he knew it. Because of that gift he deemed it not only his right but also his duty to handle the human flock as one wields a tool through which great deeds can be accomplished.

If only Francis would listen to him! If he would but let him be his representative. What could they not accomplish between the two of them! Francis with his wonderful gift of drawing men to himself, with that unsurpassed charm of his which none, not even the coldest men could resist, and he, Bombardone, the brilliant organizer, the keen, masterful, ambitious mind. . . . To what heights they might lead the Order! In no time they would eclipse the Benedictines and the Cistercian Brothers. . . .

But it was no use to think of it, no use to suggest plans to Francis. He did not understand. Despite his great virtues and his innate wit he was too obtuse. Take what happened a moment ago: "Brother Juniper ought not to upbraid thee." "But you upbraid me!" What a comparison . . . What a juxtaposition. . . . To Francis, Juniper and Elias or Sylvester were all one!

He cast a resentful glance at the singer. Suddenly he was overcome with the desire to hurt him, to upset his peace. That eternal joy of Francis was so trying!

He searched his mind for something appropriate and found a shaft so certain that it made him smile.

"I think," he said aloud, "you rejoice not only because of the weather and the apostolic approval but also because we are returning to our parts?"

"Oh, yes!" exclaimed Francis, "I am mighty glad of it. I shall see again our Portiuncula and our good old shack in Rivo Torto, and St. Damian's church, and all our vale. . . . I believe God created the longing for one's native countryside so people would know how to yearn for Him. . . . Do you not think so, brother Elias?"

"Maybe so, maybe so. I, too, shall behold our countryside with joy.

. . . But you mentioned nothing of seeing people again? I think I can tell whom you will be glad to see most of all. Clara!"

Contrary to Elias' expectation, Francis' face, far from growing red with shame, lit up.

"Right, brother! Clara, of course! Clara, Clara, the most perfect earthly creature I ever encountered . . ."

"Do you love her?" inquired Elias.

"Indeed I do. Who would not? Have you ever seen a more winsome sight? So fair, so pure! Fragrant as a flower! Her cheeks are smooth and when the shadow of her lashes fall upon them—she has such long lashes, hasn't she?—the shadow flutters like a butterfly. She is always so grave; when she smiles, it is like an unexpected gift. Like sunshine! And her eyes . . . they are clear, yet dark . . . forever gazing far yonder . . . Her soul is so beautiful, it is because of it that her body is a marvel. . . . Aye, Clara has no peer . . . One can sing of her . . . One can praise Our Lord through her. . . ."

Elias eyed him curiously.

"Well," he remarked, with deliberate carelessness, "our Rule is so weird it neither mentions celibacy nor chastity by as much as a word. . . . You can avail yourself of it and wed . . ."

"Do what?" asked Francis.

"You can wed, if you love so much . . ."

He did not finish for Francis bellowed with laughter. Mirth overcame him. He stumbled, sat down upon the embankment and holding his middle called out: "Brethren! Do you know what Elias would have me do? Take a wife!"

"Oh, stop it!" snapped Elias irritably. "Do not scream and act like a fool! It is in earnest I spoke; if you love Clara, wed her . . ."

"But I am not in love with her. I only love her! Oh, brother, it is long since I laughed so! Oh!"

"What's so droll about it? Do you deem wedlock a sin?"

"No, no. On the contrary. How could it be? Wedlock is blessed . . . Only the combination! How could a sinful beast like myself grab for himself Clara, whom God has made for His glory . . . She can belong to no one but the Infinitely Great One. . . . How could I lift my eyes unto her, I. . . ."

"Notwithstanding, you desire to behold her . . ."

"Why not? I'm an envoy, God's envoy. I tremble lest anything should defile her, turn her away from offering herself to Our Lord . . . What manner of an envoy would I be were I on such occasion to think of myself? Were I to covet Christ's betrothed? I! Perhaps if I deliver myself of my mission aright I shall be granted in the hereafter a place somewhere not too far from hers. What more could I wish for? Bold are such dreams, I know, for she will be given in heaven a mighty high place, while I . . . lest Our Lord in His mercy. . . ."

He gazed in front of him with such luminous eyes that brother Elias at once felt displeased with himself. Nevertheless he could not resist asking: "It is all very well, Francis, but you are of weak flesh, like all of us. When you carry your message are you not pestered by temptations?"

"No, not then," answered Francis with complete frankness. "In her presence they would not dare rise. As for other times. . . . In truth, brother ass will rear, yes, he will, save that I keep him on short rations, so he cannot kick overmuch. With God's help I shall keep him in harness, somehow . . . Alone, I could not . . . never. But with God's help I can manage anything, even myself . . ."

He laughed and turned around to the band.

"Why are you silent while we here talk of such droll matters? Come on! Oh, look at these woods ahead . . . Surely there must be an echo in there. Let us shout all together and loud: 'Our Lord!' "

"Our Lord," they called in chorus. The voice hit the wall of trees, bounced off, returned to them, repeating . . .

"How it comes back! Let's call again!"

"*O-u-r L-o-r-d!*"

The sound of creaking wheels come from the road. A donkey hitched to a loaded cart was advancing toward them; by its side walked an old peasant.

He eyed the brothers suspiciously. "Must be the rascals got drunk in some tavern and will holler now. Who are ye?"

"The envoys of the mightiest of all Lords," Francis called back to him. Once more he was seized with a fit of uncontrollable gaiety. He caught brother Leo's hand and both raced down the hill, like children.

"How lucky we are, brother Leo, how lucky!"

"They say it is no good to boast of luck," worried Leo.

"Nonsense, brother. What can befall us? None can take from us Our Lord's protection!"

# 9.

# The Gathering of the Children

JOHN A CAPELLO CAST ADMIRING GLANCES AT THE COMPANION WHO WALKED by his side. At last he had met a leader after his own heart. Nothing like the previous one. He moved with dignity and stateliness, well-nigh majesty. True, Pietro Cani had once told Francis how under the sharp eyes of two Venetians Nicholas had cowered and whimpered—these, however, must have been unusual circumstances. Normally, Nicholas' deportment was fraught with benevolence and dignity, a combination which enchanted John. The gesture with which he stroked his greying beard was worthy of the patriarch himself. His speech was punctuated by lofty words and phrases. When speaking he would press both hands to his heart or lift them up high and stand thus for a long time as though thrusting skyward. A true prophet! He had no objections to being addressed as "maestro." Indeed, it was at his own suggestion that John called him thus. Neither did he share Francis' ridiculous prejudices with regard to storing provision and accepting money. Thus neither of them suffered hunger or want. And the miracles were to begin any day now.

They stopped in the vicinity of every town, village and hamlet and gathered children about them. Nicholas told John he was particularly fond of children. He often insisted it was but a waste of time to convert grown people. Nothing could move those slumbering laggards. Nowhere save in the pure hearts of innocents could divine love be aroused. His dislike of elders was so strong, indeed, that he gathered children far from their parents' eyes, and whenever possible without their knowledge. The children listened to him with rapture, for he promised miracles and travels.

John and Nicholas were returning now to a region familiar to both of them—the vicinity of the Inn of the Good Guardian. About thirty children had gathered in the glade, big half-grown lads and tiny tots whom brothers and sisters must hold by the hand. The little folks twittered like a flock of sparrows, shook their fair or dark locks, skipped like wag-tails, scurried like rabbits or, to pass the time, climbed trees like squirrels.

At the sight of the two men joyous squeals burst forth from the band. The children sprang to meet them.

"Nicholas! At last! When do we start?"

"Now? At once?"

Nicholas did not reply. He lifted his eyes and his arms to the sky, then with a sweeping gesture blessed the whole band.

"Sit down," he commanded.

Quickly they crouched on the ground, staring at him with eyes bright with excitement.

"And who is he?" they asked, pointing at John.

"A friend and assistant of mine. He will visit all these places where I have no time to go, so we may soon gather, a thousand strong. . . ."

"There are already so many of us! When shall we go?"

"I told you already. Not till we have visited every village and called all the children . . ."

"And how long will it take?"

"Maybe till spring."

There was an outcry of disappointment. Till spring! Would they have to wait till spring?

"But we don't want to wait! We want to start at once."

"We want to rescue Jesus!"

"Let us start now!"

"Beloved children," Nicholas explained, "there are still too few of us."

"Oh, but there are more of us today," exclaimed Tina. "We brought Laurence."

With a maternal gesture she brought forward a slight lad, leaning upon a crutch. His left leg hung limp and useless.

"This is Laurence," she introduced him gravely. "He will come with us."

"No, no," protested the maestro quickly, "Laurence cannot come."

The boy cast him a horror-stricken look. "Why not?" he stammered out.

"Because you are a cripple, my lad."

"No matter. I, too, want to defend Jesus."

"How could you travel so far? We take but the healthy ones."

"But surely Jesus will cure me."

"If you can make miracles, if you can order the sea to open," remarked Tina resentfully, "you surely can heal Laurence's leg. He wants to come with us so much."

Nicholas controlled his annoyance and said sweetly: "Kind Jesus will surely heal him but we will take all the sick ones later. When we conquer the Holy Sepulchre we shall come back to fetch them and bring them to the Tomb."

"Yes! We will come for them later! Let's not take cripples now!" exclaimed the older boys.

Laurence sobbed and wiped the tears with his fists, smearing them upon his face. "I would fight and die if need be . . . I can walk very well with the crutch."

Tina lifted pleading eyes to Nicholas. "It is true, he walks very well."

"I shall ask the Angel Gabriel's advice," announced Nicholas solemnly. "If he permits us to take Laurence along, take him we will."

"Was it the Angel Gabriel who told you the sea will open before us?"

"Yes, the very one who announced to the Holy Madonna."

"Oh, do tell us what he looked like?"

"You will soon see for yourselves," Nicholas said. "Once you are near the Sepulchre he will stand at your head and drive the Saracens away."

"Then let us go! Let's go soon!"

"Today!"

"My little ones! I have told you already there is not enough of us. We must gather in a large throng."

"What for, if the angel will drive out the Saracens anyway?"

"So that as many of you as possible should win merit."

"And will we see the Child Jesus?"

"Indeed you will."

"Will I be allowed to take Him in my arms, Nicholas? I am so fond of babies! I wish I already had one of my own!"

"Yes, you may if you stop crying: 'I want to go at once.'"

"Oh! I won't! And Balbina whose back is crooked needs but take the Child Jesus in her arms and surely she will grow straight."

"Balbina shall come later with the sick ones. That will be the second army. The first, the hale ones. The second, the ailing ones."

But Tina would not give in.

"You will not take Laurence nor Balbina and you take such a mean, horrid boy as Walter who beats small children and has no love for Jesus! None!"

"How do you know, stupid!" shouted the accused boy, and stuck his tongue out at her.

"If you loved Jesus, you would act differently!" she replied with dignity. "Nicholas! Don't let him come!"

The maestro gave the lad an appraising glance. He was a tall shapely youth. "The kind I want," he thought.

"Walter is a very wicked boy," he said aloud, "I myself heard him curse once. But we will take him so he may mend his ways."

"But he does not want to mend his ways."

"Tina, judge not thy neighbor!"

"We can ask him: Walter? Do you want to mend your ways? See? He is sticking out his tongue!"

"Have no fear. A miracle will happen and he will want to . . . But are you sure none of you has blabbed of our expedition to the elders?"

"They know nothing . . ."

"They think we are but praying here . . ."

"They are very angry at you, Nicholas. Mother often says she will rouse the village and come after you with sticks . . ."

"Does she know I am here today?" asked the prophet, anxiously glancing to right and left.

"No."

"Those unfortunate elders! Once at the Holy Sepulchre we must pray for them! They would send men with sticks! Good Lord! What blindness. . . . What would befall should they learn of our intentions?"

"We will not tell . . ."

"Nicholas," said a half-grown lad timidly. "I have a denarius here I took out of the pot buried under the threshold where my father keeps his money. Will you take it from me? Maybe you have need of it . . ."

John, who hitherto had kept his peace, gave an uneasy start and was about to speak up for the maestro and tell the lad he must return the coin at once but Nicholas smiled gently and stretched out his hand.

"It will hasten our departure," he said. "I shall be able to hire a mule and make my rounds more speedily."

"I will try to fetch another coin to hire a mule for your assistant," cried Robert.

John made a vehement gesture. "I will not have it!"

"There is no need," admitted Nicholas. "Our whole plan might come to light beforetime. And now keep very still and I shall tell you of Child Jesus."

The children listened enraptured.

"Do you think it is right when children take their elders' money by stealth?" John asked shyly when a few hours later they were again on their way.

"As a rule it is wrong but in this case it was done to an end, to a great and sacred end. The end absolves the means. . . . The child was willing to risk paternal wrath in order to hasten the deliverance of the Sepulchre. . . . It was a brave deed."

"Francis always said God has no need of ill-acquired wealth."

"Francis, Francis! Why did you leave him if you value his opinion more than mine. I do not hinder you! Go back to him!"

"Be not angry, Nicholas. I will never go back to him. I am so happy to be with you. Tell me again: is it true the children will cross the sea?"

"I swear to you," Nicholas' voice was solemn, "that we shall set out in a throng so big it will astound the world and we shall cross the sea. I do not know whether Our Lord will order the waves to part or else move the dour hearts of Venetian merchants so that they will grant us passage, but cross we will—you will see!"

"Oh! I believe you, I believe you! I can hardly wait to see it happen!"

"They would never play with me because I am lame and now they will not let me go to Jerusalem though Jesus would surely heal me," little Laurence complained with bitterness.

"Mayhap they will come back for us," Balbina tried to comfort him as well as herself.

"Likely they will not. They will forget. What do they care? We shall not see the Holy Sepulchre and we will never be cured . . ."

"Maybe we could follow them, you and I?" Enchanted with her own idea she continued, "We will pretend we are not going with them at all, just strolling along. Always some distance behind them . . ."

Laurence lifted his head, suddenly interested. "Do you think we shall have time to cross the sea before it closes again?"

"Oh, yes," she assured him, "if we run."

"Walter will see us and throw stones at us. You know what he is like."

"It is true," she agreed. "Walter might." Though crippled she was full of energy. She shook her little head with determination. "We will walk only by night, so neither Walter nor the others will see us."

"Won't you be afraid?" he asked incredulously.

"No, I will not, even if we have to pass through woods. I often sleep in the open when my stepmother drives me out. And I am not afraid."

"Walk and sleep, it is not the same. I, too, have slept outside, but to wander all by myself along the road would scare me . . ."

"Coward! Would you rather stay here?"

"No! I am no coward and I will not stay. Maybe Jesus will send us light at night? Only what shall we eat?"

"Oh, but I have thought of that, too," she exclaimed, triumphant. "We will ask Tina to leave some food by the roadside every day. They will have plenty. Did not Nicholas say they will never lack food, for angels will bring it to them . . ."

"Won't Tina blab of our coming?"

"Not Tina. Tina is good. . . . Yonder beyond the sea there are mountains, it seems. From those mountains one can already behold the Holy Sepulchre . . . When we climb on top my back and your leg will straighten . . . and we shall run down to the others. Won't they be surprised?"


In a smoke-filled hut that huddled against the slope of the mountain, old Bertrade, the spinster, was as usual telling a yarn of dragons and fairies. But only the elders listened to her. The children, usually so fond of tales that they always pressed around her so as not to miss a single word, huddled together in the opposite corner of the room and whispered among themselves. Old Bertrade would not show that she felt hurt. From the corner of her eye she observed the little group so intent upon their own tales. Gertrude's shrill little voice rose above the others.

"Archangel Gabriel will take command and the Saracens will flee. Bells all by themselves will start pealing all over the world. . . ."

"What are you talking about?" broke in the old spinster.

Silence fell over the little flock. They would not answer.

Madonna Angelica, spouse of Sir de Trevi, was combing the hair of her little Beatrice. In the thin, tight tresses she twisted long golden ribbons, and while combing she fondled lovingly the head of her little darling. Beatrice lowered her eyes, her lips twitching as though in pain. What would mamma say when she would leave? And yet she could not stay. Jesus wanted all children to come and defend Him. He would be wroth at those who remained home. Poor mamma!

Little Beatrice sighed so deeply that Madonna Angelica leaned over her. "Did I hurt you, my sweet little flower?"

Messer Paschalis, bachelor of arts, was dozing. Flies strolled up and down over his bald scalp. Every once in a while he would whack at them in his sleep. Whenever he slapped too hard he would wake up, and opening one eye, cast a suspicious glance at his pupils. Could it be they, and not flies? But the boys were too engrossed in conversation to pay heed to their don. The shining scalp no longer tempted them. . . .

". . . Nothing will come of it, I tell you. They will stop us and turn back," insisted Jacoppo Toldi. Copper haired, white skinned, he would have been beautiful were it not for the freckles.

"But there will be hosts and hosts of us. We don't let them turn us back."

"For my part, I don't believe the sea will open, nor that we will be able to walk upon water as though it were ice . . ."

"Why not? Has it not opened before? Moses!"

"That was a long time ago. Such things happened in olden times, but not now. . . . We will rather build a large raft . . ."

"Maybe they will take us across in vessels?"

"Galleys? Are you out of your head? Don't you know you have to pay the Venetians or Genoans for the passage? Not every nobleman can afford it, how could we?"

"Dear brothers! One way or another we shall surely go . . . We will pin crosses on our shoulders like true Crusaders."

"And now across sea and land, Lord Jesus lead Thy faithful band."

"Hush, hush! Do not sing lest Paschalis wake up."

"He will not. He sleeps like a log."

"And now across sea and land . . ."

"Be still! He is awake!"

To be sure the don had opened his eyes and from sheer habit was reaching for the short cat-o'-nine tails, called "placenta," ready to belabor the heads closest to him.

"So that's how you study, rascals!"

"It is of pious matters we were talking, Illustrious Master. You have no reason to be angry."

Paschalis liked to be called Illustrious Master. He put the "placenta" away.

"And what, pray, were you talking about?"

"It was of Crusaders we talked."

"Of all things! What business of yours are they? In truth, there used to be such holy expeditions once upon a time . . ."

"And there will be again," broke in Jacoppo with conviction.

Paschalis scratched his head thoughtfully. "I know not if there will be again," he replied. "Of old whenever Peter the Hermit or Bernard the Abbot of Clairveux spoke to crowds, folks would trample each other to death to listen to them. . . . I heard it from my grandsire who used to go about with Bernard. . . . The Abbot's voice was like a church bell. When he would appear on a hillock and a throng around him and each and everyone aweeping and asighing . . . indeed 'twas something to behold . . . Today they would not gather in this way . . . They went, they all went, and what came of it? Nothing but the decimation of mankind. And the Holy Sepulchre still in heathenish hands as before . . . Must be God's will. . . . No, no, none would go now."

"None of you oldsters, you mean," mumbled the lads under their breath.

Bettina was afraid of crabs. Would water sweep them away when the sea opened? Or must they walk among them? She cast anxious glances all around her, as though from every corner menacing pincers were already threatening her. Bettina's brother Paul pondered the problem carefully. He was not quite certain. The shells would surely remain, but crabs? The mention of shells soothed Bettina. They could collect them, they would take them to little Jesus . . . the pretty, opalescent shells.

"I am going to take my pussycat," decided Marita.

"And I will gather flowers for the Child Jesus. They will not wilt if we hurry."

The ten-year-old Ignacia whom none loved, whom none would stop from going because none cared, prayed at night huddled on her pallet: "Good Jesus! once we arrive at Jerusalem make it so I will not have to return . . . and may forever remain with Thee."

Little Matteo clapped his hands in delight. He laughed merrily. He always did whenever he thought of the wonderful expedition ahead of him. His grandfather (the parents of little Matteo were dead and it was his grandfather who brought him up) watched the child with an equally radiant smile. What imagination the little lad had! He was telling, for instance, how he would go across the sea to fight for the Holy Sepulchre. Fancy such thoughts springing in that little head.

"But I shall really go, Grandpa, really I shall!"

"Why not? Do go! When will you start? Tomorrow morning or this afternoon? And what shall I make ready for his Lordship's travel?"

"I will go when spring comes," Matteo announced, climbing into his lap.

"I trust you will take me along?"

At once, Matteo's face turned grave. "I cannot, Grandpa," he explained. "Only children may go . . ."

"In that case I'll disguise myself as a child. What do you say to that?"

Grandpa disguised as a child! With his grey mustache and his red, mottled nose! At the very thought Matteo burst into peals of laughter. And so did his grandfather.

Sabina, the hostess of the Inn of the Good Guardian, shook with anger. The youngsters had just returned from their usual expedition into the woods and stood before her like two little strangers. She might jostle or hug, curse or beseech! It was all one to them. They had that far-away look in their eyes as though they saw things invisible to her eyes.

"Whatever is it he wants of you, that accursed beast?" she screamed. No answer.

"What does he call you for?"

Silence.

"Next time I shall go with you to listen to him."

They shrugged their shoulders.

"You trust a witless vagabond; don't you trust me, your mother?"

Tina lowered her head. With an effort she stammered out: "We trust Nicholas."

"And me? And me? I am first! I am your mother. Do you trust him more than me?"

Tina shrank away, cowered. At last she whispered even lower than before: "We trust him more."

"Why?" asked Sabina aghast. "Why?"

She sank upon the threshold, and sat thus for a long time, repeating dully, "Why?"

But there was no answer. Beppo and Tina, even if they would, could not have explained. They had put their trust in a stranger for he spoke loftily and of great things, while their mother had nothing but common words upon her lips and everyday troubles in her heart. . . .

Sabina's question was being repeated in those early months of A.D. 1211 by nearly all parents of Campagnia, Umbria, Tuscany, Lombardy, in the Alpine ravines in the French valleys and even on the distant banks of the Rhine. Something unheard of was happening. The children had turned against their elders. "We have no faith in you," they said. For the first time since the days of the Creation parents felt that their own offspring were judging them and finding them guilty.

"The elders lie," said the youngsters. "They are heartless, self-seeking and untrue. At church they pray and beat their breasts, but should a hungry beggar come to the doorstep they drive him away. They fight tooth and nail over every morsel. There is no charity in them. They are greedy, merciless, grasping. They would have us respect and obey them. But Lord Jesus has released us of respect and obedience so that we may go and defend Him . . ."

Skilfully fanned, the children's ardor flamed up into a blaze. The elders' ears had long ago grown deaf to lofty summons. Paschalis had been right: even if a new Peter the Hermit or Abbot Bernard were to arise none would have followed them. But the youngsters' innocent hearts craved greatness; no wonder they hastened from everywhere, the children of the rich and poor alike. Homeless little vagrants, who climbed trees and fences like tom-cats, looked upon the world with all-too-knowing eyes and moved with the stealthy agility of born mischief-makers, as well as sweet golden-haired cherubs whose eyes reflected the blue of the sky. Pasty-faced, slow-blooded girls loath to spin and carry pails, no less than cocky, keen lads always first at anything, be it good or evil. Maternal little women and flighty scatterbrains. Thin, forever hungry schoolboys and well-fed children of rich townsfolk. All of them, spellbound, followed men who promised Greatness, Beauty and Freedom.

According to their own temperaments the elders tried to defend them from the spell either with kisses or with the whip. They locked them in cellars or else showered them with caresses and gifts. None found the proper way. Neither could the distressed fathers bring themselves to set up some sensible organized action. Somehow they were ashamed even to speak of it. For as long as the world existed there had never been any trouble with children. There were enough worries and difficult problems weighing upon each adult's head; how could they bother with the children. It was enough if one left them a patrimony. It had long become a habit of elders to look upon the problems of the children as meaningless and trifling.

# 10.

## Blanche of Champagne

WHEREVER HE RODE, THE KING OF TROUBADOURS, WILLIAM DIVINI, NOW on his way to Champagne at Jean de Brienne's behest, came across groups of youngsters holding councils out in the open roads. One observant glance would have been sufficient to convince him that something unusual was going on. The children neither played tag nor hide-and-go seek; they did not divide into two camps to wage imaginary combats, attacking bulwarks made of branches and showering their adversaries with pine-cones and clots of earth. Flushed, engrossed in conversation, they did not even turn their heads to stare at the golden laurel which crowned Divini's head or at the caparisoned mules. They did not stretch out their hands to beg for a coin. Instead they would discuss something earnestly, then suddenly fall silent and stand motionless with a far-away look in their eyes. The dust would envelop them, hide them from the bard's sight, but in the next village another group would be again debating in the middle of the road.

Divini paid them no heed whatsoever. It never occurred to him, nor to anyone else, to attach the slightest importance to the doings of these youngsters who were always under one's feet. The king of troubadours was thinking of his mission and wondering whether he would achieve success. . . . If he could sail for the Holy Land with the retinue of the Countess of Champagne he would save a great deal of money. . . . Who knew, it might be more advantageous to enter her service instead of de Brienne's. . . .

He was bound for Genoa. He had decided to make part of his journey by sea, for he feared that the sudden change of weather on the Alpian summits might harm his voice. In Genoa he was directed to the offices of the well-known Venetian shipping company Hugo Ferrens and William Porcus, who, it would seem, owned the best vessels and operated a regular traffic between the coast of Italy and France and Africa and Asia Minor. Although the powerful company was known the world over its offices were located right next to the port and were miserable and filthy. When the "divine" Divini, all a-glitter in his golden laurel, called in person to insist he be given a secluded spot on board, "protected from wind, mind ye, yet not stuffy," he saw several men engaged in a vehement argument at the other end of the dusty, murky room impregnated with the smell of spices. They paid no attention whatsoever to the distinguished visitor.

". . . I hear they are driving more girls than boys," screamed one. "I told you we want nothing but boys! What am I to do with the wenches?" Another one was trying to pacify him. "No one is trying to force the girls down your throat. We will dispose of them ourselves. . . . They always are good merchandise."

"I must have a spot protected from the wind but, God forbid, not below deck. Stuffiness I cannot abide," stipulated Divini.

"Your Honor will find no cause to complain; our vessels have no equal," the factor assured him.

The galley was to sail in two days. Divini had plenty of time to roam through the city. Rather belatedly he began to wonder whether he had been right in choosing the sea route. What if sea storms should prove more harmful to his precious voice than mountain winds? At any rate he must provide himself with theriaca, a miraculous medicament indeed, which contained among other ingredients the venom of the Paradise serpent.

Whether or not thanks to that same theriaca which it took him infinite pains and a great deal of money to procure, the king of troubadours had a calm and successful crossing. In Marseilles he left the galley —filled with admiration for the Ferrens and Porcus Company—and from there he traveled on, either riding his mule or, even more comfortably, carried in a hired litter. What he saw appalled him. Traces of the bloody war between the Cathari and the Catholics were in evidence everywhere; they disfigured and saddened the once so serene Provençal countryside. Wherever Divini looked he saw charred ruins, gibbets and white unburied bones scattered by the roadside. Religious passion alone would not have wrought such devastation, but under the cover of religion other forces had been at work. The age-long hatred the Normans and Provençals nurtured for each other had increased the wantonness of the invaders, redoubled the resistence of the native population. It was those tribal animosities which had brought to ruin the fairest of all French lands, the cradle of an old civilization; which had destroyed its culture and language forever . . .

In the few inns which had escaped destruction, destitute natives told of the terrors they had experienced. Aloud they cursed the Cathari, the cause of all misfortune, and maintained God had visited this upon them because they had not driven out the heretics from the very start. They related with horror how Sir Roger de Foix, the grandson of the famous crusader, had demolished and ransacked the Abbey of Pamiers, renowned for its miracles. His mercenaries had shot their bows at the figure of Christ, shouting all the while, "Ransom thee!"

God have mercy upon us, sinners! . . . Ruefully they beat their breasts, and a moment later, after a furtive glance around, they would tell in whispers and with bitterness of the wanton crimes committed at the order of Sir Simon de Montfort who led the crusade against the Cathari. Indeed, the Antichrist himself could not excel Sir Simon. To be sure the Godless Sir Roger de Foix maimed statues, robbed monks and had driven them naked out of the abbey, but this de Montfort had ordered hundreds of men, women and children to be impaled, torn apart by horses and burned at the stake. De Montfort had no time to distinguish between the guilty and the innocent—he left that to God before whose tribunal he dispatched all those on whom he could lay his hands. . . . God have mercy upon us sinners . . .

"And all because that Lucifer has set his heart upon the seizure of Toulouse," the oldsters commented, shaking their heads.

Lately there had appeared in the stricken country droves of black and white monks of the newly founded Dominican order. Unlike the hitherto existing orders they were poor and eager to apostolize. It was they who had persuaded Papal legates to rid themselves of their brilliant retinues so that they would not offend the poor by the display of their wealth. "Our Lord," Dominic, the founder of the Order, had cried out, "bid Peter to tend His sheep. He never said that Peter should shear them. Be as poor and meek and humble as Christ was."

Pope Innocent III expected much good to come from the Dominican brethren. Indignant as he was at the crimes of the lay lords who, under cover of pious duty, settled their own accounts, he had entrusted to the black and white friars the task of exterminating heresy. Stern with themselves as well as with others, well-trained in theological arguments, they roamed the country, spying into every household. Folks looked upon them with respect and awe. A body knew well enough what to expect of his own baron but this new papal militia was still an unwritten page. . . .

Divini listened with complete indifference and without a trace of understanding to the conversation in the inns. Current events held no interest for him. War irritated and bored him, as they do any artist who in wartime feels belittled and useless. In strife any brute of a soldier proves of greater worth than the foremost among bards. In the roar of battle who would lend ear to the Muses?

He urged his men to haste, impatient to be out of the dismal country. When at last he crossed the borders into Champagne it occurred to him he had left the Inferno to enter Paradise. It was long since this province had seen war and it was renowned all over France for its wealth and prosperity. And it was not only the nobleman alone who lived amidst plenty. The simple folks likewise knew no need. Nowhere else had Divini encountered such well-built villages, such neat little towns. As for the court of Count Thibault it was famed for its magnificence and high intellectual level. Other barons would talk of it with envy and scoffingly call the lords of Champagne "merchants," for apart from its famous vineyards and the natural fertility of its soil, the great annual fairs at Troyes and Provins which attracted tradesmen from all over Europe, indeed from outside of Europe as well, constituted an inexhaustible source of revenue. Even the King of Paris could not boast such fairs. There wealth accumulated not by means of war and violence but through the wide channels of trade as normal and regular as the harvest itself, spread evenly throughout the country and created an atmosphere propitious for the development of art and science. The more so as the ruling dynasty of the Counts of Champagne had an unbroken record of over two hundred years of rule.

With admiration and envy Divini observed this thorough prosperity, this deep-rooted security and calm elegance. What a sore contrast with the ducal courts and castles of his native Italy! The latter, trampled by ceaseless wars and invasions, both foreign and domestic, resembled the devastated Province more than the fortunate domains of the Count of Champagne. In the tower of Count Thibault's castle the astrologer spent night upon night probing celestial mysteries, as his nine predecessors had done. In pursuing his studies he often availed himself of the notes they had left, neatly stacked scripts which no alien trooper or local plunderer had ever touched. In the cellar caskets filled with wine of famous vintage peacefully gathered dust, while in the beautiful library-hall precious volumes accumulated slowly and emanated an atmosphere of culture and human thought, both lay and spiritual.

It was in this library that Thibault V, Count of Champagne, spent his days. Though not old in years, he was weary and languid. He suffered from the illness called the Crusader's sickness, for it was the Crusaders, particularly those amongst them who, while in the Holy Land, had not kept their vows of chastity, who brought it back from the east. Because of his ailment tourneys and hunting no longer attracted the count; he preferred to participate in them as an onlooker while he devoted all his time to books.

The youngest and only surviving son of Thibault V was a youth of a pleasant but somewhat faded countenance. He looked better indoors strumming on a viola than in the open, mounted on a horse with sword in hand. He was exceedingly fond of music and singing, and even composed songs of his own, an activity of which he was immensely proud. Jean de Brienne had once succeeded in giving to the youth several of the songs he had composed in honor of Blanche, and had persuaded the naïve youth they were his own. The whole court sang them afterwards, to the great joy of the two lovers.

But young Thibault was a good lad and gave no trouble to anyone. His parents, not without misgivings, thought of the time when he, in turn, would have to rule, but the youth himself did not worry his head about it. If at times he felt uneasy as to his abilities to fulfill the role of Thibault VI he would climb upstairs to the astrologer and find comfort in the assurance of a propitious horoscope.

Messer Jacob Pochard, the present occupant of the observatory in the tower and court astrologer, was indeed a man of a great and thorough learning. He deserved the name of astronomer rather than astrologer, but his employers attached no importance to the distinction. Although Thibault V surpassed the run of princes and barons of his days in intelligence it never occurred to him to ask of an astrologer anything more than to give an accurate prophecy of things to come, to determine which days were lucky or evil, which propitious to bloodletting or studding mares, to draw horoscopes and warn of oncoming illness.

All this Jacob Pochard fulfilled to the best of his abilities; he was like-wise clever at foretelling the weather and could explain even the most complicated dreams. What engrossed him most, however, were the re-cently discovered tables of Toledo which determined the position of the planets, and the study of the Almagesta or the Great Syntax of Ptolemy which the Arabs had made available and the Crusaders had brought back from the East. Above all else he worshiped the genius of the great mathematician Jordanus Nemorarius, the author of an entirely new, hitherto unheard-of science which boldly overcame mathematical ob-stacles by substituting letters and signs for unknown numbers. Nemorarius had derived his discoveries from Arabian books; and this made the learned astrologer wonder whether the generally accepted opinion that heathens were ignorant and stupid sons of Baliel was not, perchance, unfounded. Indeed it seemed to him those heathens far exceeded the Latin west in science. But he never voiced such thoughts for fear of scandal.

Countess Blanche was in every way the opposite of her spouse and son. Springing from old Merovengian stock, born and bred under the warm Basque skies, she was as dark and swarthy as a hazel nut. The passing years and frequent childbearing (she had three married daugh-ters, and her two elder sons had perished while roaming somewhere abroad bound upon the usual knightly sport) had left no mark upon her smooth skin and figure. And more fortunate than her lover, she could hide her graying hair under a tight-fitting caul. One could almost feel the swift stream of blood pulsing under her smooth skin. Her form was rounded and well-set, her brow low and wide. Bold eyes she had under strong arches of eyebrows which met in masculine fashion, and a narrow arched nose. Under an outward cover of stern stateliness she concealed youthful vivacity. She governed her large household with a strong and competent hand, inspiring fear and respect. With her maid-servants she was generous though inexorable in matters of conduct. She lavishly endowed those who left her service to be wed but would drive away in shame, after ordering them to be flogged, the unfortunate ones who happened to go astray. She attached great importance to propriety, and although those near her had at times whispered of her intimacy with Sir de Brienne, she was generally considered a paragon of wifely and motherly virtue.

William Divini, upon his arrival at the court of Champagne, bowed to the Countess with servile adulation while she looked down upon him with that indulgent disdain which women of high birth were accustomed to bestow upon artists. Unperturbed, the "divine" William waited his time, knowing well this relationship was bound to change. For the present he did not divulge the true reason of his coming.

"I have heard such wonders of the court of Champagne," he announced upon his arrival, "I could not deny myself, while journeying through France, but must see with my own eyes in what measure reality exceeds the tales."

This explanation fully satisfied the two Thibaults, father and son. The youth in particular was delighted at the bard's visit. All day long he kept Divini by his side, forcing him to listen to his songs and asking what the troubadour thought of them. William praised them loudly, yawned when no one was looking, and wondered how he was to approach Blanche.

This proved more difficult than he had expected. The Countess was haughty. Lost in thoughts known only to herself—or so she thought—she sat all day long by her loom upon which she embroidered a chasuble with gold threads and pearls. Her maids-in-waiting sat by her side, modestly casting down their eyes whenever any men entered the room.

Of an evening they all sat together in the vast hunting hall lit by a fire which burned upon the hearth. Father Thomas, the chaplain, told oft-repeated tales of Elidor who spent the best part of his life underground amidst dwarfs, or of Godfried and Tancred, the crusaders. His listeners knew every word of the tales before they were uttered, yet they listened with pleasure for the stories were beautiful indeed. Sometimes Jacob Pochard the astronomer would climb down from his tower and join in the conversation. In a dull, monotonous voice he informed his noble listeners that Parisian scholars predicted an eclipse of the sun.

"How dreadful! Will some new calamity be visited upon us?"

"And must we again hide in cellars to avoid gazing at the sky?"

"Parisian scholars have ascertained," explained the astrologer, "that one may look at the eclipse provided it is through thin black cloth or soot-covered glass."

The priest slapped his knee. "Indeed," he exclaimed gloating. "It would seem messers scholars, prone to heresy though they be, admit the eclipse is nothing else but the Devil's doing."

"Far from it!" Pochard was indignant. "No, indeed!"

"How else? Have you not said yourself that one could gaze through a black curtain at that maleficence without fear of harm? Whenever blackness is involved the presence of the Devil is plain. It is he who rejoices in darkness while light is the realm of God."

"But it is only to protect eyesight! To weaken the action of the sunbeams," the astrologer exclaimed in a voice squeaky with excitement.

"Precisely. They would defeat the Devil with his own weapon. The point is, though, does it befit a good Christian to use such means?"

"Better never seek shade when the sun is scorching, revered Father, lest you fall in connivance with the Devil," retorted the astrologer, furious, and strode out of the hall without taking leave of anyone present. On the stairs he could be heard growling loudly that were he to sit another ten years in the tower, he would not come down, preferring solitude to listening to nonsense. The chaplain indignantly shook his head.

"They dislike, oh, how they dislike to admit Eternal Truth! Ah, that science!"

From the corner of his eye he cast glances loaded with reproach upon the Count. Thibault V pretended not to notice.

"We cannot remain without an astrologer," Blanche suddenly said. She liked to state all things plainly without circumlocution.

"Oh! I meant it not that way," mumbled the chaplain, afraid. "It is only that a more pious one could be found."

"But not a cleverer one. The king himself envies us Pochard. Was he ever wrong? Has anything he foretold proved untrue?"

"And how he explains dreams," added young Thibault. "I remember a few days before your arrival," he turned to William, "I dreamt that a dog sprang at me and afterwards grazed upon the grass even as a horse would. I asked Messer Pochard to explain to me the meaning of that dream. I do not recall what he said for it was very learned but I know that it pointed at your coming, truly. . . ."

"His Honor Sir Jean de Brienne, now King of Jerusalem, was also once pleased to tell me his strange and prophetic dreams," said Divini casually. "Only I could not explain them." For the first time he had mentioned Jean's name in conversation, just to see what the effect might be. Secretly he was watching Blanche's face, lit from one side by the fire blazing upon the hearth and from the other by a torch stuck into an iron holder. She was, as usual, bending over her work. She gave a start. Her face flushed deeply.

"I pricked my finger," she said. The red drop swelled and hung perilously on the finger tip, nearly staining the whiteness of the chasuble. She put her finger to her mouth and resumed her work.

The old Count suddenly became animated. "So you know de Brienne? Have you seen him? We all rejoice at this mark of honor bestowed upon him but we sorely miss a good companion. This place has never been the same since he left. He was wont to stay here more than in his own castle. We all held him dear, even the Countess did not shirk him as she would others."

He chuckled gaily. Philosopher or blind? The silk under the vigorous thrusts of the needle creaked. "I wonder whether the crown is to his taste?" continued the Count. "To be sure he was in no haste to obtain it."

"Is he very much enamored?" inquired young Thibault, chuckling foolishly.

"Of whom?" asked Divini, as though he did not comprehend. The needle circled, stood still. . . .

"Why, of his betrothed, of course! Of the princess!"

"Ah, that damsel." Divini did not turn his eyes from the hands which lay idle upon the embroidery. "I saw her portrait. Judging by it she seems . . ."

The idle hands were trembling. It seemed to the troubadour they were crying, "Go on, go on! Say it!"

". . . she seems not over-comely . . . But then a picture may not be true . . ."

"Who ever saw a true portrait? So he is not much in love?"

Divini pondered a while. "On the contrary," he said with conviction, "he loves madly, like a troubadour, like Tristan. That I know for I have often been with him . . ."

"Ho, ho!" The Count was incredulous.

"No wonder. It is not every day such fortune befalls one," the chaplain commented serenely.

The silk was creaking once more. The needle darted like lightning, feverishly, hither and yon, inside the pattern, outside the pattern. . . .

"For all that love," continued the Count, "he was in no haste to depart. It would seem he stayed in Rome well-nigh six months?"

"Through no fault of his, Your Honor. Were he but free to do so he would have flown like a bird to his beloved. Unconquerable obstacles . . ."

"It is time to retire," the Countess interrupted him rudely, rising to her feet.

"Oh, Mother!" exclaimed young Thibault tearfully, "it is not so late. I was to sing a new canzona tonight which our guest has just corrected."

"A lovely canzona," assured Divini politely.

"Then sing it," agreed Blanche, returning to her chair. With her foot she pushed the loom aside and sat motionless, staring dully at the fire. Thibault sang in a high squeaky voice, immensely pleased with himself. He kept glancing at the maids-in-waiting, seeking admiration in their eyes. At last he finished and sat down. Divini rose to his feet.

"If Your Honors will allow me," he said, "I too shall sing a canzona. The same one which last time I sang for Sir Jean de Brienne."

Black eyes looked at him from under heavy black brows without their habitual boldness. Divini took the viola from Thibault's hand.

> When grapes grow sweet and heavy on the vine
> And grieves my heart for the departed Spring,
> Enchanting lips of my beloved bring
> To love's rich banquet spiced and perfumed wine
> That sets my heart afire, and her embrace
> Hides me from Autumn's melancholy face.
>
> Then do not dim thy light, oh day,
> Enchanting day; and dusk delay.
> Invincible lust of love! Breathes one
> Who would not pray to stay the sun?

His voice rang like a bell then dropped to a whisper. The singer was putting all his great skill, all the force of expression and feeling into the words of the song. When he had finished there followed a long silence.

"That is singing and not your meowing," the Count said to his son.

Thibault blushed. Tears welled up in his eyes.

"The noble young Lord, when he attains my years, will sing even better," Divini assured him.

The lad turned to him, eyes filled with gratitude and admiration. "No, no," he protested, "I can never sing like that. Never!" He burst into tears and ran out of the hall. Without a word, without as much as a glance at the bard, Blanche rose and followed her son. The maids sprang to their feet, put away looms and skeins and hastened after their mistress.

"Yes, that was singing," muttered the old Count with approval. "No wonder the laurel was bestowed upon you. I would give it myself. Beautiful!"

"No laurel could please me more than your words, Your Honor."

The chaplain sighed perplexed.

"It is beautiful, indeed," he conceded, "but worldly, very worldly. . . . I would prefer something more pious, more profitable to the soul. . . ."

"But there is no evil in that canzona," Divini defended himself. "Cardinal Colonna himself once deigned to listen to it . . ."

"Oh! I know there is no evil in it . . . But all the same it is very worldly . . ." Father Thomas fidgeted, unable to express what he had in mind. This passionate longing was not for heavenly bliss . . . "Very worldly," he repeated once more, sauntering despondently toward his tiny chamber

"The fish is taking the bait," thought William the troubadour not without satisfaction when the Countess, followed by two maids, stepped out onto the portico where her guest was as usual listening to the poetical efforts of young Thibault.

"What are you conversing about?" she inquired, amiably enough.

"I was asking whether my verses were worth anything," sighed her son.

"The young Lord has a great and unusual gift," decreed Divini. "Some of his stanzas are noble indeed. This one for instance: 'When my beloved stands by the rose bush . . .'" It was one of the songs composed by de Brienne and attributed to Thibault. Divini knew it.

For a while Blanche stood motionless. "Thibault, my son," she said, as though suddenly remembering something, "do run upstairs and inquire of Messer Astrologer whether tomorrow is a propitious day for nesting broody hens?"

Pleased by the praise and greatly displeased by the errand the lad left them. Blanche stepped to the stone balustrade and gazed straight ahead at the vast valley at her feet.

"You can go to your work," she ordered the wenches over her shoulder.

They left. Blanche and William remained alone. The Countess fidgeted with her alms purse. The high white coif on her head trembled. Divini had no intention of coming to her rescue by opening the conversation. With head inclined in courtly respect, he waited.

"So de Brienne is much enamored?" she began diffidently. "How do you know of it?"

"From the very lips of His Honor, I should say rather His Majesty."

"Did he confide in you?" she asked him with scornful incredulity.

"Yes, so he has."

"I am surprised to hear it."

"Why should you be, Madam? In whom can one more safely confide in matters of love than in a troubadour? A knight values another man inasmuch as he is proficient with arms, a priest inasmuch as he prays, makes penance and has faith. And a troubadour—inasmuch as he loves. Love is our realm. We know its strange deceits, its hidden ways, the masks it so fondly assumes. We are no strangers to any love whatever it may be. We are not leeches of love, but its confessors . . ."

"Confessors, indeed," she sneered, "who will tattle of confidences!"

"In this you are wrong, Madam. When I repeated what I said I was but carrying out the will of my friend and master."

She drew back appalled.

"You mean to say de Brienne wanted you to tell right and left of his love?"

"It is you he wanted to hear of it."

She gave a violent start, dropped the alms purse. William quickly stooped to pick it up. As he handed her the bag he was frightened by the expression on her suddenly paled face.

"Me?" she asked breathlessly. "Me? He ordered you to tell me of his love for that . . . that . . ."

"Did I ever say that?" In contrast with Blanche's vehemence William was absolutely composed. "His Majesty hates his betrothed! She is loathsome to him! That is why he remained in Rome so long despite the insistence of the envoys!"

She came close to him, her eyes aflame. She breathed straight into his face, superb and formidable.

"Whom then does he love?" she demanded.

"Only you, Madam." He said it boldly, although he drew back a little. Would she or would she not strike him? This was a dangerous game. The Countess might well take offense, curse him, cause him to be cast into the dungeon. . . .

But love was stronger than pride. She swayed, bent over, leaned helplessly against the balustrade.

"Only me," she repeated, almost in a whisper.

"It is at his behest I came here," Divini continued with bombast as though he were reciting a poem. "In truth Isolda of the white hands was not loved more tenderly than you! Crown and kingdom mean naught to him. His thoughts are ablaze like fire. When he speaks of you his voice becomes hoarse, like the roar of a courting stag. . . . When he speaks of you his manly hands are a-trembling . . . When he speaks of you his eyes flame. When he speaks of you his heart pounds so it dents his cuirass . . ."

From recitation the troubadour had passed into a song. Thibault, who had just returned, listened to him with admiration.

"Whose is this? Whose?" he asked when Divini came to a stop.

"Mine, at your service. A modest lauda."

"Could I but once in my life compose one like it! And Pochard says neither tomorrow nor the rest of this week will be a proper time."

"Not a proper time," repeated Blanche, with an effort trying to remember what the words referred to.

"Yes, inasmuch as the moon is still on the wane . . . Not till next week."

"True . . . the moon is on the wane . . . nothing should be started at such a time . . ." She cast a reproachful glance at Divini who had at an evil phase of the moon told her of Jean's steadfast love.

"What do you think of Thibault, my Lord," Blanche inquired of her husband a few days later. As usual she sat by her loom, but in the last few days the embroidery had made but little progress.

"What do I think of Thibault?" repeated the Count. "What am I to think? It is plain enough, he is a fool."

"You must not speak of him that way!" she retorted indignantly. "Thibault is no fool. Music and singing have gone to his head, that is all . . . Much of it is this troubadour's fault. He is forever with Thibault and lends ear to his songs."

"A pity it is not the other way around. But I think the troubadour will soon depart."

"It is too late now. I know the lad. Nothing will help save to tear him away from here, show him great deeds, famous places . . . What does he see here? Where is he to acquire a taste for knightly exploits?"

"Faith, it is exactly what I wanted him to do long ago, but you would not have it. You said he was the last one left to us, poor of health. That the other ones had perished . . ."

"And to this day I shall not let him go alone. But see the world he must, and I shall go with him."

The Count laughed so hard he rose from his chair. "Where will you go?"

"It is many years since I vowed a pilgrimage to the Holy Sepulchre. I told you nothing of this, my Lord, for want of a proper occasion. Thibault and I could go together. I shall pray for the salvation of my soul while the lad feeds his eyes upon knightly life and doings."

Her husband stared at her as if she were demented.

"Don't you know the Holy Sepulchre is in the hands of infidels?"

"They allow it to be visted."

"And you would ask the Moslems leave? You? Of the House of Navarre? There is none among your kin who has not fought them! And now you will beg them? Bribe them to let you in? Blanche!"

She bent her head low, shamed but stubborn. "I do not know how permission is given, but the troubadour says pilgrims are allowed. Have him come, he will tell us."

Divini, summoned before his host, confirmed the words of the Countess. His Honor Sir de Brienne, that is His Majesty, intended to sign a pact—most likely prepared by his predecessors—which was to give the Sultan considerable concessions in return for free access to the Holy Sepulchre for pilgrims.

For once the old Lord, who seldom lost his temper, was furious.

"Is it with concessions de Brienne begins his rule? I would have never thought it of him! Has he told you so himself?"

"No, indeed," replied the prudent Divini. "His Majesty said so at an audience with the Holy Father. Everyone in Rome repeated his words and rejoiced. Many noble pilgrims, knights as well as ladies, intend to avail themselves of the chance."

"Your wish is law to me, my Lord," said Blanche. "I shall do whatever you decide."

Thibault V smiled bitterly.

"Thank you, Messer," he turned to William, "for bringing us these important tidings. If the Countess would fulfill the vow which I hear she has taken, I shall not hinder her."

And hinder he did not. He himself announced to the court that by midsummer the Countess would set forth for the Holy Land to fulfill an old vow. Almost at once preparations began. The Countess was to be accompanied by a rich retinue, as befitted the Lords of Champagne and Kings of Navarre. This was to include five knights, as many squires, twenty halberdiers and ten maids-in-waiting. Divini decided to leave shortly for Rome and upon a set date meet the Countess in Brindisi whence they would sail together. This was the only consolation for young Thibault whom the sudden maternal decision had thrown into panic. The meek youth loathed all unknown things. He would sing of heroic deeds and strange lands. But see them? Nay! Not he. Would his mother but let him remain at home! He even tried to suggest timidly that it would be better if she went alone, but one formidable look from her black eyes annihilated him completely. After this he gave up any further attempts of resistance.

His father, Thibault V, the astrologer Pochard, the chaplain and William Divini now spent evenings discussing the approaching journey. On the surface nothing had changed in the vast hunting hall of the castle. But had anyone observed the mistress of the house he could not have helped notice her listlessness. She would string the pearls on the needle only to let them slip again into the little coffret which lay in her lap. Time and again she tangled the thread, broke it impatiently, and with trembling fingers threaded the needle anew. She forced herself to pick up her work and immediately put it aside, rubbing her eyes with an expression of stupefaction. For from underneath the ornamental maze of leaves, from the complicated pattern of the embroidery there seemed to peer at her a certain hateful, though unknown, feminine face. Blanche stabbed at it with her needle, but to no avail. It was a small, thin, half childish face, as described by Divini from the portrait he had seen—the face of Marie of Jerusalem. Jean's wedded wife. How strange! But a short while ago the thought of her did not torment Blanche. Almost a year had elapsed since Jean had left her, compelled by King Philip to accept the hand of the Jerusalem heiress. Their love had come to an abrupt end. No use of dreaming of it any longer. Blanche was not the kind to waste strength in useless grief. Pride upheld her. By a supreme effort of will she stifled her love. No, she would not long for her lover. Longing feeds on hope; where there is no hope the heart heals more readily. But now Jean's envoy had arrived and all that was dead sprang to life again. Jean was summoning her, he would not accept separation, would not admit their love was dead. He loved her as of old. Confronted with these tidings her own resigned, smothered passion had burst into flames. It enveloped her like a conflagration, hid the rest of the world from her. The lover with whom she had parted forever had risen from the dead. He was alive and calling to her! But along with her resurrected love had appeared its inevitable companion—burning, gnawing envy. She was jealous of the woman by whose side Jean was compelled to live. Till the arrival of the troubadour, whenever she thought of Jean, she would console herself with the thought that he had to part with her to become King. Now it was different. The crown had become but a secondary consideration—Jean had left her to become the husband of another woman. . . . And the small, pale triangular face would once more reappear in the maze of tangled thread. . . . It haunted her day and night. A poor, sickly child, a mere pawn in the hands of statesmen, who might not even dream of love or free choice, who neither knew nor sought Jean, had become the object of a consuming, obsessing hatred which sent red darts shooting through Blanche's brain.

"I shall not incur ill-fame," thought the Countess, stringing and unstringing pearls. "I shall not meet Jean by stealth. No, I must rid us of her and take her place. That I will do! By the love of the Holy Martyrs! He is mine! What of it, even if I am forty-five? I am still young and warm in love. To none shall Jean belong but me. I will not be running away from my own home like a trull. I shall leave my husband to become a Queen. The Holy Father will surely agree to a divorce if Jean promises to reconquer the Holy Sepulchre in return. . . . But first we must be rid of her. . . ."

She tore at the tangled thread with vehemence and determination. She must get rid of Marie of Jerusalem. She must! Let her not stand in their way!

Common sense reminded Blanche at times that Jean was King only because he was Marie's husband, but she would quickly push the thought aside. Wait till the Syrian barons recognized Jean's prowess as a warrior,

Jean's brains, Jean's sword and they will not care to lose such a King just because he has changed his wife. . . .

And her face, bent over the white chasuble, would assume an expression of such wanton cruelty that the Count, watching her from the corner of his eye, would shudder. It was the very Devil the woman hid under her skin. . . . At night when the freshly awakened, unappeased lust would not let her fall asleep, her brain seethed with savage images worthy of those royal she-wolves of her own blood, Fredegarde and Brunnhilde. It was in vain her conscience tried to rouse her indignation against these visions, to banish them from her thoughts. They kept returning, insistent, convincing, irrefutable. . . . They brought hot waves of blood to her cheeks, drove sleep away. . . . "It is not my fault," she tried to absolve herself. "I was already reconciled to my fate, ready to accept cold old age . . . It was he who called me, he who roused me. If I go now I shall not return . . . She must yield to me. She must . . ."

It was because of such thoughts that all went wrong in the castle these days, and the maids-in-waiting collected every night tangled skeins of silk and wondered why so little progress had been made. What had become of the mistress' deft fingers?

And it was because of such thoughts that, at last, late one evening when the whole household was asleep, Blanche de Navarre, Countess of Champagne, stole out of the castle. A solitary figure, wrapped in a black cloak, she cast furtive glances over her shoulders. Indeed one might have thought she was not the mistress here but one of her own wenches threatened with flogging for such nocturnal escapades. She trod stealthily, cautiously . . . She was on her way to the hovel of the witch, Margot. . . .

The night was dark, moonless, pregnant with storm and thunder. A stifling, south wind breathed heat like whiffs from a bread-oven. Furious blasts rose, then dropped again as if lying in wait. Leaves rustled with a metallic sound. Poplar trees gurgled like streams of running water. When the wind abated the trees became silent and when it rose again the murmur woke, grew, swelled overhead, a sure sign of approaching storm. An evil night it was. . . . Dark powers were swooping low over the world. Who had sent them? Was it a distant planet, as the astrologer Pochard would have it? Or had the Hell made bold by human sins drawn closer to earth, as the chaplain maintained? No telling. . . . But an evil night it was. A woman who conceived that night would give life to a luckless man. A woman who might bear that night would suffer agonies and be delivered of a still-born child. Aye, an evil night. Its shadows did not refresh, its silence brought no calm. Its darkness was not rest from the labors of the day but an accomplice of crime. Venom swelled in poisonous herbs. Pure, sun-loving beasts, plants and birds lay in torment, longing for the dawn. Only the owl, the bat and the toad gloated. It was one of those nights when temptation grows stronger and conscience weaker. One of those nights when it would seem that God has turned His face away to some other part of the Universe and His Omnipresence no longer lighted the earth.

The dogs had recognized their mistress and were rubbing against her knees. They ran ahead of her but did not leap joyously as was their habit. They too were oppressed by the stifling heat, by the tense suspense that hung in the air. The watchman was not about. Blanche knew that he had sauntered away just now to the opposite side of the castle. She could hear him blowing his big bark horn. She could safely open the wicket door. She took the key from the pocket, struggled a while with the rusty bolts. At last she was outside the walls.

The dogs left in the courtyard whined and scratched at the wicket. She had to return and let them out; it was better to let them come with her. Margot's hovel was not far, on the slope of the hill. She could see it outlined against the darkness. The hunched roof, half-buried in the ground, made it look like a huge toad. Drawing her dark cloak close about her Blanche stepped up and knocked at the door. The dogs stood still, gazing at her as though surprised.

The filthy crone who lived in the hut and was known far and wide as a mighty witch was not in the least startled by the knocking. Usually her customers came at night. She quickly threw a skirt over her shift and opened the squeaky door a crack. From the inside came a whiff of mephitic air as from a pigsty.

"Step in," she said, after assuring herself the visitor was alone.

"We can talk here," replied Blanche.

"Abroad I speak not," Margot retorted insolently, while wondering to herself whose voice, whose figure this might be. "If you will not enter it is all one to me." She was about to shut the door. Blanche stepped in.

The place was dark and malodorous. Though the visitor hastily assured her no light was needed Margot began to blow upon the embers to light a resinous stick.

"I need a potent herb," Blanche announced in a voice muffled by her cloak.

"For love?"

"No."

"For death?"

The visitor's silence could only mean yes and Margot's face lit up with an evil grin. This was a request she could easily satisfy. Of herbs she had aplenty, stronger, weaker, costly, cheap. The surest ones came dear. A ducat fell upon the table. The crone grabbed it greedily and began to bustle around the room. Here she plucked a bit of herb from a bunch hanging from the beam and again some from under the bench. She crushed and mixed, all the while mumbling some incomprehensible words. Then, in whispers, she gave instructions how the brew was to be prepared and added to the victim's food; how much would bring about sudden death, how much protracted illness. . . .

"For a man?" she inquired suddenly.

Blanche shook her head.

"A woman? Old? Young?"

Too many questions! Blanche flung down another ducat and left. The dogs followed her. As she walked towards the wicket gate she knew the crone was watching her and wondering. Could it be she, the proud Countess, could it be she returning stealthily to the castle like a common wench? Could it be she grasping in her tight fist a piece of rag containing an evil herb? God! God! O! Help! And Blanche's hand would open, to drop, to fling away the accursed acquisition then again tighten and hide it on her bosom. "It is not as though I meant to poison her," she reassured herself. It was better to have the herb along when traveling. Just in case. . . .

The gale tore the fold of her cloak from her hand, lifting it high into the air like a sail. With some difficulty she drew it back and wrapped it tightly around her body. The storm was rising. From the black sky came a rumble; somewhere in the distance white lightning began to laugh! The air was even more stifling than before. An evil, evil night!

# 11.

## The Children's Crusade

SHORTLY BEFORE EASTER THEY STARTED FROM EVERYWHERE. THEIR SMALL feet trampled the spring mire of highroads. They ran from every direction, swarmed like bees. They pressed forward in a wide and low tide. Small folk surged and thronged amidst shouts and songs. Mothers and fathers ran after them, some with tears, some with threats. All to no avail. A strange madness had taken hold of the crowd of children. They broke through locked doors, overturned fences, and joining their companions, were engulfed in the stream. . . . Unknown men who directed that stream, shouted menacingly: "Do not interfere! Do not interfere! Whoever dares to interfere commits a grave sin against the Lord. It is a miracle! A manifest miracle!"

"A miracle!" repeated people in astonishment. At every stop new crowds joined the throng. From every village poured children. Each child had a cross pinned to the shoulder, either of a colored bit of cloth or made of leaves strung upon a bit of stick. When those wilted, the little pilgrims, amidst laughter, would pluck new ones from bushes along the road. "Look! Here are new emblems! We are Crusaders! Crusaders!"

Children Crusaders! The entire world quivered in astonishment. Nothing like it had ever happened before. The strange movement embraced all Italy, South Germany and a strip of France. In all churches bells rang, processions sallied forth to meet the childish throngs. By the roadside people awaited them with milk, meat and cake. They fed the youngsters, weeping with emotion . . . they blessed them. . . . If perchance benefactors were scarce, the leaders of the children's crusade would buy food after mighty bargains. They hired carts to transport the youngest ones. A crowd of mothers, torn by despair and anxiety, followed behind among clouds of dust.

In monasteries monks hurriedly scanned old parchments, seeking prophecies concerning such an unusual occurrence. Astrologers probed stars. But the stars were silent or boded no good. Bishops sent messengers by relays of horses to the Holy Father asking what they were to do? Support this movement or put an end to it? For these innocents had set out to conquer Jerusalem. Mites had taken upon themselves a task which their elders had neglected. . . .

Innocent III spent the whole night praying, beseeching for the Lord's counsel. In the morning he rose, his eyes aflame. "It is a Divine sign, if only the entire community joins in. Children are putting you to shame! Children have arisen to defend God! It would be infamy to let the little ones go alone, not to follow their example. As of old let anybody capable of carrying arms join the ranks! To arms! To arms! Save the Holy Sepulchre! Those unable to come, the weak and the ailing, may substitute an offering. Set up logs in churches for offerings. Who makes a donation will obtain the same indulgence to which pilgrims are entitled. A plenary indulgence. Oh, Christian world, arise! As of yore break loose from your roots. Follow the children! Follow the children! Save the Holy Sepulchre!"

With a hand that trembled the Pope signed innumerable letters. Three secretaries could hardly keep up with him. Letters to Bishops, to monasteries and directly to the faithful. In rapture he paced to and fro, staring straight ahead as though he saw the children marching across the field.

"Oh, why can I not go with them?" he sighed. "Why can I not lead them? I would be amongst them! Their childish faith would revive my own over-bitter, over-harsh faith. I should walk as though in Paradise amidst their voices and laughter. Indeed, angels must be leading them. There is nothing impossible for innocence. . . . Oh, blessed wave of childhood which spreads over the fields, awaken the souls of elders, mean, numb and asleep!

"Thou wave of childhood, thou seed of angels, human flower who knoweth no evil, whatever leads thee? Wilt thou really accomplish what thy elders have not? Wilt thou really fulfil what has not been fulfilled? Wilt thou brighten my old age with joy, wilt thou prove to the pagans the greatness of God Who, should He will it so, can perform great deeds with the hands of babes?"

Heedless of the astonishment of his secretaries Innocent III had stopped short in the center of the room, and raising his hand blessed the youngsters marching somewhere upon the roads. Oh, if he could go with them . . . !

The Cardinals disapproved of such thoughts. The Holy Father should not even think of leaving. His duty was to remain here, on the spot. If he left who could tell what might happen to the Church States!

To the Patriarch of Venice came messers Ferreus and Porcus, the ship owners, to announce that, moved by the enthusiasm of the innocent youth and the holiness of the cause, they offered to transport the children to the Holy Land free of charge. The Patriarch, impressed, accepted. The news spread like lightning and now no one doubted any longer the divine origin of the Crusade! It was common knowledge how hard and cunning were the hearts of the Venetians. Hitherto they had never done anything without profit! And now, of their own accord, they offered free passage! Indeed, it was a miracle!

Encouraged by this example others, likewise, hastened to help. They offered free conveyance, provisions, clothes . . . But follow the children, as the Pope bid? No one would! What? Wander again beyond the sea? Risk uncertain fate? No . . . It was asking too much! Their fathers and grandfathers had done enough of that wandering to the Holy Land. The present generation had recovered their senses. They would deposit in the church log an offering of money, dear as it was to them, and receive an indulgence—rather than risk their heads. True, crowds gathered from far and wide and stretched like a hedge along the road to watch the children pass and to cry in rapture: "God's lambs! Doves! Little flowers!" But that was all. Contrary to Innocent's hopes, none would let himself be swept off his feet. None would pin a cross upon his shoulder, desert house and possessions as of yore at the call of the Hermit! No! This was a different age.

Meanwhile children marched, rode, hastened. Their enthusiasm was not dulled. They were thirsting for miracles and greatness. Although they did not know it they were experiencing the same joys and fears their forebears had known when they had set out upon the first, mighty Crusade. Even though the page of history had turned it was the same ray that lit it now. Their small, childish cares preceding the departure, their very thoughts were a true reflection of the other ones. To be sure, then a hundred thousand people had set out and now there were not even five thousand children but it was not the number that mattered. For this was the only crusade which, like the first great one, was undertaken out of disinterested enthusiasm, in the conviction that God willed it! Not for revenge, not for glory, not for profit!

Many among the children could not go to sleep at night. They gazed into the darkness and heard voices. Others slept and had wonderful dreams which, as soon as the dawn came and birds began to sing in the thickets, they would relate to their sleepless companions. They did not know what those dreams might mean but they rejoiced in them. Nicholas could probably explain their meaning, but they saw Nicholas seldom these days. He was very busy. It even looked as though he were avoiding them, his old friends and admirers. Could he be angry at them? He had no reason to be. They had come as he had told them to. Maybe a little sooner than he had bid, for they had been stirred by what had happened with the wolf and little Ignatia. Little Ignatia had been gathering dead branches in the woods when suddenly a wolf, a snarling wolf, came upon her. She had turned white with fright and stammered out: "Do not devour me, good wolf, for I am going to defend the Holy Sepulchre." And at the words the wolf wagged his tail in friendly wise, like a dog, and went away without doing her any harm. Ignatia, breathless, had run to them and told them how it happened. And they all decided not to wait any longer but start the same night. . . .

"Nicholas dislikes your dog, Robert," the girls would say reproachfully. "That is why he doesn't come."

Nicholas did dislike Robert's dog or rather the dog disliked Nicholas. Marita's pet kitten had not followed her. When she tried to take it in her arms the kitten tore itself free, scratched the little maiden and sat upon the threshold staring at her with eyes as yellow as ducats. But the mastiff Lippo had followed Robert without being called and would not leave his master, not for a single step. At first the children were afraid of the big dog, but not anymore. On the contrary they slept calmly when Lippo watched near-by. The only strange thing about Lippo was that he hated Nicholas. He could not abide him.

"It is the devil which dwells in him," Nicholas would sigh. "I cannot allow him to come with us."

"I shall not take him on board. But up to then let him come; for what am I to do with him?"

"Do as you please, but that dog is possessed by the devil."

Nicholas would go away followed by Lippo's low, threatening growl, and Robert wondered, grieved, how he was to leave the dog in port.

Poor, dear Lippo! Maybe Matteo's grandfather who followed the crowd, together with the mothers, and every night came to hug his young grandson, would take care of Lippo. Robert would ask him. . . .

The Holy Father was inquiring feverishly of his secretaries how many applications had come in, how many men had joined the Crusade. To his horror he discovered that there had been none, well-nigh none. . . . Indeed there had gathered a good-sized number of tramps and vagrants, always eager to get a free passage across the sea, but when the ship owners announced sternly that only children would get free passage and all grown men would have to pay the usual price and in advance, they all dropped away.

During the first days of their journey Tina stole away from the camp every evening and ran back a good part of the way to meet Laurence and Balbina who were hastening in the wake of the throng. Some good fellow had happened along who was going the same way and had taken them in his cart. They were both dejected now. Tomorrow old Beppo will go no further," they complained to Tina. "We must follow you on foot. And yet you have carts and the younger children ride in them. Why will you not take us?"

"I don't know. Nicholas repeats over and over again that he will, later. . . . That he will come back for you . . . And there is no room in the carts. There really is none. . . . There are so many mites. . . ."

Tina sat dejectedly on the ground. After a while she said: "You can wait till Nicholas comes back as he promised. Everything is happening just as he said it would. People come out to meet us singing and give us food. And the Venetians will take us across without pay. . . ."

"Oh! so the sea will not dry out?"

"No. They will take us across on vessels . . . Bettina is glad that the crabs won't pinch her. Here are wheat cakes for you. Good-bye!"

They caught her by her skirt. "Tina! Old Beppo is really not going to ride tomorrow. What are we to do? We will not wait! We want to sail with you on the vessel. Tina!"

"I will try to persuade Nicholas," she promised, and ran back to camp. It was quite dark and she was afraid. The whole camp was asleep.

Only little Beatrice was still awake. She lifted her head. "Tina," she begged, "comb my hair! It is so tangled! I cannot manage it! Mamma always combed it . . ."

"I shall comb it tomorrow. Go to sleep now."

But the little girl could not sleep.

What is Mamma doing now? She is following us . . . Surely, she must be crying . . . My poor, my darling Mamma . . . she was thinking.

When Beatrice fell asleep Tina thought of her own mother. When she and her brother were going away or rather running away at night, it had seemed to them they cared but little for their mother . . . Forever screaming, so harsh . . . And how she cursed Nicholas. . . . But now Tina missed her . . . Her father too she missed a little, but above all . . . Mother.

Tossing on the straw pallet which rustled under her Tina wondered what would happen next? When would they behold the Archangel? When would they liberate the Sepulchre? And how? Oh, if only one could talk these matters over with Nicholas as they used to! And pray! They prayed, but seldom in camp. And never all together. Nicholas used to urge them to pray before, but not anymore. Maybe he thought the march would take the place of prayer. But was he not wrong? Some children were very naughty in spite of the march. . . .

In the village roosters began to crow . . . She should have been asleep long ago . . . With the solicitude of a little mother Tina's eyes once more made the round of all the little heads asleep by her side.

"What, none are going? None?" the Pope asked in horror. "No baron with a knightly train? None of the princes? Has the example not roused them, has the call not stirred them? Then I will not allow the children to depart alone. We cannot let them go to their death! Write at once— they must be stopped in port! Let them not board the vessels . . . To send those innocents right into the jaws of the infidels— Never!"

"People say it is a miracle and that the children will win more easily if they go alone," one of the papal secretaries said shyly.

"So speaks beastly laziness, not people! Shame upon the world which reasons so! I shall never allow these little ones to sail to their death. Stop them!"

"I will get the letters ready and send a messenger," the secretary hastened to assure him.

But on the very night the messenger arrived in Venice to convey to the Patriarch and the ship owners the will of the Pope, Messer Porcus had a vision sent from heaven. Strange times, indeed! Such a hard-hearted, tight-fisted merchant, one would think, and yet he had visions! Pope Urban II and Abbot Bernard de Clairvaux appeared to him just as though they were alive and threatened him with God's wrath if the children did not sail at once. "We shall lead them," the holy men had told him. "We shall direct that angelic herd. Waste not even an hour. Sail at once!"

Who would dare object to such a command? When Messer Porcus announced publicly in the square the grace which the Lord had bestowed upon him, the whole crowd roared, "Sail at once! Sail at once!"

The children themselves were quivering with impatience. The galleys lay already in port under sail. To be sure some belated group of youngsters from Germany was still expected, but they would not wait for them, just as they would not heed the letters sent by the Holy Father. "Sail at once! Sail at once!"

Venice was generous. It offered more than a thousand small white linen shifts to the little Crusaders. The example of the city was followed by others so that all the children were clothed in white. In their hands they brandished blooming twigs; their heads were crowned with flowers. They laughed, they cried, they sang, they covered the entire shore. In that crowd mothers wailed and sobbed. They pushed their way toward the galleys with determination and despair. But it was no use. The ship owners' men pushed them away without mercy. None must interfere with the fulfilment of the miracle.

"You should thank God that it was upon your children He bestowed His choice! Thank God!"

Meanwhile throngs were already boarding the vessels amidst squealings, laughter and shouts. Everything amused the youngsters, everything aroused their admiration. Only the Angel Gabriel had not appeared yet. Probably he was awaiting them on the opposite shore? Look at that mast! Isn't it high? Look at those sails. Here . . . look . . . lifeboats . . . !

The galleys (five had been prepared) were likewise beautifully adorned. From the decks hung festoons of oak leaves, their ends trailing in the water. Flags waved from the masts. At close quarters, to be sure, the impression of festivity was dispelled by the dirt and untidiness of the decks. Stains of grease, half-rotten boards. . . . But the children liked it all. Merrily they waved at those standing ashore.

Only Robert pressed his lips tight so that he should not burst into tears. He was heartbroken to leave the dog behind. Poor Lippo! He ran madly along the shore. He howled. Matteo's grandfather had promised to hold him but he himself was well-nigh out of his mind with despair. It was all because of Nicholas . . . Lippo could not abide him . . . But wait! Where was Nicholas? "Where is Nicholas?" shouted Robert, leaning over the railing. "Where is Nicholas?" a hundred small voices echoed. They began to search for him feverishly.

They searched and they found. He was in a corner of the port storehouse; it seemed as though he was hiding there. He resisted, tried to break loose, but in vain; the childish throng led him triumphantly, pushed him toward the galleys.

"We would not think of leaving without you, Nicholas. You must be with us. It was to you the Angel Gabriel pointed out the road!"

"Let me go! Let me go!" implored Nicholas. "Now others will lead you. You will find the way . . . I must return for the others . . ."

"What others?"

"The ones we left behind. . . . Balbina, Laurence, and other cripples . . ."

Tina who stood nearby burst into gay laughter. "Laurence and Balbina are already with us, Nicholas! They came in a cart hidden under a blanket . . . I have already brought them on board. They sit on deck and are so glad . . ."

"I cannot come with you. I cannot," pleaded Nicholas in despair, vainly trying to free himself from the little hands that held him fast. He shook as though in an ague, his face turned white, his voice broke.

"We will not go without you! Never! Absolutely never!"

The ship owners' men, who so far had been watching the scene without a word, now decided to intervene. One of them pushed the children aside and roughly grabbed Nicholas by the shoulder.

"What's this nonsense?" he inquired in a menacing voice. "Will you get on board or will you have me drive you there with this stick!"

Nicholas burst into tears and without further resistance climbed on board. The children, astonished, aghast, tugged at his hands. What had happened? Why would he not go? Why had that man spoken so roughly to him?

The dog howled. The crowd roared. The bells rang. Down to the port descended the Patriarch himself to bless the chirping throng. He was distressed. The Holy Father had expressly bid him not to let the children leave till he had levied an army. There were no volunteers, he had to use mercenaries. But the Papal war chest was empty, and levies would take long. In the meantime the children would have to stay in Venice, fed and lodged by the City. No one could wish that! It was one thing to offer a linen shirt and another to feed for six months, if not longer, five thousand of those small and restless locusts. That was why the Doge and the Illustrious Council had eagerly supported the commands of Urban II and Bernard the Abbot, expressed in the miraculous vision bestowed upon the ship owner. Let the little Crusaders sail away in all haste!

The ship owner, William Porcus, made no secret of it that he and his partner would withdraw the vessels they had offered so nobly should the Patriarch attempt to postpone the departure. This last consideration tipped the scale. What cost would then fall upon the Republic? A staggering cost, indeed. And likely it would be he, the Patriarch, responsible for the delay, who would be required to bear it!

And thus, helpless, afraid of the Pope on one hand and of the Council on the other, the great Church dignitary came down to bless the departure. It was all he could do. Like Pilate he was washing his hands. Already all the children were aboard. Lift the anchors! The rusty chains creaked, the helms began to rustle. The vessels, rolling heavily, executed a half turn. Between the shore, where desperate mothers struggled with port guards, and the hulls of the ships, opened a dark-green, cold ditch which grew wider, wider. . . . Matteo and Beatrice burst out into sudden piercing sobs. Hitherto they had not realized, but now they knew they did not want to go away. "No! No! Mamma! Grandpa! Let us go back! Please, let us go back!"

Their shouts had a sobering effect upon the others. Suddenly none wanted to depart.

"Mamma! Mother! Let us turn back."

But in vain they cried, shouted, and stretched out their arms. They no longer could be heard from the shore. The gale billowed the sails. The waves knocked at the sides. Ashore, wild with grief, not comprehending how it all could have happened, women threw themselves upon the trampled sand and kissed the prints of small feet. From the sides of the galleys oak leaf garlands became detached. Waves swept them to the shore, to the very lips of the mothers, as though in a last farewell.

"Look, look, seagulls! How many there are! How lovely!"

"You can't see the shore any more."

"What an old vessel! All rotten! The railing scarcely holds!"

"How does one go below the deck? Through that hole?"

"Let's go and see what the whole ship looks like. . . ."

"A shame we cannot sail side by side so we could talk from deck to deck. . . . The other ships are already ahead of us . . ."

"Those stupid kids are crying . . . Let us go below."

The two lads, Walter and Robert, approached the open hatch, but immediately a broad-shouldered mariner barred their way.

"Sit still! Don't wander about!" he ordered sternly.

"We only wanted to see. . . ."

"Sit there and be quick about it!"

His words were accompanied by such an expressive gesture that the lads drew back without protest. Scowling, they seated themselves upon the deck. All the crew was so strangely grouchy, unpleasant. . . . You could not as much as open your mouth to them. . . . On shore even the Patriarch himself came to bless the little Crusaders, and here any sailor dared threaten them. . . .

Laurence and Balbina, seated on a coil of rope, did not care whether the crew was civil or not. They felt happy, so happy indeed that it made them speechless. At last they were resting. At last they were sailing with the others. Now they were certain they would be healed without fail. Our Lord must have seen, He who sees and knows all, how much they had suffered during these long days when they lay huddled in the corner of the cart, covered with blankets by Tina . . . It was lucky indeed no one had seen them there and no one had reported to Nicholas or his men. Afterwards they had succeeded in sneaking on board amidst the crowd. Now no one would turn them back.

"If we only had white dresses like the others," sighed little hunchback Balbina.

"Maybe some kind people will give us dresses in the Holy Land? Look, how blue the sea is . . . Like the road to Heaven . . ."

"Oh, Laurence! Do look! What a strange man is coming out on deck!"

A strange man . . . All the children turned around astonished. They sprang to their feet, pressed closer to see. Who was that? Who could that be? Dressed in a long, loose, white garment. A long, black beard, a beaked nose, small piercing eyes. On his head a big white Moslem turban. . . .

He came out of the hull; three men were following him. One of them was William Porcus, who had been graced by the vision of Pope Urban II. The man with the turban was carefully scrutinizing the children. The ship-owner Porcus clapped his hands.

"Separate! Quick! The girls to the right, the boys to the left!"

Eagerly they obeyed his command. Maybe they would already be formed in ranks?

The man in the turban walked between the two lines. He spoke loudly in a tongue the children did not understand. He was excited. It would seem he was angry at something. The ship owner shrugged his shoulders. He answered in the same alien tongue.

"And you, why do you sit here? Get up!" He suddenly turned in anger at the two little cripples seated on the coil of ropes.

Abashed, surprised, they sprang up. Laurence with his twisted short leg, Balbina the hunchback. So they, too, were to stand in line? How wonderful! But the man with the turban burst into loud, scoffing laughter. He gesticulated vehemently, the ship owner's face turned purple with anger.

"Who allowed you to come on board? Who brought you here? Only the hale were to come!"

"Jesus will heal us," whispered Balbina, all atremble and with tears in her eyes.

"Who allowed it? Are there any more like you? Speak up?"

"No . . . we alone . . ."

Tina came running, terrified.

"It was me . . . I hid them in the cart . . . Because they, too, want to defend the Sepulchre!"

"Then you can take care of them, for I will not feed them! Cripples!"

"Handsome merchandise, indeed," remarked the Moslem in Arabic sarcastically.

"There's only two of them. They don't count, they are outside of the quota. I knew nothing of them. And the rest . . . just see for yourself!"

He sprang towards the girls. Before little Beatrice, who stood first in line, knew what was happening he had torn off her linen frock, turned her around naked, tapped her shoulders, lifted her chin, slapped her knees.

"Mamma! Mamma!" screamed the little girl.

"Shut up! Stand still! This is merchandise for you. And all are like that. Come here . . . you!" He stretched his hand to grab Tina who stood motionless, speechless, with both hands pressing her dress to her breast. "Come here, don't you hear me?" In his hand flashed a short leather whip. The Moslem said something as though to calm him. Porcus dropped his hand. He stepped over to the boys. He ordered them to take their shirts off. He examined breasts, backs, eyes, teeth, legs. He tapped them, setting their legs as though they were horses, praised, smacked his lips. The Moslem scoffed. He, too, grasped narrow childish shoulders, tapped breasts, lifted eyelids. The children stood dumb with terror. What did it all mean? Beatrice, huddled on the deck, continued to sob, "Mamma! Mamma!"

"Hey, there, be still!"

Once more the whip appeared. At last the two horrible men walked away to the other end of the deck. There they began to quarrel. They screamed and jumped. They counted something and then screamed again. They sent the third man, who had kept silent, below the deck to bring someone. After a while he returned with Nicholas.

The children sprang to their feet.

"Nicholas, Nicholas! What is happening? Where is the Angel Gabriel? Who are those men! They want to beat us! They yell at us, Nicholas!"

Bent in two, clutching his head in his hands, Nicholas did not hear them, did not answer them, did not look in their direction. He hurried toward the others. Robert, Beppo and Tina ran after him.

"Nicholas, didn't you hear? Why don't you answer? What is happening?"

"Get out of here!" Whistling, the short leather lash fell upon their necks, backs . . . "Get out," yelled the ship owner. "Stand in line . . . or else you'll be sorry."

"Oh God! Oh Lord! Mamma! Mamma!"

How dreadful it was to be small and not understand! What did they want of them? What did it all mean? . . . Linen dresses, blooming twigs, wreaths, blessings . . . gifts from the crowd . . . God's might that was to watch over them . . . mothers in tears . . . the Patriarch . . . the procession . . . the glory . . . the fame . . . the Angel Gabriel . . . What had become of them all?

"What does it mean, Tina?"

"I don't know. I don't know," whispered Tina, white as a sheet. "But don't weep lest they beat us again."

"I know," cried Robert. "I know! They have . . . sold us!"

"Sold us? How? To whom? What for?"

But the lad would say no more. He drew into an obstinate silence. He was weighing something in his thoughts. The others stared at him in horror. Sold? True, the pagans bought children . . . maybe the man in the turban was a pagan . . . ! "Mamma! Mamma! Mamma!"

Oh how dreadful to be small and helpless! As little and as helpless as a nestling! Only a while ago they had been so happy, secure, supported by the Omnipotent! Nothing could threaten them; all hastened to their help, and now . . . ? All those people who thronged the shore to bid farewell to the little Crusaders . . . Why had they not sailed with them? Why were they allowed to sail alone on vessels where were hidden the man with the turban and the man with a lash in his pocket? Why was there no one here to protect them? Why did Nicholas neither hear them nor see them?

Sold . . . Sold . . . ! In the midst of childhood, in the midst of carefree youth! The weight of it crushed them. They did not care to live any longer! They wept bitter tears. In vain they called their mothers.

Their mothers! Probably they still stood on the shore, staring at the water upon which their loved ones had sailed away. Their hopes and loves, their greatest joys, nurtured under their very hearts, carried in their wombs, suckled at their breasts, cradled in their arms. . . . Probably they still knelt upon the sand, kissing the tiny footprints and stretching their arms toward them. . . . Probably it seemed to them that they could still perceive the white sails. . . . And they guessed nothing . . . nothing . . .

"Mamma! Mamma!"

Unconsciously they all repeated the one word, not knowing whether they were calling the Sacred Mother or their own mothers left behind. Huddled and terrified, not understanding, they were seeking some protection, some help. A hand that would save them . . . They dared not move lest the man with the lash return. And only that one word: "Mamma . . . Mamma . . . Mamma."

Two sailors with hard faces brought pails with food. It was awful but some children ate, for they were all hungry. Tina beckoned to Laurence and Balbina.

"Oh no," protested Balbina through tears, "he said we were not allowed to eat."

"Eat my share, I am not hungry," and Tina turned away her pale face, suddenly grown old, so no one would see she was crying.

"Mother was right," said Beppo, his mouth full. "Too bad she did not break Nicholas' neck as she threatened. He deceived us. And now he hides like a snake . . . I wonder what became of the other one that was going around with him . . . John? Is he here?"

"No! he boarded another ship."

It was true. They had forgotten. There were five galleys. Maybe no heathens had hidden on the other ones? Maybe those other vessels continued happily on their way under the guidance of the Angel Gabriel? Maybe they did not know of the misfortune which had befallen their companions? Maybe they could give them some sign?

"But what sign? And is it possible, Tina?"

Tina bit her lips. "I think," she said with an effort, "there, too. . . ." For now she remembered. . . . The man with the lash was the same one whom, out there in the square, the Patriarch had solemnly thanked for his noble offer to transport the children. . . .

Dusk fell, night was coming. No one paid any attention to the children, no one put them to sleep or showed them where to rest. They slept like animals, wherever they happened to crouch. They sighed heavily in their sleep. When the night passed, the turbid daylight revealed wilted flowers, clothes soiled with the dirt of the deck, frightened little faces and eyes red with tears. This was no longer the joyous crowd of pilgrims, the army of little Crusaders, the heroic children of God, but a herd of slaves sold to misery and hardship.

Even before the sun had risen in the sky and lost its red glow, a terrible tumult burst on deck. The crew ran to and fro. A lifeboat had disappeared. Someone had unchained it, lowered it into the sea and rowed away. Porcus fumed. Again he wielded the whip. "How many are you?"

he bellowed at the children. "Count, count!" He pushed them around, lining them up once more. The younger mites, still sleepy, rubbed their eyes with small fists and began to cry. "How many are you? Anybody missing?"

He counted feverishly. Two were missing! Two of the number he had finally established after painstaking, protracted bargaining with Mohammed Ali!

"Which ones are missing? Who? Speak up or I'll skin you alive!"

"I think . . . I think," stammered Tina, terrified, "Walter and Robert . . . the big ones."

Porcus turned to his men.

"Hurry up, you cattle! Lower the boats and be after them! And you," he turned to the children, "below deck! Quick! Below, I said."

He drove the children in front of him, cursing and counting them anew. In the meantime a new tumult broke out on deck. Holes had been cut in the remaining boats. The fugitives had cunningly insured themselves against possible pursuit.

"Not a difficult task," mocked Mohammed Ali, who in the meanwhile had come out on the deck and tapped with his staff at the rotten boards of the boats.

"Accursed pups! Although I grieve mostly on your account, Mohammed, because the merchandise became your property after it was delivered yesterday."

"Your speech is useless! You know well that the merchandise will be mine only after you deliver it at the port. For the present the losses don't concern me."

"Nor me!" screamed Porcus. "But repair those boats! Hurry! We shall overtake them yet."

The skipper of the galley, with a gloomy secretive face, raised his voice. "We shall soon repair the boats, Porcus, but I shall not send them anywhere. Those lads will perish anyway. And we will need the boats . . ."

His hand pointed to the sky which had turned a dull grey. Porcus' eyes followed his gesture; he spat into the sea viciously.

"A storm is coming?"

"And what a storm! May the Saints protect us."

"Will we have time to escape it?"

"Yes, if we change our course at once to the north . . ."

"You know that's impossible! North? Back? Right into the Pope's hands? Are you mad, Benito? We must follow the course!"

"Not with these galleys . . . You took these rotten boxes to make a bigger profit . . . Old rot which can be sunk without grief, pretending a mishap for which you were promised a pay . . . !"

"You lie! The vessels are still good, and besides there's no telling whether the storm will come."

"Ask your partner the devil not to send it. Maybe he's not longing for you, yet."

Below deck, in the cramped windowless space, it was dark, hot and stifling. There was the stink of decaying provision, and plenty of rats. Huge, swift, they ran over the children's feet, afraid of nothing. Not so the children who screamed in fear. They pressed close together, filled with horror. They sobbed in motherless despair.

They no longer knew how many hours they had been crouched there. They had lost all sense of time. They were again very hungry but no one brought them food. Outside something dreadful must be happening; that's why they had been forgotten, for the entire vessel tumbled from side to side, creaked, climbed up then dropped down. They could hear an incessant roar. Children and rats alike were tossed about like balls. At times it seemed to them they were lying on the floor then all at once the floor would become the ceiling. Painfully they rebounded from the walls, falling in the dark with the dull thump of inanimate objects. The tormented little heads knocked helplessly upon the boards. Pale lips still whispered their gospel of childhood: "Mummy . . . Mummy . . . Mummy."

"And where is Jesus?" someone's voice, as though astonished, asked in the dark.

"Where is Jesus?" repeated the others. "Where is Jesus?" Men could betray, deceive the poor children, but Jesus would not do it, surely. "He must come! He must rescue us!"

"Let's ask Jesus," called Tina. "Come, now!"

And amidst the roar of the creaking masts falling upon the deck they shouted in a desperate chorus.

"Jesus! Kind Jesus! take us away from these evil men. . . ."

"Let us return to Mummy . . ."

"Don't allow them to beat us . . ."

"Oh, water is coming in, water . . ."

"It's up to my knees!"

"Get out! Get out!"

With the strength of despair they broke the door. The steps were already flooded with water. Water poured from above, rose from below. And the roar was such that even though they shouted they could not hear each other. Outside it was almost dark and the sea, a horrible swollen sea, was high overhead! Looking up they could see the crest of waves crowned with foam.

Clutching to the ramp, struggling with the gale and the water the stronger ones came out or rather crawled out on deck. The younger ones had remained downstairs and the water was flooding them now. . . . No one paid any heed to them. . . . No one cared any longer. . . . What did merchandise matter when the buyer and the seller were about to perish? William Porcus, the man with the whip, convulsively clutched the stump of the broken mast, his face contorted with fear, such horrible fear that suddenly hope sprang up in the children's hearts. "The evil men are afraid—surely Jesus must be angry at them." Tina stretched out her hand in front of her. "Look, look at that cloud," she screamed, trying to raise her voice above the roar of the waves. "It is Jesus coming to punish those evil men!"

More dead than alive, with weariness they now watched with growing hope the dark blue column shaped like a huge funnel which reached from the waves to the clouds and with increasing speed advanced upon the sinking ship . . .

Robert and Walter rowed bravely all night long till daybreak. The wind was in their favor. It blew from the south and pushed them toward their native shores. But by morning they were exhausted. When the storm caught the little craft, they were indeed close to the shore but unable to hold the oars in their sore hands. The storm which had sunk four galleys carrying the little Crusaders did not fuss much with a miserable shell and two boys who knew nothing of the sea . . . Walter at once went down. Robert, who was a good swimmer, fought long for his life. He let the waves carry him without resistance till a sudden blow on the head made him lose consciousness. When after many hours he opened his eyes, he was lying on the shore. The sea was once more calm, the sun shone brightly and hurt his eyes red from salt water. He lay prone for a long time. At last he rose to his feet and, stumbling and staggering as though he were drunk, he started in search of people. He was dreadfully hungry and weary. Food, food! But along with consciousness memory had returned, the memory of what had happened, together with gnawing grief and anger. He craved for the sight of man not only to ask for food but to spread the news of what the ship owners had done. Let everyone know in whose hands they had placed the children! Let everyone hasten to the rescue!

He dragged along the coast not knowing where he was going or whether he was proceeding in the right direction. As he went he plucked still green, tasteless figs, he chewed on ears of unripe corn, trying with them to deceive the pangs of hunger. Suddenly, he stopped. Towards him, equally staggering, advanced a woman. Her clothing revealed noble rank, although it was dirty and torn. Her head was bent. The high head-dress, characteristic of the wives of noblemen, nodded to left and right and the long coif which descended from it was rumpled and torn as though the woman had spent all the preceding stormy night abroad. Four armed men followed her at a respectful distance.

Robert recognized her. So many times had the men of Nicholas and those of the ship owners respectfully but implacably removed Madonna Angelica de Trevi, the mother of little Beatrice, from the children's camp that he remembered her well. But could she be this stooping woman with the insane look in her eyes?

"Madonna! Madonna!" cried Robert, falling at her feet.

She did not recognize him and drew back in terror.

"Madonna! I was on that vessel. . . . I escaped . . . Beatrice and all of us . . . sold!"

"Where is Beatrice?" she screamed wildly, convulsively clutching his shoulder.

"Sold . . . all sold . . . There are pagans aboard . . . They wanted to whip us . . . They tore off Beatrice's dress . . . The Venetians have betrayed us and . . ."

He did not finish, for with a horrible scream she fell on the ground in a dead faint. Hurriedly, as though with relief, the squires ran to her and lifted her up.

"Hey, lad! Come with us to the Patriarch! You shall tell him what you have told us here."

"First give me food," he implored.

"Where will we get food from? We, too, have not eaten since yesterday . . . The Mistress has gone completely mad. Come now, hurry!"

They carried the lifeless form. Robert dragged behind. They stopped the first cart they met on the way and ordered the driver to take them to the palace of His Grace the Patriarch Sanuti. When he insisted upon being paid first they stuck their fists under his nose.

Dumbfounded by the news the Patriarch sat death still while a burning blush of shame rose to his sunken cheeks. He listened to the chaotic story of the boy. At times he rubbed his eyes. No, it was impossible. This must be a dream? "My child, are you sure it is so?"

"Upon the guiltless death of Our Lord," Robert assured him, "it is true. The man with the turban came out from below the deck. They whipped us and stood us in a row. They tore our clothes off . . . They felt us, tapped us, looked us over like cattle . . . They quarreled and wrangled . . ."

"O God! Merciful God!"

The Patriarch covered his eyes. Whose fault was this? Whose? His! The Holy Father must have had a premonition . . . he had ordered that the children be stopped. . . .

The Patriarch sat motionless, dejected.

"Send quickly to His Highness the Doge," he called to his secretary. "May it please him to come! As for this lad, give him food and clothing and guard him lest he go into the town and spread rumors beforetime . . ."

The secretary ran to carry out the orders and the Patriarch continued to clutch his head with both hands. God, merciful God! The city even now was all atremble over the fate of the children, because of the terrific storm last night; the mothers who had not yet departed for home would not leave the port and were unceasingly asking questions of returning sailors. And they whined because no one knew anything. What if they were to hear the truth? To learn of that horror worse than any storm. What would happen? What if the crowd turned to rioting . . . ?

Peter Zano, by the will of God, Doge of Venice, Dalmatia, Croatia, half of Constantinople and lands conquered by the Latins from the Empire, was a rather colorless man. Old, greedy Henry Dandalo, the conqueror of Byzantium, was dead and buried on the spot of his victory in the Basilica of St. Sophia. His successor did not measure up to him either in brains or in courage. The evil tidings dazed and terrified him. Heavily he slumped into a chair facing the Patriarch.

"What are we . . . what are we to do?" he stammered out.

The Patriarch had had time to recover. "We must organize a pursuit," he said, "and until it starts we must not divulge the news. No telling whether the unfortunate things would not have been drowned anyway, so why should we add to their elders' bitterness to no avail? If we catch up with them we shall punish the guilty. Let God judge us!"

"Yes, we must say nothing!" Peter Zano agreed. "What would be said all over the world? Because of two scoundrels ill-fame would fall upon the whole nation!"

"Listen! What might the tumult be?" the Patriarch interrupted him.

They moved over to the window. Great Heavens! the tidings they wanted to hide must have spread somehow, for a huge crowd had gathered in the square. People poured out of sidewalks, canals. Water splashed, oars creaked, boats rubbed against each other . . . the whole square was paved with heads as though they were cobblestones . . .

There was a roar of voices. "What has become of the children? Where are the children? You sold them to the heathens!"

"Where are the children? Hey, speak up! Which one of you sold them?"

"You took money for our children!"

The crowd roared, surged. The Patriarch and the Doge looked at each other and bit their lips.

"Let us go out and address them!"

They both stepped out upon the balcony which hung over the square like a swallow's nest.

"Woe! Woe! Herods! Give us back our children!"

"Children! Children!"

"Be still, keep your peace, Christians," the Patriarch called out in a ringing voice. His voice was strong, his face as if carved in stone, though his heart trembled. "Do not despair! Do not repeat vain abuse! The news of the misfortune is not certain. A poor lad half-crazed with fear, and saved by a miracle from the storm, has come ashore and tells incredible things. We know not whether to give credence to him. Let no vain fears take hold of you! Indeed it is easy to encounter an evil man, for Satan sows seeds everywhere, but a crime like this seems hard to believe. His Highness the Doge is sending out a pursuit. If Divine Providence has saved the innocents from the storm the pursuit will catch up with them and get the traitors . . . The rascals will meet a fitting punishment, the children will be saved . . ."

"Save the children," roared the crowd. The sobs of mothers rose above the din.

Peter Zano moved in front of the Patriarch.

"Orders are already issued," he shouted. "Four of the swiftest galleys are setting sail. The crew of oarsmen has been increased. They will row incessantly with all the oars. They will overtake them. Go to the port to watch their prompt sailing . . ."

Convinced, the crowd split. Half turned towards the shore, the rest disappeared into the churches. The two dignitaries, relieved, returned to the room.

"Who has tattled? Did I not say the lad should not be let out," the Patriarch demanded.

"We did not let the lad out," his secretary assured him. "He has eaten his fill and now sleeps like a log. Maybe Madonna de Trevis . . ."

"You ought to have stopped her too!"

"There was no order, and alone we dared not."

"The accursed rascals," mumbled the Doge. "Porcus and his companions . . . I have known long they were gallows birds, but I did not think they were so bad as this . . . Although at first their enthusiasm looked suspicious to me . . ."

"Why did you not warn me, Your Highness?" asked Patriarch Sanuti reproachfully.

The Doge scowled disdainfully.

"And why did your Grace agree to the departure of the children despite the Holy Father's command?"

The Patriarch made no reply. Neither of them had any right to reproach the other. They were both guilty. They had become accomplices in the crime. Oh, God have mercy!

"Is there any hope that they may be overtaken?" he inquired timidly.

Peter Zano shrugged his shoulders. The golden chain upon his breast tinkled slightly.

"None whatsoever," he admitted. "In the first place I am certain the vessels were wrecked. How else? There has been no such tempest in ten years. Few vessels can stand a gale like that. And it would seem that

Porcus took his worst galleys. The villain reckoned wrong. He thought the weather would hold till the end of the moon. . . . But even if they are not wrecked we will not overtake them . . . How do we know where they sailed? Maybe they are already in Tunis?"

"Good God! So the pursuit is aimless!"

"Absolutely aimless, but necessary to calm the rabble. Otherwise they might tear this palace down . . . The children are surely lost. . . . And the disgrace will stick to us. . . . Even a hundred years from now the people will hold Venetians responsible for it. Mark my words: the news of this will spread throughout the whole world like a pestilence. . . ."

# 12.

## Brother Pacific

AND INDEED THE NEWS SPREAD. WITH THE SWIFTNESS PROPER TO EVIL tidings the rumor of innocent children sold into slavery was rife in hamlets, villages, towns and castles. Everywhere it aroused horror. Those who but a short while ago had joined in processions to bid farewell to the departing children stood now horror-stricken and wild with rage. They recalled those God's lambs who had marched with such radiant smiles and such trust, and at the thought that there had been men infamous enough to abuse that trust, to deliver them into the hands of heathens, even the most placid ones ground their teeth. Woe! Woe! Verily, the world must be doomed that such horrors have become possible? Verily, it must have reached the limit of evil. Verily, there must be no greater difference between it and hell than between the hoof of a colt and that of a mare. Verily, God must have forsaken the earth and given it into the power of Satan.

All Italy, South Germany and a part of France had been touched by the tragedy. There was no hamlet where children were not mourned; where mothers did not sob. Mothers! They had had a premonition . . . they had struggled to the very last moment . . . they would not have allowed it!

Now they wailed and reproached their husbands for their cowardice. They abused them, they spat at them, drove them from their beds, urged them to go and rescue the innocents. To be sure the sea had washed ashore several hundred small bodies at the island of St. Peter; it had washed ashore the wreckage of ships, but who could tell by these splinters from how many galleys they had come? There had been five vessels; maybe not all had sunk? Maybe the rest of the children were alive and awaiting rescue?

And what the Pope's summons could not accomplish was now fulfilled spontaneously. Men gathered, armed, some driven by grief, others by shame. The fact that here, in the very heart of the Christian world, the accursed heathens had stretched out their hands for the children was a blow bitter enough to arouse the most callous. The innocent would not have perished if, as the Pope had urged, the men had gone with them! They had fallen victim to the lethargy of grown men! And hastily, knightly trains made ready their arms, offerings poured in, men volunteered everywhere. Women urged them. Make haste! For Mercy's sake make haste! Let the Holy Father appoint a leader! Let a fifth mighty crusade set forth!

Like a ball rolling down an incline, like an avalanche sweeping everything before it, the Crusade grew. But two months before people had held for a fool anyone who would want to go to the Holy Land. Now they turned away with disdain and called coward anyone who was not going. French, Italian, even English barons proclaimed their willingness to go to the Holy Land. Sussex, Arundel, William de St. Omer, Savary de Mauleon, Enguerrand de Boves, Simon de Joinville, Walter de Nemours, Albert de Castel Gualteria. . . . Each with a strong force . . . Avenge the infamy! Show the pagans it was hands off the Christian seed!

William Divini was returning from Champagne and could not make heads or tails of the change. Like everyone else he had learned while still at the court in Troyes of the Children's Crusade and its dreadful end. He had been sincerely moved and intended to compose an appropriate song. The tune was already in his head; the words could wait till his return. No doubt his countrymen would supply him with many valuable details which would lend color to the composition.

Thus no one could reproach the king of troubadours that he had not taken sufficiently to heart the loss of five thousand innocents. But it was one thing to compose a song and another thing to take up a sword. Divini looked with deep horror at what was happening all around him. He met people whom he knew who had long since turned their helmets into hen-nests and who now swaggered in full armor in the roads as though they were King Richard. Their number grew constantly. In Rome, a specially summoned Council was in session at the Lateran and it was rumored that the Holy Father himself intended to lead the Crusade. Incredible! This sudden war enthusiasm was beginning to irritate the bard.

"You used to scoff at those who rushed to the Holy Land and now you will go?" he railed at his acquaintance, Sire de San Marino.

The knight pondered a while before he answered. "It is true I scoffed. But those children! One cannot forget or forgive that . . . !"

"It was through no fault of yours they perished!"

"It does not matter whether the fault was mine or somebody else's Such monstrous villainy must be erased by some great deed. Otherwise one could not live; one could not be called a Christian."

"I see," agreed Divini, more out of civility than conviction. "I see, and in a few weeks, I too shall start!"

He did not add that he was starting for entirely different reasons and that the prospects of war greatly diminished his enthusiasm for the trip.

He dragged himself along drowsily from stop to stop, a bit sour because the laurel upon his cap did not impress people as of yore. A cross upon the shoulder—that was the fashion of the day. Could it be Godfried's times had returned? Wandering minstrels sang new songs which he had not heard before. Mostly the themes dealt with the Children's Crusade. Roadside beggars spun out stories of the Holy Father and the sea.

". . . so the Holy Father bid that he be carried in all Peter's majesty upon the shore and he threatened the sea and beseeched it to return the children. . . . And he cried: 'Oh, thou unfaithful sea! Hast thou ceased to be a Christian sea?' And the sea lay dead as though asleep, smooth like set lava. And the Holy Father prayed and prayed and then cried again: 'Wilt thou not reply, O Sea? Can it be thou feelest guiltless? Indeed thou hast saved the little ones from dishonor. Thou hast delivered them gently into angels' arms? Belike I should thank thee, forgive? Aye, thou art right O Sea! I am not wroth with thee any more. I forgive thee but them I forgive not. And God, Himself, cannot forgive. I desire not that He should forgive. . . . They will never obtain forgiveness. . . . But thou, Sea, forgiven, absolved, pardoned, hearken to me—return the bodies of the little ones! . . .' And at these words the sea heaved as though a sudden wind had arisen. It foamed, it leaped to the feet of the Fisherman's successor and that very night it swept ashore many a hundred of drowned bodies upon Peter's Island at the cape called the Rock of Recluse where now they are building a temple, the Temple of Innocents. . . ."

Thus sang the beggars. Divini collected all such yarns avidly. They would be useful for the song he had in mind. But even this did not improve his mood. Not far from Rovigo he encountered the insane Madonna de Trevi. Unable to keep still she was travelling all over the country riding upon a mule under the watchful eye of a duenna and several men whom her despairing husband had assigned to her. Whomever she encountered she told of Beatrice and implored him to go to the children's help. Divini, who the year before had known her as a young and beautiful matron, gazed with genuine grief at her aged, altered face, the spasmodic quiver of her lips and wild eyes while she recited in a ghastly whisper!

". . . they tore the shirt from her and wanted to whip her. . . . My darling . . . They felt her like a beast for sale . . . My Beatrice . . . I gave her into the Angel Gabriel's care and it was not the angel but Satan? Have you not heard of it? Satan has extorted our children from us! Go and fight him! Go! Rescue, help the children and us and yourself!"

"That I shall do, by all means, milady," he assured her courteously and rode away. Try as he would he could not forget the sight of her poor face or the sorrowful sound of her voice.

In a heavy mood he stopped for the night in a hostel. Just as in his favorite canzona, sweet clusters weighted down vineyards by the roadside the air seemed sticky with strong, ripe scents, fruits and herbs and the very summer at its end were scintillating with perfumes. Inside, however, the air was heavy and filled with the stench of sheep cheese. Divini opened the window and leaned out. He stood thus motionless till dusk had turned into the darkness of night. His mind was sensitive to beauty and the evening was beautiful indeed. As though to welcome the night there rose from the gardens ever stronger, ever more intoxicating, the perfume of flowers and breath of herbs. Bats flew by swift and silent. . . . In the thicket night birds called to each other. From somewhere low in the grass under the tree there came muffled but in the silence distinct young human voices and laughter. The troubadour's servant Silvio, and of course with a girl!

On a night like this . . . no wonder! Divini smiled indulgently though not without melancholy. Suddenly he heard them talking of him and he began to listen.

"What is it he wears upon his cap, your master?" the girl was asking.

"Laurel," Silvio informed her, not without pride. "The Holy Father himself gave it to him, meaning he is a king."

"Ha, ha . . . what sort of king?"

"The king of singing."

"An oldster like that, and he still sings? Surely his hair must be white under his cap?"

"It is not."

"Dark?" she asked incredulously.

"Not dark either."

"What then?"

"There was once a man," began Silvio sententiously, "who had two mistresses. One was old and the other young. The young one plucked his gray hair so he would look younger. The old one plucked out all his dark hair so he would resemble her. . . . At last they fixed him up so . . ."

". . . that he was bald," she exclaimed, chuckling. "Now I know. . . ."

"Don't speak so loud! Old as he is and bald-headed, my master sings beautifully!"

"What of it? An old man's singing cannot warm!"

"You would not run after him?"

"Indeed I would not. Likely he stinks of the grave?"

"Nonsense! He rubs himself with scents every day."

"Maybe just so, because he stinks. . . . Fetch me some of those scents . . . ! Oh, do! My sweet one, my black-eyed one. . . ."

"I'll fetch them tomorrow. . . ."

The man in the window drew silently back into the room. Old, old, stinking of the grave. . . . Only a little while ago he would have laughed at such talk. Tonight he could not laugh. For the first time it occurred to him that maybe he was really old? Angrily, he pushed the thought away. Did he not feel young, spry, full of life? Why should he pay heed to what a silly little goose was saying . . . At her age, anyone over twenty seemed old . . .

"To be sure," thought Divini, "it was long ago that I was twenty. I am now . . . why think of it . . . Still, I am young, indeed I am . . ."

He threw himself on the wide, squeaky bed without undressing. Under the stiff sheet straw rustled loudly. The opening of the window seemed to him like a dark-blue surface breathing freshness into the stuffy room. The king of troubadours stared into that surface sorrowfully. He felt already he would not be able to go to sleep tonight. "He stinks of the grave." What an expression! No telling who would be the first to go . . . This little goose might die and turn into a stinking cadaver even sooner than he would . . .

"But you too shall not escape death," suddenly rang in his ears. He gave an uneasy start so that the straw rustled once more . . . No, he would not escape death. . . . None had . . .

None. . . . How strange that people almost never give it a thought . . . He, Divini, could not recall that the realization of this fact had ever come to him before: Not till tonight, because of that wench's talk! Or maybe it was not the talk that brought it on? Maybe on such a night as this everyone lying frightened and sleepless imagines, as though to spite the pregnant scent which rises from the soil, that he is departing, dying? Maybe everyone feels his own death—like Divini right now, his own limbs growing rigid and numb, the mortal fear and cold sweat upon his brow, and hears the inescapable question: "What now? What next? What next?"

"What next?" he repeated almost aloud and sat upon the bed. What? A great responsibility, the day of reckoning, the horror of eternity. . . . A voice that would say: "Mene, Tekel, Upharsin. The measure, the number, the sentence. I measured thee, I weighed thee and I cast thee away for thou art empty and wanting. . . ."

Every hour of life gone by suddenly acquired meaning. Each was called forth from oblivion. None was lost, none was hidden. They existed somewhere, alive in the void, and now at the voice of the Judge they would arise and tell their story. And the soul, helpless, naked and trembling with fear, would listen to the testimony of the hours of its own life.

Divini desperately rubbed his eyes. What was happening to him? He must be ill! Never, never had such thoughts visited him before. He felt an urge to pray. It was long since he had done so; troubadours were not known for great piety. Wandering minstrels openly wove into Christian antiphonies the pagan names of Venus, Jove and, above all, Bacchus. To be sure Divini was too much of an aristocrat and true artist to imitate such pranks, nevertheless he knew well those blasphemous drunkards' prayers. And now they, too, wandered around in his head, substituting their thoughtless aping for the proper word of prayer. He wanted to say: "In secula seculorum," and instead said "In pocula poculorum laudabut te, dolus vobiscum," and "cum gemitu tuo," as though prompted by some malicious imp. And William Divini, who among friends often mocked at belief in the Devil, now looked fearfully around and crossed himself, and again confused Our Heavenly Father with Bacchus, and the Holy Virgin with Venus. When at last, shortly before dawn, he fell asleep, he dreamed of the Devil, first in the guise of a man with a calf's tail, then a dragon, a Negro, a snake, a red-hot iron and in the form of a shining eye set in a dark, dull surface. That mocking eye stared at the troubadour till he awoke and its memory tormented him throughout the whole day. It took many a goblet to banish the image, but for all the wine he drank he was unable to recover his calm. His soul, stirred by the question "what next," would not recover its previous serenity. Somewhere in the corner of his brain stuck like a splinter the awareness that sooner or later he would be asked to render an account of the meaning of his life. The meaning of life? Divini did not know it. He had never thought about it till now. He like most people did not wrong others deliberately; he sang, he was fond of women, games, honors, good wine and good food; he disliked bad music, stench and competitors . . . What else? Was this enough? Was it too little?

These doubts made him absent-minded during the rest of his journey. Absent-mindedly he looked at what was going on in the country. To only one thing he remained sensible as of yore: the marks of respect paid to him, the king of troubadours. But here, too, he was made to suffer. For those marks did not seem to him sufficient. He was used to greater esteem. At times it seemed to him that people had simply forgotten his existence. The Crusade, the death of the innocents were absorbing all minds. The king of troubadours and his gold laurel drew no attention. Not in a single town did the Councilmen come out to welcome him with an oration. When he departed there was no train of noble youths to accompany him. And yet that was how he was treated of yore! "They have all gone mad with that Crusade," scoffed Divini. "In Rome it will be different; they know me there." And he prodded his she-mule.

But in Rome it was even worse. He found the city full of people preparing to depart for the Holy Land. To Divini no one gave a thought; people scarcely recognized him. At the Lateran the Synod was meeting. Bishops, Archbishops, and Cardinals had gathered from every part of the world. Their retinues filled the squares. Though imposing enough they did not strike one with the magnificence of former days, and it was being said that much had changed among the clergy in the last year or so. Some attributed this change to the constant, stern admonitions of the Pope, others to the Children's Crusade, still others to the beneficial influence of a man they referred to as the fool of Assisi, who a year ago was in Rome and had provoked general laughter. Today nobody laughed at him. The number of his brethren reached half a thousand, it would seem. They were constantly wandering up and down Italy, preaching a life according to the Gospel, and lately the Crusade. It was said that this fool, Francis himself, had recently come to Rome again and awaited the departure of the Holy Father with whom he was to sail for the Holy Land.

For Innocent III intended to lead the expedition personally.

"I shall not command 'go' but 'come,'" he had said to the Council. "Weak of body, holder of an office which it does not befit to take up arms, I shall not fight with steel. But I shall do as Moses did, who when Israel fought with the Amalekites, knelt upon a mountain and prayed to God. So shall I kneel upon a hillock or on the bow of a vessel and shall call to the Lord for a victory for you. . . . I shall go. . . . Oh, why did I not go before . . . then the innocent children would not have perished. . . ."

His voice broke and the Pope wept, for he was unable to speak calmly of the cruel end of the Children's Crusade. "Expeditio derisoria, expeditio nugatoria . . ." the Cardinals recalled their first definition . . . But the Pope shook his head.

"It is a sacrifice, a sacrifice that ought to shake the world. Truly, I tell you, woe to men if they do not wake up now!"

He shook his thin hand, sick, looking like a ghost, and the men who watched him wondered whether the Holy Father would have strength enough to stand the long voyage and the hardships of camp life. Some thought that the Holy Ghost would support him. The Holy Ghost, the Paraclete, whose imminent coming was predicted by the Abbot Joachim di Fiore, worshipped generally as a saint. Please God, it would be so. Much hope was set in the leadership of the Pope.

Unnoticed, honored by none, Divini wandered through the city of his birth, as familiar to him as his own house. He was filled with the unpleasant sense that something had happened: either he had become a stranger to the city or the city a stranger to him. Everything irritated him. His steward Giano, whom he had trusted, had emptied his cellar of the best wines. The horses were skinny; the servants obviously had stolen the money he had left for oats. His creditors—and in spite of his fortune he had many of them—upon learning of his proposed departure fell upon him like vultures. Even more persistent than creditors proved his friends who lauded Divini's generosity. Knowing his vanity of old, they were able, by means of deft flattery, to open his purse. Of yore the divine William had felt happy among these younger sons of barons, would-be poets, bards, minstrels and even common shysters and spongers. Today even their company bored him. Gloomily he listened to their jests and shouts, while he fingered his face. For some time it had become a habit with him to feel his cheek bones timidly, as though in secret. His friends thought he was searching for wrinkles, but it was not of wrinkles that Divini thought. Morbidly, feverishly, he was feeling under his skin the sockets of his eyes, imagining his own skull after death! It had come over him once at the barber's. For the first time it had occurred to him that the bony edge which he could feel right under his eye was but an empty hole through which stared Death, as drawn by patient Benedictines upon the pages of psalters. A death skull, and he was carrying it around and it alone would still remain after his body had decayed, fallen apart . . . The sneering, blind horror would be all that would remain of the divine William. And some day even the bones would crumble into dust. . . . Then nothing would remain . . . And what would become of the soul?

"Surely someone must have bewitched me," worried the troubadour. "I must be bewitched. De Brienne spoke once of a witch in Troyes; he even gave her name . . . Margot, I think. I must have encountered her, not knowing who she might be, and she must have cast a spell upon me? Why did she? Surely I have done her no wrong. . . ."

At other times it occurred to him that he must be beset by the vapors of dull sorrow called acadia which frequently tormented monks in monasteries. Its victims knew no joy, their souls pined away in gloom. To counteract the ailment he took elixir vitae, a famous medicament compounded of the juice of apples of paradise, cinnamon, crushed amber, lapis lazuli, ground pearls and hammered gold. It was believed that the smallest amount of that medicament would make anyone merry and many had proved the effect of it upon themselves. But even the elixir did not help William. He did not grow merry. The feeling of hollowness which tormented him must have been deep rooted and he did not know its cause. Could it have come because once, accidentally, he had deliberated upon the vanity of the world and himself? He was no child, after all; he must have known of old that he would die like everyone else; that every hour brought him closer to the grave . . . not farther away from it.

With this mood still upon him he beheld without enthusiasm Julia entering his bedchamber one morning, evidently in secret connivance with Silvio. Julia, the lovely wench whom he himself several months before had brought to Jean de Brienne. In the course of the last year the maid had developed from a child into a woman and had grown still more beautiful. Her coyness had increased at the same rate as her looks. She was conscious of her own worth and had become supercilious towards men.

"What do you want?" asked Divini.

"Well, I was told Your Honor had returned so I came to inquire what was to become of me?"

"How is that? What is to become of you? I don't need you. . . ." She gave him a quick, slightly mocking glance. "I thought maybe I could be of use . . . either as a servant or just so . . . inasmuch as Your Honor called me last year. . . ."

"What of it? I did not promise to keep you permanently. I gave you a ducat. . . ."

"My stepmother took it away. . . . Now she drives me out to bring another one . . . all because of Your Honor? What shall I do now . . . ?"

She hid her face in her hands and began to sob, loudly, insincerely. Divini gazed at her, unimpressed. Silly wench, he thought, truly you should weep because you will die, because your looks will rot . . . Worms will devour you . . . Have you heard of it? Worms! . . .

"Don't bawl," he said aloud, "here is another ducat."

She stopped crying immediately and grabbed the coin. Her face lit up in a smile but she did not go.

"Couldn't I stay here for good?"

"I don't know," Divini replied. "I will see . . . I will consider . . . Now you can go."

Reluctantly she departed. Divini ordered his horse to be brought and rode off through the city. It was full to bursting. It overflowed like a swollen river. The preparations for the great Crusade absorbed all minds. At the stalls violent wranglings were in progress. As usual in such cases the prices of some goods had fallen sharply while others, particularly the price of horses and all kind of armor, had increased tenfold. At times, indignant at the traders' demands, the customers would seize a stick or a sword. A fight would begin and along the entire street all the stalls would be hurriedly closed. A detachment of Papal guards would rush to the spot to restore order but in some other alley other tumults would arise.

Divini rode along slowly. Absent-mindedly he observed the confusion. Suddenly a throng gathered in a square, more silent and closely packed than the others, attracted his attention. He turned his mount in that direction. A street preacher. He must have been standing on a stone or a tree stump, for his head and shoulders showed above the heads of his listeners. His arms were lifted high, and there was something about the ardent gesture which brought vague memories to the troubadour's mind. Was this not perhaps that newly famous madman of Assisi whom he had once wanted to show to the Frangipanis and found swinging on a board? Yes, yes, this must be he. Just as the year before the men who surrounded him kept absolutely still, hanging upon his words as though bewitched. And drawn by the force of the general tense attention Divini dismounted, flung the reins to the lad, and dived into the crowd. He pushed his way through, unmindful of the stench, until he found himself quite close to the speaker.

The speaker was crying: ". . . Many among you have vowed to go to the Holy Land, but how shall you go before you make a crusade in your own hearts? It is from there you ought to drive out the pagan first so that Our Lord would have no reason to be ashamed of His defenders!

"The sword and the Cross will not avail when a Saracen hides within the soul and thinks more of the booty than of the Holy Sepulchre. First you must conquer the greed within you. It is an all-important task. Greed is the mistress of Satan even as the Holy Lady Poverty is the love of God. Most evil comes of greed. But a while ago a most atrocious crime has been committed. Evil men have deceived and brought to death children whom Our Lord held dear. Those traitors lied to the children! They delivered them to doom. And they lost their own souls; they made a compact with the Devil. What made them do it? Nothing else but greed. They did it for the sake of money. Of money! What is money that for its sake people fear not to commit crime? A crime of which Satan himself would be ashamed? Money! There is nothing in the world more foul and more dangerous for men. . . . Look around: the worst wrongs, injustices, inequalities and cruelties spring from greed, from the craving for money! Whoever loves money, cannot love either God or his neighbors. Money means violence for some and slavery for others. While loving money none can be free or happy. This one, because he craves it, that one because he has already won it and fears that others might take it away. Why should we love money—that most effective of the Devil's tools, instead of loving God? If we are to love, why not love what is best; if we are to serve why not serve the One who is unchangeable, will not betray, will not desert? Our Lord is freedom and who would not be free? There is nothing in the world as priceless as freedom. . . .

"And who would not like to escape from that mean fear in which we live constantly, and stretch and laugh merrily and feel under a mighty protection? We live in constant fear in this world; of old age, of pestilence, of weakness, of thieves. . . . We fear the Devil, witches, witchcraft and evil spells . . . And yet we are Christians and need fear nothing! The Devil compared to God means no more than the moon compared to the sun, than a viper compared to a lion. What can he do to us? It is God alone we should fear, for there is no foe from which He would not protect us. Witchcraft and evil spells exist only where the Lord is not, when the door has been closed before Him. . . . And there hides fear, horror, danger! Beloved brethren! Ever since I serve the Lord I am so happy. For I acquired those very things—freedom and the fact that I am not afraid. Why, I can mock the Devil, or pity him. And that because of God's grace, of course. Not because of any merit of mine, for merit I have not and never shall have, for I am but common, human dirt. All I have is this—that I have leaned upon the Lord, rested upon Him . . . And that I love Him with all my heart. I love as much as I can. I fain would love ever more and more were I but capable of it. It is all I have. Love Him with me! Be happy even as I am and free! I know how it is to live in the world . . . Nothing but misery, fear, disappointments . . . For the world is shiftless and the soul craves constancy.

"Aye, the world. . . . Today they praise you, tomorrow they will abuse you. . . . Today you are famous, tomorrow humiliated . . . Today they bow to you, tomorrow they kick you. . . . Today you are fair, tomorrow you will stink of the grave. . . . And what have you of all that torment?

And what good do all your riches do you? It will not stand by you on the day of the Judgment. Nothing will defend you from the Lord, neither earthly honors nor any skill. Learning? Aye, learning is good, but only when it teaches what a man lives for upon this world; what he has to accomplish here and how he can help his fellow-men. If it does not do this it remains but chaff. . . ."

Simple words tumbled feverishly from his lips. The speaker was not an orator. He did not lead his listeners along a logical line of reasoning, did not draw conclusions. But in his unpretentious appeal there rang such deep conviction and ardor, such concern for the listeners, that his words fell upon the soul like hot lava. They reached right into the heart. And William Divini, that refined artist, accustomed to listening to the greatest masters of the word and able to point out their errors in dialectics and reasoning, now stared at Francis, breathless. The crowd surged, pressed against him, but he paid no heed. His cap slid from his head, fell upon the ground, was trampled, and he did not notice it. He stared and listened. He could not resist the impression that the speaker was addressing him in particular; thinking of him; answering his most hidden thoughts and torments; that the man knew all about him and was stretching out a hand.

"And these words of mine," concluded Francis, "the words of an unworthy servant, I address to all of you together and each in particular . . . To the priests and the monks and the little children and the young maidens and lads and the poor and the kings and the princes and the scholars and the singers and the musicians and the craftsmen and the laborers and the farmers and the lords and the servants and those who live in chastity and those who live in wedlock and in innocence and in great sin and the old and the hale and the small and the big, belonging to any nation and speaking any tongue. Indeed to all my brethren who live and shall live in the future. And I beg you and I implore you and I beseech you to love Our Lord more than aught else, for otherwise you cannot achieve happiness here nor salvation hereafter. Everyone and everywhere at all times and in every place, it is Him we must call, it is Him we must praise, it is Him we must rest upon! It is Him we must follow, Him our only Lord, Omnipotent Creator and Redeemer, the Infinite, Invariable, the Lord who is eternal light and salvation and blessing and greatness and might and truth and peace and calm, the

Supreme Lord, best, most charitable, one and only worthy of love, admiration, obeisance and glory, now and forever . . . Amen."

He was out of breath. He leaped down from the stone which served him for a rostrum and almost fell into the arms of the listening William Divini.

"Brother," said the troubadour in a voice that was not his own, "brother, take me away from the world and give me peace."

Francis did not seem at all surprised. He put his arms around the troubadour's neck and hugged him, smiling as though greeting a long lost friend.

"May the Lord's peace be with you, brother. Stay with us. What is your name?"

"William Divini."

"It is not a seemly name for a mortal man. We shall give you another one. You seek peace, therefore we shall call you Pacific."

"Pacific," agreed Divini meekly.

He wanted to continue to hold Francis' hand but the throng pressed from every direction. The speaker was assailed by questions. Some sobbed, others promised they would make peace with their enemies or return money taken by stealth. A monk was pressing questions; whether Francis was right; whether he was sure he was right to weaken in people their fear of the Devil? Would that not lead to disregard for evil? After all it was a well-known thing . . . But already a well-dressed youth was pushing the monk and his doubts away.

"Brother Francis!" he was shouting, "I came to join your Order."

"Is your desire sincere?" asked Francis incredulously.

"Indeed! It is why I came here. I came from Lucca. My family belongs to the most distinguished in the province. But I care nothing for miserable honors. Neither do I care for earthly bonds, as I told Donna Lucia who scorned my love."

"Tut, tut, brother," laughed Francis, "go back to your Donna Lucia!"

"What do you mean? Will you not accept me? Me who came all the way from Lucca? My family. . . ."

"I will not accept you!" cried Francis angrily. His hands trembled and his eyes flamed. "I will not accept you! You came here to spite your love, not because you want to serve the Lord. I can see right through you! Deceive not God and me, His unworthy servant!"

The youth vanished, crestfallen. Francis calmed down and turned to the troubadour who stood motionless. Before he had time to open his mouth, however, someone timidly tugged at his sleeve.

"Giacobbe Setteoli, wife of Graciani Frangipani." William recognized her, not without surprise.

She was confused and embarrassed. She paid not the slightest attention to the presence of William. Probably she had not recognized him at all. She gazed imploringly at Francis.

"Brother," she stammered out, "I want to talk to you of the salvation of my husband's and my own soul. Would you come to our house?"

She folded her hands pleadingly, certain of his refusal, for she had heard but a moment before how he had rebuked the youth. But Francis looked with friendliness into her honest grave eyes. "I will come gladly, sister, the first day I am free. Where shall I look for you?"

"Casa Frangipani," yelled several urchins in the crowd. "Casa Frangipani."

"Yes," Giacobbe smiled, "everyone here knows us. They will show you the way." Pleased and grateful she turned away.

"We too shall go now, brother," Francis said to William. "You must meet all of us. There are a great many of us, but only a score here in Rome. Mostly my oldest and best beloved companions . . . And what was your calling till now?"

"I am a singer, a troubadour."

Francis clapped his hands.

"Why, that's wonderful. It is long since I wanted to have a singer in our midst. You will sing us the glory of God. So far I was the only one to sing, but my voice. . . . merciful God! Our Lord is patient so He puts up with it . . . But now, brother Pacific, you will teach us to sing beautifully . . ." He gave Divini's arm a friendly squeeze. "Little brother," he said, smiling his angelic smile, "little brother, surely you must know that if you belong to us you must give away all your possessions and dress as we do and possess nothing—according to human understanding."

"I know," bravely replied Divini. "I will remain with you. I will return to my house no more."

Francis shook his head.

"It is not enough, little brother. It is not enough to leave. You must distribute. Distribute in such wise as to relieve human want . . ."

"To whom ought I distribute?" asked Divini alarmed. Suddenly before his eyes stood creditors, friends, Giano the steward who had emptied his wine cellar, the servants who had starved his horses. . . .

Francis kept his eyes fixed upon him. He seemed to see and read every one of the troubadour's thoughts.

"First of all, brother, you must pay all your obligations, and the remainder you must give to the poor . . ."

"Where shall I find them?"

"As though there ever could be a lack of poverty! Don't you know how much of it there is here in Rome? How many people are swollen with hunger, gnaw at bark and see no bread for years? Aye, brother . . ."

"I don't know how to go about it," fidgeted Divini.

"It does seem hard at first," agreed Francis gravely. "Well I remember the day when years ago I first came to Rome. I was foolish and vain. But Our merciful Lord had already looked upon me and something was dawning in my brains. And once, entering a church, it occurred to me that indeed those poor men who sit on the church steps and in the name of Our Lord beg for alms, are luckier and more honored than those who distribute the alms. For were Our Lord to come amongst us in person He would sit among these poor. And He would stretch out His hand to the rich, proud passers-by as for centuries He is stretching His hand to people. And this thought clung so to me that I exchanged my clothes with an old beggar. I gave him my clothes and I took his rags . . . And I sat in his place all day long and I ate what I received in alms. . . . At first it was not easy to beg . . ."

"I am not afraid," William assured him, but he had slowed down his pace.

"Afterwards in Assisi when I had found out a little more how insignificant and small I was, I went around begging for bricks to repair St. Damian's little church . . . On a street corner I suddenly encountered my old cronies and companions whom but a short while before I had led in fight, drink and mischief . . . They beheld me . . . a beggar with my hand outstretched . . . They dropped their eyes, blushed . . . They were ashamed for me . . . And I, merciful God, instead of being proud to be a knight of Holy Poverty, I fain would have hidden underground! I could not say a word and just stood burning with shame, the sweat upon my brow . . . because they were so splendid, so handsomely dressed, and I . . . a bedraggled beggar . . . a wretch . . . and because I had acted like a fool . . . But at the same time I felt that if I did not stick it out I should run away and then I would be lost, for having once wasted God's grace I should never lift myself to a better life . . . And I vanquished myself with God's help . . . and I went straight up to them. 'For the love of Our Lord,' I said, 'help a poor man.' . . . No sooner did I say it than I felt better. And I felt like laughing at the sight of their gaping mouths, not like blushing with shame. . . . But before it was hard . . . Aye, the world clutches us hard indeed. . . . Would you, brother Pacific, have me or one of the brethren come with you?"

"No," said the troubadour, "lest others think that I have been persuaded; that it is not of my own sincere will I am acting . . . I shall attend to everything myself and soon return to you."

"Go then, brother, and may the Lord's peace be with you!"

They parted. Silvio, who with growing surprise had watched the long conversation between his master and a tattered beggar, hastily brought the horse. In his hand he held the laurel adorned cap which he had picked up from the ground and carefully dusted. The troubadour instinctively put it on his head. The servant held the stirrup for him. When they started Divini came to himself and took off the cap.

"Take this as a keepsake from me," he said, handing it over to the lad. "Those leaves are wrought of pure gold. Each is worth a ducat. You will be rich."

"Your Honor will not wear it any more?" exclaimed Silvio amazed.

"No, I will not."

"It does not matter that the velvet is crushed, the leaves can be sewed on to a new cap."

"I will not wear it any more. It is yours. Those two horses and saddles, too, for you are a good lad . . ."

"And what about Your Honor . . ."

"I will not need them any more . . ."

Silvio was so amazed that he even forgot to rejoice at the gift. He was stricken dumb. He fell a step back, holding the cap in his hand piously and suspiciously staring at his master. What had happened to him? Had he gone mad? Or had he committed some crime and was about to run away? Maybe he was a heretic? No telling, nowadays. . . .

They rode in silence. The troubadour was painfully conscious of the lack of a cap upon the bald head used to a covering. The previous blissful sensation that someone else was speaking and acting for him, that someone else was leading him by the hand, had vanished without trace. Divini, who, in spite of his artistic nature, was fundamentally a mediocre man, had remained himself, with that persistent human common sense and that incredible and weird decision reached but a moment before.

. . . So he was to distribute all his possessions? His beloved gems, clothes, books, precious glassware, beautiful furniture? He was to distribute them? Why? What for? Indeed those who called Francis of Assisi a madman were right, a thousand times right! Tomorrow all the city, and the recipients first of all, would laugh at him . . . They would laugh . . . The thought of the inevitable ridicule with which he would cover himself paralyzed him . . . What would the world say? The world was strong, Francis himself admitted it. Death alone cared nothing for the world's opinion and tore worldly bonds asunder as it pleased. But a living man? A man who had grown up in that world, who was born to it, who counted more with it than with God, who feared it more than God? Not only was God invisible and the world obvious and insistent. No, it was not only that! God never mocked and never humiliated anyone and the world always did. And man is a creature who more than death fears ridicule and the humiliation that comes of it. That is why Satan had made ridicule his chief weapon and the world followed Satan's suit!

And thus struggling with his thoughts, William Divini felt that it was God himself who had called him through Francis' words, and at the same time he suffered at heart and repeated to himself: "I shall not do this folly, I shall not!" "That's right," common sense confirmed, "why should you be a fool? Give generous alms, let them know you are charitable, but do not deprive yourself of everything! Don't burn your bridges. What if you strip yourself of everything and then find that you cannot stand living among beggars . . . Leave something for yourself, for instance the gems . . . the marvelous gems which queens have envied. . . . Hide them, bury them in the ground in a spot no one but yourself will know and distribute the rest, if such is your will . . ."

"No, no! I cannot do that," William argued with himself. The torment which was gnawing at his heart showed upon his face and Silvio felt pity for him. It would seem that it was not prison that threatened his master or else he would hasten. So what could it be that grieved him so? It must be because he had given away his well-beloved cap . . .

"Your Honor," he said, riding up to him. "I will return these leaves gladly . . . I know they came from the Holy Father . . . The goldsmith will straighten them out . . ."

"What do you want?" William asked, not comprehending.

"Your Honor surely grieves over that cap . . . But I will . . ."

"I do not grieve and I shall not take it back!" shouted the troubadour so vehemently that Silvio drew back terrified. They were nearing Divini's house. Under the colonnade a woman's dress made a vivid splash. Julia! She was awaiting William in the hope that she could wheedle another ducat from him. In the side door stood his old housekeeper, Martha. Divini had no doubt that she was awaiting him to warn him of Julia and report some most dreadful and probably true thing concerning the wench, or protest against her presence in the house. Down the stairs descended Giano with an air of self-importance. Doubtless he must have had new wrangles with the creditors with whom, according to Martha, he connived. From the dining hall came a gay noise and the sounds of the viola. Evidently his companions were enjoying themselves while awaiting the return of their host. . . . And William suddenly realized that among all these people there was not a single one who was dear to him; who awaited him with true friendship. If he were to remain among them he would continue to be lonesome, as hitherto . . . horribly lonesome, with the ghost of death forever more pressing and importunate. And finding strength in this realization he dismounted.

# 13.

## The Test

T HE OLDEST AND DEAREST COMPANIONS ARE HERE WITH ME," FRANCIS HAD told Divini. And indeed it was so. Of the newcomers there were but three in Rome: brother Caesar from Spira, brother Thomas Calano and brother Illuminatus. The last was a simple man; the two others had higher education. On the whole, the Order had been joined lately by a great many learned men and Francis was beginning to worry about it. Contrary to the story spread by his opponents he was not opposed to education, he only asked that it should serve towards a better knowledge of Divine laws, and not to set oneself above others. What virtue was there in knowledge? What merit in learning? Oftentimes a small man, humble of heart, was closer to Our Lord than a great scholar. It was not learning that chafed Francis, but the sense of superiority of the learned, and their complicated speech, comprehensible only to the initiated few, and their tendency to associate only with their equals in education.

"The time will soon come," he was wont to say, "that our learned brothers will not want to listen to such simpletons as brother Juniper and myself, and they will say it does not behoove them to have an unlearned man for their leader. What am I to do then? Maybe old as I am, I'll have to enter the Academy."

He would chuckle at the mere thought. No one took this fretting seriously, nevertheless, as the Order grew, two tendencies became increasingly more apparent: the original one and a new one against which Francis stubbornly fought. The advocates of the new tendency, the brethren Elias, Sylvester and John Parenti, wanted among other things to create Franciscan schools in which every new brother would study the fundamental principles of theology, thus allowing them to preach with a modicum of knowledge.

"The brethren need not preach learnedly," Francis protested. "They need to love our Lord and our fellow men and live according to the Gospel. It is enough! It is through example that one converts, not through words!"

"But you must admit, Francis," Elias expostulated, "it would be worthwhile. Brothers could defend the faith against imaginary errors."

"Defend the faith? What for? Faith will defend itself as long as its followers are worthy of it. And God forbid that the brethren should engage in any arguments."

The "learned" brethren would give up, unconvinced. They begged Francis that at least he consent to curb the gaiety of their companions, which was apt to shock people. People valued dignity, disliked vain mirth.

"Thank God," retorted Francis unperturbed. "Let them sing and laugh. There is nothing worse than sadness. Verily, it is the Babylonian disease!"

"Why Babylonian?" queried Elias, screwing up his eyes.

"It is the fruit of corruption. Innocence is joy, sin is sorrow. Let these lower their heads who do not belong to the Lord."

He would retire from the "learned" ones hurt, in spite of his outward serenity, by these eternally recurring attacks. He sought rest among his best beloved friends, Angel, Leo, Rufin. As though to spite the "learned" he would ask brother Pacific to sing. The ex-king of troubadours did not let himself be asked twice and would sing as beautifully as he could:

*Oh sister charity,*
*The warm compassion of thy face,*
*The fragrance of thy holy grace,*
*They perfume even Death's embrace.*
*No sacrifice I would not make,*
*Even death itself, for thy sweet sake.*

Francis would listen delighted, and join in. When the singer had finished he began to think out loud about the previous conversation.

"Brother Elias and brother Caesar would fain seem more serious. It seems to me they are wrong. We err, it is true; we are often not worth the name of good Brothers Minor but it is not because of singing. Oh, if we could but achieve brotherly perfection! That is how I imagine a perfect Brother Minor . . . faithful to poverty like brother Bernard, pure and simple like brother Leo, noble like brother Angel, civil to everyone like brother Masseo, pious and honest like brother Gilles, exalted in prayer like brother Rufini, detached from the world like brother Lucides who after a month cries 'Transfer me from here to another place for I am beginning to get used to this place!' gay and strong like brother Juniper . . ."

"And of you? What should he have of you?" inquired brother Leo, staring at his master with adoration.

"Of me? Of me there is nothing he could have save maybe that I love you all equally just as a hen loves her chicks . . ."

These arguments acquired special importance now, when Francis was about to leave for the Holy Land. Only two brothers were to accompany him: Illuminatus and Caesar. During his absence a deputy appointed by him was to rule the Order. So far the deputy had not been chosen.

Francis wanted to follow the procedure which so far had never failed him: after an ardent prayer in common to open the book of the Gospels and from the first verse upon which his eyes would fall draw a hint as to how to act.

"I have always done so," he insisted, "and it always came out right, and I knew that my sinful mind was not opposing the Lord."

Brother Sylvester smiled indulgently. "In that way one can solve only general problems pertaining to the spiritual side of life, but not the choice of a vicar. You will not find the names of the brethren in the Gospel."

"It is true," conceded Francis with a sigh.

Brother Elias conferred feverishly with the brothers Caesar, Thomas and John. "We must not allow him to appoint Leo or Pietro Cani! A fine thing it would be to be led by them. Or brother Juniper, his favorite? That nitwit would cast ridicule upon the whole Order."

"Francis, too, does all he can to bring ridicule upon the Order, yet it does no harm," the ex-judge, John, reminded him.

"Oh, Francis! He is unique, unique! People would always follow him even if he ordered them to stand on their heads! Because it is he . . . I do not know myself why it is so. . . . It is his gift . . . But we must think of the whole . . . of the future . . . Let Francis talk, sing, address the little birds . . . We must build! Build! God bears me witness it is not my own elevation I desire but God's glory and this we will accomplish better if we are a strong Order than if we are a weak one . . ."

"You are right," approved brother John warmly. "As far as I am concerned, I shall do what I can for Francis to appoint you his vicar."

"If you think it will be profitable for the Order," agreed brother Elias modestly, "I shall accept the task . . . You see for yourself what tremendous possibilities lie open to us now . . . A year ago none could have dreamed of them . . . Our Order is famous. . . . The brethren in great demand. Truly it would be a sin not to take advantage of that God-given success . . . But Francis! What can you do with Francis? A few days ago Cardinal Colonna offered to take one of us for his confessor . . . Just think of it! Other Orders strive for such honor . . . such an important and influential post . . . And Francis refused! Simply refused!"

"Incredible? Why?"

"Because the Brothers Minor can council the little ones but not the great ones . . . Besides . . ." He broke off, for into Bishop Guido's courtyard where they camped as usual, a man whom they did not know entered with great dignity. He was no longer young, low of stature, dressed in the full gown of a scholar and the biretta of a professor. He peered around as though looking for someone.

"In the name of Our Lord what is it you desire, messer?" boomed brother Masseo's bass at him.

The newcomer turned eagerly in his direction.

"I am the astrologer Pochard of the Parisian school Sorbonne. I am seeking the honorable William Divini, troubadour and poet. I was told in town I would find him here."

"We never heard of one of that name," brother Masseo assured him.

"I thought at once it was some error," the astrologer replied, relieved. "What would he be doing here?"

He was withdrawing toward the exit, gathering the folds of his long gown about him. Francis, who had heard the conversation, stopped him. "Brother Masseo does not know that William Divini is the lay name of brother Pacific. You will not find William Divini anywhere but brother Pacific is here . . . Here he is . . . What? No brother Pacific? He was here but a while ago? Surely, he will return at once."

"I shall not wait, no, I cannot wait," hastily exclaimed the astrologer.

"Please tell him that I was here. My name"—his voice became solemn—
"is master of liberal science and in particular of astronomy and as-
trology, Jacob Pochard. I was sent by Her Ladyship Blanche de Navarre,
Countess of Champagne, to whose court I belong . . . The honorable
Divini was supposed to go with us to the Holy Land. It is for him I
came. The Countess will wait for a week, for the vessel has been damaged. Please repeat this to him. I doubt whether he shall come with us,
if, as I hear . . ." He made a circular motion of his hand with an
expression of embarrassed pity, shrugged his shoulders slightly and departed, straightening the stiff, formal biretta on his head. Red and
embarrassed Pacific emerged from behind the well where he had been
hiding.

Francis chuckled. "Hey, brother! So you hid yourself! It would seem
you are in no haste to see that astrologer, whatever his name may
be . . ."

"Pochard . . . No . . . I am in no haste. I spent six months at the
court of his masters, but I would rather not recall it . . ."

"What were you doing there?"

"I was persuading a woman to leave her husband and commit adultery with another man," confessed Pacific in one breath, and suddenly
stopped, stricken by the sincerity of his confession. Yes, yes, that was
what he was doing and nothing else! To be sure it was called differently,
it was dressed up in beautiful words, but the essence was the same.
Words! Words! How many words! The right to live and love . . . A
troubadour the priest and confidant of those in love . . . Absolved by
love . . . The unconquerable passion of two noble and separated lovers
. . . A love that would not be curbed. . . . Words, vain words . . . The
truth, the stark naked truth of it was just that; he was persuading a
woman to leave her husband and live in adultery with another man as
faithless as herself. . . . It had seemed different to him, then. . . .

It suddenly occurred to him that the environment in which he lived
now was probably the only one in the world where there was absolutely
no need of lying. He had said this horrible thing openly, without beating about the bush . . . ! There was no lie wherever Francis was. Ever
since Divini had come here he had not even once had the need to lie,
and yet in the world even the most honest of men lied constantly. . . .

"Those were grievous ends, indeed," sighed Francis, shaking his head.
"Was this woman the Countess the astrologer mentioned?"

"Yes."

"And what will happen now?"

"She will sail for the Holy Land without me."

"Don't you think, brother, you ought to go to her and plead with her not to commit the sin to which you prompted her?"

"By the gifts of the Holy Ghost! Do you require this of me?"

"I do not require. Nor do I order. But I think you want to do it yourself, brother."

Blanche de Navarre, the Countess of Champagne, restlessly wandered upon the seashore. The harbor was well-nigh deserted. Fishermen's nets were spread upon stakes. Boats were turned upside down. There was not a single galley except the damaged one on which she had arrived and which carpenters were repairing now. The delay was driving the Countess to desperation, and imagining that her impatient presence would hasten the moment of departure she spent all her time in the harbor. She would not even go to Rome. What did Rome—which she knew of old—mean to her when Jean was not there? Let the carpenters work day and night, let them finish at last so she could sail!

Her irritation was increased by the news which was on everybody's lips that the Crusaders' armies were to depart shortly. She realized that when the Holy Father with all the knights should arrive at Acre, the duties of a king and a captain would absorb Jean so much that he would not have time for his mistress. No matter how much he desired it he would not be able to stay by her side. She must start at once to arrive ahead of them! And shaking with impatience Blanche would run to and fro upon the shore, urging the carpenters wrathfully, abusing the skipper, and praying to God to delay the departure of the knights and give her propitious winds and a quiet passage.

From impatience she had grown thin, darker and quick-tempered, irritable. Young Thibault, who had always feared his mother, now hid where he could lest he find himself alone in her presence. On the least excuse sharp reproaches would pour upon the lad's head. Blanche would have liked to see him a Crusader! It was a shame! All living souls were hastening to accept a Cross from the Pope's hands and only the young heir of Champagne was going as a common pilgrim!

Thibault junior felt not the slightest desire for fighting and pretended not to understand his mother's broad hints. Besides, he was seriously grieved by the absence of William Divini. He had looked forward to the troubadour's arrival; he had so expected him! And the troubadour did not come! The astrologer Pochard had brought from Rome incredible tidings: it would seem that Divini had joined a mendicant's order and had become an itinerant monk! This seemed so absurd as to be incredible. Divini a monk! One might have expected anything else but not this transformation! Thibault could not get over his grief and astonishment. As for Blanche she was so absorbed by her own problems that the news barely penetrated her consciousness. She conceded it was an unusual occurrence indeed and added that as things stood the astrologer would take the place reserved for the troubadour. Otherwise there would be an odd number of those participating in the expedition, a bad omen!

Thus the learned Jacob Pochard had fallen into a snare of his own making. For it was he who had stressed the necessity of an even number. Thanks to that, old Thibault had ordered him to accompany his mistress to Italy, from where he was to return after the troubadour had joined the party. The prospect of a short but free stay in Rome, of visiting the Roman libraries, had greatly appealed to the scholar. He had calculated the whole thing so smoothly! And now, owing to William's incomprehensible folly, he was forced to continue on his way! He felt for the prospect even less enthusiasm than young Thibault, if such thing was possible, and still less courage to explain to the Countess that an even number could be as easily achieved by hiring an additional servant. The impetuous woman filled him with veritable dread. He mumbled timidly that maybe this or that could be arranged; that he had left behind pressing tasks commenced at His Lordship's request. . . . Blanche paid no heed. She did not even understand what the astrologer was driving at. She had but one thing in mind: what would happen to de Brienne and herself? How would the Crusade affect their future? Would Jean reconquer Jerusalem and achieve such fame and importance that the Holy Father would not refuse a double divorce and a new wedlock. Or perhaps she too would take the Cross, as women had often done of yore, and would fight by his side?

Hour after hour she would pace upon the shore pondering her problems. The wind tugged at her coif. Whenever she passed her tongue over her lips she could feel the salty taste of the sea. The squires and maids in waiting who accompanied her waited patiently, seated in the shadow of a rock. The banging of hammers on the galley rang loudly in the silence. A few sun bleached vagrants sat close by the water watching the vessel. An itinerant monk, or was it a beggar, happened by and stood at a distance. He gazed at the sky, then at the sea, then at the lady. Every once in a while she would reach as far as the rock and turning around would pass by his side unseeing, her clothes rustling. He stood a long time, not daring to approach her. He advanced a step, then drew back again. He wiped the sweat from his brow with the sleeve of a coarse cloak. His heart hammered in his breast. Here was a test, a test compared with which all the others seemed child's play. What was he to say? How was he to begin? What would he answer if the Countess asked him whether he felt happy now and did not regret what he had done? Would he be able to answer with an accent of truth that he was happy? For in reality he was not certain himself as yet. He had not as yet accustomed himself to his new personality, at times it seemed to him he was dreaming. And so he stood and stood. At last he crossed himself. From old habit he pulled down over his stomach his ash-brown cloak as loose as a bag and girdled with a hemp rope. Then he stood in the Countess' path.

Without giving him a glance she took a copper out of her alms purse and flung it in his direction. He did not stoop. He was following her. She turned around annoyed.

"If you need anything, address yourself to my servants."

"It is Your Ladyship I want to see. I . . ."

The voice sounded familiar. She gave him a careful glance, then screwed up her eyes uncertain.

"It is I, Your Ladyship . . . William Divini."

"Divini!"

"So I was called once . . . Now I am brother Pacific . . ."

"So it is true? Where is Thibault? He was expecting you. Wenches, call His Lordship!"

"Your Ladyship! Pray call no one! It is with you, you alone I want to speak! I implore . . . !"

With a motion of her hand she stopped the maids who had already started running. "Then speak up . . . Well, well . . . I should never have recognized you . . . Pochard told us it was true, but we would not believe it. What has happened? Were you suspected of heresy? Was anyone persecuting you that you had to hide under this garb?"

"No, Your Ladyship. No one forced me. It is of my own free will that I wear it."

"No one will believe that." She smiled. "However if you will not tell we shall not inquire. . . . It was kind of you to come to bid us farewell, at least . . ."

"I came for a different reason, Your Ladyship," he whispered, his voice hoarse with emotion.

"I am listening."

She seated herself upon a flat rock, gazing at him expectantly. For a long while he remained silent wrestling with himself. At last he exploded: "Your Ladyship! Do not go to the Holy Land! Return to Troyes!"

She sprang up as though stung.

"Why? Why?" Terror seized her at the thought that Divini had received some information that Jean had stopped loving her and no longer wanted her to come. "Why? Has he written you? What has happened?"

"He has not written. Nothing has happened. Only it is . . . a sin!"

"A sin?" She burst into laughter and sat down again. "Good God! How could you scare me so? A sin! A preacher indeed! A moralist! Brother . . . Pacific—is that right? I must say truthfully that a canzone suits you better than a sermon. . . . Your viola and your old vestments befitted you better, too. . . ." Her scornful glance swept the dejected figure of the ex-king of troubadours from head to foot.

"I know my appearance is ludicrous," he admitted humbly. "Nevertheless please listen to me, My Lady! It was sinful of me to bring to Troyes the message of the Honorable Sir de Brienne. Now that I see it, I must warn you, beg you, implore you not to do it . . . !"

Again she laughed, loudly, youthfully. She nodded her head in commiseration. "A goodly jest," she said. "I go back! Never!"

"Think of your husband, of your marital vows, of your son . . ."

"Where were they, my husband and my son, while you urged me to depart?"

"I sinned, I did not see . . . I regret . . . it was my fault . . . be more honest and better than I was . . ."

"There is no one I need sacrifice myself for." Her face darkened. "My husband knows and secretly accedes. It is long since I have been wife to him. He could not bear it were I to follow anyone else, but Jean is a kinsman and a king . . . Thibault will breathe freely once he gets out from under my thumb . . . And I want to live! I have a right to live!"

"But it is precisely that we have no such right, Your Ladyship . . . We have usurped it but there is no such right . . . There is but one law —Divine law. Sir Jean de Brienne is bound to another woman . . ."

"She will yield to me . . ."

"Even if she should the Syrian barons will never allow it! They will never agree to a divorce!"

"She will yield to me," she repeated threateningly, involuntarily touching the bodice of her dress. In the glitter of her eyes there was something that filled Divini with horror.

"Your Ladyship," he continued, "I am the only one to blame. You can punish me, curse me, even flog me. But renounce the thought of that journey . . ."

She shrugged her shoulders contemptuously. "Do you expect me to forget what is my life, my last and only joy? To forget? To renounce it? Let God punish me if He will! Let Him damn me! I prefer to go to hell as long as I have Jean now!"

"Eternity is long, life is short," he whispered.

"For one moment with Jean I will relinquish eternity!"

"It is blasphemy!"

"Today it is blasphemy, and yet but a while back you sang it yourself!"

"I was a fool . . . I did not understand!"

"It is now you are a fool. A droll jester! Do but glance in the mirror and see what you look like!"

He lowered his head, crushed. His old masculine vanity was bleeding. Oh, how he wished to run away from her eyes, her sneers! Yet he did not yield.

"Madam! Go back! All I said before is a lie!"

She sprang up like a wildcat. "What is that? You lied that Jean . . . that . . ."

"No, it was true."

"Thank God!" Heavily she slumped back upon the stone.

"All I sang was a lie . . . All those canzonas and romances . . . Life is different . . . harder. . . ."

"Stop! Then you spoke like a man, now you speak like a cadaver!"

"On the contrary! It was then I felt a cadaver inside me; today I am alive! I beseech you once more! Nothing will come of it but sin and ill fortune . . . !"

"Stop!" She stamped her foot angrily. "Enough of your nonsense. You are out of your head. Jean is mine and the other must yield to me. She must . . . !"

"Your Ladyship! You would not dare . . . !"

"I will dare all, even the worst!" In her rage again she touched the bodice of her dress. She staggered as though she were drunk. Despair seized Divini at the thought of what he had done. The irresponsibility with which he had unchained the passion of this possessed woman filled him with horror. He suddenly beheld her as he had found her upon his arrival at the court of Troyes; gloomy, but calm. It was he who had aroused her by agreeing to act as de Brienne's envoy. At that time he deemed it an honor, a duty, to help lovers . . . A duty, indeed! Now no one else but he would be responsible for all the evil that would come of it . . .

Sincerely horrified he fell to his knees. "Madam! By Our Lord's Passion! I implore you! Go back!"

She pushed him violently so that he fell and sat upon the sand, clutching his head in both hands. He felt helpless and beaten. And she stood breathing hard with wrath, towering high above him.

"Oh God, have mercy!" he moaned.

"What is it you are after?" she screamed, annoyed beyond all measure. The squires and the maids were watching them from a distance and no telling what they might be thinking. And what if Divini was not a madman? What if priests or Marie of Jerusalem had bribed him; what if this was but a masterly staged act in order to divert her from Jean. . . .

She shook his shoulders. "Get up! Speak! Speak up or I'll have you flogged! Who sent you? Who ordered you to come here?"

"Who sent me?" he repeated, not comprehending, while with an effort he struggled to his feet.

"Who sent you? At whose orders are you doing this?"

"By the salvation of my soul. I swear no one else but my conscience."

The sincerity which shook his voice convinced her. She calmed down and jeered contemptuously.

"His conscience! What an envoy Jean chose! The old fool! His conscience!"

Swiftly she walked away. He did not attempt to follow her. What for? No word could banish her lust; force her to consider. Unfortunate woman! May God grant her peace!

And suddenly Divini was filled with a sense of physical relaxation and freedom. He had sinned, but now he had done everything in his power to mend the evil he had wrought. He had confessed his guilt. God would forgive him. For Jean and Blanche he would pray every day. . . . How fortunate that he no longer belonged to the same world. . . . For the first time since he had taken orders, for the first time in long months, he felt absolutely happy and serene. He felt like singing. He must compose some new, beautiful chant for the brethren . . . And without glancing back he set out on his way, humming to himself, picking words and tunes. They came easily and he was pleased and hardly noticed how the road passed by. . . .

# 14.

## Vae Vobis

GRACIANI FRANGIPANI WAS DISPLEASED THAT HIS WIFE HAD BROUGHT THE tattered fool to the banquet-room. True, people were talking a great deal of him lately, and it would seem that the Holy Father himself held him in great respect; nevertheless, he was a queer bird and nothing else! A fool, and not even a droll one at that! And as for what some people said—that he was a saint—it was perfectly ridiculous. A saint indeed! Just look at him now! See how he eats. . . . Saints were more abstinent!

And in truth, Francis was eating with relish. He had declined to sit by the board, explaining that he had lost the habit of sitting upon a bench, and had seated himself, plate in hand, upon the floor by the hearth. Immediately the dogs surrounded him, the famous Frangipani mastiffs, obstinate and suspicious, and he fondled with pleasure their ears tattered in many fights and their menacing muzzles. Delighted at the petting they sprawled before him and would even turn upon their backs, showing their spotted bellies in a sudden impulse of trust and friendliness. Giacobbe from where she sat at the board looked upon the sight.

"You have made friends with them at once; usually they dislike strangers."

"It is a brother they feel in me, not a stranger!"

"I thought you would forget your promise and not visit us before departing. The troops, it would seem, are already embarking in Ancona."

"They are, and we likewise shall sail any day now. I cannot think of it without trepidation. My sinful feet will tread the same soil upon which Our Lord walked. . . . I shall behold the very places where He taught and blessed and suffered. . . . I can hardly wait for the time and I live in constant anxiety lest something delay it . . . But I did not forget to come to you. To be sure I did not expect I should come upon such a banquet. . . ."

"Are you angry?" she asked anxiously.

"Angry? Why? This food is so wonderful. I never partook of anything like it. How is it made?"

"I am so glad you like it. It is the white of eggs crushed with nuts and honey and cooked together. . . ."

"Very good indeed. . . . Our Lord in His kindness has bestowed upon us so many senses so that we might feel joy! The eyes . . . to gaze upon mountains or upon trees, or the sky . . . a never ending pleasure. Hearing . . . particularly when one hears music or the splashing of water. Smell . . . the perfume of flowers. And now taste . . . to eat food like this . . . Why, it is wonderful!"

The feasters smiled at his naïve enthusiasm. Giacobbe gave her guest a second helping. "Eat, pray, if it is to your taste."

He thanked her gaily. Then he glanced around and thinking no one was looking at him he stretched out a hand behind him, grabbed a fistful of cold ashes from the hearth, added it to the dish and mixing thoroughly, continued to eat, voicing praises and smacking his lips.

"And such a greedy glutton is held in high esteem by the Holy Father," mumbled his host in disgust.

But Giacobbe had noticed the gesture of her guest. "Why have you added ashes to the sweets, brother Francis?" she inquired, staring at him with her frank eyes.

He became confused, blushed and did not know what to answer. At last he stammered out: "Brother ash is clean . . ."

"Ha, ha, ha!" guffawed Frangipani. "A wonderful seasoning indeed. Ashes!"

The dinner was over and he rose heavily from the table, followed by the others. Giacobbe brought a low stool to the hearth and sat upon it, facing Francis.

"Are all the brothers departing with you?" she asked.

"Oh, no! Only two will keep me company. It is very cruel of me, for everyone of them would fain go, and really I should remain and send them . . . But the Holy Father has authorized me to go . . . We cast lots for those two others. The rest will work here for us . . . There is a lot to be done . . . There are scarcely fewer heathens here than overseas and the road of contrition is still deserted . . ."

"Who will rule over the Order during your absence?" It seemed to her his face had darkened.

"Brother Elias Bombardone . . . The majority of the brethren wanted him . . . I had to obey their will . . ."

"You had to obey? So, in your opinion, he will not be a good vicar?"

"Oh, no, not at all! He surely will be the best one . . . Surely . . . Why, it is not hard at all to take my place. He only must in all follow the Gospel and simply take every word of it. People twist and change. They say this is to be understood so and so . . . this was written for different times . . . for different men. Sinful talk! Men are always the same and the words of Our Lord are eternal. And they must be taken simply. Those twists are but the customary deceit of learned men. . . ."

She could not repress a smile. "It would seem as though brother Elias is a learned man."

"How did you know?"

"Bishop Guido has told me of all of you, one after another."

"I fear His Grace has presented us in a much better light than we deserve. He is our best friend and sponsor . . . Verily brother Elias is a learned man. But he promised me he will not let his reason guide him but the Gospel and his heart. . . . For there is another important thing for the leader of brethren; he must love them . . . And he must always forgive . . . even the worst offense. And if a brother were to sin and not ask forgiveness, the leader should come to him himself and put his arms about him and ask, 'Dear brother, don't you really want me to forgive you?' And he must do it even were the brother to sin a hundred times and more. . . . For it is in this wise Our Lord acts towards us . . . Forgive me for talking so much."

"I could listen forever."

"You wanted to ask me something, didn't you? I will be glad to help if I can. And I speak so much for I feel happy with you. It is as though I were not speaking with a woman but with a brother . . . Would you be angry if I call you brother Giacobbe?"

"Do! I will at once lay my cares before you, but first tell me some more . . . I would know more about you and . . . Sister Clara?"

"So His Grace has told you of Sister Clara too? How wonderful! I rejoice so when I can speak of her to someone! Clara is already in a convent. It was on Palm Sunday that her nuptials with Our Lord took place. Nothing threatens her any more. No one can degrade her or destroy. . . ."

"Her parents, it would seem, were very much opposed to it?"

"Much indeed. They would have preferred to give her in wedlock to a mortal man she did not love rather than to God. Was it not strange of them? Clara stole out at night from the castle. Others do the same for the sake of evil and ugly things; she did it for the sake of Christ. . . . We awaited her in the chapel . . . My heart pounded so, it was dreadful! Whenever a leaf rustled in the woods I thought, 'Here she is!' And then no one came. Then again I thought they would not let her out . . . she will not come . . . At last, late at night, we heard steps; they were coming, she and her duenna. 'Light the candles for the nuptials,' I said to the brethren. And I went out to meet her . . . She stood in the path, so beautiful, so radiant. . . . She had a golden, stately gown. . . . It shone in the dark like a stream . . . And we took each other by the hand and I led her into the chapel and there the brethren had already lit the candles.

"It was as bright as daylight. The birds woke up in the bushes and began to twitter. She put on a black frock and I sheared her hair. You cannot imagine how long and soft and golden it was. . . . She gave it to the Lord without grief . . . Afterwards she wrapped a black kerchief over her head and we led her with torches as befitted a bride to the convent of Benedictine nuns in Isola Romanesca . . ."

Giacobbe listened attentively with her eyes wide open in the peculiar way she had . . . "And what next?" she inquired.

"What could be next? She remained there. But soon with the approval of the Holy Father she and several other sisters will move over to St. Damian's Convent with their own rule . . ."

"Will you see her sometimes?"

"How could I? They will take a very stern rule. So Clara and I have decided . . . I shall never see her again . . . not in this world!"

"May she not need your guidance or advice?"

"The Holy Father will give her a good confessor."

"Surely she would rather seek your advice than a stranger's."

"She does not need my advice . . . She knows all better than myself. Hers is a soul chosen by God."

"If she loves you she will hanker after you. Maybe she would want to see you sometimes, touch your hand?"

He laughed and shook his head. "Clara loves no one save Our Lord. Besides, I cannot imagine how anyone would find pleasure in touching this paw." He lifted his palm; though calloused with work and tough it still retained its slender fingers and its narrow, aristocratic shape.

"But sometimes one human being is fond of another."

"It depends. If I should suspect that what you say is true I would lose all my admiration for Clara . . ."

"Why?"

"For she can love nothing but what is purest, ideal, eternal. If Clara were to love a moral vermin like myself . . . why, it would be dreadful!"

She smiled sadly. "You have persuaded me. I shall not argue any more!"

"I should say not," he exclaimed triumphantly. "You scarcely can imagine how wonderful she is. Like a flower and a diamond at the same time, and besides . . ."

A sudden commotion interrupted the conversation. Someone was running across the courtyard. Someone was calling aloud. The dogs sprang up, growling. Graciani Frangipani appeared in the doorway.

"The Holy Father has been taken ill!"

"The Holy Father is dying," came from the courtyard.

"Merciful God," exclaimed Francis, aghast.

"He sent for you," finished Frangipani, as if surprised.

Without a word Francis ran out of the room, his bare feet thudding upon the stairs. Frangipani, already outside, yelled for mounts to be brought for himself and his lady. Dogs howled. The squires feverishly helped the hostlers to saddle horses. Throngs were already flowing towards the Lateran; apparently the news of the illness of the Holy Father had already spread throughout the city.

Bells pealed. Dusk was falling; translucent, purple dusk. Innocent III was conscious, fully conscious. Death was claiming him unexpectedly. Up to the day before he had hoped that he would have enough strength, that it was God's will that he should lead the holy expedition, and today he was dying. His old, worn, ailing heart, too weary of its bitter role as the helpless conscience of Christendom, was giving way at last and no efforts of the physicians could restore it.

After receiving extreme unction Innocent gave orders to be carried out upon the balcony that dominated the square. He wanted once more to look upon the city, the crowds, the army which someone else would lead to the Holy Land. When he beheld the innumerable throng standing in mute silence in the light of torches, he wept and asked to be lifted from his couch. He raised his hand as though about to speak to those present and to the entire Christian world as well.

The balcony was lit with scores of tapers and from below people saw the Holy Father being lifted. They fell to their knees and the Pope called out:

"Woe to you, woe, should you fail to carry out the Divine deed!"

His voice was barely audible, but those around him picked up his cry and flung it down as the last request of the dying man. And the people, returning late that night to distant squares and hills, talked into the night of that white ghost of the Christian conscience, of the lifted hand and the words: ". . . Vae vobis, vae vobis, is opus Dei deseretis!!"

# PART TWO

# 1.

## The King

SIR AYMAR DE LAYRON, LORD OF CESAREA, RETURNED ONCE MORE TO ROME, this time as envoy of Jean de Brienne, and every fortnight, by means of a Pisan galley, sent news of the Crusaders' armies which were gathering in Italy. The skipper of the galley demanded a great deal of money for foregoing his usual ports of call, but the letters arrived at Acre promptly and awakened hope and joy in the hearts of the knights. No one had expected that after the conquest of Byzantium it would be possible to rouse Europe to a new, a fifth, expedition! It was known that this new zeal was due to the ill-fated Children's Crusade. As to that, however, the news in the East was rather vague. According to the stories brought by visitors from the West countless throngs of innocents, led manifestly by an army of angels, had embarked upon vessels in Venice, Genoa and Marseilles and set out on their way. In the open sea they were caught in a storm. The storm was unchained by Satan and his cohorts bent on stopping the angels. For the second time in the history of the world Archangel Michael engaged Lucifer in a hand-to-hand fight and cast him into the sea. God had taken the children, guileless witnesses of this awesome encounter, to Heaven so they would not tell of things no mortal may behold. The sea had brought their bodies and lined them up on shore in a spot designated to the waves by the Holy Father. . . . And the elders had caught the arms which had slipped from childish hands. . . .

So people said, and Jean de Brienne, old soldier that he was, incredulously wagged his head. He did not try to get at the truth, however, for what did it matter to him? Who cared what particular miracles or events had rekindled the extinguished ardor of French and Italian barons? The important thing was that such ardor existed; that in Ancona, Brindisi and Bari huge forces were gathering, thirty thousand strong, it would seem, and any day now would set forth under the leadership of the Holy Father. Sir Aymar sent detailed reports concerning the number of men and the various arms. Thus it was known in Acre that awaiting the signal of departure stood in armed readiness the brave duc de Nemours, Jean d'Arcy, the Sirs William de St. Omer, Robert de Hainaux, Erard de Chacenay, Albert de Castel Gualteria, Simon de Joinville, the English knights Sussex and Arundel and many others. The main thing now was to use these forces properly, to prevent the expedition from turning to nothing, as the third and fourth Crusades had done before.

"We will not let it pass, provided Your Majesty is given command," old Ibelin of Beyrouth was saying to Jean. During the minority of the Queen he had acted as regent of the Jerusalem kingdom. "The Holy Father will be the spiritual leader but he will neither deploy the troops nor lead them in battle. . . . This must fall to you for the sake of the Holy Sepulchre."

"When I was taking leave of the Holy Father he told me, 'I shall call, you will lead,' " admitted Jean. "I trust he has not forgotten . . . I have already worked out a plan of campaign and have dispatched it to Sir Aymar to submit to the Holy Father . . . For as I see it the troops ought not to sail here but straight south."

"How is that, Your Majesty? Not to the Holy Land?"

"No. And I shall tell you why . . ."

Before he had time to do so, however, the newly appointed Bishop of Acre, Jacob de Vitry, who had arrived from Rome only a month before, broke in in an aggrieved voice: "Not on its direction hangs the success of the campaign, but on the spirit that shall animate the knighthood. . . . Your Honors. Your Majesty! We in Europe hear a lot of the corruption rampant in the Kingdom of Jerusalem and we dismiss such tales as slander. But since my coming here I am aghast to discover that the reality is worse than the blackest rumor would have it! We, in Europe, deem that though Jerusalem be lost, divine spirit and a longing to recover the sacred mementos still prevail in what remains of the Kingdom. Unfortunately, it is not so. . . . The population is turning Arab. In Tripoli I had to preach through an interpreter who translated my words into Arabic so that Christians might understand me. In the ports, Venetians, Genoans and Pisans fight with each other for supremacy and have no wish whatsoever for the Crusaders to win. They openly admit it is better for them to hold the ports themselves and let the Saracens keep the rest of the country, for the sales are greater that way and the transportation of merchandise easier . . . They make no secret of it. Indeed, it is dreadful to hear them!"

"But Your Grace, the Kingdom of Jerusalem—it is these brave knights, not Venetians, Pisans and Genoan merchants who came here without our leave," corrected Jean displeased.

"I would not slight the brave knights but, indeed, it is not to the merchants alone my words refer! What depravity everywhere! Surely nothing worse can be found even among infidels. . . . All live in sin. . . . The sacred law of matrimony has gone into oblivion . . . Crimes at every step. . . . It is nothing for a man to poison his wife or for a woman to poison her husband in order to wed a paramour . . ."

"Your Grace exaggerates," Jean laughed. "There is a great deal of wickedness, it is true, inasmuch as peace-loving men will not come to us because of constant wars, while thieves, vagrants and robbers fleeing the arm of justice flock to our shores. Any gallows-bird all along the Mediterranean coast hastens here, for well he knows that for lack of men we accept anyone . . ."

"Then don't!" the Bishop almost shouted. "You will never accomplish your goal with stained hands! And what I said before I still maintain . . . Crime is rampant everywhere . . . In every alley you can find booths in which witches openly sell poison . . . Procuresses will leave no one alone, not even a priest . . . There no longer exist in this hapless kingdom such things as an honest couple, an honest husband, an honest wife . . ."

"Oh, no!" exclaimed the Queen with childish indignation. Seated in her big armchair she was so inconspicuous, she so seldom opened her mouth, that most of the time no one remembered her presence . . . Now all eyes turned to her with surprise. At once she was overcome with shame and confusion. . . . True, she had a right to participate in the Council, inasmuch as the crown belonged to her and not to her husband. Usually, however, she did not avail herself of the privilege. State matters did not interest her; when confronted with them she felt small and lost. She had come today only to get a chance to see Jean. She saw him so seldom nowadays! Since she was with child he had altogether ceased to visit her, to spare her strength and health, he said. It was true her health was poor and it took all her strength to bear her condition, but the presence of her husband would have been a great help and solace to her . . . This, however, she dared not tell him. She admired Jean and despite the difference in years had soon come to love him. . . . He was so clever, so brave! The barons held him in great esteem and what was rarer still, obeyed him.

Jacob de Vitry nodded.

"The just indignation of Her Majesty proves clearly how remote her pure soul is from all sin. That is the way it should be; the duty of all anointed heads. Both Your Majesties are far above human infirmities even as stars are above this earth . . . If only people would follow the example of virtue which you set them . . ."

Queen Marie became even more confused at the praise and cast a quick glance at her husband. But Jean was not looking her way. Only the old Lord Ibelin of Beyrouth gave her a paternal smile. It was he who had brought her up; not only ruling during her minority but acting as both father and mother to the little orphan. And he had come to love her as he might love his own child. The more so because he had no grandchildren of his own. Her happiness meant more to him than anything else in the world.

Ibelin was pleased with the choice of king; an older, serious man and a true knight to boot. The unmanageable barons had real respect for him. Even the Great Masters of the three Knightly Orders: the Templars, the Hospitallers and the Teutonic Knights of the Most Sacred Virgin of Jerusalem did not protest overmuch. At first the whole Syrian knighthood had resented the fact that the new king made but little of the honor they had conferred upon him and was in no haste to ascend the throne. That sulkiness, however, had passed and Jean's indifference had added to his prestige. Every one of his predecessors had striven and schemed to obtain the crown or let a woman do the scheming for him. De Brienne had been appointed against his will by the king of France and the Holy Father. He did not owe the honor to anyone here, was under no obligation to any local baron. And in war experience and statesmanship he equalled the best among Jerusalem kings. Even his lack of wealth did not detract from his prestige. He handled money with a scornful superiority which proved how little he cared for it. Modest clothes, a modest retinue, could denote either impecunity or love for a hard, soldierly life. On state occasions he appeared in the full glory of crown jewels and regal clothes (which Sibille had brought with her from Jerusalem thanks to the magnanimity of Saladin) and, by God, all had to admit he knew how to wear them! In everyday life he still wore his leather jerkin, faded from long years of service. From his wife or the Council he would accept nothing. At any time he was ready to depart as he had come, free, proud and independent. Therein lay his strength.

In addition, luck had been with him in the first years of reign. He had concluded a six years truce on equal terms with the Sultan Malik al-Adil. This youngest brother of Saladin, who at one time was to marry an English princess, though he did not resemble his brother, had retained some of the latter's friendliness toward the Latins. It was hard to tell whence this friendliness came, for Malik al-Adil was no sage and did not devote his time to religious speculations. It was generally said that all Ajubits had been imbued with that attitude by their preceptor, the Emir al-Bara, who was the son of a Christian captive. If this were true, the influence of the long-dead woman had proved lasting, indeed. The Ajubits were never the first to start the war with the Franks. If they declared war at all they did so reluctantly, forced by the treachery or aggressiveness of the barons and they were always willing and eager to conclude a truce.

The younger generation, al-Muzaam, who ruled in Damascus, Malik al-Kamil, Sultan of Egypt, no longer understood such restraint. In fact, the destruction of the Franks was their supreme goal. They considered it a disgrace that a strip of coast and a few ports should be left to the Latins and bear the proud name of the Kingdom of Jerusalem. Compared with the magnitude of the Moslem Empire which embraced all of Asia Minor and North Africa this territory was no more than a fly to an elephant. Was it not ridiculous for the elephant to conclude treaties with that buzzing, annoying pest?

But old Malik al-Adil knew by hearsay the story of the conquest of Jerusalem and from his own vivid recollections the inexplicable defeat inflicted upon Saladin by the leprous lad at Montgissard, and stubbornly maintained that the strength of the Franks could not be measured by their number. With unconcealed satisfaction he heard that instead of the previous young hot-heads a grey-haired, experienced knight more inclined to peace than to war had ascended the throne of Jerusalem.

This satisfaction had brought forth the six years truce which gave the tiny kingdom a much-needed period of respite.

"I would not have that truce broken too soon," said Jean, when Bishop Jacob de Vitry, weary of enumerating all Syrian evils, lapsed into silence. "As I said a while ago I have sent to the Holy Father a plan of the new Crusade different from all previous ones. According to that plan we shall not break at once with Adil. To strike at Palestine itself is neither convenient for us nor dangerous to the Saracens. The attack ought to be launched upon Egypt."

"Upon Egypt?" all exclaimed, astonished.

"Yes. We must avail ourselves of the fact that the Holy Father has collected a big flotilla and strike either at Alexandria or Damietta. Strike at the roots, as the saying goes, not at the branches. The Moslem power lies neither in Palestine nor in Damascus but in Egypt. From there comes the wealth of the sultans! From there their might! They would sooner lose anything else than the Egyptian ports. If we are successful in taking Damietta, mark my words, they will be glad to return the Holy Land in its stead."

"Bold plans, these," mumbled the Master of Templars, William de Chartres, without conviction.

But old Ibelin warmly supported the King.

"This is not a new scheme!" he exclaimed. "According to the chronicle of the Archbishop of Thyr, King Amalryk had a similar plan. He even concluded a treaty with the Basileus Manuel to assure himself of the assistance of the Greek fleet. . . ."

"But will the western lords agree?" objected Raoul of Thiberia.

"They may think we are trying to lure them away from the Holy Land, as Dandola lured the others . . ."

"If the Holy Father gives me supreme command, I will persuade them."

"Surely His Holiness will give it to no one else," Ibelin said with conviction, "for he will find no one more worthy of it. Your Majesty has no peer, either in virtue, knowledge of the country, or in rank. To be sure, there is one of royal blood among the Crusaders—de Nemours—but there is no crowned head . . ."

"Will the Polish duke not come?" asked Sir Dzierzek. He had been sitting silently in a corner of the room. Sir Dzierzek was almost as old as Ibelin of Beyrouth. He had come from Poland with the third Crusade. Taken prisoner, he had escaped to Acre and there had fallen ill. It took him long to recover. When at last he was well, he could not bring himself to return to his country. He had grown used to these parts and like birds which forever make ready to depart and never do, so Dzierzek was always talking of leaving Syria but did not leave. He was brave and trustworthy and people respected him. Unable to pronounce his name they simply called him Sire de Pologna.

Sir Dzierzek had no reason to feel particularly lonely, for often his countrymen or some news of Poland would reach the Holy Land. Indeed, but a year before, at the time of the ill-fated Hungarian expedition Duc Kazko of Stettin, son of Boguslas, came to Acre and brought a score of knights.

The young duke had met a knightly death during the siege of Mount Tabor. When his knights, left leaderless, were about to return to their native land Sir Dzierzek vowed to leave with them, but at the last moment he changed his mind and stayed. He was homesick at times, but over twenty years spent in Syria had left their mark. He had thought the Stettinians uncouth and ignorant; besides, he was afraid of want. Before he set forth he had left his domains to the abbey of the Premonstratensian Fathers in case he did not return; it would be awkward now to evict the monks from a property which for a quarter of century they had tended and considered their own. And so it seemed likely he would remain here to the end of his days, particularly as the Holy Father himself was urging the brave knights not to desert those last Palestine posts.

"The Polish duke will not come," the Bishop of Acre now informed Dzierzek.

"We had news of it before I left Rome, for six Polish bishops were present at the Synod. Before the Holy Father they excused their duke who despite his vow would not participate in the Crusade . . ."

"Does Your Grace know which one they spoke of? For there are several . . ."

"Lesko, I think, Duke Cracoviae."

"Lesko of Cracow and Sandomir? Yes, yes, I know! What has detained him?"

"The bishops said that the duke, because of his great corpulence, could not undertake a long journey. They also said it was his habit to drink beer and mead, and one cannot find those beverages here; nothing but wine and water, neither of which agrees with his nature. . . . Therefore, in place of the vow he had made, he begged the Holy Father to accept an expedition against the heathenish Prussians whom he would gladly convert to the best of his abilities. . . ."

"So he will not come . . ." sighed Dzierzek.

"What heathens?" inquired de Brienne. "I never heard of them."

"A most ferocious tribe; Christ has no more bitter foe in the entire world than those Prussians," answered the Great Master of the Teutonic Order, Herman von Salza, forestalling Dzierzek's reply.

The latter was so surprised that he stuck the point of his moustache in his mouth and left it there. . . . What did the man know of the Prussians? What business of his were they?

Jacob de Vitry did not share the opinion of the Great Master.

"The Archbishop of Gniezno Kietlicz told me," he said, "they are a completely barbarous tribe with no castles nor proper weapons. It is because of their ignorance, not out of wickedness, that they still cling to paganism . . ."

"Archbishop Kietlicz was right," corroborated Dzierzek.

The deputy Great Master Herman von Balke cast a sulky glance at him. He was a rotund man with a pasty, sallow face, cruel and sly. Herman von Salza relied upon his judgment and held him in great esteem because of his cunning.

"It is just as we say," snarled von Balke. "No barbarians, but fierce fiends the Prussians are. To fight them is as meritorious as to fight the Moslems. Perhaps even more for they are a greater threat to the Church. It is far from Cairo or Damascus to Rome but Prussia is quite close. Christendom is not secure as long as these pagans dwell on its northern border. . . . The oldest, the most venerable German bishoprics are constantly threatened by them. . . ."

Dzierzek opened his eyes wide and stared at the speaker. The others also listened attentively and wondered how it was possible they had not heard of such a fierce foe.

Garin de Montaigne, the Great Master of the Hospitallers, smiled maliciously. "I have been told already—though I would not believe it—that Your Grace intended to move the Order to Europe . . . Could it be you intend to fight those Prussians who, though naked and without swords, are more dangerous than the Saracens themselves?"

Van Balke flushed angrily.

"For the time being we remain faithful to our vow to fight for the Holy Sepulchre. Sneers, though, I will not have. The lion fights with nothing but jaws and claws yet the bravest feel awe before him. The Prussians have no armor, but their number and their devil-inspired courage make them more dangerous than any other heathens. Let me but ask Sire de Pologna whether the Christian Polish dukes would not have harnessed those northern demons long ago if they were strong enough to overcome them?"

Sir Dzierzek found himself in an awkward position and stopped chewing his moustache. He could not abide Herman von Balke and yet by denying what the latter said he might cast suspicion upon the bravery of Polish knightdom. However, he was released from the necessity of answering, for Jean de Brienne suddenly raised his head.

"The bells are ringing," he said, and motioned with his hand for quiet.

Silence fell. Someone pushed the window shutters open.

"They are ringing in the cathedral."

"And at St. John's."

"At the Holy Trinity, likewise!"

"Is the enemy approaching the walls? Can it be fire?"

"This is not the tocsin."

Raoul of Thiberia sprang to the door to run for news. In the door he collided with de Brienne's squire, Willfried. At the heels of Willfried came a strange knight.

"My name is Gerard d'Avesnes," he said. "I have just arrived on a French galley, the bearer of evil tidings: the Holy Father is dead!"

"And the Word was made flesh . . ." moaned Bishop de Vitry.

"May his soul rest in peace," said the three Great Masters simultaneously.

"The Holy Father is dead . . ." repeated de Brienne. "And what about the Crusade?"

"The knights are not returning home yet. They await a new leader."

"Your Majesty must hasten to Rome in person now," mumbled Ibelin, and de Brienne gave a confirming nod.

"Indeed, these are evil tidings you bring us, Sir," he said aloud. "Evil and portentous."

"I hurried as much as I could. Though I am only a pilgrim I availed myself of the kindness of the Countess of Champagne and came on her galley . . ."

He broke off, amazed at the effect the words produced upon the King.

"The Countess of Champagne, did you say?" Jean exclaimed. "Of the house of Navarre?"

"Yes, Your Majesty. She came to fulfill her pledge of a pilgrimage to the Holy Land."

"My kinswoman! Where is she biding?"

"At the hospitium for noble pilgrims."

"Tomorrow morning I must pray her to move to the castle. . . . Yes, yes, thank you for the news. . . . So the Holy Father is dead? What a loss for the whole Christian world! I am glad to welcome you, Sir. . . . Please remain here as our guest! Your Honors! In view of the mournful tidings we shall suspend the Council now . . ."

"But Your Majesty," remonstrated Ibelin, surprised, "it seems to me that just because of these tidings we should decide at once what is to be done. Your Majesty must lead the Crusade. You know the western lords. How many who are inadequate will be all too eager to avail themselves of the Holy Father's death to bid for leadership!"

"I cannot push myself till asked," retorted de Brienne. "Besides we can talk it over tomorrow. Or the day after," he added absent-mindedly.

"What tidings! Good Lord! what tidings!"

"Grievous tidings, indeed," sighed the old lord.

"Grievous? How so? Wonderful, wonderful, I'd say. Oh, yes! You think of the other news. Yes, grievous indeed . . . and so unexpected . . ."

Stepping briskly he walked out of the hall without a glance at his wife, who had risen from her chair and followed him with her childish brooding eyes. It was his custom to bid her a ceremonious goodbye and entrust her to the care of the First Lady, the wife of Sir Aymar of Cesarea. Confused and with an awkward gesture, she took leave of those present and started for the door. The ex-regent, old Dean Ibelin, who loved her as though she were his own child, quickly stepped up to her and reverently led her to the exit. Suddenly overcome with gratitude she leaned upon his strong arm.

Once in his chamber de Brienne dismissed Willfried as well as his two servants who had rushed in to attend to their master. He wanted to be left alone. Alone with that sudden joy of his. He threw off his jerkin, opened his shirt at the neck and feverishly began to pace the room. Blanche was here! Here! Here! He had no longer expected her, no longer awaited her—and she had come! She was here, in Acre, close by! Almost three years had passed since he saw her last. Three years! Suddenly it seemed incredible to him that he had stood it so long. . . . She had come . . . William Divini the troubadour had carried out his mission. . . . Oh, let him ask any reward he pleased. . . . Jean was ready to give him anything . . . anything in his power . . . the man had brought him Blanche . . . ! Blanche was close by, quite close. He was suddenly seized with a mad desire to leave the castle and run to the hospitium . . . He felt young, hot-headed as of old! He had lived three years without her but now not one hour longer! Not a minute! "Steady now, mind you are a king," he reminded himself. "Tomorrow she will be here . . . You will bring her yourself. . . . Tomorrow . . . only till morning . . . no longer . . ."

On tiptoe he went over to the adjoining chamber. He stepped cautiously lest he awaken the squire who slept in the hall. The devoted lad would be sure to rush to his side asking what His Majesty desired, and His Majesty desired nothing. . . . It was only that the windows in this chamber opened upon the port and the hospitium. He opened the carved and gilded shutters. The sharp, chilly March night struck at his face. Jean leaned out to prevent the shutter from banging against the wall and suddenly felt the low, too low, window sill pressing below his knees. He drew back with a slight shudder, unwittingly reminded of his predecessor, Henri de Champagne, who in this very same castle—although from the other tower—had at night fallen out of the window. The real cause of the accident had never been established. Many insisted that Henri, not accustomed to the Syrian lowset windows, had simply lost his balance and fallen out.

"Nonsense," thought Jean. "No grown man would jump out of a window of his own free will to break his neck. . . . Nonsense . . . Besides, why should I think of Henri when Blanche is here. . . . Blanche! Why are the bells ringing so? Of course, the Pope is dead. . . . That's the hospitium over there . . . That must be the roof. Over there, between the Church of the Holy Trinity and the city scales. . . . Under that roof Blanche lies asleep . . . Asleep? Surely not! She could not fall asleep tonight no more than I could. She is awake . . . maybe she stands by the window and gazes in this direction? They must have shown her the royal castle. . . . Perhaps I should light a candle and give her a sign? I am mad . . . like a minstrel. . . . Surely she must be lodged in the state chamber downstairs, not in the garret. . . . And only from the garret could one see signals sent from here. . . . At best the guard would see the light and rouse the town in the belief that Ismailites had stolen into the castle . . . No, my beloved one . . . I shall not light you a flame tonight, but I burn so myself I wonder how I'll be able to last the night . . . For you are mine. . . . Until tomorrow then, my love. . . ."

# 2.

# The Lover

BUT EVEN BEFORE DE BRIENNE LEFT THE CASTLE THE NEXT MORNING young Thibault, accompanied by the astrologer Jacob Pochard, came to call on him. De Brienne had had time to regain his self-control during the night and received his kinsman cordially but not without formality. In a seemingly indifferent voice he inquired whether Lady Blanche had made a good voyage.

"Mother is well, though very petulant," replied Thibault, while unconsciously he drew the back of his hand over the nape of his neck. "The voyage was unpleasant. We were supposed to come here three months ago!"

"Why such a long delay?"

"First our galley was damaged and others would not depart because of the inclement weather . . . Then there was the turmoil produced by the Holy Father's death. . . . I thought we should never get here . . ."

"I understand my gracious kinswoman proposes to undertake a pilgrimage to the Holy Sepulchre?"

"Why, yes. . . . She says she had taken the vow . . ."

"Yes, I remember hearing of it many years ago. I am happy I shall be able to assist her in the pilgrimage. The truce with Sultan Malik al-Adil is still in force and pilgrims provided with a letter of introduction from me can travel to Jerusalem unmolested. The trouble is it takes a long time to issue such a letter and get the Sultan's approval. You must be patient. I shall go at once to Lady Blanche and beg her myself that you all move to the castle where you will find more comfort than the hospitium might offer. Did William Divini come too?"

"He was supposed to come, but imagine, Uncle Jean, he became a monk!"

Although de Brienne was completely absorbed by the thought of Blanche he could not help guffawing at this piece of news.

"What? Divini a monk? You don't say . . ."

"But it's true. He has become a monk in a beggars' itinerant Order . . . Mother has seen him. . . . He is a droll sight, it seems . . . Mother says he must have lost his mind for he was absolutely raving . . ."

"It is I who came instead of the troubadour," remarked the astrologer, stepping forward with a sigh.

"Welcome, Messer Jacob. As it happens we are just now short of a court astrologer so we shall welcome you gladly. I will order an observatory installed in the tower. And what about you, my lad? Have you already taken the Cross?"

"No," mumbled Thibault, displeased.

"Never mind. You'll take it as soon as the troops land. We shall yet make a knight of you, mark my word! And now let's be on our way!"

Blanche stood on the threshold of the pilgrim's chamber, seemingly motionless, her head bent stiffly.

"Welcome, dear cousin! God help the Holy Sepulchre!"

She nodded without a word. Her lips whispered inaudible words. He guessed they were repeating his name: Jean, Jean, Jean. Her maids behind her dropped deep curtsies.

Without a word they entered the room. Neither of them knew what to say. Thibault was saying something but they did not comprehend his words. They were both awed by the flame that burned them, by their inability to control the trembling of their hands. They could not trust their voices. And all these people around!

Blanche was the first to recover. "I have brought you, my cousin, a confidential message from my husband, Count Thibault."

Straight-backed and stiff she went into the adjacent room. Jean followed her. With wild passion they fell into each other's arms.

"You!"

"You!" she repeated like an echo.

They fell silent, closely entwined, swaying. . . .

"I will take you at once to the castle . . ." mumbled Jean incoherently. "We will be able to see each other freely, there . . ."

She tore her face from his and drew back a little, just enough to cast him a glance.

"Is your wife there?"

"Yes, of course she is, but I never see her any more. Only when people are around . . . She is with child. So . . ."

She frowned.

"But I would have to see her?"

"No more than absolutely necessary . . . She will give you a friendly welcome. A good gentle child she is . . ."

"But I will not set my eyes on her! I hate her! I won't be able to conceal it! I do not want her friendly welcome! No, I shall never come to your castle . . . At least, not as long as she is there . . ."

Helplessly he dropped his arms. "What shall we do now? I have already announced your visit and ordered chambers to be made ready."

"Tell her I have pledged that so long as I have not accomplished the pilgrimage I shall remain here, even as a common, poor pilgrim would. Take Thibault with you and the astrologer and all the others. We will be more free to see each other thus . . . I will not live under the same roof with your wife!"

"But you cannot remain here alone," he exclaimed.

"I shall keep the squire la Salle with me, and Genevieve whom I can trust . . . Jean, Jean. . . . I thought I'd never see you again!"

"Nothing can separate us now," he whispered huskily. "Come to the castle. She will not annoy you. Why, she is no more than a child. . . ."

"I told you I will not," she cried.

He stared at her with deep admiration. That was the way he loved her! Proud, wild, passionate. No, no! Nothing could separate them. Nothing greater than their love could ever happen, greater or more important. It was worth any sacrifice. . . .

Marie of Jerusalem took an instant liking to young Thibault. They suited each other well. The youth was beside himself with joy when he found out that the Queen would gladly listen to his songs. As for Marie she was sincerely grieved because the lad's mother had taken such a strange vow which prevented her from taking abode in the castle. What a pity! Marie thought of the Countess of Champagne as an amiable, elderly lady, as gentle as her son, with whom she could have made friends and in whom she might confide many a thought and worry. Maybe cousin Blanche could tell her more of Jean's disposition and likings? Marie knew so little about her husband and was so eager to discover what he enjoyed and what annoyed him . . . what his wife might do to please him and what she should avoid to spare his feelings? Obviously, Jean had much love for his family. She was told that ever since his kinswoman's arrival he had become more cheerful. Probably he was gloomy because he was homesick. . . . She should always talk with him about his native land.

Jacob Pochard, the astrologer, was getting settled in his new observatory in the castle's tower without much enthusiasm. . . . The stars here were different, unfamiliar, he could not find his way among them. He felt lost in that strange horizon, he whose eyes traveled upon the French firmament as though it were a familiar highway. Here not only the stars had become tangled and confused. So was his destiny. And for the hundredth time at least Pochard cursed his own cunning which made him insist that the number of the members of the expedition be even, that cunning which supposedly was to secure him a pleasant and profitable trip to Rome and had driven him instead to the Holy Land. God alone knew for how long. No one so far spoke of return. To make things worse, on the one hand they were all threatened with the tempest of War—Oh, where art thou, peaceful Champagne?—and on the other, right under the astrologer's nose, things were happening of which he could not think without distaste. He tried to close his eyes upon them, to ignore them, but to no avail. They pressed upon him, they reminded him of all the kindness the old Count, that friend of books and learning, had bestowed upon him, as well as his instructions to take good care of his wife! Take care of the Countess! Good Lord! How could the worthy master of starry science take care of that menacing feminine element, that embodiment of passion itself which was the Countess? He might as well take good care of thunder, of storm, of tempest! Why, this was an element one had to protect oneself against or better still cautiously avoid by keeping out of its path. But Messer Pochard could not do that. He could at most curse himself as well as William the troubadour who had brought about this journey. And curse he did.

After casting an annoyed look at the unfamiliar sky, Jacob Pochard decided, for want of anything better to do, to draw the horoscope of the young Queen and her future heir . . .

The old Lord Ibelin of Beyrouth walked slowly to the Queen's apartments. Three times before asking to be announced he stopped, pondered, wavered. Should he or should he not see her? Maybe it would be better to turn back? Still he entered.

Marie greeted him with such obvious delight that the old knight felt his heart melt in his breast. That dear, poor, little queen! Why poor? He had become accustomed to think of her as an orphan and now he reprimanded himself. Why, she was no longer poor. Not at all! She had a brave husband and would soon give birth to a lusty little prince, who, God willing, would rule from Jerusalem, not from Acre.

Thus thinking he carefully studied the face of his foster child. Somehow she looked too pale . . . Her small thin face, not devoid of a certain charm, seemed even tinier than before. Was Her Majesty feeling well? Were the leeches taking good care of her? Had she no troubles or worries?

Marie smiled with strain but protested quite warmly. She was feeling very well. Madame Aymar of Cesarea, the first lady of the Court, was taking wonderful care of her, fussed over her, forced her to eat, brought her dainty tid-bits. . . . No, her guardian had no cause for apprehension. Everything was going well.

"God be praised," said Ibelin, relieved, and immediately plunged into the matter which had brought him here.

"Why doesn't His Majesty do something to be appointed captain of the Crusade? In Rome they are fighting tooth and nail over who will take command. The new Pope, Honorius, is no warrior by nature and though he urges Christian barons to set forth for the Holy Land, he, himself, does not intend to go. He is to appoint their leader. Sire de Cesarea sends missive upon missive imploring the King to come in person or at least to authorize him as the royal envoy to request the command on his behalf. And His Majesty has given him no answer so far. This is urgent! And more important than aught else. It is a miracle that the troops have gathered and are willing to set forth. A miracle sent by merciful God. We cannot permit it to go to waste. And it will go to waste if any of the western lords takes the lead. They know nothing of conditions here, of the Moslem fighting methods, of the disposition of the people. They lack the most important thing—experience. Richard of England, Philippe of France, Leopold of Austria, Andrew

of Hungary accomplished nothing not because they lacked courage but
because they did not have the necessary experience. They do not know
the East; they fail to realize the most simple things. They will not admit
that we have what's most essential to success: a thorough understanding
of the Moslems. I pledge my head should anyone else but His Majesty
lead the Crusade it will fail. If they appoint one of the Cardinals or
Western Barons it will come to naught as did the previous Crusades. It
wrings one's heart to think of what Richard of England could have
accomplished had he but listened to the sound advice of those of us who
have spent all our lives here. We cannot allow it to happen again!"

"I thought it was settled that the King would lead the expedition,"
broke in Marie, surprised at this long oration.

"It was all settled as long as the Holy Father Innocent was alive, who
would have surely appointed him supreme commander. But not now!
The Holy Father died quite unexpectedly without appointing anyone.
Sire de Layron writes that lay Barons and Cardinals are already storm-
ing the Holy See to get the appointment. Time is passing. Three weeks
have gone by since d'Avesnes brought the news of the Pope's death,
and His Majesty has done nothing so far. Yesterday the third messenger
arrived. Sire de Layron writes he fears that the King had sent him a
letter but that it was intercepted by hostile forces. And that he does not
know what he is to say and does His Majesty apply for command or
not? Sire de Layron reckons it is not too late yet . . . but soon it may be
too late. . . . When there is no encouragement, no pressure from our
side, it will be no wonder if they elect someone else."

Marie listened with great concentration. "Have you talked of this
with the King?"

"I tried several times but I had no luck. His Majesty was busy. He put
me off without lending ear to what I had to say: 'I will attend to it
tomorrow,' he said. And that 'tomorrow' lasts already three weeks."

He broke off, then continued in a soft voice. "That is why I came to
you, Madame. I know well you have no liking for state matters, but this
time the liberation of the Holy Sepulchre and the recapture of your
kingdom are at stake. You must persuade your royal husband!"

"I?"

"Who else can do it more easily than a wife?"

Marie lowered her eyes. With a sigh she repeated. "Of course . . .
who else?"

She broke off and sat silent and pensive gazing at the points of her golden slippers. She was afraid to lift her eyes. She could not lift them. They were brimming over with tears. And at the same time she felt a spasm of bitter laughter. So Ibelin expected her to persuade Jean? Why, anyone could see Jean more easily than she, his wedded wife. She had not set eyes upon him since the last council meeting and the arrival of d'Avesnes. She could not even imagine when and where she would see him again. But this she would tell no one. She would not admit it, even to her old guardian. And so she lowered her head even more and said nothing.

But Ibelin noticed the tear which had fallen upon the silk of her dress and suddenly felt cruel. "Oh forgive me, Madame," he begged her, "I understand it is not an easy matter for a young wife, particularly when she is expecting a baby, to persuade her husband to leave her and go to war. . . . I understand. . . . But you must conquer your heart for the sake of your duty. . . ."

"I will," whispered Marie.

And again that morbid, weird laughter swelled within her, choking her throat. Ibelin rose with great dignity, kissed her fingers and bowed low. He would have gladly stretched out his hand and fondled the small head of his ex-charge but etiquette would not allow it, unless she herself chose to press against her guardian as she used to do when she was a little girl.

The old man expected she might and stood as though waiting. But Marie did not move. Oh! how she wished she could huddle close to the broad chest of that one and only man who truly loved her and cry out her sorrow and tell him all! But it was impossible. It would sound as if she accused her husband, and Ibelin's heart would surely turn away from Jean. And, holding back her tears, with a royal nod she dismissed the old knight.

Ibelin was heavily descending the stairs when someone cautiously took hold of his arm. It was Eudoxia, Marie's old nurse. A simple woman, but honest and devoted. When the present Queen was still a tiny, sickly child they had often watched over her together, the Lord of Beyrouth and this uneducated highlander from Liban.

"Your Honor," she whispered into his ear, "things are faring badly with the King. . . ."

"What are you talking about?" He stopped, stupefied.

"Yes, yes. For weeks now he has been spending his nights away from the castle, they say."

There was a sound of steps downstairs and the nurse vanished like a ghost. Irritated, Ibelin resumed his descent. His straightforward, chivalrous nature found such secret staircase whisperings repellent. He spat angrily. Had old Eudoxia lost her mind? Could the doddering old fool not tell what was possible and what was not? How dare she come to him with such silly old-wives' tales! The King spends his nights away from the castle. . . . The idea! The King had no need to steal out at night to see anyone. . . . If he ever wanted a paramour they would obligingly bring him to the castle anyone he might fancy. . . . Besides the thing was a lie. Jean had been King for over eighteen months; there had been time enough to get to know him well. A stern, serious man, not a hot-headed youngster! Crazy woman!

Marie sat motionless. Only the child stirred restlessly in her womb; and equally restless were the thoughts that beat in the Queen's brain. Why did Jean make no effort to be given command over the Crusade? Why was he neglecting such an important matter? After all, it was his duty to reconquer Jerusalem. Had he not pledged during the coronation to devote himself to that end? Ibelin insisted it was her, his wife's, duty to remind him of it. How was she to go about it? Should she go herself to his apartments? Or send someone to bring him here? To beg him to come? Surely, a wife had a right to see her husband. . . . She would apologize for summoning him. She would say: "Forgive me, Sir, for disturbing you, and listen to me. No one save you can command the Holy Expedition. . . . I was just talking about it with Ibelin . . ." No. It was better not to mention Ibelin and speak only for herself. . . . Simply ask him, as though she knew nothing of the matter: "My Lord, have you already been appointed captain of the Holy Crusade? For I fear lest someone less worthy be appointed in your stead?" Yes that will be just right. . . . I will send the squire or Eudoxia at once. . . . No telling. . . . Perhaps I should have acted long ago in this way . . . Maybe he was waiting for encouragement from her? To be sure never, neither by word nor gesture, have I shown him my desire to see him. . . . I was ashamed. I thought he would divine it himself. . . . But maybe men are not good at divining such things. . . .

Quickly she rose from her seat to call her nurse. But Eudoxia was nowhere in sight. She must wait for her return. For after all she would

send no squire. . . . No. . . . What would she do, if, oh, dreadful
thought, Jean refused to come? Just to think of it made her cold and
hot all over. Marie was proud. If Jean refused to come, the shame of
being deserted, the brand mark of the unwanted wife which hitherto
she had kept her own secret, would become common knowledge.
Eudoxia would not tell but it was better not to share humiliation even
with Eudoxia. Humiliation should not be shared with anyone. No, she
must go alone. . . .

Her eyes fell upon a small silk-covered door next to her bed. That
secret passage cut in the thickness of the wall connected the two bed-
chambers: the King's and the Queen's. It was carefully closed and few
people knew of its existence. With an involuntary sigh Marie thought
that probably never before in the lifetime of any other Queen was the
little door as seldom open as it was now. Oh, those previous queens!
How well she knew from hearsay and chronicles those fair and wild
aunts and grandmothers of hers, those wilful lovers whom the old people blamed for the loss of the kingdom, Those Sibillas, Messalinas,
Alixes, accursed, beloved, sung about. . . . She was of the same blood
as they, and yet she had so little in common with them. Her fate was so
unlike theirs. Why? Could it be that her mother, the beautiful Isabelle
four times given in marriage, felt tired of this constant passing from
hand to hand and did not wish to bestow upon her daughter the lure of
femininity which she considered a curse rather than good fortune?
Could it be that her father, the comely Conrad de Montferrat, murdered
by stealth, had had a premonition of his untimely death and while be-
getting the child thought more of the future than of the present life?
Who could tell?

Yet ill-favored and unloved, devoid of charm and beauty as she was,
she must go and speak with her husband. . . . She must go at once, for
the welfare of the kingdom hung in the balance. . . .

Carefully avoiding glancing in the mirror which stood opposite, lest
her own reflection rob her of courage, Marie cautiously opened the small
secret door. Inside the narrow, long passage it was dark, stifling, alarm-
ing. In that close, unventilated space, it seemed as though the hot breath
of those who had hurried through it still hung in the air. Perspiration
stood out on Marie's temples. At last her groping hand encountered a
door. It opened noiselessly. She lifted the rustling silk hanging and
found herself in the lighted chamber facing the huge royal canopied bed.

Jean stood in the middle of the room. He was alone. He must have been undressing, for he wore only a shirt and tight, dark breeches not unlike the ones the knights used to wear. At the rustle of the curtain he turned around and stared astonished at his wife as though he did not recognize her. She had appeared so unexpectedly! What had happened? Had she learned the truth? Was she spying on him?

"What has brought you here, Madame?" he asked.

Marie made an awkward motion with her hands, unable to say a word. She had hoped he would come to her, lead her from behind the great bed, the proximity of which filled her with confusion, seat her upon a chair and sit by her side and talk . . . Then she would tell him everything she had planned to say. But he did not budge.

"What has brought you here?" he repeated in a voice edged with annoyance.

"I wanted to . . ." she mumbled timidly. "Forgive me for coming . . . I wanted to ask . . ."

"What about?" asked Jean, hiding his own apprehension under a cover of roughness.

But Marie had forgotten the phrase so carefully prepared in advance. She was lost in confusion, while his impatience grew. Out there Blanche was awaiting him!

"I wanted . . ." repeated Marie, looking around helplessly, "I wanted to ask whether you have already been appointed the leader of the Crusade?"

Ah! So it was this she had in mind! Jean imperceptibly shrugged his shoulders. Of all things! To bother him with this when he was hastening to rejoin Blanche!

"Why, that was decided long ago," he replied. "I am only awaiting the arrival of the flotilla to take up my post."

"But you said the expedition should be directed not here, but against Egypt."

Bother! He had forgotten she had been present at the council.

"Yes, but I will meet them at the proper time in Cyprus," he assured her.

"As their captain?"

"Why, yes. I told you it was decided long ago . . ."

"It was decided by the late Holy Father Innocent. No telling whether they won't make a change now."

What did she want? What had come over her? Who had been speaking to her?

"I will beg no favors," he said stiffly. "If they find a better man, let them . . ."

Marie clasped her hands. "But this is a matter of recovering the Holy Sepulchre! Of restoring the kingdom! No one can lead the expedition better than you!"

He deigned to give her a half-hearted smile. "I am grateful for the high opinion you seem to hold of me. But have no fear. I shall do everything in my power to obtain the nomination . . ."

"Will you, my Lord?" she insisted.

Not without effort he restrained his growing impatience. Blanche was surely anxious by now! "Indeed, I will," he promised. "And now you must return to your own chambers, Madame. In a moment I am expecting several of the knights to join me in a privy council . . . Ibelin of Beyrouth, Raoul of Thiberia . . ."

"Ibelin?" she repeated slowly.

"Yes, Ibelin, Raoul and others. It would be unseemly if they were to find you here. Good night, Madame!"

She lifted her eyes to him. She was about to say: "That is a lie! Ibelin came to see me but an hour ago. He himself has sent me here . . ." But the words stuck in her throat. Silently she turned around and lifted the curtain.

"Fear not!" he called after her as she disappeared into the passage, "the care of the Holy Sepulchre is uppermost in my thoughts."

She did not reply. The curtain fell back, swayed, grew motionless. The door creaked ever so slightly. Jean stood still for a moment as though waiting. But no, she would not return. She was gone.

Quick! Quick! How long had Blanche been waiting! . . . This door must be locked. . . . How careless of him to have left it open. . . . Hurriedly, he finished dressing himself in his squire's garments. He clapped his hands. Willfried appeared at the door.

"I am ready. You can go!"

Willfried ran down the stairs and out into the courtyard. It was his old friend Jacob who was on the watch this side of the castle.

"Père Jacob," inquired the lad, "would you like to earn another denarius?"

"Hm . . . why not?"

"Well then . . . leave the wicket ajar as you did on the previous nights and pretend you do not see me when I sneak out."

"Now? Right away?"

"Not yet. I must still return to the castle and wait till His Majesty falls asleep. Mighty hard to fall asleep, the King is."

"You will be sorry for this some day, yet, you rascal! What if the King wakes up?"

"He has his valets!"

"But he might want you, not them. What then?"

"I'll be hanged, I know," sighed the lad, "but think what fun I'll have in the meantime? If you only knew, Père Jacob, what a one that wench is!"

"Wenches are nothing to me. Not any more. What about that denarius?"

"And before daylight you will likewise leave it ajar so I can return?"

"You can return as long as I don't see you."

"As soon as I whistle you'll open the wicket and hide yourself behind that corner where you always take your naps."

"I never take naps, you impudent cuss! Say, are you sure this denarius contains no lead?"

"Try it with your own teeth. His Majesty himself gave it to me."

"He will give you something yet, only it won't be a denarius. Come to your senses, lad, before it is too late."

"Sure I will. . . . Only I'll let you put aside a few more coins before I do . . ."

The lad turned on his heels. The old man, gloating, hid the coin in a fairly heavy purse. Willfried gleefully ascended the stairs, moving stealthily as though afraid someone might see him. He was pleased with himself. The maid-in-waiting of the Countess, Genevieve, whom according to general belief he visited at night, was to be rewarded for her part of the conspiracy with a large dowry. But Willfried wanted no reward. He would have felt insulted if it were offered to him. No, not for money he was doing this, but out of pure devotion to his master. He was proud of the confidence placed in him. Besides, what fun he had! Old Jacob was forever prophesying that these pranks would lead him straight to the gallows. In the hospitium everybody looked askance at Genevieve. The housekeeper—so the culprit could hear—loudly deplored the blindness of her mistress, that stately, pious, haughty lady!

She was not going to stand it much longer. She threatened to tell the Countess. What would happen then, Willfried wondered. In the meantime he bribed the housekeeper just as he bribed Jacob and the watchman at the hospitium with good, royal denarii.

What a power a denarius is! Everyone was willing to close his eyes as long as he knew that he would get it in return.

While Willfried and Genevieve kept watch, one in the royal chamber, the other in her lady's alcove, the lovers enjoyed perfect freedom. Now, that the fresh spring breeze was blowing from the sea they did not care to remain in the stuffy little chamber. The hospitium as well as the castle was outside of the city walls, therefore they were able to go out at night upon the seashore, wander amidst the rocks, sit close by the water. . . . The nights were still cold but a pearly freshness rose from the waves. The distant, barren Judea lay gray and drab, regardless of the season, but here in Galilee the trees were bursting with burgeons, the grass swelled with fresh, juicy greenness. Jean and Blanche lay on the pasture till the blue night turned white and whiteness changed to the rosy hue of dawn. They cared not whether they were seen or not. They were neither King nor Countess—just a simple couple. If anyone were to see them entwined he would think they were a port wench and a servant from the castle. Let them . . . let them think anything they pleased. . . . They had never known such freedom before. In Troyes they had been very careful. Sometimes during a hunt they had succeeded in separating themselves from the rest of the hunters under the pretense of losing their way in pursuit of the deer, and had spent several hours alone. But this happened infrequently. Besides the equerry, Sir Mountbart, would suspiciously survey their mounts afterwards, and mumble something under his breath. He wondered why, contrary to the story they told, the horses were neither weary nor foaming but rested, as though they had been standing all the while hitched to some upturned tree. . . . No, indeed, it was no easy matter to achieve even a moment of freedom. No wonder that now both of them revelled in the pleasure of spending whole nights together and refused to think that this bliss could ever come to an end.

"I reckon," said Blanche, standing upon the seashore, small waves breaking and splashing upon the stones, "I am too old to become pregnant, but if I did I would not be sorry."

"What would you do?" asked Jean anxiously.

"I would bear and bring up your son. Our son . . ."

"But he would be a bastard . . ."

"No, he would not. We are meant for each other, you and I. Sooner or later I shall be your wife. . . . Will you then recognize him?"

"How could I not recognize him? Our child! Oh, my beloved. . . . Only when will this come about?"

"She will not live long . . ." announced Blanche, staring at the waves.

"How do you know? Why?"

"The astrologer told me. . . . He has drawn her horoscope, didn't you know it?"

"No. What does it say?"

"It says it could be prevented but not easily. Stars are not very propitious to her . . ." she burst into malicious laughter.

He cast her an almost fearful glance. He did not want Marie to die. Let her live unaware of anything as hitherto. True, he wanted to wed Blanche, but after obtaining a divorce. He felt no hatred for his wife. Why should he hate her? He suddenly remembered her as she had stood tonight behind the great bed, helpless, made shapeless by pregnancy, appearing so unexpectedly against the background of the silk curtain. At first he had simply been scared by her; he had taken her for a ghost. She had come to ask if he would lead the Crusade? Strange. What had made her think of it? Of course he would lead. . . . He must lead. . . . To be sure, he had somewhat neglected the matter. He had not even noticed how fast time had passed. Now he must be sharp about it . . . lest they make a fool of him. . . . "No I will not allow it," he reassured himself. "Whom else have they there? No one! Nothing but green youth or small fry. . . . Nevertheless I must do something. . . . De Layron wrote several times . . . I shall write him today. . . ."

"What are you thinking about?" Blanche, perplexed by his silence, touched his hand.

"I was thinking our happiness will soon come to an end. . . . I must busy myself with the Crusade. . . ."

She heaved a deep sigh. "Hurry not overmuch. . . . Just a little longer. . . . A little . . ."

Yes . . . just a little longer. Be it a few days! When once he started upon the expedition those glorious, glorious nights would not happen again. . . .

The sea continued to splash at their feet. It was still dark in the murk but in the curve of the waves a green hue was beginning to flicker. Over the heads of the two lovers like the bow of a gigantic ship rose the sacred mount of Carmel. Its rocky spur jutted out into the sea. Somewhere, high above, invisible in the darkness, the cavern of the prophet Elijah stared upon the waves. People were afraid to go inside, as though the voice of the prophet calling God still thundered in its bowels. At the very tip of the stony spur, blurred by the suffused light of daybreak, stood a man now. He was not looking at the two lovers nor at the sea. He gazed inland. It seemed as though his eyes, piercing the murk, saw Mount Tabor and the roofs of Nazareth and the distant Capernaum and the entire Holy Land which remained in the power of the Moslems. Indeed, it was a derision that this strip of shore should belong to the Christians! They held the cavern of Elijah whence they could call the Lord. . . . That and nothing more. . . .

"Why, it's Gerard d'Avesnes," whispered Jean, after a glance at the figure. "Quick! Let's go away from here!"

They turned back. Besides, it was getting late. They had remained too long upon the shore, forgetting they were a long way from town. They must hurry now. Daylight was quickly invading the world. In a short while the sun would emerge from behind the mountains. Its forerunners, those golden fingers, similar to the rays which once crowned the menacing face of Moses, were already sweeping the sky. Jean and Blanche hastened their pace. In the churches bells began to peal. Women were coming out to fetch water. Holding with one hand the tall clay amphoras balanced on their heads, they cast contemptuous glances at the wench who had spent the night abroad with a man. The white top of Hermon already flamed and glowed in the morning dawn. Camels treaded softly upon the roads. The miserable wretches who slept in the open climbed from under the cover of rags and tatters, stretched their limbs and flung juicy remarks at the belated couple. In the royal castle Willfried was rubbing his sleepy eyes. Why was his Majesty not back yet? Had some evil befallen him? In the hospitium Genevieve mused bitterly while she watched the rising sun. What good would the promised dowry do her when through her mistress's fault ill fame would be cast upon her name. It was not of Madame people spoke ill but of her, Genevieve. Already now they were pointing at her. . . . The false gossip may readily reach her native land, and if it does she will surely find no husband. . . .

The belated lovers were almost running now. In the vicinity of the hospitium they parted without a word. Jean was gloomy. Something irked him. Not something, many things. . . . The thought that Blanche might be with child . . . The bodings of the astrologer . . . Marie's questions with regard to the Crusade . . . And above all the fact that he had been fleeing from Gerard d'Avesnes.

The old de Brienne, Jean's father, would never have exposed himself to such a humiliation. Neither would Ibelin. Both belonged to an older sterner generation which could not imagine such things as donning the clothes of servants and stealing out of one's own castle at night. Aye, they might without qualms break with an ironclad fist bonds that had become onerous. Braving the threat of anathema they might repudiate their lawful but unloved wives and take another unto themselves. This they might do. But they would not stoop to deceit. The world had changed much lately, under the influence of troubadours and their love songs. It had come to believe that love was the supreme mistress, and that any humiliation incurred for its sake was no humiliation as long as the beloved woman came of noble stock. De Brienne shared this creed. Had he not himself composed canzonas? Nevertheless, he returned somber to the castle and would not even as much as nod at Willfried in response to the latter's eager glances.

Once in his chamber, he threw himself upon the bed, to catch a moment of rest. But sleep would not come. For the first time since Blanche's arrival he thought of their common future. They had not talked of it so far. Jean did not even know whether Blanche gave the matter a thought. Probably not. All she did was to glory in the joy of his presence and hate Marie. She awaited her death . . . Marie's death . . . Was Messer Pochard out of his mind to recount such things? And come with them to Blanche of all people . . . ? Again Jean saw his wife as she had stood here by his bed. He saw her small, triangular face, her heavy deformed figure. . . . The poor child . . . No, she must not die . . . Besides, her death would mean the end of Jean's reign . . . He would have to return to France, and what then? Would he and Blanche be strong enough to flout the public opinion of all of Champagne? Public opinion might be indulgent to a King but never to one who had ceased to reign. No, he would not go back. He might take the Cross and set out upon the expedition even as a simple knight. But what about Blanche? Would she go with him? As what? A camp paramour?

Oh, Lord! All these cares . . . so many cares! And in addition all those letters of Sir Aymar de Layron still awaiting his answer. . . . Perhaps after all Marie was right? He must attend to it at once. . . .

As soon as Willfried, whom de Brienne had sent upon some errand, appeared in the guardhouse his companions surrounded him roaring with laughter.

"Come on now, out with it. What time did you return this morning?"

"They say it was after first milking!"

"Sure it was. I saw him from the window stealing through the wicket. And how he ran! In the mist he appeared so tall I did not recognize him at first. . . ."

"Wait till the King finds out!"

"Before he finds out we shall be off to the wars, and then no more love, either," Willfried retorted, chuckling.

"Before we set out you'll be worn to a thread. You poor wreck! When do you get any sleep? On duty in the daytime, on duty at night. . . ."

"It's not so bad. I sleep nights. Only not alone and not here. . . ." He was about to depart when suddenly a poorly clad man who had been standing for a long time in front of the gate stepped timidly forward and bowed low.

"Your Honor, I am seeking service. I thought I could be of use in the castle?"

"We do not take strangers," Willfried replied haughtily. "Once already Ismailites have sent murderers in the guise of Christians and slain the king."

"It is from Europe I came . . . I am a scholar, a master . . . My name is Matteo Pesaro."

"Many claim they've come from the old country though none has seen them aboard a galley."

"Neither has anyone seen me, if the truth be known, for I came gratis, hidden among boxes and crates, but it is a fact I came from the old country and I can prove it. I know Your Honor. We once spent the night in the same inn, near Rome. The inn was called The Good Guardian. Sir Jean de Brienne, the present King, was on his way to Rome to meet the envoys. You were with him. You drove two wayfarers out of the room. . . ."

Willfried searched his memory, puckering his brow. "I remember," he admitted. "Out in the courtyard there was a bunch of some sort of beggars. And in the room we found two rascals whom we threw out . . . One of them even grumbled. . . ."

"I was one of these travelers, but it was the other one that grumbled . . . Pietro Cani. . . ."

"How do I know it is so when I don't recollect your face?"

"How would I know those details unless I was there?"

"True, you could not," admitted Willfried. "Well, I'll bring you to the steward. Maybe he will find you something to do."

"I could be of use to the astrologer . . . I write skilfully."

"We shall see. But say, didn't you tell me you arrived here by stealth, hidden on a galley. That means the executioner was at your heels. Lively now, tell me what you've done?"

"A heretic, a Catharus with whom I unnecessarily became acquainted, accused me of heresy to turn away suspicion from himself . . . I barely escaped."

There was a matter-of-fact sincerity in the voice of Matteo Pesaro, the itinerant scholar. Willfried observed him keenly from the tail of his eye. "How do I know he was accusing you and not telling the truth?"

"The truth? Only a fool could give credence to the explanation of Genesis as given by the Cathari. They . . . never mind. Take me to the Bishop. I'll expound my credo before him. He will see I am a good Christian."

"Forget it. We are not as strict here as they are in the West. Come now. I'll take you to the steward."

They crossed the courtyard. Suddenly Willfried stopped short. "How long ago since you left Rome?"

"Three weeks."

"What about the expedition?"

"Well, the troops stand in readiness . . . Because of it prices soar and people complain. And no telling when they will set out for they have no leader. . . . They quarrel, they bicker . . ."

"How's that? Isn't our King to lead them?"

"At first I heard they were speaking of him, but not lately . . . No doubt but that the Holy Father will appoint one of the Cardinals . . . That's what everybody says . . ."

"No! No! It cannot be. Let's go to the steward. Afterwards I shall hasten to His Majesty. Perhaps he will want to see you."

# 3.

# The Leader

BECAUSE OF HIS CONCEIT AND DOUR DISPOSITION, CARDINAL PELAGIUS WAS not popular. He had been nicknamed the Red Cardinal because of his particular fondness for this color. Not only his own vestments but his litter, the harness of his horses and mules were crimson. He always looked as though he were bathed in red. A crimson reflection bathed his swarthy, secretive face. At heart he was not wicked, neither was he a schemer. Nevertheless, he was excessively conceited and nurtured a deep rooted hatred toward all lay lords. With regard to the rabble he was haughty but charitable, for he considered charity one of his ecclesiastical duties. As for barons, knights and dukes, he could not abide them. He was absolutely convinced that all of them, no matter what their undertaking, had nothing but their private interests at heart. Mentally, he contrasted them with himself, Pelagius, who thought of nothing but the good of the Church. To be sure the interest of the Church was usually synonymous with his own; this, however, he would not admit. Otherwise he was sincere in everything he did. And it was in all sincerity that he desired to increase the power and authority of the Church.

This was what the late Pope Innocent, dead but two months, had been striving for, and Cardinal Pelagius was wont to refer to him as his model and authority. There was a difference, however; Innocent looked upon secular power as a means to achieve general peace; it was to aid him in bringing together his beloved United Christian States of Europe, in which all nations would live in common freedom, mutual respect and peace. The mind of Pelagius did not embrace such wide and distant horizons. To him the establishment of the secular power of the Church was an end in itself.

Obviously, according to the Cardinal, it was clear that none but an ecclesiastic could lead the new Crusade. Neither Jean de Brienne nor Walter de Nemours nor Simon de Joinville. The leader must be a member of the clergy. Innocent III was dead. The present Holy Father did not feel capable of military leadership; the duty, therefore, clearly fell upon one of the Cardinals. For with regard to the lay lords the Holy See had had plenty of bitter experience. Each time it was Rome, and none else, who instigated the Crusade, roused men, spent money, granted indulgences, alleviated financial burdens, levied powerful armies and entrusted them to the hands of the nobles who either led the expeditions ineptly or diverted them from the real goal, as in 1204 when instead of attacking the Moslems they struck at Byzantium. No more of that! The Holy Father must appoint a captain from the body of the Holy College. And who among the latter was more capable of assuming command than Pelagius, that born warrior? The Cardinal was convinced he had the making of a great captain. Was he not brave to the point of recklessness, stern with himself and with others?

The Holy Father Honorius was not so sure of it. He would have preferred the King of Jerusalem. Innocent had often repeated in front of him that he would be the spiritual leader while de Brienne would take actual command. Upon the Papal desk still lay the plans of the future campaign prepared by Jean and sent to Rome shortly after Innocent's death. This plan, advocating an initial attack upon Egypt, was strikingly clear, carefully prepared and broad in conception. The Pope thought the plan should be carried out by its author. But Jean de Brienne gave no sign of life. He must either be ill or had run into some internal troubles which would not allow him to leave Acre. His envoy, de Layron, complained he did not even receive an answer to his urgent letters. Indeed, grave must have been the reasons which prevented the King from striving to obtain the command over the campaign.

Meantime, the troops waited idly, boredom gnawed at the men, and the dearth which Matteo Pesaro had mentioned to Willfried grew every day. The prices of bread, meat and olives had risen to unprecedented levels, just as they had done after the German invasion. And again those smart tradesmen, the Genoans, Pisans and Venetians, who managed to make profit from everybody and everything—be it victory or defeat, their own countrymen or strangers, a war already in progress or one about to begin—supplied provisions and amassed fortunes. They had no

reason to complain and their zeal continued to wax high. Theirs alone.
As for the others . . . it was but human that enthusiasm should wane.
Even a flame when not fed turns to ashes. The impulse which had
aroused them had lost its compelling force; last year's sacred indignation had paled and subsided. Spring was coming and with the spring—
field labors. Those labors were beginning to loom in the Crusaders'
minds more important, more pressing than the expedition. Childish figures no longer haunted people's minds. Upon the island, which now
bore the name Innocents' Island, where the sea had swept ashore hundreds of small bodies, rose an imposing basilica. And as it grew the
memory of the children themselves waned as though the basilica were
a sufficient compensation for their death. And only the demented Madonna de Trevi, mother of little Beatrice, continued to roam throughout
the country calling in a distraught voice for all to take the Cross. Only
mothers still wept and would not allow their husbands to turn back;
the mothers who insisted it was not certain that all the galleys had sunk;
that perhaps some of the little tots were still alive and moaning in pagan
bondage. Only the mothers. . . .

Anyway, it was natural enough for people to grow indifferent, for
everyone was sick of that protracted waiting. Six months of waiting!
It was about time matters were settled one way or another—either let
them set forth or return home. What were they waiting for anyway?
The Holy Land was not so far away. In the olden days their grandsires
had traveled there on foot, circling the sea. They had wandered several
years across waterless deserts and mountains full of precipices. Nowadays those travels sounded like fairy-tales. People had grown wise, they
had discovered that the safest and shortest way was by sea. An even,
broad way. True, storms would break out at times and vessels would
sink, but then a man could perish on land too, when his hour struck.
And, weather permitting, in a couple of weeks one could reach the Holy
Land nowadays without trouble or effort. Didn't the merchants travel
back and forth as though going from fair to kermess and back to fair
again? If only the captain were at last appointed.

So many wise heads and still no leader! Strange was the world, indeed! In all that swarm not one man, not a single man whom all would
accept. One might have thought no choice would be easier, for this one
was good and so was that other and this third one even better. . . . Yet,

if you looked closely you would soon find there was no one. They all fretted over it whenever they met in council. Walter, Duc de Nemours, his friend Jean d'Arcy, both covered with glory that they had won at Bouvines, Robert de Hainaux, William de St. Omer, Simon de Joinville, Erard de Chacenay, Milon de Nanteuil, Bishop of Beauvais and Andrew de Nanteuil his brother. At heart, each of them thought he himself would make the best captain, but none had the courage to say so aloud. None had the necessary strength to force himself upon the others. They had brought a score, sometimes a few hundred knights, and up to a thousand men-at-arms at best. Not enough to back one's words with the clatter of swords. And so they kept silent, fearing ridicule, which to a knight was worse than death. It even happened that one would say politely to another: "You should lead!" secretly hoping the other would answer: "You are the worthier one," and others hear and join in.

Practically all would be ready to accept Jean de Brienne. Or for that matter any other king. A king was a king and would give no rise to mutual envy. But the crowned heads showed no haste. De Brienne gave no sign of life. The young but sly Frederick II, though he had promised the Pope to take the Cross, did not even think of fulfilling his pledge. He said he would not set out till he had defeated Philip of Swabia and Otto of Brunswick. Philip of France had already fought in the Holy Land and considered he had done his share. Andrew of Hungary, likewise. The Polish duke dreaded the lack of mead and beer; the Czech was busy with internal dissensions. There was no one.

"I had always believed de Brienne was to lead," de Joinville was saying. "He was never slow to take up arms. I've often seen him in strife before."

"It seems an evil fever has been sweeping Acre . . . maybe it got hold of him."

"Everybody says Jerusalem has a healthy, dry climate, while Acre is surrounded with marshes."

"I have heard the Holy Father intends to send a mission to King Philip to beg him to appoint a leader just as before he appointed a King."

"The King will surely nominate one of those who fought at Bouvines," remarked Bishop Milon politely. His brother flushed angrily, for he had not taken part in the battle.

"No telling . . ." retorted de Nemours with feigned indifference.

But the sedate Simon de Joinville denied the rumor.

"Impossible! The Italian and English Lords would never consent to the choice made by the King of France! The English in particular! Only the Holy Father can appoint the chief commander. You will see, he will choose one of the Cardinals. . . ."

"A Cardinal will be commander only in name, in reality someone else will have to direct the operations."

"I am not so sure of that. The Holy College does not lack men who will gladly grasp the sword and keep the authority for themselves."

"Whoever is to get command, let him get it soon. For in no time now, men will begin to disband."

"It is a wonder they have not disbanded! And they seem so placid this year! I don't recollect a single riot, not one big fight or plunder, and few complain. . . ."

"That's because there is no famine."

"Nonsense! Men are more prone to mischief on a full stomach than on an empty one. . . . Out of idleness. . . . We all know how it was at other times. The more ample the provisions the worse the strife. . . ."

"I likewise have marveled at the fact," the Bishop of Beauvais bore out the speaker, "and have made inquiries as to what may be the cause. According to the centurions it is due to those beggars-monks, the Minor Brethren whom the Italian knights so fiercely dislike. . . ."

"Why should they dislike them?"

"Because the founder of the Order, Francis, whom some consider a half-wit and others think a saint, persuaded the daughter of the Sciffio of Assisi and Sasso Rosso to join his Order. The Sciffi are a powerful family. They have stirred up other nobles against him. But the Holy Father backs the beggars. Besides they care nothing for the castles and seek only the company of the very poorest, so all that wrath harms them but little. . . ."

"I've noticed many times some bedraggled fellow addressing the soldiers while they listened to him with gaping mouths. . . . Must have been one of these monks. . . . Does Your Grace truly believe they can exercise such influence?"

"I was repeating only what the centurions say. Only a while ago one told me: 'We could never hold anyone in camp, not a single house would escape looting, were it not for the Minor Brethren!' "

"Incredible!"

And, indeed, Francis and his companions did not remain idle. Francis in particular was indefatigable. He was to be seen everywhere. Filled with pious awe brother Leo, surnamed "the lamb," confided in brother John Parenti what for long had been weighing upon his mind. Surely, the Lord must have bestowed upon Francis the gift of being present in several places at once. Otherwise, how was one to explain the fact that he was heard here and there and yonder. . . . When Francis heard of it he merely laughed and made fun of brother Leo. This, however, did not alter the Lamb's deep conviction.

But even Francis was becoming weary and worried over the delay. They were supposed to start last year. . . . What were they waiting for? . . . Were they to stay here till everyone forgot the goal they had set out to attain?

"So far we still lack an adequate leader," the Holy Father Honorius explained to him. Ever since he had ascended Innocent's throne he had taken up the latter's trust in the weird fool from Assisi.

"None but Our Lord ought to be leader."

"But how is this to be done?" smiled the Pope indulgently.

"Why, Your Holiness, what could be more simple? If only everyone loved Him and obeyed His command and always thought of what Our Lord would have him do—all would fare well! And there would be no disagreement or strife, for the words of Our Lord are the same for all. . . ."

The Pope continued to smile as one does at the vagaries of a child.

"Christ did not allow the drawing of swords . . . How then are the troops to go? Unarmed?"

Francis' face beamed.

"That's it! Exactly! Unarmed! In the name of Our Lord's love!"

"How would they defeat the pagans?"

"They would have no need to defeat them. They would convert them!" And joyously he sprang to his feet, dazed by this unexpected thought for the first time put into words. Hitherto they had been all calling for the heathens to be exterminated. Why must they be exterminated? Convert them instead!

"An obdurate sinner will never convert himself, unless a sword dangles over his head."

"It is no conversion, whatever is brought by sword . . . it's fear. And Our Lord wants none to be afraid and forced. . . ."

With these words he departed, serene as ever. The Holy Father followed him with his eyes. How he envied Francis! How far he was from such serenity. The Crusade of which he must appoint a commander, which stood idle, devouring tremendous sums of money, filled him with bitterness. Today again the Cardinal of Albano, Pelagius, had come to see him and insisted that he be entrusted with the command. He would know how to lead. He was willing to take upon himself full responsibility for the success of the venture. Should he fail, let God and man judge him. He would have no other thought, no other care, save the success of the Crusade. He would not rest till he vanquished the Crescent, recovered the Timber of the Holy Cross, and set it up again in the temple of Jerusalem. So help him God!

He had spoken with great enthusiasm and with deep and sincere conviction. Honorius had promised him a definite reply two days hence. Oh, if only Jean de Brienne would arrive in the meantime! If only he would send word!

Cardinal Cencius Savelli, the present Pope Honorius, was very old. He had never taken active part either in the administration of the Church or in politics. For many years he had held the office of the Exchequer of the Holy See. He had a great knowledge of figures, none of men. And he knew it. He knew he could not adequately assay values which could not be expressed in figures. That was why he tried whenever possible to follow the line of his predecessor whom he had always worshiped. Hence the trust he set in Jean de Brienne. Hence his confidence in Francis, though every word of the latter seemed unreal and funny to the learned accountant.

But what had Innocent thought of Cardinal Pelagius? No one knew. To be sure, Pelagius asserted that the dead Pope had thought highly of him, but others kept silent on the subject. Innocent was not loquacious. He seldom expressed judgments. What is more, he strictly advocated complete equality among the members of the Holy College and never admonished or praised any of them in front of the others.

So what was Honorius to do? Oh, Holy Ghost, merciful God, enlighten him . . . ! Pelagius was harsh, vindictive, unpopular; but all he said, he said with complete sincerity. He had courage, was not afraid of responsibility. Those indeed were great qualities. Perhaps the Pope ought to entrust him with the plan of campaign prepared by Jean de Brienne, appoint him leader and let them all at last set out on their way?

Aye! let the troops embark. Let the arm lifted for over a year fall upon the heathen's heads! God help the Holy Sepulchre!

# 4.

# Damnation

GERARD D'AVESNES NEVER SUSPECTED THAT HIS APPEARANCE ON THE ROCKY spur of Carmel had routed a pair of lovers. This was a favorite spot of his and he often visited it. That natural watch tower which overlooked the sea, the bay and the entire valley, drew him for certain private and extremely painful reasons.

He had come to Palestine with the intention of making a pilgrimage to the Holy Sepulchre. That was why he had joined the retinue of the Countess of Champagne. He had reckoned that as soon as they reached Acre they would set out on their way. So, at least, he had been told on board. Apparently some unexpected obstacles had arisen upon their arrival, for now no one mentioned the pilgrimage. Several weeks had gone by and the Countess, her son and her retinue were still biding in Acre, as though awaiting something! But what? Perhaps in view of the imminent campaign she preferred to enter the reconquered Jerusalem in knightly fashion instead of paying the Sultan a tribute to gain admission. The knight found such a motive understandable enough.

As for himself, impatient as he was for the troops to arrive and for the fighting to begin, he meant to fulfil beforehand an all-important vow.

D'Avesnes was a man of small means. Nevertheless his coffers contained a sum at which no magnate, however rich, would sneer. One thousand gold byzantines. This gold was to serve to redeem the sin of his beloved wife, Margaret, who lured by a lover left her husband, and when in turn the lover deserted her jumped into the sea from a rock, not unlike this one. . . .

Aye, she herself had cut short her days, thus committing a fearful crime, a sin against the Holy Ghost; she had given herself up to the powers of Hell. Nothing could help her now, nothing could save her. Even prayer was of no avail.

D'Avesnes had loved the unfortunate woman with a tender passion, so that he was even willing to forgive the wrong she had wrought him and take her back, dishonored as she was, caring not what people might say. And even now he was constantly thinking of her. Of the torment she must be suffering in Hell, the poor soul, of the fire devouring her delicate limbs, those long slender hands. Her flesh, always so avid of caresses, must now be shrivelled and charred, yet never consumed by the flame. In vain she begs for a drop of water, for never can she be refreshed and the torture will go on and on and on forever. . . . States, kings and nations shall vanish and still the sinner must suffer for her misdeed. Nor will she ever atone for it. Whatever happens in the universe, she will continue to smother in flames, never know sleep, respite or peace. For ages and ages and into eternity. There were times when the realization of this horror struck Sir d'Avesnes with such unutterable despair that he was ready to blaspheme and mock divine justice. At night he would jump out of bed and roam the fields as though he were demented. Feeling that he was going mad he had sold his patrimony, sold all he possessed, obtained a thousand Byzantian coins and set forth for the Holy Land. Here he would found something that might particularly please God and His Mother and thus compel them to mercy. True, there was no retreat nor exit from Hell, but the Mother of God could overcome any obstacle should the sinner turn to Her. Greater is Her mercy than the gates of Hell, deeper Her kindness than the abyss of damnation. Had she not rescued the unworthy monk whom the Devil had come thrice to fetch, once in the guise of a bull, then a dog and lastly that of a lion? Had she not fed with Her own divine breast the criminal condemned to death by starvation? Was she not ever ready to hasten to people's help? Indeed, in their sinful madness men might renounce God, yet none would ever forsake His Mother. For well they knew in such a case nothing could rescue them. . . .

It was this faith that brought Gerard d'Avesnes to the Holy Land. In this faith he pondered how he could best please the Mother of God, and thus secure her favor. Once he had intended to use his gold to adorn the Holy Sepulchre. But so far Jerusalem had not been reconquered and it might easily happen that he would lose his life in the campaign without fulfilling his intention. It was better to act now. Acre constituted the last Christian outpost in Palestine. This outpost was not adequately guarded nor protected. What if he were to contribute to its protection?

Wouldn't God find such a deed more pleasing than aught else? The
longer he stood upon the rock the more the thought appealed to him.
Why shouldn't he build a castle upon this very spot? It would protect the entire harbor. A truly unconquerable watch tower. Under its
guard Acre would be safe. But would it be possible to erect a building
upon this rock? Would the sum he possessed prove large enough to
cover the cost?

He spent hours pondering over the matter, increasingly attracted by
the plan. It seemed to him he could already see the walls rising from the
rock, and the image began to take the form of the feminine figure forever present before his eyes. Her arms upraised in a gesture of distress
found a counterpart in two lofty turrets. Where the head rose from the
shoulders a bastion would appear. To safeguard Christendom there
would rise a castle, as ransom for the soul of that unfortunate sinner,
Margaret. He would call it the Castle of the Pilgrim.

Once he had made up his mind, d'Avesnes was eager to set about his
purpose, even though he missed the presence of his friend Robert de
Hainaux, with whom he had exchanged pledges of brethren in arms.
De Hainaux would have been of great help to Gerard now, for he was
adroit, brisk, did not avoid people nor meditate upon the horrors of
Hell. To be sure he likewise had troubles but they were neither as important nor as deep as Gerard's. While d'Avesnes ate his heart out because of the suicide of an unfaithful wife, de Hainaux suffered because
his grandmother had not committed suicide. That grandmother of his
had taken part in the Crusade and had fallen captive to the Saracens.
It seemed as though she lived for many years and had children there.
Robert could not forgive his father's mother for that breach of faith. In
his opinion she had brought dishonor upon the entire family.

". . . My father did not remember those times for his mother left him
at home, still a baby, to follow my grandsire to the Holy Land," he
would recount. "It seems they were very much in love. After he lost her
my grandsire was beside himself with grief and to the day of his death
no one ever saw him smile. He would not even look at his son—that's
my father—for the child reminded him too much of his lost wife. My
father was brought up by strangers as though he were an orphan. . . .
At first all thought her dead and praised her for dying so valorous a
death. Then, after my grandsire's death, at the time of the leper King,

rumors spread that she was not dead at all . . . that she lived in a harem and was faring well. . . . By the Blood of Saint Martyrs! She— born a Montferrat, the Countess de Hainaux! Others would not let themselves be taken alive!"

"Come now, it is better she did not take her life and lose her soul," d'Avesnes would sigh, and the two friends would plunge into a long oft-repeated argument as to whether suicide was such a dreadful crime as the priests would have it or not. According to the precepts of chivalry it was better to take one's life than to live dishonored, and no one blamed such a deed. . . .

"People may not blame, nevertheless God always forbids suicide," insisted d'Avesnes. He would close his eyes as though blinded by the blaze that devoured the wretched sinners. Who but the spirits of suicides inhabited crossroads and haunted places? Where did ghosts come from if not from among those who had been denied burial in consecrated soil?

"Nonsense," protested his friend, "the Church herself praises virgins who took their lives to escape infamy. . . . God would surely forgive my grandmother, nay would deem it a merit had she saved a worthy family from shame. . . . As it is . . . what am I to do? My heart craves the Holy War yet fear grips me lest among the heathens I should encounter a kinsman. . . . I wish Hell had swallowed her before she had ever lain in a pagan's bed!"

"Hush! For Heaven's sake!" implored d'Avesnes. Not that he cared much about Robert's grandmother, but the profanity shocked and pained him. If men would only consider—be it once in a lifetime—what Hell meant they would not fling the word about in such careless fashion.

Now, however, the two friends were separated. De Hainaux with the entire Crusaders' army was still biding time and growing bored in Ancona. Therefore d'Avesnes set about his business all by himself. He easily obtained permission from the King, the blessing of Bishop Jacob de Vitry and the assurance of both that should his funds prove inadequate they would supply the balance out of their own. Builders there were aplenty and good ones, better than in the west. The news that a foreign knight was building a castle to protect the town from the sea quickly spread and was greeted with admiration and satisfaction. The knights of the Templarian, Hospitalian and Teutonic orders already circled around the generous founder in the hope of becoming the future garrison of the fortress. He paid no heed to them, however, and in silence he supervised the work.

As a matter of fact, the work was easier than had been anticipated. Much to everybody's surprise the rock proved to be not monolithic stone but the remnants of some antique, mighty building. Under a thin layer of soil brought by the wind, under a measly cover of turf, the first strokes of the pickaxes uncovered old, sound walls of glazed bricks of beautiful, still unfaded colors. Inside those walls, which were strong enough to serve as foundations for the future structure, workmen found small, strange objects wrought in gold, silver, crystal and bone; hairpins, bracelets, clasps and small statues of unknown gods with ugly faces and big bellies. The men were afraid to touch them because of the evil spells that they might cast, but the sight of gold was a strong temptation, indeed, and here and there a man would spit thrice, cross himself, and hide in his bosom a brooch of some unusual shape. In addition to these small gems they unearthed many clay vessels which fell to pieces when hit by a spade and small quardangular tablets hard as stone and thickly covered with tiny fissures. These could be of no use to anyone and were thrown aside upon a pile. When the time should come to clear the lot they would be flung into the sea.

Matteo Pesaro, who had lately been taken into service of the royal castle as assistant scribe, heard of the strange discovery and hastened to the spot to take a look at the excavated wonders. He had chosen a bad time, however, for a storm was coming up. The sea, dark as steel and tumultuous, spat upon the rock and almost reached the newly started structure. The workmen hurriedly collected their tools and advised everyone to leave. It had often happened that billows swept everything off of the rock . . . Most likely they would today, for the sky was growing ominously dark.

"But in that case the sea will wash all this away," exclaimed Matteo, distressed. He took off his cloak and loaded it with the clay tablets and broken pottery. He collected as much as he could lift and asked the workmen to hoist it on his back. Fat Jonathan, the mason, willingly obliged but not without scoffing and jeering at all men of learning. What need had the scholar of all that rubbish?

"He will grind it to powder and sell it to leeches for medicaments," guessed Eusebius, the carpenter. "He is not such a fool as you think!"

Painfully Matteo plodded back to the castle, lashed by gusts of wind, blinded by dust, bent in two under his load. At last he deposited his precious burden on the floor of the chamber which belonged to Messer Jacob Pochard, his new acquaintance and friend.

"What have you brought here?" the astrologer inquired sourly. He was in a bad temper for the Queen might at any moment send for her horoscope and that horoscope . . . Oh! Why did he ever begin the damned thing!

Matteo told the astrologer what he had found. They both sat upon the floor and began to scrutinize the shards.

"This is a script," declared the astrologer in a voice choking with excitement. "An unknown script . . . Not a pattern; not a haphazard impression, but letters. . . . Only look how even the lines are. . . . Some signs are repeated. . . . Oh, if we only could guess what they mean!"

"Yes, these must be the books or documents of people who once lived upon this earth. But when? At the time of Abraham? Perhaps earlier! Maybe before the Deluge! Maybe the man who drew them had seen the Noah's ark!

"They must have carved these signs while the clay was still soft. . . . Look how it dragged here behind the chisel."

Feverishly they handed the tablets to each other, brought them close to their eyes, drew their fingers over the surfaces as though they had hoped to pierce their secrets. Suddenly they felt bitterly conscious of their own lack of knowledge. The earth was so old, so full of mysteries, so many peoples had lived upon it, and what did they know of it? The learning of which they had been hitherto so proud was of no avail when it came to studying the past.

"Those men were no barbarians," continued the astronomer, scrutinizing the shards. "Just look at these patterns. Today a potter could not work such an exquisite one!

"No telling whether these tablets don't contain the mystery of transmutation of matter which it seems was known to men of ancient times. Or the evidence in support of Plinius' assumption that the earth is round, a theory none will accept today inasmuch as it is believed that the earth rests upon water. . . . Who knows?

"It has often occurred to me that our division of nature into creating but uncreated, creating and created, created but uncreative, and uncreated and uncreative is not absolutely accurate. . . . Maybe the proper classification is revealed in these tablets. We hold it in our hands yet are unable to read it!"

The sound of the opening door interrupted their laments. One of the Queen's valets entered and stopped short, surprised at the sight of the two learned men seated on the floor.

"Her Ladyship the Royal Housekeeper, Madame de Layron, is coming," he shouted, and darted out guffawing with laughter.

"Saint Apostle, my holy patron," moaned the distressed astrologer, painfully rising from the floor, "surely she is coming for the horoscope."

"Tell her it is not ready."

"I dare not. They might think me a fraud. And the horoscope is ready, has been ready these many days, only . . ."

He broke off for Madame de Layron swept into the room. She was rotund and stately. Her face said plainly that it was not pleasure but an order that had brought her here. Without conviction she sat upon the edge of a stool they advanced for her and quickly glanced over her shoulder to see whether the maid in waiting, Sabina, stood behind her. Her inquisitive eyes circled the room.

"What is that?" she inquired, pointing to Matteo's findings.

"An ancient script, unknown to us, dug up from the ground."

"What about?"

"That we don't know, for we have no knowledge of the letters."

"Pagan, perhaps?"

"No doubt," admitted the astrologer.

"Throw it out in that case!" she exclaimed. "Do not keep it in the house! Evil may be hiding·in it . . . No telling . . . It may be a Devil's incantation!"

"We shall take it out at once. Do not worry, Madame. Now please tell us to what we owe the honor of your visit?"

But the lady had not yet finished her inspection. "It seems," she announced, "that other astrologers keep all sorts of stuffed beasts, owls, bats and bottles with powders."

"The alchemists, Madame, not astrologers. An astrologer only gazes at the stars for which these instruments suffice . . ."

"It's all one to me," she admitted haughtily, "astrologers, alchemists, medicos and rat catchers. Much wind, little profit . . . Any crone knows more than they do . . . I came here because her Royal Highness wants to visit His Majesty's kinswoman, the Countess of Champagne today, and as you belong to her Court she has sent me to ask you whether she will not disturb her in her prayers at this hour of the day."

Messer Pochard opened his eyes so wide that they appeared as round as an owl's.

"Her Royal Highness . . . ? Go out visiting . . . in this weather?" The housekeeper shrugged her shoulders.

"Just what I said . . . In this gale! And for the first time, too! For Her Majesty does not know the Countess of Champagne yet . . . I tried to persuade her . . . But she would not listen. Such obstinacy happens in her condition when a craving comes . . . She says she wants the Countess to use her kinswoman's influence upon the King so he will go to Rome and apply for the captaincy . . ."

The astrologer continued to stare. The housekeeper, loquacious by nature, continued:

"I do not wonder the King prefers to wait for the confinement . . . In two or three weeks Her Majesty's time will come. It's better when the husband is home at such times . . . But the Queen will not have it. . . . She has heard that the King holds his kinswoman in great esteem. And it seems the Countess has vowed she would not come to the castle before she accomplishes her pilgrimage. So the Queen wants to go to her, herself . . ."

By now, the astrologer had had time to recover.

"She cannot go," he decreed sternly, "I am just completing the Queen's horoscope . . . It shows clearly that Her Majesty should not at this time either leave the castle or make new acquaintances . . ."

"Why?" the housekeeper asked, visibly distressed.

"Saturn combined with Mercury creates aspects unfavorable to travel. Likewise they command that she beware of strange faces, be they as venerable as that of the King's cousin, the Honorable Countess of Champagne."

"Thanks for the forewarning . . . I shall at once tell Her Majesty. . . . I told her right away she should not set out in this gale . . . And throw away those horrors!" With her foot she pointed to the shards and left, her dress rustling.

The astrologer heaved a deep sigh. "You don't suppose the Queen will go, do you, Matteo?"

He did not hide from Matteo what to all who had arrived from

Troyes had long since ceased to be a secret. Often in their idle moments they discussed and pondered those feminine problems. On such occasion they exchanged many remarks fraught with great dislike for women and a complete lack of knowledge in the matter, typical of men of learning.

Matteo scratched his head. "How am I to know? If she is that stubborn, she might go."

"In this gale? In a minute it will start pouring. Well, I guess I'll go to forewarn the Countess, anyway."

The gale blew directly from the sea. In the West black, heavy clouds wallowed in the sky, glittering with lightning. There was no sound of thunder, for the roar of the sea drowned everything. Clouds of gritty dust rushed along the road. Disregarding the oncoming storm King Jean had arrived at the hospitium to visit his kinswoman. He did so openly once a week. He had come to apologize to the noble pilgrim for the delay in her journey. It was long since he had sent a message to the Sultan but the messenger had not returned yet . . . No one knew what had delayed him . . .

Dressed in a sumptuous stiff robe, her head surmounted by a high coif, Blanche sat in a carved armchair. Jean in a similar chair faced her. By the door stood the host of the hospitium in an attitude of profound respect. Willfried hovered behind the chair of his master, Genevieve behind that of her mistress. The King and the Countess exchanged measured, ceremonious remarks. Outside the gale roared as though a cavalcade was tearing by.

"Will your Majesty permit me to leave?" the host of the hospitium inquired after a while. "I must see that the windows upstairs are properly closed or else the wind will tear off the shutters."

His Majesty gave him leave. Immediately Willfried and Genevieve vanished likewise. They found it dull to wait at the door and decided to withdraw to a cubby hole. They exchanged glances filled with curiosity, for they hardly knew each other, though the whole world looked upon them as lovers. It was they who supposedly stole out of the house at night and roamed the fields till dawn. Genevieve was a public sinner, Willfried a seducer. Back in their own country he would have been long time driven out and she brought to pillory. Here, however, no one paid much attention to such things.

"And a lucky thing, too," remarked Willfried yawning.

But Genevieve shook her head angrily. "They do not care because they are half-heathens, but how they wag their tongues! Rumor flies with the wind like an evil seed. It will reach back home yet and if it does my father will surely kill me!"

"Not kill . . ." protested Willfried.

"Yes, kill," she insisted, "what do you think? Father is a nobleman, high-born . . ."

He cast her a keen glance. True, she did look like a noblewoman, comely, tall, black eyed. "My own is likewise high-born and yet I won't worry."

"Why should you worry?" she cried angrily. "It's upon the girl shame and dishonor falls, not upon the man."

He stretched out a conciliatory hand. "Don't you think that as long as they will talk, it might be just as well to give them good cause?"

Genevieve did not reply.

Left alone Jean and Blanche continued for a while to sit in their big, carved armchairs. Soon, however, they moved to the alcove. There was not much room here as the big bed filled most of the space. A soft, heavy curtain separated it from the room. Jean stretched out on the bed. Blanche took off her high coif, leaving nothing but a lace caul which made her look young and beguiling.

"I am sending a missive tomorrow to the Holy Father," said Jean when she came to rest by his side.

"Tomorrow . . . It means that very soon . . ."

". . . our happiness will come to an end."

"I will go with you to war."

He laughed while he caressed her shoulders. "That's impossible. You know it yourself!"

"But why shouldn't I? There were women Crusaders!"

"That was when they fought for Jerusalem. It was a great honor to enter the Holy City. This war will be altogether different. Far away . . . in Egypt . . ."

"But you will be still fighting for the same cause."

"In a way, yes. But differently. . . . Those other expeditions were more like armed pilgrimages. This time it will be a deliberate, military campaign . . ."

"Then what am I to do with myself?" she whispered in a disappointed voice.

"Wait. If God allows me to reconquer Jerusalem the Holy Father will not refuse me a divorce."

"But the war may last several years!"

He made no denial. She continued with growing vehemence. "Several years—when I can hardly stand another day! It chokes me, sickens me! I can't go on living this way! Break clear! You must choose. Either she or I . . ."

"I have chosen long ago," he argued gently. "I never see her any more . . . And truly, I cannot see in what way she hinders you!"

"In what way? Because I have to sit here like a servant, at the mercy of my own maid! Because I have to slip out like a wench, because I see you on the sly . . ."

"In Troyes it was even worse . . ."

"In Troyes I could stand it, and today I will not."

"Hush! I think someone has come in."

"No. It must be the knocking of the wind. Genevieve would not come unless I called, nor would she let anybody in . . . I won't take it . . . It stifles me . . . Look what I carry here in my bosom . . . I never part with it . . . No, it's not a scapulary. It's herbs, from Margot. Do you remember the witch Margot? I went to her before I left. She gave me that. I can get rid of whomever I please . . ."

"Hush! Hush!" he whispered horrified. "Have you no fear of God?"

"God?" she repeated vehemently. "What difference does one more sin make? I don't care whether I am damned if only at last I could be myself. Be it for one day!"

She drew close to him, her feverish face as beautiful as ever. Outside the storm continued to rumble and it still seemed to him someone was walking, then stopping, and listening to their conversation. Besides, Blanche's words terrified him. So she had gone to Margot to get poison! How much she must love him to dare such a thing? But this fleeting gratification of his masculine vanity only flickered through his mind and was replaced by horror. He drew away.

"No, anything else but not that. Don't ever say such things again. Neither you nor I is a murderer. God forbid! I would gladly cast off both kingdom and wedlock, and take you for my own against the whole world were it not for the approaching war . . . If I were to leave they might call me a coward, say that I fled from battle. I will sacrifice anything for you but not my honor. You would not want it yourself to have it said of me . . . When the war ends we shall leave together . . ."

"I cannot wait for the end of a war which has not yet begun!"

"Someone has moved the door," he whispered with renewed apprehension.

"You are hearing things. All doors bang in this wind. Anyway, go and see."

Jean slid from the bed and drew the curtain a little.

"There is no one there," he announced relieved.

Blanche put both of her hands under her head. "That's exactly why I cannot wait any longer!" she exclaimed. "I cannot stand it! Always atremble lest someone come in . . . Spring up because the door has creaked . . . Hide like a rabbit . . . take servants into our confidence . . ."

He did not reply. It irked him too! But what else could they do? How could it be helped? For a long while they lay in silence.

"I must go," he said at last, lowering his feet to the floor.

"Don't go away. No one will be surprised if you wait here till the storm subsides. Don't you hear how it pours?"

"The rain will not stop soon. It will last till morning."

"But we must decide something," she cried suddenly in despair.

"What is there to decide? There is no way out!"

With a gesture of finality he rose and left the alcove. Heaving a sigh Blanche got up and began to arrange the elaborate scaffold upon which her coif rested. There was a sound of voices in the hall. Jean opened the door to call Willfried and to his surprise beheld Messer Jacob Pochard crouched and dripping with water.

"What brought you here in this rain, Messer Jacob?"

"The downpour met me on my way, Sire. I wanted to forewarn Her Ladyship that Her Majesty the Queen intends to call on her but I came too late. So I am only waiting to get dry and will be starting on my way back presently."

"Her Majesty intends to come here?" repeated Jean dumbfounded.

It was the astrologer's turn to show surprise.

"Has she not been here but a minute ago? I just met her litter already on its way back!"

"There was no one here!" shouted Jean, his voice trembling a little. "Willfried! Did anyone come?"

Flushed and confused the squire emerged from the shadow. "I . . . I don't know . . ." he mumbled.

"Did you stand here all the while?"

"No," confessed the lad, almost in tears.

Jean was about to explode but he checked himself. He turned to the astrologer.

"Why did Her Majesty intend to come here?"

"Her Majesty the Queen meant to ask Her Ladyship to use her influence upon Your Majesty so you might hasten to take command of the Crusade!"

"And she was here?"

"I saw her litter . . . Anyway, we can ask the host."

"No," shouted Jean. "Don't ask anyone."

He paced the room shaken to the core. . . . Marie had been here! Had she entered the room? Had she heard their conversation? She could not have heard, not in that roaring gale! So she was here; he had been right. She had slipped in as she always did, noiseless like a mouse, just as she had once slipped into his chamber . . . Helpless and shy she could do things no other woman would ever dare to do . . . She was here . . . And she had left without a word. Why? What had she heard?

Wrapped in her high, white coif, Blanche followed him with her eyes. A wicked smile hovered on her lips. She did not seem perturbed. The wretched Willfried cowered at the door like a whipped dog. In the vestibule the astrologer was wringing out his cloak. Big drops of dirty water dripped to the floor. Outside the storm seemed to subside. Jean continued to pace the room. He knew he ought to return but could not find the courage. A clatter of hoofs resounded under the portico; a messenger from the palace.

"Where is His Majesty?"

"I am here."

"The Mistress of the Household begs you to hasten, Sire. Her Majesty is in childbed!"

"Good Lord!" Jean exclaimed. Willfried was already leading his horse around. The King sprang into the saddle as though he were a youth and plunged into the night. Puddles splashed under his mount's hoofs. Willfried caught the mantle his master had left behind and tore after him. The host of the hospitium clambered down the stairs and stood by the door, dumbfounded and aghast. The Queen in childbed? Surely this was premature . . . Good Lord have mercy upon her! And to think that she was here less than an hour ago. . . .

The astrologer was busy smoothing out his wet cloak. Blanche stood still, her head lifted defiantly while she listened to the vanishing sound of hoofs. She turned to Messer Jacob.

"What do the stars say about her?" she asked imperiously.

"The present aspects of stars are unfavorable to women in general," replied the savant.

She cast him a scornful glance.

The child, a tiny girl, Isabelle, was so weak that she had been baptized at once, for no one thought she would live for more than a few hours. Against all expectations, however, once she was put to the breast of a buxom nurse she seemed to improve. Perhaps after all it would be possible to keep her alive. The Queen, however, was sinking fast. She had fallen prey to the wicked fever which consumed women in childbed upon whom someone had cast an evil spell. It was in vain Bishop Jacob de Vitry in person brought Holy relics and placed them upon the bosom of the Queen. Uninterrupted services were held in all churches and a swarm of leeches surrounded her bed. The prejudices which the Latins once had against Greek and Armenian physicians had vanished long ago and Jean summoned everyone known throughout the country. He himself did not for a moment leave his wife's bedside. He watched over her as did the old Ibelin of Beyrouth, the Mistress of the Household and the old nurse, Eudoxia. His distress was absolutely genuine. He felt guilty, horribly, shamefully guilty. In addition uncertainty gnawed at his heart. Had his wife been in the chamber that day? And how long had she remained there? He could not ask anyone, for he would thus betray that he had lain with Blanche in the alcove and had not been in the chamber. Tensely he scanned the wax-like face of the sick girl, whose sharpened features revealed the approaching end, and vainly tried to penetrate their secret. She seemed conscious but did not look at anyone. Her small face more than ever resembled the sad face of a white ermine. Only an ermine would bite viciously and Marie never knew how to bite. She was going away in silence, just as she had lived, not sharing her thoughts with anyone.

Thibault, sincerely distressed, called every day to inquire on behalf of his mother after the Queen's health, and Jean, hearing how in a voice strangled with tears, Madame de Layron replied that the Queen was worse than yesterday, shivered at the thought of how Blanche would rejoice at the news. From himself he sent no message, no word to the hospitium. He was unable to. He begged the leeches to apply all their learning. He promised them all he possessed if only they would save the Queen. But the leeches spread their hands in a gesture of hopelessness. What could they do when Her Majesty would take neither medicine nor food? This was true. Marie with revulsion (or was it fear?) looked away from anything handed to her, compressing her lips in silent but stubborn refusal. It was in vain that Jean, leaning over her, begged with belated tenderness that she drink a few drops of a strength giving cordial. She closed her eyes and mouth, refusing by a scarcely perceptible motion of her head. Finally the leeches decreed that the uterus had risen and pressed upon the stomach which in turn pressed against the lungs and throat and made swallowing impossible. They still tried to rub her with hyssop, famous for its miraculous effects, and Madame de Layron had put under her pillow the stone called agate, a talisman with which the eagle protects its nest from snakes, and which she had somehow procured after infinite pains. But even that did not help.

Stifling her sobs, the old nurse Eudoxia advanced to the bed, holding a tumbler with a potion.

"Do drink this, at least, my dove . . . Try it, my sweet little bird . . . This potion always helps . . . You think it's hot? No, it's not hot, fear not!"

As though to convince her patient she took a sip of the brew herself and held out the tumbler pleadingly. Marie watched her attentively. Then she opened her dry, parched lips and took a few swallows almost with avidity. Jean felt a stab at his heart; she had drunk the potion because the nurse had tasted it first. Could it be that she refused food and medicaments because she feared to be poisoned? Poisoned? In that case she had not only been in the room but must have heard all their conversation! And she was afraid . . . She probably recalled the words of the Bishop who said that for people here it was a trifle to poison a wife in order to marry a mistress. And she was afraid! That poor, dying child feared poison from her husband! From him . . . ! The realization hit him like a blow. He staggered. Oblivious of the others he fell to his knees.

"Marie," he called, "I swear upon the salvation of my soul, I never meant you ill!"

Did she hear him? Did she understand? Did she believe? He never learned. For she did not open her eyes again and did not say a word. That very night she died.

As soon as the magnificent funeral which lasted several days was over, Jean de Brienne summoned the Council and solemnly resigned the crown. He asked only to be allowed to participate in the coming war. But the Council would not consent to the abdication. With unwonted unanimity the Barons and the masters of knightly orders insisted that the King remain as Regent ruling on behalf of the tiny princess Isabelle.

"We trust you, Sire," said the old Ibelin of Beyrouth. "We desire no other master. God has taken unto himself Our Mistress." His voice broke—he could not recover from the death of his ex-charge. "His will is sacred. But you, Sire, must remain. Who should act as regent if not the father? If you should desire to enter into new wedlock we shall not oppose you as long as the marriage be concluded with our consent and in no way impeaches the right of Princess Isabelle. . . ."

Thus spoke Ibelin of Beyrouth. Others, Bishop de Vitry, Raoul of Tiberia, Dzierzek of Poland, Milon de Plancy and the rest joined in. After a moment of hesitation, Jean consented. But he moved out of the royal chamber, insisting that, as Regent, he had no right to sleep there. People wondered at those exaggerated scruples. He knew, however, that in that room he would never be able to rest. He would be forever seeing Marie lifting the curtain, timidly entering the room, standing by his bed just as he saw her the last time before she was taken ill. She would stand there, with that sad little face of hers and ask him: "Why did you do this to me?"

So Jean remained. He took the Regent's oath to reign on behalf of a nestling not bigger than a knight's fist, mewing helplessly in its swaddles and referred to solemnly as Princess Isabelle.

"Her mother looked exactly like that when I took over the Regency," old Ibelin would say, heaving a sigh, "and yet she grew to womanhood."

Jean plunged feverishly into the work he had neglected for months. Before the reply from Rome arrived, everything must be ready for the campaign. He sent envoys to the young Duke of Tripoli, Raymond, and haggled with Genoans over the charter of vessels. The sly tradesmen made exorbitant demands. Even Greeks used to be more honest than that! But the Greeks' galleys were no more. Indeed it was strange to think that there was no longer any Basileus nor his magnificent Court, no fleet, no complicated ceremonies nor haughty officials bearing strange weird Greek names. The present Emperor of the Latin Byzantium, a countryman, even a kinsman of Jean's, could not help much even if he were to try. He had no power whatsoever. A servant of the Venetians, that was all he was. Venetians ran everything. And the Greek population hated the Latins with such bitter hatred that even in daylight it was dangerous to show oneself unarmed in the city "protected by God."

It was no use to expect assistance from these quarters; nothing remained but to accept the shameless demands of the Genoans.

Those problems absorbed de Brienne completely when one day Thibault came to see him on behalf of his mother. The youth was so insignificant and useless that it was easy to forget his existence and Jean was almost surprised to see him.

"Mother would have you come and see her, Uncle . . ."

Blanche! Indeed, he had not forgotten her. She had been incessantly on his mind, though they had not seen each other since the funeral and had not exchanged a word since that other memorable evening. Yet it seemed to him that by visiting her now he would be doing a new wrong to his dead wife; a wrong not less than the previous one. Nevertheless at her express bidding, he went.

Upon his arrival he was aghast at the change he found in Blanche's face. She looked ten years older.

"I thought I would never see you again," she whispered when he entered.

These were the very words with which she had greeted him three months before. The memory of that moment and of that joy flashed through his mind. They held each other in a long, passionate embrace.

"I thought you no longer loved me. I thought they had forced you to swear you would never see me again."

"I would never consent to take such an oath," he replied. "Besides no one asked me to . . . nobody knows . . . Marie did not tell a soul . . . I could marry when the mourning is over and if you were free . . ."

"Thank God for that," she sighed relieved.

But Jean's face was still gloomy. "The others don't know, but there is an obstacle within me, Blanche. I have not stopped loving you and never will, and yet I can't think of anything now, not even of you . . .

Not till I forget . . . She thought I wanted to poison her. . . . Did you
know that?"

"Have a Mass said for her soul."

He laughed bitterly. "Hers? My own, you mean. I need it more than
she does. She who committed no sin . . ."

"Neither did you! You would not . . . remember?"

"I have let you speak of it . . . Don't remind me . . . For the Lord's
sake, don't. And do not hold it against me that I shall not visit you
now . . . for a time . . ." He broke off, unable to express the too
complex feelings which he himself was unable to understand.

Blanche stared at him, her eyes wide with horror. "But you cannot
abandon me!" she moaned. "Remember, it was you who called me! It
was at your summons I came here."

It was true. She had scored. In the attempt to justify himself, so
common to all men, Jean had forgotten it, unconsciously had looked
upon her as the guilty one, the temptress. But it was he who had called
her. It was he who sent William Divini to bring her. He himself. . . .

His heart felt even heavier than before. "I shall not abandon you,
Blanche, nor will I ever cease loving you, but leave me alone for a while
. . . give me time to forget . . ."

"Do as you like," she said dejectedly. "Find out whether I could not
really go to Jerusalem? At least I would accomplish the pilgrimage . . ."

"I will do my best to arrange it for you!" he exclaimed with spirit.
"You shall go . . . In the meantime I will recover. . . . On your return,
having fulfilled the pretended vow, nothing will prevent you from
taking abode in the castle . . . You can remain there while I go to
war. . . . Maybe things will righten themselves. . . ."

"Let us hope so," she whispered dully.

They soon parted. But even now the projected pilgrimage was to
come to naught. In the palace the Barons already awaited Jean; letters
from Rome had arrived.

Impatiently, without pausing to divest himself of his mantle, de
Brienne broke the seals, unfolded the parchment. There were two
letters, one from the Holy Father. Jean scanned it hastily. The blood
rushed to his head. Without a word he handed the letter to Ibelin.

"God help the Holy Sepulchre," Ibelin exclaimed after he had read it.
And he repeated the contents aloud: "The Holy Father, Honorius,

advises his beloved son, Jean de Brienne, that to lead and command the Fifth Crusade he has appointed by the will of the Holy Ghost and after long prayers at the Apostle's Grave, Cardinal Pelagius of Albano . . ."

The second letter was from Cardinal Pelagius himself. In his capacity of commander in chief he summoned the King of Jerusalem and his troops to take up their posts under his command. In three weeks the Crusaders' fleet would be in Cyprus. The knighthood of Jerusalem was to await it there, under penalty of excommunication.

Silence fell over the room.

"He will not frighten us," wrathfully exclaimed Herman von Salza, Master of the Teutonic Order. "Let them anathematize! If they do, they will soon withdraw it themselves! What does a Cardinal know of the science of warfare? How can he lead a campaign?"

"For a monk, Sir, you don't seem particularly submissive to the will of the Holy See."

"We are humble servants of Christ, Our Lord, but we will not take orders from a priest!"

"My advice would be to pretend obedience," suggested Gerin de Montaigne, Master of Hospitallers. "The Cardinal's rule is sure to be feeble. It will be easy to supersede it and direct everything according to our lights."

Jean shook his head in denial. He had once met Pelagius at Pope Innocent's court and now he recalled that tall figure, drenched in crimson, the hard, bird-like eyes, the rash, offensive words. No, the rule of that man may be ill-advised and inept, but never feeble. He would not easily surrender it to anyone.

"Who brought the letters?" he inquired in a dull voice.

"De Layron of Cesarea. He will be here presently, he has only gone to change his garments."

Indeed, almost at once de Layron entered the room. He bowed low to the King and before being asked, began to expound his griefs. "Your letter arrived too late, Sire. They waited more than three months. The Holy Father would not have anyone but you. Every other day he sent secretaries to inquire whether I had not heard from Acre. At last, as the men threatened to disband, he appointed the Cardinal of Albano and gave him his blessing. Only then . . ."

He stopped, for Jean rose without a word and left the room. De

Layron stared after him, perplexed. "Could it be I offended him?" he asked.

"No, it is not that. He simply grieves at learning the truth. For we, likewise, kept telling him, reminding him. Even the late Queen pressed him. But he would do nothing . . . true cunctator that he is! A brave knight but a cunctator!"

"Maybe it was not cunctation alone that held him back," suggested von Salza with a subtle smile. But no one paid heed to his insinuations.

# 5.

# At the Gates of Damietta

SIR DZIERŻEK SAT ON THE BANK OF THE NILE IN THE VAIN HOPE OF FINDING some coolness amidst the thick growth of papyri. With his sleeves he wiped the perspiration from his brow, chased away swarms of flies, panted and complained: "This God-forsaken, accursed country!"

"No country is that," corrected Francis de Assisi who sat by his side. "All lands are equally in the hands and might of Our Lord."

"I wager the Saviour has given this one to the keeping of the Devil . . . In the Holy Land, too, it's hot at times, but nothing like this. It seems as though the wind blew straight from the oven. Flies pester the life out of one . . . Not to mention. . . . Out with you, adder!" he shouted, as a small crocodile climbed out of the water and made straight for them. The knight flung his spear at the beast; the lizard promptly hid underneath the bank.

"He did you no wrong," remarked Francis aggrieved.

"It turns my stomach to look at those beasts. To be sure, this one was small, but I myself have seen beasts bigger than a cow that will swallow a man as easily as a pike swallows a bleak. And I've been told by Scholasticus, the secretary of the Legate, that a few days' trip down south there are even more of them. Often it seems they will lift their backs and turn over a boat so they may devour the crew. That's how cunning they are! Only if perchance they swallow a virgin they weep in grief and come out on shore groaning . . . Then a body can kill them . . . So at least, Scholasticus says. . . ."

"Incredible!" Francis was amazed. "How does Scholasticus know?"

"That I don't know. Maybe from books, maybe he heard it from Copts. It seems that in this Nile there lives an animal called a river horse or a Nile horse, larger than an elephant, all swollen with jaws wide as a door . . ."

"Truly, it's a wonder what a variety of creatures Our Lord has wrought. So many lands, each with its own different nature . . ."

Francis looked around, his eyes filled with wonder. Nearby grew a cluster of tall palms. A strong wind blew in gusts from the west; it carried desert dust, tore at the plumes of leaves, rustled among papyri. The dome of the sky was turbid and faded from the heat. A ruddy haze covered the horizon. Hawks like black dots hung still in the air as though they had soared beyond the reach of the gale and attained perfect, motionless silence. Behind Francis' back the sea lay like a blue-gray wall; to the south, far away, small triangles of pyramids shone white, like distant sails. None of the Latins had seen them close so far and they wondered at those mountains so unlike any others.

Not far from Francis and Dzierzek an Egyptian peasant, a fellah, was turning a big wooden wheel equipped with dippers. The wheel rolled heavily, creaked. The dippers plunged into the river and rose in the air, spilling and splashing half of their contents to no good purpose and pouring the rest in a canal dug above the river level. The man had been working thus since dawn, heedless of the heat. Nor was he alone. Every hundred steps or so rose similar wheels turned by weary, grey men. Those patient toilers seemed indifferent to heat, to everything in the world. Regardless of war or peace they tended their perennial chores that reached back to Moses' times, as invariable as the song of crickets and the twitter of swallows. Thousands of years of Pharaoh's rule, then the Roman, Greeks and Moslems had swept and tumbled over their heads; none had brought the slightest change in their wretched existence. That existence could not grow worse, for it reached the limits of squalor; it likewise could not be more diligent. And no one cared to make it any better. Probably they did not care themselves. A great army of men, a sight hitherto unseen on the shores of the Nile, had come from foreign vessels, filled the estuary of the Delta, and still the fellah as always turned the water wheels; still his wife washed their rags in the river, trampling them rhythmically, one step forward one step back. They perished under the foot of war like trampled grass whenever they found themselves in its path. Driven by whips they dug trenches, built bulwarks, raised palisades without asking in whose defense they were to be used. And, as they had done for a thousand years and more, they turned heavy waterwheels.

Francis looked at them with friendliness and commiseration. Indeed in his drab cloak, small, slight as he was, his head wrapped in cloth, he even resembled a fellah or one of the dervishes more than his armored and proud fellow Crusaders. Perhaps for that reason he was not popular among them. The fact that Dzierzek entered into conversation with him only proved how bored the knight was. For, like everybody else in the camp, he considered Francis a complete fool who by some obscure reason enjoyed the unjustified confidence of the Holy See.

"A devilish country," he insisted again. "No trace of sand anywhere around, yet my nose and throat are full of it. I can hardly breathe. Or that flood last month! Not a cloud, no rain, and the river swells, swells! It flooded the whole valley. . . . Then, for no good reason, just as it swelled so it began to retreat. . . . What else? Could it be sorcery? A devil's trick, I tell you! Oh, if a body could only go home!"

"Back to the Holy Land? I, too, crave to go there."

"No doubt it's in the Holy Land I shall end my sinful days, for I've pledged myself to remain in the Lord's service. . . . But right now it was my native land I had in mind. . . . Thirty years have gone since I left it . . ."

"And what is it called?"

"Poland."

"I have never heard of it!"

"You don't say! It is not as though Poland were not known to the wide world. A big country it is, rich, populous . . . Forests, fields, pastures. . . . It has no fierce mountains as other countries have nor is it ever too hot there. . . . A mild land . . . Rivers flow through plains . . . Along the river, birds . . . a multitude of birds . . . People till the soil, work hard . . . They do not go out to conquer and plunder as others do, not they . . . An honest people . . ."

"And do they believe in Christ?"

"How else? We are Christians, have been for ages . . . Good Christians, too. Open-handed with church and convents. A peaceful country . . . Once the knights return from war, they sow and tend their husbandry in person, just as farmers do . . . They do not sit idle. In all the waters fish abounds . . . And beehives up on the trees. . . . Bees are held in high esteem as though they had a human soul . . . For that matter any beast useful to man is made much of. . . ."

"I like this country of yours! Where does it lie? How does a body go there?"

"From Italy the way leads across Germany. From here, through Hungary."

"My brethren demur at going to Germany, where on several occasions they met with drubbings. They will rejoice when I tell them now that once they've soothed the Germans they may continue on their way to Poland . . ."

"Let them come. In my country surely none will drub them . . ." He fell silent. With a palm leaf he tried to drive the flies away.

"To be sure," he remarked, "it is thirty years since I saw it last. Still I reckon nothing has changed much. Things do not change easily in my country. Life goes on as of old. I fain would return there. . . ."

"Of course. We may meet with sister Death anywhere, but surely, it is more pleasant to die among one's own . . ."

"No telling but that every man of us shall die here. It is three months since we stand thus without gaining as much as an inch. Luckily the Cardinal's been taken ill. May he ail long!"

Francis jumped up indignantly. "This is sinful talk, Sir. How can you wish sickness upon anyone?"

"Sin or no sin. I still wish him not only sickness but eternal glory to boot. There is none in the camp who would think otherwise. Faith, it's only as long as the man is sick that we have a chance of success. Don't you remember how it was at first? Nothing but bickering, arguments, offenses. . . . Only now, since our King has taken everything in hand, matters are beginning to go right. . . ."

"One should not judge anyone, much less wish. him ill," Francis firmly insisted. He glanced around, looking for an excuse to interrupt the conversation. His eyes fell upon the man who turned the water-wheel.

"He needs help," he exclaimed, and started straight for the man. By signs he explained he wished to take the other's place. The fellah's black, bird-like, frightened eyes stared at him in surprise. What did this stranger want of him? He carried neither sword nor stick so there was no need to flee. Judging by his faded and cheap robe he could not be rich. What? He wanted to work? Let him work. Wiping the perspiration from his brow with his forearm the fellah drew a little aside. Francis stepped by him and together they began to turn the heavy wheel.

Sir Dzierzek observed these doings from a distance with scandalized pity. He shrugged his shoulders and getting to his feet, walked over to where his horses stood. His servant held them in readiness in the scanty shade of the palms. The knight mounted his bay and started at a slow pace along the river bank. Although it was well past noon the heat had not abated. The wind was growing stronger, the air increasingly stifling. The faces of both master and servant dripped with perspiration. The horses lowered their heads and stepped gingerly, groaning and snorting.

"Is a storm coming or what?" wondered the knight.

"Must be a storm," agreed the lad.

They were making for the camp whence came the rhythmic knocking of axes. The Crusaders were constructing another, the fifth, floating seige tower which was to be used to capture the bastion that guarded the Nile and the approaches of Damietta. The bastion stood on an inlet which the Arabs called Bur-al-Silsil. It had once been the site of an Egyptian temple of the cat-headed goddess, Basta. All that remained of it were two pillars watched over by statues with the heads of a cat and a jackal. Upon the ruins of the temple the Arabs had built a bastion with powerful bridgeheads. From those bridgeheads massive iron chains extended across both arms of the river, barring the way to all vessels. It was impossible to break the chains and proceed upstream to the walls of the city without first taking the bastion. That was why the Moslems guarded it like the apple of their eyes.

For three months now, despite constantly renewed efforts, the Crusaders had made no progress. It was in vain they anchored galleys and built upon them great wooden towers with a drawbridge jutting at the top; it was in vain they sailed those rams close to the islet. Each time the Moslems had succeeded in setting the wooden structures on fire, forcing the assailants to retreat. Behind the safe barrier of chains stood the Sultan's flotilla, and still farther, on the left bank of the Nile, the Sultan Malik al-Kamil and his army lay in wait. The Sultan had a large force with him, including the best regiments of Mamelukes called Dagmarits and Boharits, the sons of valor and the sons of lions. They were commanded by the Turk, Bibar.

Impervious to the heat and storm the King of Jerusalem, Jean de Brienne, his neck protected from the sun by a white cloth falling from under his helmet, without his cuirass, his jerkin open at the neck, personally surveyed the structure of a new gigantic ram. It was bigger than any of the previous ones, a veritable floating castle, five hundred yards in circumference. The tower, completely covered with iron shells and hides which were to protect it from fire, surrounded with a palisade and surmounted by a roof, stood upon a platform which in turn rested on four of the largest galleys. Four masts already with sails rose from the platform's corners. From the front protruded a heavy iron spur which was to batter the bastion's gates. In the tower and inside the palisade there was room for three hundred men.

Jean had grown dark and gaunt; nevertheless he felt much better than he had felt in Acre. Soon after the troops arrived in Egypt the Cardinal had been taken ill, and of necessity the command fell to the King of Jerusalem. He made good use of it and met with no protest. War had brought him back to life. He had neither time nor desire to reflect what would happen next, what turn things would take once the Legate recovered, nor what Blanche, who awaited him aboard her galley, might be thinking of.

For the Countess of Champagne had also come to Egypt, presumably because she would not part with her son. In vain Jean had tried to persuade her to remain in Acre where in the absence of the King old Ibelin was in charge, and to await him there in peace. She would not hear of it. She had come to loath Acre and the hospitium. As the memories of that other, blissful spring grew more remote, her dislike of the places which had witnessed her all-too-short happiness became deeper. Nothing could make her stay in Acre alone, without Jean! To return home would be even worse. And so she came here and for the last four months had not left the deck, hardly spoke to anyone, indifferent to all that was not Jean. And Jean never came any more. The war, the capture of Damietta, absorbed him completely.

But was it only war? Was it only because of his eagerness to fight that they were now like two strangers and he no longer needed nor sought her? No! Blanche had no illusions. It was the shadow of the dead woman who stood between them. Even though Margot's herb, never used, still remained hidden in her bosom, Marie was avenging herself.

"We have killed an orphan," Jean had said once while still in Acre. "A poor orphan, and we have killed her. . . ." Blanche had at the time vehemently denied the charge. She still looked upon Marie as the woman who had a claim upon Jean, her own Jean. That woman had vanished from life through no fault of theirs. Why should they grieve?

But Jean was not to be persuaded, until at last his incomprehensible scruples began to irritate her. That was perhaps the reason why he had ceased visiting her. He had a good, plausible excuse: while war was in progress there was no time for love.

Yet Blanche continued to wait idly, hopelessly, doggedly. Impatiently she awaited Thibault who, still blissfully unaware of what went on, every day brought his mother news of her lover.

Moored right in front of the Countess' galley stood the huge, magnificent galley of the Legate. Over her bow, covered with crimson cloth, flew the Papal flag. On the deck, shaded by sails, the supreme commander of the Crusade lay on a sumptuous bed, so emaciated he appeared a mere ghost. Malaria, a frequent visitor to the marshy lowlands of the delta, had sapped his magnificent physique. The pallor of his sharp face stood out in painful contrast to the background of the red coverlet thrown over the bed. Only his black, close-set eyes remained as keen and full of life as ever. They scurried to and fro in their perpetual thirst for news. Weak and ailing though he was the Cardinal wanted to know all that went on, insisted on being told everything. He continued to consider himself the responsible leader of the campaign. He was convinced that his illness was the worst misfortune which could have befallen the Crusade.

If only he were well Bur-al-Silsil would have been taken long ago; by now Damietta would be encircled and about to surrender . . . If only he were well!

"The work on the big ram is progressing briskly," his chaplain, brother Philip, tried to console him.

"Hold your peace, brother, rather than talk of things you know nothing about. Brisk, indeed! It's four weeks since they loiter over it and you call it brisk!"

"It is a mighty big engine," muttered the monk.

"Even if it were the biggest the world has ever seen, were I only there it would have been ready a fortnight ago. Mark my word. Well I know how they go about it. I can well imagine. Don't I know those lords? Half the time they waste in talking and the other half in arguments. I've seen it before . . ."

"Truly, Your Grace, one never hears of any dissensions any more . . . It's a wonder, indeed. . . . Everybody's doing his best, willingly obeying the King of Jerusalem. . . ."

The Legate closed his eyes to signify the conversation was ended. He could not abide to have Jean de Brienne praised in his presence. The chaplain drew aside. After a while the sick man asked again.

"Has the letter to the Holy Father I dictated yesterday been sent yet?"

"I don't know, Your Grace . . . It was Messer Scholasticus who . . ."

"Call him . . . Where is he?"

"I don't know, Your Grace. He left before noon with Messer Pochard and the scholar Pesaro to see some old Egyptian stones!"

"They have altogether lost their wits over those stones! What good can those heathen relics do?"

"That's just what I told them, Your Grace. What will they have with that heathen filth with which the land is simply littered."

"Let Scholasticus come to me as soon as he returns. And you, brother Philip, run to the camp and find out when the ram will be ready at last. Ask the men, mind you, the carpenters, not the knights. Hear that wind! Just what we need . . . We could use the sails . . . We may have to wait for weeks for another wind like that one . . . Surely they can't pull such an engine upstream on oars alone. . . ."

"No, indeed not, Your Grace."

"They have wasted such wind! They did not finish in time. And all because I am not there. Oh, Lord, grant me health! Not for myself but for Thy glory! Make haste, brother Philip!"


The furious gusts of desert wind were indeed unusually propitious to the Crusaders, and Jean de Brienne, contrary to the Cardinal's expectations, was fully aware of it. As he stood on the bank of the river he kept glancing in turn at the ram and at the river swollen by short waves running against the current. The water beat hurriedly at the bottom of the craft as though prompting to action. And the ram was almost ready. Only the stairs to the tower were still missing, but stairs could be easily replaced with ropes or ladders.

With sudden resolve he turned to de Layron who stood by his side. "Sound the bugles," he said. "All at their posts! In the name of God we shall charge!"

De Layron ran as fast as he could. A moment later bugles began to blare. Knights and squires sprang to their feet, rubbing eyes smarting from dust. What? Were they going to attack now, with the night so close at hand? In this blizzard of sand? In the midst of tempest? But the trumpets continued to blare and without further question every man hurriedly donned hot armor on jerkins drenched with sweat, bodies weary with heat, and hastened to join the ranks. Walter de Nemours, Jean d'Arcy, Gerard d'Avesnes, fearing lest someone get there ahead of them, were already climbing like cats onto the tower. The detachments of de Joinville and de Nanteuil drew up in battle formation along the shore, ready as soon as the chain was broken to rush upon the island, using the barges for a bridge. As if incited by these preparations the gale redoubled in fierceness. It roared, it rumbled, swept men off their feet. Never mind the wind! Four hundred men at arms took to their posts on board the battering ram.

"Let the chains go!" shouted Jean from the deck, "God help the Holy Sepulchre!"

The roar of the gale drowned his voice but the men understood his gesture. The sails, so far uselessly flapping in the wind, swelled, stiffened. At the same time the oarsmen cut the water with their oars. Creaking and moaning the huge raft shoved away from shore. Atop the tower d'Arcy and de Nemours, arching their backs like lions about to spring, held the drawbridge in readiness. If they succeeded in throwing it over the parapet the chain tower of Bur-al-Silsil would fall to the Franks.

But those inside the bastion had by now spied the approach of the assailant and the stone crenellations were swarming with defenders, some with flares and burning torches, others with boulders. Greek fire spurted from flexible pipes. It flowed down the iron-sheathed walls of the floating tower, spread upon the water and ran over the waves swept by the gale.

"The sons of the Devil will not set us on fire! Never fear!" shouted de Layron in Jean's ear. De Brienne nodded absent-mindedly. His whole attention was directed at the bow of the craft whence jutted the iron spur. Would they succeed in steering the raft so that the spur might strike at the fortress' gate? In the gathering dusk, in the midst of the tempest, it was well-nigh impossible to issue orders, but those who manned the sails knew well what was asked of them and the craft was gliding straight for the gate. The Moslems on the parapet were already thrusting out poles, timber and iron shafts. To no avail! The speeding engine struck the stone citadel, the statues of the goddess Basta and the god Anubis with such terrific force that the deck of the craft split asunder and the knights tumbled from their posts. But the iron shafts snapped like reeds. The wooden tower almost touched the stone one. The battle turned into a hand-to-hand struggle. A hail of stones reverberated on the iron sheathing. Burning torches fell and went out. On both sides dead and wounded rolled into the river. At once crocodiles began to swarm around them. Flames glowed red, reflected by the waves.

Across the river bedlam broke loose in the city. From minarets meuzzins were calling Allah's help. On the walls dervishes performed their incantations. But in the Moslem camp at al-Adilijah the Sultan did not lose his head. It seemed likely the Franks might take the bastion. A new obstacle must be erected without delay. Whip in hand the Janchars rounded up men from the town. All men. Moslems as well as Copts, Malekites, Jews. They drove them to the shore where stood an old Egyptian mastaba or tomb. Tear it down! Load the stones upon the Sultan's galleys moored close to the bank! Stones covered with hieroglyphs and pictures of men, beasts and gods rumbled over the decks as frightened men rolled them on board. Make haste! Make haste! Whips whistled. Along with the loading, carpenters were erecting on the decks strange, box-like towers, weird superstructures almost as high as the masts.

The Cardinal tossed restlessly on his great bed, groaned, fretted. As before he bemoaned the slow pace of work so now he was torn by despair because they had charged heedlessly, without his knowledge or leave. There could be no doubt; they would accomplish nothing and only waste the ram. Had he not been told only yesterday there was several days' work still to be done?

Drenched in cold, malarial sweat, mortally exhausted, he tried to rouse himself, listened, dispatched messenger after messenger. He expected the worst and would not believe his ears when suddenly a joyful tumult broke out all around. The chaplain, panting, rushed to his bedside: "Our men have scaled the citadel! Bur-al-Silsil is taken!" Wild screams rose from both shores. To be sure the Moslems had succeeded at last in setting the ram on fire and it burned now like a gigantic torch brightly lighting the water, the crocodiles, the reeds and the city hidden behind its walls. But the Franks no longer cared. They had attained their goal. Without waiting for the barges those on shore hastened to the citadel, clutching the chain like apes.

They found the bastion full of their comrades. The Moslems had been slain or hurled into the river. Fourscore axes simultaneously tackled the chain, hacking the links open. At last the iron splashed into the river. Both arms of the river were free. The road into Egypt stood open.

No sooner had daybreak dispersed the murk over Pharaoh's land than the Crusaders' galleys, which for three months had stood idle, began to move up the Nile along the walls of Damietta. No sound came from the walls. The sun had just risen but was already beating fiercely upon the world. The knights, staring with eyes red from lack of sleep, beheld the Sultan's flotilla waiting in front of them. A tight row of vessels closed the river below al-Adilijah.

There was something odd about that fleet. Not a man in sight, just as there was none on the city walls. No sign of preparations for combat. Instead clumsy unfamiliar scaffoldings rose high from every deck. Bare timber. The vessels careened heavily as though overloaded. Gangplanks had been thrown from deck to deck and the Franks saw a few men running on them, fleeing to the shore.

"If they reckon they will stop us long with this trap," muttered de Brienne, "then they are out of their minds. It will take us no longer than a couple of Paternosters to burn this boon." Even as he spoke his men were placing chests lined with clay and containing Greek fire on the bow of the first vessel. Others wrapped arrows dipped in tar. Servants blew upon iron pots with live coals. Raise the sails! Quick! We are almost there!

By God! What was that?

All at once, amidst complete silence, as though by magic, the Sultan's vessels listed and began to sink. Humbly, obediently, they sank into the water. Some leaned to the right, some to the left, forward, backward, like men mortally wounded. A whirlpool formed around them. The water gurgled and rose in a wave. The wave struck at the bows of the Latin galleys.

Fuming with rage the Latins dropped their sails. The oars hit the water in reverse. A bad business to collide with a wreck. The Sultan's craft sank deeper and deeper. The turgid water hit the banks, frightening the dozing ibises and crocodiles away. At last the vessels disappeared altogether, only the tips of those odd, clumsy superstructures protruded from the surface. The hulls, pierced at the right moment and loaded with stones, had come to rest at the bottom of the river, forming an obstacle which none could move, save, perhaps, the next flood; a tougher barrage than the chains of Bur-al-Silsil. Hidden under the water the wrecks could neither be burned nor dragged out. A dahabiya, the narrow fishing craft of the natives, might slip through the unsightly scaffolding but not a galley. The Nile was closed once more. The fruit of yesterday's victory was lost.

"I knew it, I knew all along they would not accomplish anything without me," sputtered the Cardinal wrathfully. "They never asked me, and now, see what has come of it!"

# 6.

# Al-Azrak

"S IRE," SAID WILLFRIED, "THAT OLD COPT BEN ELIAS HAS COME AGAIN AND begs to be received."

"Let him go to the devil," muttered Jean angrily. "I have no time to listen to Copt nonsense."

"He says he has something very important to tell you."

"I can guess. . . . That the sun will set this evening . . ."

"Maybe not, Your Majesty. He seems an old, respectable man. And he implores so . . ."

"I wager he wants to extort a few coppers . . . Here give him this denarius and tell him to go."

Willfried retired and Jean once more lost himself in somber reflections. How was he to overcome the obstacle of the scuttled ships? The problem tormented him day and night. He thought of extravagant and impossible schemes. To drag the galleys along the shore on oiled timbers? Maybe with one but not with sixty galleys. The Sultan, discovering what they were about, would doubtless avail himself of the confusion, charge the camp and burn or destroy the immobilized vessels. No use thinking of it. But what else could be done? What else? The powerful walls of Damietta would never surrender to anything but a real siege. The city could be taken only by hunger. And in order to surround the walls and cut off food supplies one must command the river above and below the city. But the Nile was closed. Closed for many years. None could sail upstream, neither a Christian nor an Arab. . . .

Willfried returned crestfallen. The unconscious familiarity which had developed between them in those days when they donned each other's clothes had vanished and Willfried as of old approached his master with respectful awe. "Your Majesty, the old man flung the denarius into the

river and says that is not what he came for. He has important news, he
says. And he promises he will say no more than three words . . . "

Jean shrugged his shoulders. "Oh, well. Let him come. Only tell him
I will not have long discourses. I know those Copts. Once they start
talking they are worse than Greeks."

Willfried darted out. Jean angrily pursed his lips. Although kind by
nature, like all knights he felt an invincible aversion toward Greeks,
Copts, Malekites, Maronites, Armenians and all those people who,
though they claimed to be Christians, were according to the Latin lights
not true Christians at all but something apart, inferior, transitory. Any
Crusader, if he were to own the truth, had to admit that he preferred the
heathen a hundred times to those would-be co-religionists whom they
referred to scornfully as weathers.

This aversion, strangely enough, was shared by the Moslems as well.
Hence the Copts, many of whom had settled in Egypt, were the butt of
constant and bloody persecutions. To be sure one of the Prophet's wives
was a Copt and the Koran commanded that these people "with dark
skin and curly hair" be spared. Nevertheless, every few years as regu-
larly and irrevocably as season follows season, slaughters and massacres
would break out.

Ben Elias, who now timidly slipped into the tent of the King of Jerusalem, was an old man. His beard, according to the custom prevalent
among the Copts, was dyed black. This artificial blackness lent his
countenance an undeserved look of false dignity. His clothes, too, were
black, black being the color worn by the Copt elders and clergy. He
bowed low to the King, carefully drew the curtain of the tent and said:

"Defender of Christendom, Lion of Judah, Hope of the Faithful; I
am allowed to say but three words: Here they are: the old riverbed
al-Azrak."

"I don't understand what you mean!" de Brienne scowled.

"I am saying only three words as I was ordered. The old riverbed
al-Azrak."

"What riverbed?"

"Defender of Christendom, Hope of the Faithful! In that case it is
best that I should make myself clear. Yesterday while I sat in the street
I beheld the commander of Damietta whom they call Djemal ed-Din,
and the great Mufti of mosques of Damascus, named Ibn Giusi. Ibn

Giusi was saying: 'My eyes have shed tears till they are dry. The Father of Rivers is closed forever. Slender dahabiyas will no more sail to the sea.' And Djemal ed-Din replied, and I heard him myself, I, your unworthy servant: 'Hold your tears, great Mufti. When the Franks depart, the Ruler of the Faithful will turn the river into the old bed of al-Azrak and we shall raise the ships.' This I heard with my own sinful ears, whereupon I set forth and departed from the city telling the guard I was going to Cairo, and I deceived their eyes and here I am . . ."

"What meaning has this for us?" inquired Jean. At first he had listened absently; now he became attentive.

Ben Elias lifted his eyes to the sky with an expression as though propriety alone prevented him from lifting his arms as well. "Defender of Christendom! It seems to me the words are full of portent. For can you not forestall the Sultan and turn the water of the Nile yourself?"

"I see. You say there exists an old riverbed which . . ."

". . . can be easily connected with the Father of Rivers. It is called al-Azrak, which means the Blue Canal. It was named so because its stagnant water carries no mud and hence seems blue. Upstream it suffices to dig through two dams; downstream more work will be needed as sand has obstructed the bottom and reeds have overgrown it . . ."

"Come, you must show me where it is."

"Have mercy, Defender of Christendom! Any fellah will point the way. All you need is to ask where al-Azrak is. Do not compel me to show myself with you outside this tent. I left my family in Damietta . . ."

"All right. You can remain here. I will not forget the service. Ben Elias, I would not see you at first—I was wrong. What you told me is of utmost importance, indeed. Tell me also, if you can, how many troops has the Sultan?"

"The Sultan has forty thousand of cavalry and incalculable multitudes of troops of foot. Half of the latter are good soldiers and the rest just rabble, herded by the whip from all over the place. In Damietta, in Cairo, in Alexandria Moslem officers go from street to street shouting: 'By order of the Ruler of the Faithful: whoever fails to join in the fight against the giaour shall hang after sundown.' And before evening they return to make sure no one is hiding. They search every house and hang those they find. And so people join from fear. Likewise there are the Bedouins, who think only of loot . . . They care no more for the Prophet than they do for Christ. One can never be sure whom and when they will strike, you or their own side."

"Does the Sultan think he can accomplish much with that army?" inquired Jean contemptuously.

"How am I, a poor Copt, to know what the Sultan thinks? They say in town he is waiting for his brothers to arrive with great forces. It would seem he has already dispatched three messengers. The Sultan al-Muzaam of Damascus and al-Asraf of Mesopotamia were expected to come last month . . . No one knows what has detained them. I have heard people say by the wells that the old Sultan Malik al-Adil is very ill and his sons will not leave him lest someone seizes their heritage . . ."

"Another reason why we must not tarry," thought Jean and he added aloud: "But if they have rounded up and herded all men then you Christians likewise must be in the Sultan's army?"

"No, Defender of Christendom. They do not trust us. When you approached Damietta, Djemel ed-Din summoned our elders to appear before him. I, your unworthy servant, was there too. Djemel ed-Din said: 'You must go and fight the giaours.' And we replied: 'You have spoken, Lord. We shall go.' Then he continued: 'I am sorry for you, for before you reach the camps you shall be slain, as all know you hold with the Franks.' Our knees began to tremble, for by the Holy Tree under which the Sacred Virgin rested this was likely to happen indeed. Our superior said in all haste: 'We have set aside out of our wretched poverty one thousand denarii.' To which Djemel ed-Din replied: 'You speak wisely, abuna. But what is a thousand denarii? In my eyes you are worth twenty-four times as much. Do you hear me, Christian dogs? I value you at twenty-four thousand denarii. If you pay, you can continue to sit in your burrows.'

"We fell upon our faces babbling for fright, for we are poor people, and then he added: 'Know how merciful I am—I consent to fifteen thousand denarii provided you bring it at once.' And so we must give! Poor men that we are, we had to satisfy that pagan Beelzebub. And still we expect to die at any time . . . Blessed be the will of Our Lord! A sinner is born to suffer and bend under the load of human hate and contempt."

"I am grateful to you, Ben Elias, for the news you brought and shall reward you as much as our means permit. Tell me what will you have?"

"I did not come here for the sake of reward, Defender of Christendom. I came here because it was you, the Latins, who overcame Byzantium . . ."

"What has Byzantium to do with this matter?" exclaimed Jean amazed. "I reckoned you helped us either for the sake of reward or as Christians might help Christians. Does it not matter to you that the Cross shall win?"

"The Greek yoke was the worst my people had ever known," Ben Elias explained. "Neither Romans nor Arabs have ever persecuted us as much. We used to hold in great esteem the old Greeks—the Hellenes. But we hate the Byzantians. When we heard Byzantium had fallen services of thanks were held in all churches. The Moslems were likewise overjoyed and so the rejoicing was general. The Cross shall win only when we win. Ours is the oldest, the most venerable of all churches. We accepted Christianity during the lifetime of Jesus Christ . . ."

Although Jean could hardly wait to summon his knights and consult with them about the news he had just received, once more he stopped abruptly, amazed. "In the lifetime of Our Lord?" he repeated. "How could that be?"

Ben Elias solemnly lifted his hand. "We were instructed by the Most Holy Virgin Mary in the days when she and the Divine Child abided in Egypt."

"So?" exclaimed Jean. "I should like to hear of it, but not today. Now I must hasten to the Council. My thanks for what you have told me."

Again Ben Elias bowed to the ground and departed, stroking his beard with great dignity. Willfried, who stood at the entrance of the tent, gazed after him mockingly.

"He says the Holy Virgin herself instructed them in true faith," he said to Francis who had just emerged from the royal kitchen carrying a jug of water mixed with vinegar, and was sauntering toward the fellah who worked nearby. "Only a fool could believe such stuff. As though the Holy Virgin would ever talk to those rams! The black, filthy louts. I've heard that on fast days they will not even wash!"

But Francis, transported, put the jug on the ground.

"It is true!" he cried. "The Holy Virgin did live here. And I, unworthy sinner that I am, have completely forgotten it. I, unworthy sinner, could dream of nothing but the Holy Land when this, too, is a Holy Land. Oh, he must tell me about it!"

He ran after the Copt and pleadingly tugged at the man's coat. Ben Elias, alarmed, looked back, and with a frightened gesture gathered the cloak about him. But at the sight of Francis, so utterly inoffensive, he quickly regained his composure and a note of superiority crept into his attitude.

"Do tell me of Mary, Our Mother," Francis begged. "Where did she abide while she was in Egypt? What do you know about her?"

Ben Elias would gladly and at length have told of his faith to any more noble listener, but upon Francis he cast only a perfunctory and haughty glance. "You call yourself a Christian and you don't know?"

"No, I don't. I am not a good Christian. I am a miserable creature, the most despicable creature in all this camp. Still I love Our Mother. . . . Do tell me about her!"

"The Most Holy Virgin lived in Cairo for three years, six months and two weeks," Ben Elias deigned to inform him. "For abode she used a grotto which we hold in great respect . . ."

"I should say you would! What else?"

"Not far from the Heliopolis grows a sycamore tree in the shadow of which the Most Holy Virgin was wont to rest, and a spring from which she drank . . . That spring heals any ailment."

"Good Lord! And what else?"

"The ruins of a pagan temple where the deities lie in fragments ever since they fell off their pedestals when the Holy Virgin stopped nearby."

"Is this Heliopolis very far from here?"

"Right beyond Cairo. But the Sultan will not allow anyone to go to Cairo."

"If I only saw the Sultan I would plead and beg him till he would let me."

Ben Elias contemptuously shrugged his shoulders. "No infidel may see the Sultan face to face, lest he is an envoy. And it does not seem likely they will make you one."

"No," admitted Francis, crestfallen.

His skin yellow, wasted by fever, Cardinal Pelagius tossed restlessly on his bed. Was it a fevered imagination or was the vessel really rolling? From where he lay he could see the sail of a ship. It was swollen with the wind. So they were sailing! Whither? No doubt they had taken advantage of his sickness, the Barons and that accursed de Brienne, and had turned back! They had become discouraged and would renounce Damietta!

Summoning what was left of his strength he lifted himself and clapped his hands. "I forbid! I forbid!" he stammered out.

His chaplain, frightened, ran to his bedside.

"What is it, Your Grace?"

"I forbid them to turn back! Under anathema!"

"But we are not returning; we are sailing upstream!"

"Upstream! Merciful God! How can it be . . . the barriers . . ."

"The King of Jerusalem has opened up the old riverbed and let the water through. . . . It is along that bed we are sailing now. In no time we will be in front of al-Adilijah, in front of the Sultan's encampment! The Nile belongs to us, Your Grace!"

"God . . . God . . . ," whispered the sick man. Perspiration broke out on his brow. He fell back, exhausted, happy. "Why wasn't I told immediately?"

"We did not dare to trouble you, Your Grace."

"Trouble me? Such tidings would have restored my health."

"Your Honor will soon recover now. Everybody says the fever torments men only close to the sea. The further south one goes the healthier it gets."

"I will recover if such be Our Lord's will . . . I feel better already. Onward! Onward! No denying but that the King of Jerusalem hit upon a good plan . . ."

"Apparently the Copts told him about the existence of this canal."

"So? Well, no wonder. How could it ever occur to him? Still, it is a good thing he took their advice . . . He might have refused. A lay lord!"

Whether it was because of the joy he felt at the overcoming of the barrier or because they had moved further away from the marshy estuary of the delta, at any rate the Legate was beginning to feel stronger. As yet too weak to get up and issue orders, he already wanted as of old to be kept informed of everything that went on. Nothing irritated him more than the fact that Jean did not come to him for advice. De Brienne, on hearing of these grievances, appeared unbidden on board the Cardinal's galley.

"Your Grace," he said curtly, "where two are in command the foe is sure to thrive. When Your Grace recovers his strength I shall return the command which by right belongs to you and which I have exercised so far without detriment to the name of Christ. But as long as Your Honor is unable to mount a horse, indeed unable to raise himself in bed, I shall retain command."

"In no time now I shall recover my strength," the Cardinal assured him. "Little as you wished me health, no doubt Our Lord has provided otherwise . . ."

"I have never sinned against you, either in thought or in word, Your Grace," retorted Jean drily and left, cut to the quick. Pelagius, propped on his pillows, followed him with hostile eyes. Immediately afterwards he received the Podesta of Genoa, Bartholomeo Doria, who—so he said—had arrived for the express purpose of inquiring after the Legate's health.

The somber face of Pelagius lit with a wan smile. Because of the grudge he bore all knights he was ready to welcome the representatives of any other estate.

"What is your opinion, messire?" he asked the Podesta. "Can the attack upon the Sultan's camp be postponed till I am well? In truth, I would rather lead it myself than entrust it to others."

Thoughtfully, Bartholomeo Doria closed one eye.

"The attack must be launched before the reinforcements come," he said at last, twisting a ring on his finger, "but as to when these reinforcements might come, God alone can tell. Maybe soon, maybe never. . . ."

"Never?" the Cardinal propped himself on his elbow, fixing his guest with piercing eyes.

"Old Sultan Malik al-Adil is mortally sick. Our merchants have just brought the news. He is sick from grief and fear of the Mongols."

"The Mongols?" the Legate repeated surprised. "How so? Do not the Mongols live somewhere at the end of the world, a year's journey from here, in the country of Gog and Magog?"

"That's where they used to live. But of late their great Temugin, Genghis Khan, whom they call the Unvanquished, has gathered these unruly hordes and has flung them across the world. Already all of Asia belongs to him. I have good knowledge of these matters because we have a trading port in their capital, Kharacoum. A fierce people they are. Our men call them Tartaru, for verily, they must spring from Hell. None can stop them. They sweep onward like locusts . . ."

"Does that Genghis Khan lead them in person?" asked the Legate, his curiosity aroused.

"No. In his stead he sent two of his leaders; Subutay, the old Lion and Djebe, the Lightning. Like lightning and a lion those two speed south. It seems they have already taken Bokhara and are advancing upon Samarkand. They threaten not to stop till they have reached Baghdad. And reach it they will if such is their intention. That is why Sultan Malik al-Adil trembles for his domains and his sons are reluctant to come to the aid of Egypt."

"In that case those Mongols are in reality our allies?"

"Indirectly, yes. Islam is now clutched between two mighty prongs."

"Which means now is the time to act," sighed the Legate. "We shall never recover the Holy Land if we fail this time."

"It is not enough to recover the Holy Land, Your Grace. We must get a strong hold upon Damietta and Alexandria . . . Egypt should not be only a means but an end in itself. Egypt is the source of Islam's power. If we were to leave Egypt in the Sultan's hands, our hold on the Holy Land would never be secure . . ."

"It seems the country stretches far into the desert," remarked Pelagius cautiously.

"It does and for that reason we must not endeavor to conquer all of it. The ports will suffice, Damietta and Alexandria. Whoever holds the ports is the master of the country."

"Still, it would be no easy matter to hold and defend them?"

"We would gladly take it upon ourselves for the love of Our Lord," cried the Podesta with fervor. "Our fleet could guard the shore without any additional reward. . . . At best the reimbursement of costs . . ."

"I shall think it over," promised the Cardinal.

"I am convinced that with your superior and keen mind Your Grace will see my point. The knights, of course, will think otherwise, no doubt of that. They are incapable of perceiving anything beyond the next battle: I trust Your Grace will pay no heed to their words."

"I have never heeded anything the Barons might say," snapped the Legate, pressing his thin lips. "Brother Philip, call Master Scholasticus. Let him write down what His Honor the Podesta was told about the Mongols."

"Master Scholasticus is not here," said the chaplain, chagrined.

"Not here? Is he again roaming the countryside with the astrologer and the scholar in search of heathen deities? This cannot go on! Wait till I get well!"

Jean left the Legate's galley with a rankling thorn in his side. What was the use of deceiving himself? The Cardinal's health was returning and so would his command. "I shall not dispute it," de Brienne promised himself. "I will withdraw and let him do as he pleases!"

But even as he said it he was aware it would not be easy to give up the work he had begun, to abandon men who trusted him and assume the role of a simple knight. And yet were it not for his own neglect, he and he alone might have been leader. Both by papal choice and common consent he was destined for that post. It was he himself who had forfeited it. How could it have happened? What had come over him in those days?

Unconsciously he lifted his head and glanced at a near-by galley whose high bow cast a deep shadow upon the water. On that carved bow stood a figure leaning over the railing. Jean gave a start. This was Blanche looking at him, Blanche whom he had not seen in two months!

His first impulse to go away with no more than a wave of the hand gave way to a sudden need of seeing her, of pouring out his heart to her. Was she not the only human being with whom he could speak openly?

He motioned the oarsmen not to row ashore but to row to the galley. With his usual agility he climbed on deck. The crew bowed low to the King. Fortunately there was no one at the bow where Blanche stood except her maid-in-waiting, Genevieve.

He noticed how much she had changed. She looked older, gaunter. She neither reproached him nor asked what he had been doing these many months. She was only grateful, infinitely grateful that he should have come to her at last. She, that once so proud Blanche!

But Jean felt the need to excuse himself. "I cannot leave the camp," he explained. "You know how it is. Everything rests upon my head. That was why I insisted that you remain in Acre. But never mind, in a few days the Legate will be well again . . . he will assume command. Then I shall be free."

He tried to make it sound casual but his voice broke.

"No, no. No one could possibly be the leader now save you," she insisted warmly. "The knights won't let you go . . . you must stay in command. I am not complaining; I just wait, I wait and wait. God! How I wait! I wilt and shrivel in my heart, waiting like a soul in Purgatory. But you must retain the command!"

"I might have had it, but now I shall not," he retorted in a hollow voice.

"Because of me?" she whispered.

"Because of you? No. In what are you to blame? It was my fault, my own . . ."

He rose and began to wander restlessly around the deck. Blanche followed him with her eyes, trying to hide her despair. Here he was, that beloved man for whose sake she had left everything, and yet so distant, so alien . . . He never came to see her any more. Indeed, he would not have come even today, had he not seen her standing at the bow. She had noticed how he seemed to hesitate for a moment. And now that he had come he did not even try to touch her, to caress her. It seemed incredible that hardly a year had elapsed since they had loved each other with such mad, hungry passion, since they had been so happy!

Jean, turning around suddenly, met her eyes and tried to smile. A blow could not have hurt her more than this forced smile.

"I must be on my way," he said. "For the time being I am still in command, and in the camp is where I belong."

"But you just came," she protested shyly.

"I can't stay . . . don't grieve, my love. Maybe, God willing . . ." He meant to say that glorious, happy days might yet return for them, but he found himself unable to utter the lie; he did not believe himself. "Let me go. You can see for yourself how dull I am. I'd much rather you did not see me this way . . . I have so many troubles right now . . . The Legate, and the war, and this weird country which we don't know at all! I have the constant feeling that it conceals some trap . . . I don't know whether we ought to attack or wait for a more propitious time. But if we wait, the Sultan's reinforcements may arrive . . . And I am tormented by the lack of news from Acre. How are things there? How is the child . . . It's a long time since Ibelin wrote me last . . ."

The child. Blanche cringed inwardly. Yes, Jean had a child, a tiny little girl, Marie's daughter.

And as he uttered the words the half-forgotten shadow of the dead woman, the pitiful little face of the mortally wounded ermine once more rose between them.

What was that? Suddenly Jean leaped to his feet and listened intently. He ran to the rails, peered at the boat. There, too, Willfried stood listening. His ears had not deceived him: in the camp bugles were blaring

the alarum. Without taking leave of Blanche, without a glance at her,
Jean slid down the rope ladder.

Frightened hippopotami were fleeing upstream. The crocodiles, those
wise lizards once worshipped and held sacred, were scurrying downstream. Behind them was the experience of many thousands of years of
dealing with man; they knew the ways of the humans; they could ap-
praise them judiciously. The more armed men crossed the Father of
Rivers, the more fiercely they shook their spears and drummed upon
their shields, the more abundant would be the food for the rightful inhabitants of the river, the more bodies would float down to the sea. On
such occasions one could fill one's belly enough for several weeks. Only
the bumps over their eyes showing above water, the great reptiles keenly
watched the doings of man. Not since the times of Antony and Cleopatra
had there been such multitudes here. They clapped their jaws in glee.
Every creature has its time. Just as every year the Nile will flood the
country, so every once in a while men will slaughter each other so that
the crocodiles may gorge themselves.

But men did not know what went on in the reptiles' minds. They
pushed forward frantically. It seemed as though all Egypt must have
been ransacked to collect all these boats with slanting masts. The river
was covered with them. A moving bridge. Like a swarm of locusts,
arrows flew in clouds. The war cry of "Talil"—there is no might nor
power save God, and "Tacbir"—God is great, God is great, there is
none beside Him—swept overhead. The first sounded like the scream
of eagles, the latter like the croak of vultures.

Willfried, with hands that shook from haste, drew Jean's armor tight
and fixed the strap of his helmet. The King was ready. He sped to a
hillock from which one could see the river and the valley. Noise, haste,
confusion surrounded him from every side. The bugles continued to
blare. It was so many months since the troops had been standing idly
that they had almost given up expecting that the fight might break out
at any moment. Now it had come upon them unexpectedly on a blister-
ing hot day when all of them wished only for a cool spot. And so the
Franks were in a frenzy of haste, ashamed that they, old warriors, should
have been caught unawares. Jean, motionless, watched the innumerable
swarm of boats from the hill. It seemed the Sultan had thrown all his
forces into the fight. Up the river, also, something was moving. Shading

his eyes with both hands he could clearly see that upon a bridge placed on barges the cavalry was crossing the river. Their multi-colored cloaks shone in the distance like butterfly wings. Jean surmised at once that the cavalry had been ordered to circle the camp and, while all the attention of the Latins would be directed at the river, strike from the back. So much was plain. Plain, too, was the fact that the enemy outnumbered them ten to one.

"Master of the Hospitallers," he called to Odo de Montbeliard, "I entrust the defense of the camp to you. The cavalry is coming from behind. Let the knights follow me! God help the Holy Sepulchre!"

At breakneck speed he rushed down to the river where already boats were beginning to touch shore. The bank was muddy and soft. They must send their mounts away and on foot form a solid wall along the shore, planting their feet firmly in the slippery mire. They must stand shoulder to shoulder in a rampart of armor, flashing the whirlwind of their swords. They stood thus three, four, ten deep, immovable and stolid. The space in which the enemy could land was relatively small. A few fathoms up and a few fathoms down the river the bank formed a steep cliff, easy to defend. Arrows and spears bounced back from shields and armors. The wall stood motionless and waited. It would not be an easy task for the heathens to leave their boats and land. The terrible swords were beginning to go into action. Whirling and cutting, right and left. Their bodies heaved in that mighty swing, so celebrated in song.

Much had changed in the world and in the way of knights since Roland IV in the gorge of the Ronsenval Pass, since the days of the First Crusade and the battles of Dorilea, Antioch, Jerusalem. So much, in fact, that the grandsons of today would have found no common language with their grandsires. In one thing, however, they still would feel the common tie of blood—in fight. Minds, hearts, souls had changed, valor remained unaltered. Theirs was the same wild joy at flinging one's life in the face of the foe as that of a sling in flinging a rock in the air. Theirs the same unconscious instinct of battle, prompting the hand to an unerring thrust. Theirs the old battle cry, the knightly call rising from the ranks, testifying to their knightly lust. The boats pressed, the more distant rows of the crowd pushed against the first ones in an attempt to break through the wall of iron. In vain. Behind the rampart of bodies hewn down and sliding into the river, the knights stood as before. The fight continued, seemingly hopeless, for the number of knights would not increase, while the Sultan's men continued to surge in ever growing throngs, still pushing their way into the boats, obscuring the sun with swarms of feathered arrows, filling the air with screams and the sharp stench of sweat.

Slowly, more and more bodies of Moslems and Christians floated down the river. The turbid-grey waters of the Nile turned red, and among the handful of defenders standing on the shore many a heart might have felt weary and many a shoulder grown numb. Yet they did not. One against a hundred! No matter! It had happened before! And the greater the number of enemies the more glorious the death, the more lasting the posthumous fame.

The sun was broiling hot; armor hissed whenever water splashed upon them; helmets pressed on skulls like red-hot pots, but the fighting men did not feel it. In spite of the fall of faith, in spite of the softening songs of troubadours, the old valorous greatness reappeared faithfully at the hour of battle by the side of the Franks, justifying the legends and old tales of knights who single-handed could stop armies.

A wild tumult arising from the camp signaled that the cavalry had joined the battle. The camp was surrounded with a ditch and protected by a stockade of thorns; therefore the enemy would not overcome it easily. Odo de Montbeliard would know how to keep them off for a time. Raising himself on his toes Jean stared over the heads of the fighting men. The bridge of barges, upon which the cavalry had crossed the river, caught his eye. No large detachment had been left on guard, he noticed. And suddenly a mad, breath-taking thought flashed through the king's mind.

He looked around. Directly behind him, calm and deliberate as though he were cutting down oaks somewhere on the Vistula, Sir Dzierzek hewed the heathen. One bristling tip of his mustache jutted out through the bars of his basinet; the other he probably chewed, as was his custom.

"Sire de Pologne," Jean called over the din of battle. "Sire de Pologne! Gather in the rear not less than a hundred knights. Take them across the river and on to yonder camp!"

Sir Dzierzek hastily left the place he held in the ranks and pushed his way to the rear. His post was immediately taken by Sir d'Arcy, easily distinguished even from afar because of the peacock feathers on his helmet. At that moment a boat larger than the others struck the shore, on board it the gigantic standard-bearer, Samila, holding the standard in both hands. Quick as lightning, agile as a lynx in spite of his heavy armor, d'Arcy leaped from the shore right on to the boat. With one blow he mowed Samila down, grabbed the standard and flung it into the river. A scream of rage rose from the Moslems, a shout of triumph from the Franks. A hundred armed hands stretched vengefully towards Sir d'Arcy but already others sprang to his help. They routed the crew. Overpowered, the boat formed an advance rampart which would serve as a bridge head for the defense.

In the rear, the knights summoned by Dzierzek already sat in the saddle waiting, wondering where he might lead them. There were over a hundred of them and as many squires. Astonished, they saw that he did not turn back to the camp to go to the rescue of the Templars and Joanites, as they had expected, but in full gallop led them along the river across reeds and rushes. Frightened herons and ibises rose screaming in the air. In spots the ground was boggy. The horses sank in the mire, painfully dragging their feet free. In no time, it seemed, they reached the bridge and knocked down the boatmen and the soldiers guarding it. Now the boards sagged under the hoofs. The mounts shied and snorted. Now they were on the opposite shore. "Onward!" At full speed they rushed upon the Sultan's camp!

The charge was totally unexpected. The Sultan, certain that with his overwhelming strength, he could wipe out the Christians completely, had not kept a strong detachment by his side. When he was told that cavalry with alien armor could be seen on the bridge, he rejoiced at the news, thinking these were prisoners which had been brought to him. But the presumed prisoners were already inside the camp looking for his tent. Their voices, resounding from their basinets, rang like bells: "God help the Holy Sepulchre!" and that other battle cry, old, infallible, which came unconsciously to the lips: "God wills it!" "God wills it!" They rode down the terrified men. There were many armed men in the camp, but they all belonged to the group which Ben Elias had scornfully defined as rabble, the men who had been driven here with a whip under the threat of gallows, wild Bedouins who craved nothing save loot. Leaving everything behind they fled now in panic; the thought of resisting never occurred to them. What? The Franks have already crossed the river? Then Allah had turned away his face from the faithful!

Close by the Sultan's multi-colored tent stood a guard of Baharites, the "sons of lions." Surely they would not flee! But the Sultan had lost heart. Seeing the total defeat of his camp, the routed throngs, he was certain the entire Franks' force had crossed the river. How—that he could not understand. But anything was better than to fall in their hands. Surrounded by the Baharites he hastily fled in the direction of Cairo.

He fled, as once Emir Kilich-Arslan had fled from Dorilea, Emir Kerboga from Antioch and the great Saladin from Montgisard. And, like them, beside himself with rage he pondered in what lay the strength of the Franks. How could such a tribe, normally cowardly, quarrelsome, conceited and treacherous, forever fighting each other, suddenly rise to the heights of superhuman deeds? It was in vain he pondered! None could have explained the mystery, the Franks themselves least of all.

A hundred knights had taken the Sultan's camp without suffering any casualties themselves. Without tarrying Dzierzek set afire the stacks of straw and hay they found in the camp. Let flames and smoke inform his own side of what was happening. Leaving half of his men on watch he returned with the rest to the river to guard the bridge in case Bibars' cavalry attempted to cross it again.

But those by the river had already seen the conflagration and heard the uproar. The uproar came from Damietta where crowds had surged on the walls amidst moans and laments. Likewise the commander of the Sultan's army, Bibars, caught sight of a band of his own men speeding southward with the green speck of their standard fluttering over their heads. It was the Sultan's guard! The Sultan was fleeing!

Unable to understand what had happened, Bibars withdrew; his place was by the Sultan's side. He did not attempt to retake his own bridge, bristling with a bridgehead of spears, but retreated to the south along the left bank. He would ford the river near Cairo.

After the departure of Bibars the innumerable throng on the boats was left without leader or command. Jean had thrown a part of his men at arms over the bridge to support Dzierzek and the Moslems saw they were surrounded. The enemy had taken both shores. There was no retreat.

Below them the Crusaders' flotilla stood at anchor. Above them the bridge was occupied by the Franks. Some of them tried to climb on to the right bank and make their way into Damietta. Others fought to the last; still others let the current sweep them blindly downstream towards the galleys. There, however, preparations were already under way. Cardinal Pelagius, supported by his chaplain on one side and his secretary on the other, stood on the bow of his crimson galley and directed the operations: "Pour boiling water! Throw torches! The accursed sons of the Devil! Quick! Spears and arrows! Roll boxes with Greek fire from the hulls! Don't let them come near the bow! Let them drown! Let them perish!"

Howling with fear the bands flung themselves desperately here and there.

Among the general tumult and confusion, while the river crowded with men and boats rose and spurted in every direction, while the blood-curdling din rose higher and wider and rebounded from the Libian rocks, no one either noticed or objected to the doings of a small, gray man who with two companions ran excitedly to and fro along the bank and heedless of arrows, stretched his hand to those who drowned and took aside the wounded, saving Christians and Moslems alike.

The sun had scarcely turned red when the defeat of al-Kamil was completed and Damietta surrounded. Cardinal Pelagius watched his men bustling on the river, capturing what remained of the Moslems. Others, leaning out over the railing, pushed away with long poles the bodies which had collected around the vessels and formed veritable barriers. Let them drift with the current and poison the air elsewhere.

Cardinal Pelagius felt deeply moved. Truly God in his mercy had granted them a fair victory! For the first time he thought of Jean de Brienne without active dislike. The man had led the battle well enough today; no worse in fact, than he, the Cardinal of Albano, would have conducted it himself. . . .

What was the meaning of that uproar ever louder, ever more insistent? The Legate knitted his heavy brows. His good feelings vanished without trace. It was the knights carrying Jean de Brienne high, and shouting so that even here one could hear them distinctly: "Long live the King of Jerusalem! Long live our leader!"

"Be still! Order them to be still! I won't allow it! He is not the leader. I am. . . . I . . ." the Cardinal snarled in rage. But his strength failed him. He fell back limp into the arms of his horror-stricken secretary, his teeth chattering in a new attack of fever more severe than any of the previous ones.

# 7.

## The Offer

THE OLD SULTAN MALIK AL-ADIL WROTE FROM HIS PALACE IN DAMASCUS:
". . . In the depth of the night my star woke me and I trembled. I
told my envoy: 'Drive thy mule in all haste and stop not on the way.
And when thou water the beast at the well stop no longer than absolutely
necessary.' For I wish those words to reach the favorite of the Prophet ere
I gaze towards Mecca seated in my grave. These are my words: Expect
no quick help from thy brethren. Allah grant they may not need it themselves. They stand sabre in hand amidst their warriors yet they are much
oppressed. The wrath of the Prophet in the guise of the miserable tribe
of Mongols is drawing close to us. Take my advice, son of Turanshah.
Rid thyself of Franks in Egypt. Give them Palestine and they will be
pleased and they will leave the shores of the Nile blessing thy name.
For they care naught for land, which they have aplenty, but only for the
tomb of the prophet Jesus. Give them likewise the timber upon which the
prophet Jesus died. It is in Damascus. I shall order it to be delivered at
your request. Thou shalt make durable peace with them and thus acquire
an ally in the struggle against the Mongols. Thou shalt be able to come
to our rescue instead of beseeching our help. Hearken to these words of
mine, O Son of Turanshah. May the Prophet guard thy days."

Sultan al-Kamil, lost in thought, scratched his chin. The little brush
used to drive flies away slid from his lap. A slave picked it up and on his
knees handed it back to him upon flat, open palms. Two black Nubians
stood behind the Sultan holding ostrich-feather fans which they waved
lightly and almost imperceptibly. The Sultan stared at the letter he had
just read with vague apprehension. This was truly a posthumous message, as a second messenger arrived at the same time as the first messenger bearing the news that the old Sultan Malik al-Adil was dead. By
and large today was a day of Iblis, a day of evil bodings. Djemal ed-Din,

the Commander of Damietta, had informed him but a while ago of an incredible thing: the much trusted guardian of food stores set aside for the event of siege, had proved a dastardly thief and traitor. The stocks of flour, olive oil and dates which were to last the garrison two years simply did not exist. When they had vanished no one knew, as Djemal ed-Din, trusting the steward implicitly, was not wont to examine the contents of warehouses.

No need to tell that the steward had bolted before the discovery was made.

"May Allah punish him!" sputtered the Sultan, blanching with rage. "May he destroy his accursed seed! Damietta, the pearl of the state; Damietta, of the unvanquished walls, without food! Let me never hear the name of Djemal ed-Din again! Woe to his head if the Franks will not take it off themselves! Accursed be his house and his kin! He did not come out of his walls when the Franks attacked me in the camp of al-Adilijah! He did not verify the stores in time. It would have been better for him never to have seen the light of day!"

"I always wondered, Oh, Ruler of the Faithful, at the trust you put in the Emir Djemal ed-Din," broke in Bibars, with impudent familiarity.

"Be still, for you are no better than he! Allah has not seen fit to grant me leaders! Had I but a single one!"

The face of Bibars contracted like that of a bad dog.

"Oh, Ruler of the Faithful, how was I to expect that a body of cavalry would be enough to throw fear in the heart of the Sultan and the camp?"

"What did you say?" The Sultan turned upon him in rage. "What did you say?"

"I said that if you care not for me, Oh, Ruler of the Faithful, Favorite of the Prophet, I can leave even today . . . with my men."

Al-Kamil bit his lips and made no reply. Rage tore at his heart but he felt helpless. The troops worshipped Bibars and at his orders might even abandon the Sultan. Al-Kamil was not popular among his army and he knew it. In the first place he was not a warrior; books and songs were closer to his heart than the sword. Besides he was uneven, moody, weak. Bibars, on the other hand, was a born soldier and a leader of genius. To be sure, he had lost the last battle ignominiously; still he did not consider himself responsible for the defeat. And anyway who could tell what thoughts brewed behind the low, wide brows of that Turk? Had he really the Sultan's success at heart?

O! how evil was this day.

Abdullah, the messenger of Djemal ed-Din, stood by the door, awaiting an answer. Naked, huge, black, he was a skilled swimmer. Thanks to this ability he was able to get out of the fortress guarded so closely that a bird could not have flown through. He had been lowered from the walls at night. He had crawled like a serpent through reeds and dived into the river patrolled unceasingly by a fleet of boats. In one stretch he had swum across, never showing his head above the water till he reached the opposite shore. Once there he had crawled again through reeds until he had eluded the guards.

"You may go back," the Sultan said.

Abdullah gazed at him imploringly. "Without an answer, Oh, Ruler of the Faithful?"

"With this answer, Abdullah: Djemal ed-Din may consider himself lucky if he perishes from the hand of the Franks, not mine . . ."

The messenger fell to his knees. "Oh, Ruler of the Faithful," he moaned, "let your eyes strike me like thunder but deign to tell this much: is the Sultan of Damascus coming to the rescue?"

"He is on his way," replied the Sultan with indifference, playing with his uncle's letter. "He is already on his way."

"Thank you, Ruler of the Faithful, Favorite of the Prophet. Thank you. We shall endure it till he comes. We shall endure. . . ."

Bowing, he left. Al-Kamil cast a gloomy glance at an old imam with a flowing white beard who sat opposite him upon a low ottoman. This was Ibn Giuzi, the great Mufti of the mosque of Damascus and in addition a historian of great repute. He had arrived in Egypt several months before to adjust some details of rite. The late Sultan Malik al-Adil had held him in great respect and had often sought his advice. Meeting the eyes of the Sultan, the Mufti stirred and cleared his throat.

"You ought, Oh, Ruler of the Faithful, to take the advice of your uncle, the son of Ajub, whom you shall not meet again till the day of resurrection in the valley of the great Judgment!"

"I have no leaders! I have no leaders!" complained al-Kamil, clutching his head with his palms. "If I only had leaders I would show these giaours!"

"Sometimes it is better not to have leaders," said Ibn Giuzi cryptically. "Ruler of the Faithful, make peace with the Franks and beware of Bibars."

"I cannot take away the command from him for the army will not accept another. I would have him strangled or blinded but I fear, lest the Mamelukes rebel."

"That is why I told you, Oh, Ruler of the Faithful, it is sometimes better not to have leaders."

"Damietta, my Damietta! The gem of Egypt!" the Sultan continued to lament. "Damietta without food! A jackal's puppy would have shown more wisdom and foresight than this Djemal ed-Din! My Damietta!"

"By making truce with the Franks, Oh, Ruler of the Faithful, you shall save Damietta!"

"But at what price! All Palestine!"

"If you continue the war you will not save Damietta. Hunger is stronger than man."

"I shall send envoys," decided the Sultan with a sigh.

Cardinal Pelagius was slow in recovering from the sudden attack of fever and so his secretary, the learned Scholasticus, continued to enjoy his freedom. The inseparable threesome, he, the astrologer and the scholar Pesaro, lived in the last three months in a constant frenzy of discovery, blind to all that went on around them, indifferent and deaf to everything except the mysterious past of Egypt which stared at them from every stone; the first European scientists to stand on Egyptian soil. To be sure Italy and Provence were likewise full of traces of old times and worship, not to mention that the astrologer and the scholar had come in touch in Syria with Phoenician relics buried at Mount Carmel. All that, however, was nothing compared with Egypt. The magnitude and the profusion of Egyptian ruins exceeded all imagination. The innumerable columns and pylons covered with ant-like inscriptions (they guessed at once that those tiny pictures carved in granite with such painstaking precision must be a script), statues with animal heads, human figures wrought with undreamed-of skill and perfection, obelisks boldly thrusting into the sky and glittering with the relics of gilt under the layers of birds' droppings. At sunset towards Cairo the triangular mountains of pyramids blazed with glittering surface of granite.

During their ceaseless wanderings the three companions had found their way into Copt cloisters miserably built of manure, clay and straw, looking from the distance like huge wasps' nests. It was in these stinking windowless hovels that Copt monks, dark, filthy and unlearned, dwelt. Scholasticus spoke with them in Greek. It was from them that explorers learned the names of sphinxes, pyramids, obelisks. It was they who told them that the statues of men in cauls, with narrow strips of beards attached to their chins, snakes upon their brows and hawk wings wrapped around their heads and necks, represented the Pharaohs, the immortal and invincible rulers. "Their tombs are over there." They would point to the pyramids. "Even up to these days much gold can be found in them. In the olden days people used to find gold even in the common tombs, but the Bedouins have looted everything. What they did not sack has sunk into the ground. No use going in there . . ."

Nevertheless the three friends did go in. Torch in hand, they entered sepulchral chambers whose walls were covered by paintings. The colors, preserved by the darkness, shone vividly; the designs remained unmarred. Moving the torch along the murals they learned of the daily life of the people who had built the tomb in all the minute detail of work, play, prayer, struggle, birth and death. On the stone floor, as though to supplement the picture, stood various household articles, arms, vessels, and small statues. They touched the objects with feverish hands, thinking perchance they had been bewitched and carried into some other mysterious world. In the middle of the main chamber stood the sarcophagus itself, the very core of the tomb. The stone lid of the sarcophagus had been thrown aside by the plunderers who had once come to loot the place, and leaning over the dark depths of the granite box they could catch the sight of the bier which rested there shaped like a human body and with a painted face. This bier both terrified and attracted them. Trembling like thieves they made bold to open it. It seemed to them all the figures painted on the walls stirred menacingly. Surely the deity with a jackal head has bared his teeth! Nevertheless the lust of exploration proved stronger than fear. They lifted the carved and painted lid. They beheld another bier just like the other, save that on the first the eyes were closed while on the other one they were wide open. These eyes incrusted with enamel, with leads of copper and white of crystal stared at them so lifelike and keen that the three men were seized with terror. Their feet shaking they left the tomb.

Sunshine lit their blanched faces. Above, as usual, hawks hung like motionless specks in the blue sky. Somewhere, far away creaked the immemorial water wheels. They rested a while and returned once more.

Curiosity, one of the four cardinal lusts of men, drove them back to the tomb. They lifted the second lid. Inside lay the dead wrapped in a yellowish tissue. The tissue proved not to be a shroud as they had thought at first, but a narrow band of cloth in which the body had been swaddled from head to foot with countless wrappings. They summoned all their courage and lifted the form. It seemed oddly light, stiff and hard. They dared not go on with their exploration, refraining from tearing off that strange swaddling cloth, brownish in hue and exuding a strange perfume. They replaced the body in its bier and left the place, convinced at heart they would return here some day and when they did would not depart till they had probed into the mystery of this swaddled form. Then they would unwrap it to the very last and would see it with their own eyes, regardless of what those figures and deities on the walls might do.

When they emerged from the tomb they were not even aware of hunger though they had not eaten since morning.

"There! If we could only go there." Pochard pointed with his hand to the far-away, rosy pyramids. "There, to those royal tombs . . . There where it seems lies the great Sphinx, the enigma of the world. Who solves it will become immortal . . ."

"The monks say no one knows its beginnings, but they were not human hands which wrought it . . . It was born with the earth itself . . ."

They lapsed into silence and continued on their way, unable to control themselves nor this strange mixture of fear, helplessness and passion for discovery that tore at their hearts. They looked around them with unseeing eyes and were almost startled at the sight of troops, tents and the usual bustling of camp life. The scarcely tasted antique world had completely swallowed them; they had fallen prey to the incurable desire to see, to understand, to know. . . .

Aymar de Layron, Lord of Cesarea, and Gerard d'Avesnes entered the royal pavilion with unaccustomed solemnity.

"Your Majesty! The Sultan's envoys have arrived and ask to be received."

"Do you know what they come to say?" asked de Brienne, lowering his voice.

"We know. The Copt interpreter told us. In return for our leaving Egypt they give us all of the Holy Land and the Timber of the Holy Cross."

Jean bent his head and for a while remained silent. "Tell them," he said at last with outward composure, "that I shall see them after sunset when the heat abates. In the meantime ask them inside and give them a fitting welcome."

The knights departed. Jean drew a deep breath, crossed himself twice and stretched both arms before him. Victory! Victory! Jerusalem recovered! The Holy Sepulchre once more in Christian hands! The plan he himself conceived, the plan of attacking Egypt, had proved miraculously effective. . . . A warm wave of joy and pride swept over his heart. He, de Brienne, would carry inside the sacred walls the recovered Timber of the Holy Cross even as Emperor Heraclius had once done. He forgot all previous torments, troubles, griefs. The blessing of God was upon him. In less than a year, without excessive sacrifices, he had recovered Godfried's heritage! O kind, merciful God!

The news of the envoys' arrival had spread like wildfire throughout the camp, and in the open space in front of the tent a crowd began to assemble. Silently the Barons of Syria pressed forward. So far they bore only the empty titles of their domains, those lords of Jericho, Ramla, Naphuse, Bethlehem, Tiberias. Now they were to return to those places won in struggle by their grandsires. They were once more to take up watch in the unconquerable castle of Kazak, called the Rock of the Desert, water their horses in the Jordan . . . And they stood, gazing at their King, in a silence more expressive than words.

All at once, as though a current had run through their bodies, they lifted their right arms. "We shall not lose that soil again! So help us God!"

"What's happened? What's happened?" inquired the Podesta of Genoa, pushing his way through the throng.

"The war is ended," said Jean with force. "The Sultan is ready to give us back the Holy Land in return for our withdrawal from Damietta."

"And is Your Majesty going to accept the terms?"

"Only a fool could reject them. It is the Holy Sepulchre that matters to us, not Damietta."

Bartholomeo Doria blushed and fidgeted. "How unfortunate the Legate will not be here in person to receive the envoys' good tidings," he remarked.

"His Grace is still ailing, though he will recover soon on hearing that we are taking him to Jerusalem. He is a harsh man and a proud one but he loves Our Lord with all his might."

"Yes, oh, yes," the Podesta agreed eagerly. He lingered awhile, then left. No one paid any attention to him, for others were already pressing forward; servants and scullions, archers and shield-bearers. Brother Francis pushed his way through them and tugged at Sir Dzierzek's mantle.

"Brother knight," he whispered warmly, "what has happened?"

"Jerusalem is ours and so is the Timber of the Holy Cross," replied the Pole and turned away to hide his moist eyes.

"Ours," he repeated. "The Sultan is ready to give them back to us if we only go away from here."

Before the knight knew it Francis had thrown his arms around his neck and kissed him warmly on the cheek. Sir Dzierzek did not seem scandalized; he only cleared his throat. Francis darted to the King, threw his arms around his knees and staring with his luminous eyes into the King's face, whispered: "Is this true, Sire?"

"Yes, it's true," Jean replied, placing his hand on Francis' shoulder. He felt so happy that even this baffling little fool seemed close to his heart.

The envoys, led by the white-bearded Mufti Ibn Giuzi, bowed low, touching in turn their breasts, brows and lips in sign that they concealed no treason either in their hearts, minds or mouths, then sat upon the stools pointed out to them, pleased that the King did not abase them. The Copt, Ben Elias, who knew Latin and was generally used as interpreter stood behind them. Ibn Giuzi was saying:

"In the olden times no ill-will existed between the Kings of Jerusalem and the Favorites of the Prophet. The late Kings of glorious memory, Amalryk, Baldwin and their predecessors, lived in neighborly agreement with the great Sultan Sal-ed-din and his forefathers. The Ruler of the Faithful, al-Kamil, son of Turanshah, would fain restore this friendship so seemly between knights. This is what he ordered me to say: 'Let the lion-like Franks return to their domains and leave ours. We shall give them in return possession of Palestine within the boundaries this land had under the rule of the lad with a leprous-body and the soul of an eagle.'"

"And the Timber of the Holy Cross," Jean reminded him.

"This is so, oh, King! The Timber of the Cross of the prophet Jesus. Your envoys can come to fetch it from Damascus . . ."

Ibn Giuzi stopped speaking and stroked his beard in sign he had finished. Jean was already opening his mouth to answer when suddenly a commotion at the entrance attracted his attention. He saw a flash of crimson in the parted curtains of the tent. Leaning upon the arm of his chaplain, in came the Legate of the Pope, Cardinal Pelagius. Crimson covered him from head to foot, flowing loosely over his emaciated frame. Between the pallor of his cheeks two black Spanish eyes blazed angrily. Unsteadily he advanced, glaring at the envoys. Jean, with his usual self-control and presence of mind, rose from his seat and gave him his armchair. Ibn Giuzi stared with unconcealed astonishment, the rest with apprehension. Ignoring the envoys the Cardinal addressed Jean:

"Who gave you leave, Sir, to receive envoys without me, the leader appointed by the Holy Father himself?"

"It was my right to do so," Jean returned, "as deputy of Your Grace in time of his illness."

"I am much better now."

"That I did not know. And we refrained from giving you the news as we meant to cheer Your Grace with the glad tidings of an accomplished fact."

The Cardinal leered. "What can those tidings be? Tell me! For I have already heard something of them and I did not find them so good."

"The Sultan," Jean summarized briefly, "offers a permanent truce; the return of the Holy Land within the boundaries it had in the time of Baldwin IV and the Timber of the Holy Cross in return for our withdrawal from Egypt."

"And you, blind that you are, would accept it?"

"We undertook this expedition to reconquer the Holy Sepulchre."

"To reconquer it permanently! Permanently, Sir Jean de Brienne, King of Jerusalem! To secure it forever! You will never accomplish this without Egypt whence Islam derives its wealth and power. We will not move from here till we get hold of Alexandria and Damietta."

Jean blanched, aghast.

"Does Your Grace realize that the plan he proposes means a long and very costly war? Does Your Grace realize that any war can turn either way? Why should we forsake what we have already won and what constituted our aim for the sake of some illusory gains?"

"To a true knight there is but one outcome of war: Victory. None but the faint-hearted will withdraw from a half conquered town! Where is the interpreter?"

Fearfully, Ben Elias stepped forward.

"Tell them," said the Cardinal harshly, "that I am the leader, I alone have authority to speak here. I do not accept the Sultan's terms. Damietta must be ours. This is my last word. They need not trouble to come again for I shall not change it."

Silence fell in the pavilion. Silence in which only rapid breathing could be heard. Only the old master of the Templars nodded his approval. Although for a Templar he was an exceptionally peaceful man so that the Order under his rule had lost much of its aggressiveness and influence, he still held fast to the old principle which claimed that any war with the pagan was better than peace.

Ben Elias lowered his head. Before his lips could repeat the cruel words his thoughts flew to his family in Damietta. And because of these thoughts he suddenly abandoned the impersonality of an interpreter. "Your Grace," he muttered in his broken Latin, "war is a horrible thing. Christians should not crave war."

"I am not here to listen to your advice," retorted the Cardinal haughtily. "Attend to the business for which you were summoned here."

Ben Elias repeated the Cardinal's words. Ibn Giuzi started from his stool, his shocked gaze seeking Jean. But Jean turned his eyes away. Without a word the envoys rose to their feet, bowed and departed.

Cardinal Pelagius, though exhausted and weak from over-exertion, felt pleased with himself. He had been in time. Were it not for him the Barons would have let themselves be lured by a mere bone thrown to them by the Sultan and would have even deemed it a boon. Boon, indeed! The conquest of Damietta was only a matter of months. It would be folly to withdraw now!

"The Barons wanted to accept the truce and leave Egypt," he informed his secretary, Scholasticus.

The savant stared at him aghast. "Leave Egypt? Now? But that's dreadful, Your Grace!"

"Of course it is. You, a bookworm who knows absolutely nothing of life, can see it would be dreadful, and yet the Barons could not. Oh, well. . . . Why wonder? They never understand anything."

# 8.

# The Overdrawn String

IBN GIUZI WAS RIGHT WHEN HE SAID THAT HUNGER WAS STRONGER THAN man. Give it time and hunger will conquer any, even the strongest man.

Gaunt as a skeleton, Djemal ed-Din, the negligent commander who had failed to verify in time the stores of food entrusted to a dishonest and sly steward, was penning his last letter to the Sultan.

This letter would no longer be carried by the faithful Abdullah. The Franks had spied him at last and caught him in a net. Tied and shot out of a catapult the bloody pulp of his body was sent flying upon the city ramparts. The net had remained permanently set, inflicting another painful loss upon the beleaguered city. Heretofore the Moslems were wont to throw slain oxen, camels and sheep on inconspicuous floats into the river and let them drift downstream as offal. They timed it so that the carcasses would pass by the city walls in the dead of the night and oftentimes the defenders, leaning out of the corner towers, succeeded in fishing them out with hooks. Now even this help had stopped. Nothing drifted downstream save the corpses flung from the town. By their number and degree of emaciation the besiegers were kept informed of the progress starvation was making inside the walls. Any day now they expected Damietta to surrender.

The bodies were thrown into the river although to an orthodox Moslem the thought of a body deprived of a proper burial in the ground was hard to bear. There no longer was anyone to bury them. Even for the price of forty silver coins it was impossible to hire a man to dig out even the shallowest grave. Likewise you could have offered twice as many gold pieces for a handful of rice, dates or flour. There was none.

For lack of a diver the letter was to be tied to an arrow and shot far behind the Franks' lines. Maybe one of the faithful would see it, pick it up and carry it to the Sultan.

Djemal ed-Din wrote: ". . . The dawn was against us and the sunset still remained adverse. Thus speak to thee, Oh, Ruler of the Faithful, Ruler who has no equal upon earth, the inhabitants of a city which once was happy and blooming and today lies abandoned. Even in the hour of death, however, we have remained steadfast to thee. Our steadfastness is like nutmeg which in big and small crumbs alike, keeps the same scent. Oh, Ruler of the Faithful, if thou canst do so, hasten to our help or else give us a sign to tell us we can surrender to the foe. For our hand is no longer able to lift the sword nor have we strength enough to moan. There is no one to defend the walls. This is our last cry."

The letter never reached the Sultan. The Franks intercepted it.

They ordered Ben Elias to be brought so he might translate the contents. But Ben Elias had disappeared. Some said he had drowned himself from grief upon seeing the skeleton-like bodies of his children drifting down with the current.

And so no one read the last letter of Djemal ed-Din.

One day in September, in the year of Grace 1219, the Sires de Joinville, de Hainaux and d'Avesnes climbed onto a corner tower. They had been observing it for many days as their posts were right across, and had noticed that for some time now no one stirred either in the apertures nor on the ramparts. Neither was it lighted by night. The place seemed silent as a tomb. Committing themselves to the care of Archangel Michael the knights tied ladders with ropes and set them against the wall. They entered. First the three friends; twenty others followed. In the upper storey of the tower, seated by a long-extinguished fire, used to send light signals, sat a man—more like a skeleton—staring at them with dull eyes. He was still breathing but he could not move any more. Two others, similarly moribund, lay down stairs. After putting them out of their misery the knights locked themselves up in the tower and waited till morning. When dawn lit up the world they hoisted upon the top of the tower the standard of the Kingdom of Jerusalem and shouting, naked swords in hand, rushed out into the streets.

They sought the foe; they expected him. But foe there was none. Nothing broke the terrifying silence in which their armored steps reverberated like thunder. There was no foe; only wherever their eyes fell, in the streets, in the courts, in beautiful houses, corpses lay. They

THE OVERDRAWN STRING 293

were so emaciated that they did not decompose. The blazing sun had sucked dry whatever flesh famine had left upon the bones. They lay one on top of the other, skeletons covered with brown skin. Wide open, dry eyes seemed to stare in expectation. In the entire city there was not a sound of life, nor a live beast. No bird, no cat, no rat, no dog or lizard. Not even a plant. Trees had been first stripped of leaves and bark, then their pulp chewed; the roots pulled out.

The knights, aghast, opened the gates and the troops began to enter. No one had ever experienced or seen anything like this before. No! This was not their idea of what the conquest of a city should be. They were used to something altogether different. First assault would follow assault. Siege towers would creak, battering rams thump, dust and rubble rain upon their heads while missiles, fire, boiling water, stones and arrows poured down over the ramparts. Both sides would be seized by a frenzy of rage and destruction. At last the walls would be taken; the victors rush into the town. They would run through its streets, drunk with bloodshed, covered with blood, lusting for murder. When the frenzy of slaughter left them, they would split the loot, rest, then sing a "Te Deum" of thanksgiving. That was the normal course. Those were things one understood.

But to enter a city of corpses? To conquer a graveyard? No, there was no glory in that. The conquerors of Damietta felt downcast and shamed. A strange horror oppressed their hearts. This first hold the Latins had gained in Egypt was an event of tremendous importance. In France, Italy, England and Germany bells would ring to celebrate the glad tidings. Here, however, no one felt rapture. Somehow it was difficult to rejoice or feel proud of the victory.

Only Cardinal Pelagius was pleased. Who was to blame that all those wretches had died? They could have surrendered! Why didn't they? Damietta had been taken—that was all that mattered. Almost completely recovered he rode up and down the streets of the town looking like a monument in crimson, and issued orders. Remove and cart away the corpses. Bring settlers to fill the empty houses and shops. Anybody was welcome; Copts, Armenians, Jews, even Moslems. The wealth of Damietta was famous and volunteers came in droves, Genoans first of all. As though they had been only awaiting this moment they arrived in scores, bringing their families and servants; opened trading posts, strove to obtain special privileges. Venetians also would have been glad to settle in the city but the Genoan Podesta reminded the Cardinal in time of the

villainous part Venetian shipowners had played in the drama of the
Children's Crusade. How after committing such a crime could the slayers
of innocents be allowed to profit by the wealth won by Crusaders?

The Children's Crusade! It was the first time it had been mentioned
—and only for the purpose of removing a competitor! It had happened
but a short while ago—less than four years—and already no one remembered it. The circles on life's surface had closed again, the memory had
vanished in the past. Maybe here and there a mother still continued to
weep; maybe the half-demented Madonna de Trevi still rode up and
down Italy calling: "Save them! Save the children!" Nevertheless the
Legate acknowledged the justice of the Podesta's remarks and forbade
the Venetians to settle in Damietta.

Sultan al-Kamil spent all his days seated motionless in his fabulous
palace of Cairo and lost in gloomy thoughts. It was not so much the
accursed Franks who were on his mind, as Bibars. The Sultan hated that
Turk in whose presence he never felt master nor able to control his fears.
Whenever Bibars spoke to him the Sultan felt as though the commander
of his troops was examining him with his eyes, seeking on his neck and
his breast the spot where his dagger would plunge. It seemed to him, too,
that not only the soldiers but likewise his courtiers, slaves, dignitaries,
servants, everybody in fact, made more of Bibars than of himself, the
Ruler of the Faithful! How hurriedly, how humbly they bent in two
whenever the man entered! The thing to do was to have Bibars killed
at once. But this was not easy. Why was it so simple to send to death even
a thousand men, and so hard to annihilate one Bibars? The reason was
simple. There was no one to do it. Unless he, the Sultan, did it himself
. . . with his own hands. But this the Sultan did not dare. Bibars was
taller and stouter than he. No doubt but that he would forestall his
movement and kill the Sultan instead. Yet, no one else could be entrusted with the task. Was there anyone in whom he could confide? Anyone of whom he could be sure? Who would not go to Bibars and warn
him of the orders just received? The Sultan did not trust anyone. Ibn
Giuzi, the only man with whom he could speak openly, had returned to
Damascus to plead for help. To be sure Ibn Giuzi would not have killed
Bibars either, but perhaps he would arrange with the Old Man of the
Mountains to get rid of the fellow. The Old Man of the Mountains never
failed. Too bad Ibn Giuzi was away! By Allah! And what if Bibars had

already guessed the Sultan's scheme and forestalled him? What if Ismaelites, sent to murder the Sultan, were already here, among his slaves? At the thought perspiration dripped from the brow of the Ruler of the Faithful.

While those thoughts pressed upon him from every side and made him feel like an antelope surrounded by lions, in a sudden flash he saw a way out. Escape! Leave everything, mount a horse and flee from Cairo! But soon reason returned. He was the nephew of Saladin, the Great Sultan. He could not dishonor the dynasty of Ajubites. But then what was he to do? Unless . . . there was still another possibility . . . Peace! Yes, peace was the only way out. Peace at any price. Once he had made truce with the Franks he could go anywhere he pleased, even visit the Franks themselves; he could set out to his brother's rescue or simply leave for one of his more outlying castles. Peace!

And without advising anyone of his decision he entrusted a new mission to the court chamberlain, Ibn Djelila. The terms which the latter was to submit to the Franks were unheard of, dazzling Only a man living in mortal fear, his mind and heart torn by anguish, could have made a similar offer. In return for peace, immediate permanent peace, he would give the Franks Damietta, the Holy Land, the Timber of the Holy Cross, and bind himself to pay an annual tribute of a thousand Byzantian gold pieces.

Never before had any Sultan proposed peace on such terms. No wonder Cardinal Pelagius was beaming. He had completely recovered and was now receiving the Sultan's emissaries in full splendor, draped in crimson and seated upon the throne in what used to be the Sultan's palace of Damietta. The dome-shaped ceiling of the great hall was bound by a ring of windows set with cut crystal the color of amethyst and sapphire. The light that sifted through fell soft and mysterious upon the walls inlaid with ivory and glittering like a precious coffret. Jean de Brienne sat by the Legate's side upon a lower chair, the rest of the knights stood around in a semicircle.

After hearing the envoy through the Legate turned to them.

"See what I have achieved, Messers Barons. I prevented you from making an error six months ago. I know what was said of me at the time. I saw how you glared at me. Now you see for yourself who had been right. The faint-hearted and cowardly—or I?"

He looked down upon them, gloating in his triumph. How they must hate him—this King of Jerusalem, these knights whom he humiliated so, whom he abused with such impunity! What did he care? They had to listen, for it was he who had been right. He had won!

He turned to the interpreter. "I am truly grateful to the Sultan for his sincere wish for peace. Nevertheless I cannot accept his terms." And amidst general stupefaction he continued: "If the Sultan gives us the entire coast called the Delta, I shall make truce with him at once."

"An overdrawn string will snap," said Jean de Brienne in a low voice.

"That's what you said before. I will not give in. If the Sultan is ready to give Damietta he will give up the rest."

"The entire coast," he repeated firmly, turning to the emissaries. "This is the answer you can take to the Sultan."

Al-Kamil impatiently awaited the return of Djelila. He had ordered that he be brought at once.

"What do you bring?" he asked, trembling with excitement.

Ibn Djelila fell upon his face. "They want all of the Delta, Oh, Ruler of the Faithful! They want all of it."

"Thou filthy swine!" In a fit of fury the Sultan smashed the head of the emissary with his golden truncheon. Let him die; the man who had seen to what extent the Sultan had abased himself could not remain alive.

The slaves hurriedly carried out the quivering body. Al-Kamil breathed relieved. The act of violence had restored his courage. . . . His arm was still strong. Could he but smash Bibars' head, too! The accursed infidels! They had scorned his plea. They demanded all of the Delta! All! They might as well have demanded his, al-Kamil's head. What would Egypt be without the Delta? Truly they must be possessed. Possessed by the demon of pride and evil. Never again would he turn to them. Never! He had recovered his senses. Anything rather than a truce with the Franks. He would not leave them Damietta. He would fight till he had driven them out of Egypt. Compared with them even Bibars seemed less menacing, less hateful. After all he was one of his own sort, a true Moslem. A faithful of the Prophet, not an unclean swine like those others. War upon them! War to the last, to death!

And for the first time in a long while he sent for Bibars, his commander in chief. He addressed him with authority, nor did he wonder what the other might think. Never mind that! What mattered now was to smash the Franks.

"Truly, it is a shame they should still be there," Bibars agreed. He was stupefied at the change he found in his master. Had he received some news? Was al-Muzaam coming to his aid? In that case, Bibars would have to postpone his ambitious schemes. . . .

"Truly it is a shame," he repeated. "I heard, Oh, Ruler of the Faithful, you were pleased to kill Ibn Djelila with your own hand. Indeed I deem it too great an honor for that miserable jackal."

"I killed him," calmly replied the Sultan, "because he suggested I should leave Damietta to the Franks."

Cardinal Pelagius had agreed to grant an audience to brother Francis. He felt so happy and pleased with the world that from pure kindness he would willingly spare a few moments to speak with the simple-minded friar.

Francis seemed smaller, greyer and more miserable than ever. He seated himself on the floor at the Cardinal's feet.

"Reverend Lord Legate," he said, "is it true that the Sultan's emissaries have again proposed peace and you have turned it down?"

"Yes, I turned it down," the Cardinal confirmed. "I want victory complete." He cast Francis a suspicious glance and asked sharply: "Who sent you here with this question?"

"Who sent me? No one. I came of my own will to implore you, revered Lord Cardinal, not to do it. The victory is won. The Sultan wants to return the Holy Land."

"And he offers Damietta to boot! But I want all of the Delta. All the ports! Only then will the Holy Land be safe, Islam smashed and the States of the Church great. . . . Do you know what the greatness of the Ecclesiastical State means? The power and might of the Church!"

"So many people, so many, have died in Damietta!"

"They were heathens!"

"That's just it. They died without ever hearing of the Lord Jesus. We lost their souls. They were dying of hunger. Tiny children withered like leaves in the drought. Mothers had to look upon their torments before they died in turn. They all died without comfort or hope. And all because of Christians! And now must they continue to die?"

Oh, enough of that whimpering! The Legate could barely refrain from ordering the moaning half-wit out. He restrained himself for the sake of the Holy Father who held him in great respect. Likewise the late

Pope Innocent had sent for Francis in the hour of his death. Besides, Cardinal Pelagius was not a bad man. Whatever he did he did in good faith. Therefore he decided to calm and enlighten the poor fellow.

"Sacrifices are inevitable," he patiently explained, "when great ends are to be achieved."

"But the end is already achieved."

The Cardinal knitted his heavy brows. "Listen when I speak, mendicant. I told you that to make the Holy Land safe we must weaken Islam and strengthen the Church State. These rich ports, this soil, will belong to no one but the Pope. Is that clear? Thanks to them the Holy Father will become a ruler equal to the mightiest Emperor. He will be able to impose his will, account to no one save God, bend the proud necks of the Barons, declare himself the supreme Mediator in all earthly problems. He will be able to reward and to punish. This last in particular, for who fears anathema today? But once the Holy See has at its disposal a powerful army and a fleet, once the wealth of Egypt begins to pour into the Papal treasury . . ."

Francis, in despair, hid his face in his hands. "Lord Jesus did not possess anything and did not order Peter to strive for worldly power!"

"But He made him a rock and what is rock like in this world if not power? He told him to live and act among people, not among angels. Therefore we must think and build in the human way, in the worldly way . . ."

"He told us to be perfect like Himself and follow Him in everything! And the Holy Gospel . . ."

"Ridiculous dreamer, do you think you can conquer the world by the words of the Gospel! The world would crucify the Church even as it crucified Our Lord. . . . Of what account are the weak today? The weak will not conquer the evil!"

"It is the mighty who are weak and will not conquer anything. Because always there will be those even mightier than they who will overcome them. But anyone who possesses nothing in the worldly sense and relies completely on the Lord is invincible, for God stands by him . . ."

"God helps those who help themselves. We are the triumphant Church, the struggling Church. We march forward heedless of sacrifices, for so duty commands us to do. We must conquer all who will not think according to the Church teaching, destroy paganism and set the Church above all else!"

"Destroy paganism, yes, but not the pagans," cried Francis, choking with tears. "They are our brethren! In what are they to blame? They have never heard of Christ . . . They only knew their Prophet . . . They believe in him as best they can . . . There are among them good and honest men . . . I was told of the charitable sheik Hassam who, though rich, shared everything with the poor and gave everything he had and died of starvation like the rest."

But Pelagius had had enough. Anyhow his chaplain had just announced the arrival of his Honor Bartholomeo Doria, Podesta of Genoa. With a motion of his hand the Legate dismissed Francis. The Podesta entered the room; somehow he seemed less brilliant, less sure of himself than usual.

"I have heard of the mission Your Grace had turned down," he began, without preliminaries of any kind, "and I am sorry I did not come sooner to dissuade Your Grace from this step."

"I did as I consider fit," the Cardinal retorted haughtily, "and I would not act otherwise."

"Your Grace, I have just received through my men news of which the Sultan himself is not aware. . . . No one knows of it . . . Important news . . ."

"What news! Speak . . ."

"The Mongols have abandoned Baghdad and are moving on Ruthenia. The war spear stuck in front of the Subutay's tent points towards the West. . . ."


"The Mongols march on to Ruthenia!"

God knows how the news had slipped through to the knights. Not all understood its threatening portent. It was Sir Dzierzek who was moved the most. "Woe!" he exclaimed. "We should have forced the Legate, even rebel if need be, but by all means make truce, recover the Holy Land and return to our lands."

"Why?" asked the others. "Isn't Ruthenia, likewise, somewhere in Asia? We never heard of it."

"Ruthenia is not in Asia. It takes no more than four days to get from Ruthenia to Hungary and it has a common border with Poland. Ruthenians are our neighbors!" And although so many years had gone by since he had left his country, he suddenly saw it as if he were there, those flower-covered meadows of which not so long ago he had been telling Francis, and a dark foreboding clutched his heart.

# 9.

# Christian and Moslem

WITH GREAT TENDERNESS FRANCIS TOOK LEAVE OF BROTHER ILLUMINA-
tus and brother Caesar who, weeping, implored him to remain
or let them come along. Turning a deaf ear to their pleas, he set forth at
a brisk pace. He stepped so boldly and calmly that it never occurred to
the Sultan's outpost to ask him what right he had to be here? In his grey,
miserable cloak, his head wrapped in cloth, he looked like a dervish or
a madman, and madmen were considered saints by the Moslems. This
belief was further confirmed when he would come to them and with a
friendly, childish smile inquire: "Cairo? Malik? Soldan?" the only Arabic words he knew. Laughing they would point out the direction and so
he went on, scorching his feet upon the hot sand.

"Soldan? . . . Soldan?"

His progress was slow. Here a fellah was turning his water wheel and
had to be helped. Yonder children played in the road, beautiful Arab
children disfigured by clusters of flies that clung to their eyes. Francis
drove the flies away and fondled the coal-black little heads. Bedouin
bands roaming on the outskirts of the city in search of plunder passed
him on his way. Their vulture-like swarthy faces peered from under
black or white cloth, the whites of their eyes flashing wildly. They
would allow no stranger to get by alive but neither would they think of
attacking a dervish. When he looked at them smiling as was his wont,
they put their palms to their lips in greeting. Their small but incredibly
beautiful horses raised clouds of dust with their hoofs. No sooner had
they vanished than a patient little donkey would emerge from the dust
leading a string of weirdly rocking camels. Women in black robes returned from the wells carrying tall clay amphoras upon their heads.
Francis watched it all with great curiosity. Everything interested him,
he smiled upon them all. He did not feel a stranger, an enemy among

those people. The world that surrounded him, though to be sure not Christian, was still God's world. God had created it and now it waited for the glad tidings. And Francis felt a great desire to remain here; he would learn the language and tell these people of the Lord.

For the time being, however, he knew but two words: Malik, Soldan, which he shouted whenever afraid of losing his way.

Any dervish was allowed to come to the doors of the Sultan's palace but it was not easy to get inside. The guards did not let Francis in. Not in the least upset by this failure, he calmly seated himself under the wall and contentedly stretched out his sore and road-weary legs.

The Sultan was just returning from a ride. His robes and his turban shone with jewels, likewise the bridle and trappings of his mount were studded with gems. A band of beggars and dervishes ran behind the horse shouting and stretching their hands.

"Soldan! Soldan!" yelled Francis at the top of his lungs.

His foreign pronunciation attracted the Sultan's attention. "Who is that man?" he asked the commander of the guard, who stood bowing before him.

"Oh Ruler of the Faithful who has no equal! Some poor pilgrim craving the sight of your face. He must have come from afar. Look at his feet. Maybe he came from Mecca itself. Allah has tied his tongue and he cannot say anything else save your name."

Al-Kamil was an Ajubite, the nephew of the Great Salad-Din, therefore like all of his lineage he spoke Latin, considered as one of the prerequisites of a ruler's education, fairly well. He cast Francis a keen glance.

"Say, Dervish! Didn't you come perchance from the Christian camp?"

"Yes, I did," exclaimed Francis delighted. "That's where I came from to you, Reverend Sultan!"

"I knew that at once. Hey, thick heads!" he addressed the guards in Arabic. "This man is a giaour!"

"A giaour?" Two guards leaped upon Francis, naked daggers between their teeth, rapacious hands stretched toward him. The Sultan stopped them with a motion of his hand.

"Let him be for a while, only watch every gesture he makes. I want first to find out what brought him here."

A black slave bent in two, his forehead almost touching the ground.

The Sultan, stepping upon his back, dismounted. When he entered the palace Francis followed him, the two guardsmen, knives between their teeth, at his heels. The Sultan stretched comfortably upon a low ottoman. Francis sat in front of him on the floor.

"Did they send you here to kill me or to bewitch me?" inquired al-Kamil with scorn.

Francis shook his head. "Kill you, Messire Sultan? Indeed not. And no one sent me. I came myself."

"What for?" It flashed through the Sultan's mind that the man was a spy and would betray the plans of the Franks in return for gold. "Speak up, whatever you have to say. If the matter is truly important I shall reward you generously."

"The matter is of extreme importance and I am expecting a great reward from you, Messire Sultan. I would like the war to end. I implored our leader, the Legate of the Holy Father, to make truce and stop the fighting. For the heart cannot bear so much fierceness and at last the patience of Our Lord will be tried. The Legate would not listen to me, so I came to you."

Disappointed, al-Kamil peered at the huddled grey form at his feet. So the man was neither a murderer nor a spy, but a madman. Or was it only a clever pretense? He would find out.

"I can't help it that your leader is stubborn. Ought I perchance to relinquish all Egypt to the Franks and withdraw with my people into the desert to starve."

"That wouldn't be fair," replied Francis earnestly. "Egypt is your land, Messire Sultan, and no one should take it away from you. But you must do something else, something very profitable and beneficial, which will likewise put an end to the war . . ."

"What is it?" asked al-Kamil, his curiosity aroused.

"Embrace the Christian faith," Francis said with great simplicity.

The Sultan guffawed with laughter. None of those present understood their conversation and they stared with surprise at this fit of mirth.

"Embrace Christianity?" he echoed. "I will give you better advice: you embrace Islam, bow to the Prophet, and the war will also end."

It was Francis' turn to burst into laughter.

"How could that be, Messire Sultan, when our faith is the true one and yours is not? Who would ever exchange something better for something worse?"

Again words not to be uttered in the presence of a true Moslem. Involuntarily al-Kamil glanced around, scanning the faces of his court. What if someone understood? But the faces remained indifferent.

Reassured he nodded his head. "So your faith is the true one and mine is not. How will you prove this to me? I cannot renounce the faith of my forefathers on the strength of what some vagabond tells me?"

"Of course not." Francis had to admit the truth of the remark. "Indeed I am the most miserable and lowliest servant of Our Lord. Nevertheless His might is such that even through an instrument as unworthy as myself He can, if He will, show His magnificence. . . ."

"Let Him show it. I am waiting . . ." The Sultan stretched himself comfortably upon the cushions. He felt sincerely amused; he was having rare fun with that grey little man. "What will your Lord show me?"

"Our Lord can do anything He pleases. He can make the earth split asunder under our feet or the sky tumble on our heads. You, Messire Sultan, can order a great bonfire and have me thrown in it and, if such be His will, He can make me come out of it unharmed . . ."

"By Allah!" said the Sultan, squinting his eyes, "I am tempted to do it."

"Then why don't you?"

"Aren't you afraid?"

"No. I am not afraid, for my Lord is about me and nothing can befall me save what He means me to bear and what I duly deserve, and whatever He means me to bear He will adjust to my strength . . . I am not afraid, but I beg you, Messire Sultan,—and it is only just—let one of your men enter the fire with me. And let the one whose faith is false be consumed by flames and the one whose faith is true come out unharmed."

The Sultan turned to his court. "This dervish arouses my curiosity. He says he is willing to enter a bonfire with one of us in order to prove whose faith is better. That would be merry indeed. Come on! Which one of you will take up the challenge?"

They listened to him with apprehension. Was the Sultan speaking in jest or was he serious? They stirred uneasily, each trying to hide behind his neighbor's back.

"Oh Ruler of the Faithful," Sheik al-Atir exclaimed, "we are not dervishes."

"In that case fetch me a dervish."

Two slaves darted out of the room. The Sultan glanced at Francis who with complete unconcern was holding his thin, scarred heels in his hands.

"The dervishes will be here in a moment. You cannot draw back now!" the Sultan said.

"I will not draw back. I shall consider myself happy if this trial convinces you, Messire Sultan."

"You may burn."

"I may. It will mean that Our Lord wants to enlighten you in some other way, without my unworthy intervention . . ."

"But that will not bring you back to life."

"Our Lord in His mercy will give me eternal life, for I shall die for His glory."

"But it won't be pleasant to shrivel in the flames before you get there, will it?"

"Our Lord suffered more for us. Why shouldn't we suffer for Him, too?"

"Did your God suffer?" The Sultan lifted his brow, shocked.

"He suffered dreadfully. More than anybody can bear. And that is why we love Him so. Who else would have done so? He, the God, the Lord of everything, laid down His life for us, took our ills upon Himself, carried our pains, bore wounds for our evils, was ground to dust for our sins and His death healed us . . . That is why we must love Him more than aught else in the world. A mother does not love her children as much as He loves us, sinful men."

"In that case it's but just that you should love Him. But why should I have faith in Him? I for whom he did nothing?"

Francis gasped. "Why, He did it for you as much as for any one of us."

"I know nothing of it."

"But He knows, Sultan. And He loves you."

"Me?"

"You are His handiwork, His beloved child. . . . For no one in His eyes is either better or worse. You don't know Him, but He knows you. He knew you before you were in your father's seed, in your mother's womb. He guards every one of your steps. A hair does not fall from your head without His will. He looks at you. You can, whenever you want, turn to His protection. . . ."

He spoke with such conviction that the Sultan felt abashed and looked away. He gazed around with inquiring eye. "Where are the dervishes?"

"The slaves have not returned yet. Probably they are still looking for them."

"Looking for dervishes? There are always crowds of them lying in front of the palace." He yawned with feigned indifference and returned to the conversation.

"What does your God require in return for His bounties?"

"Nothing save that we love Him and try to become like Him . . . So He orders us to love every man as if he were our brother. . . . And share everything we have with others and wish no harm to anyone and thank Him for all that comes from His hand . . ."

"I have often been told," the Sultan interrupted him, propping himself on his elbows, "that the sons of Aiuba, of immortal fame, had a preceptor whose mother was a Christian. That woman, it seems, spoke of your faith and of your faithful much as you do. Lured by her stories, the old Emir al-Bara—that was the name of the preceptor—and the glorious sons of Aiuba nurtured friendly feelings towards the Christians. They sought in them merits described by that captive as the mark of your faith. They never found them. The Christians are untruthful and cruel and fight among themselves like dogs. They are grasping and dishonest. No one equals their arrogance. And so the Emir and his pupils discovered that the stories were but a delusion born of longing, for the woman was pining for her country. Now you again come with similar fables. . . ."

"The woman of whom you speak, Sultan—God bless her soul!— spoke the truth. And my words are also true. True, there are evil Christians, for human nature is weak and prone to sin. But despite their sins and errors Our Lord pleases to show His will through them and carry out His designs sometimes against their will. For His might has no limits even as His mercy has none. And through Him even the most wicked, untruthful, grasping and dastardly man can turn into a hero and a saint. And that is possible nowhere else save in Christianity!"

He broke off for in rushed a panting slave who prostrated himself before the Sultan.

"Oh Ruler of the Faithful, there are no dervishes," he stammered out. "They would not come . . . they fled . . ."

"I ordered them to be brought without being asked," the Sultan said angrily. "You deserve to be thrown into the fire yourself. Where is the other one? Has he done as well?"

Just then the second slave came in. He had had more luck for he was driving, or rather pushing before him a reluctant dervish, half naked and hairy, in a weird straw cap.

"Here he is, Oh Ruler of the Faithful," the slave said and flung the dervish like a carcass at the feet of the master. The man fell flat on his face and lay motionless, moaning.

"Rise, wretch!" snarled the Sultan angrily. "This infidel wants to submit to the trial of fire to prove which faith is true. I order you to accept his challenge!"

"Have mercy, Oh Ruler of the Faithful! Kill me at once! Spare me, an innocent, the tortures!"

"Why is he not afraid?"

"He is a sorcerer, Oh Ruler of the Faithful. He will cast a spell upon the flames so they will not touch him and burn only your servant!"

The Sultan eyed Francis suspiciously. "He does not want to enter the fire with you. He fears you are a magician."

"I am no magician," Francis retorted gaily, "and if he is I don't care. Our Lord is stronger than any magician. What can magic do against Him? Is your God not stronger than sorcerers?"

The Sultan flushed and kicked the dervish who still lay limp with terror at his feet. "Rise and bear witness to the greatness of the Prophet!"

But the man would not lift his face from the floor and continued whimpering until at last the Sultan had him thrown out of the room. Once released the dervish bolted as fast as his legs would carry him, his sandals clattering upon the marble paving of the courtyard.

Al-Kamil turned his angry eyes upon his courtiers. "This stranger," he said in Arabic, "will deride us and the Prophet. Miserable cowards, will none of you dare?"

"Oh Ruler of the Faithful," sighed Sheik al-Atir, his face pale as death, "no doubt the man is a magician. It is better to chop his head off at once. If his God is so mighty, let the steel of the ax bounce back from his neck . . ."

"I can have his head chopped off without the benefit of your advice. I want him to find out that our faith is as mighty as his!"

"Oh Ruler of the Faithful, Favorite of the Prophet. Everyone of us is true to our faith! We will be happy to die in a holy war, as the Prophet teaches us to. We would not even be afraid of flames. What we fear is that thanks to the magic wrought by this giaour the true believer shall perish in flame and true faith be dishonored. We know nothing of magic. We are warriors. If only the saintly Ibn Giuzi or the charitable Sheik Hassan who died in Damietta . . ."

"Ibn Giuzi, the great Mufti . . ." Al-Kamil saw before his eyes his stately, white-bearded figure. "No, Ibn Giuzi would not walk into the fire," he thought. "He is too wise, too learned to do it . . . Why is it that my men are afraid and you are not?" he shouted angrily at Francis. "I don't want any trial," he suddenly announced. "You may go . . ."

"I will not go, Messire Sultan, until you promise me you will fulfill my prayer."

"What prayer?"

"That you will learn to know Our Lord and once you know Him, accept Him?"

Al-Kamil laughed hoarsely. "You poor fool! If any of my men understood your words they would tear you to pieces before I could stop them! I can promise you one thing; if I meet more Christians like yourself, if I meet a hundred—nay, ten, hear you?—if I meet ten I shall change my opinion of your Christians. . . ."

Francis looked perplexed. "Messire Sultan, I fear that will be difficult, for, truly, it is not easy to find in the camp any creature as stupid and contemptible as myself."

"So I gather. You can go. You are leaving like a child, unaware that you have put your head into the lion's jaws. For I have sworn hatred to the Franks and ordered that none who comes here be allowed to depart alive! But you I shall let go free. Not only that, I want to reward you. I have not even noticed how two hours have gone by while I talked with you. Time usually drags for me. Therefore, as a reward for the entertainment you have provided, I shall give you as much gold as you can carry . . ."

Francis lifted his arms alarmed. "Gold? What would I do with it? I don't need any gold."

"You don't need gold? You don't want it? It is the first time I behold such a giaour!" He turned to his men. "This infidel wants no gold!"

"A magician! He will make it himself," mumbled the Sheik.

Francis observed them smiling. "Messire Sultan! I don't want gold but instead pray give me another precious gift. Allow me to visit the spot where the most blessed Virgin Mary and the Holy Child dwelt."

Al-Kamil fell to thinking. "Indeed I have heard that the Copts worship a tree and a spring near which Miriam, the mother of the prophet Jesus, used to sit. I consent. You can go there. I shall give you a rope with my seal. With this sign you can go safely anywhere, even to Jerusalem."

Francis joyously sprang to his feet. "God will repay you, Messire Sultan! God will repay you! How wonderful! I shall go there at once!"

Al-Kamil watched him from the corner of his eye, a strange smile hovering on his lips.

"Here near Cairo you run the risk of being cut to pieces as soon as anyone notices you are a giaour. Therefore I shall detail a slave for your protection. He will likewise show you the spots held in respect by the Copts. After that he shall take you to the advance posts of the Franks and then return to me. Remember, the slave belongs to me and you must send him back."

"Of course, Messire Sultan. I don't see, though, what need I have of brother slave? No one has killed me so far and no one will, if Our Lord wants me to stay alive."

"The slave shall go," said the Sultan, "and return." He turned to al-Atir. "Have one of the Christian slaves brought here."

The Sheik gaped. "The slave will escape to his own camp, Oh Ruler of the Faithful! Why should you lose a worker?"

"Do as I tell you."

A moment later a miserable looking man clad in grey slipped into the room. Francis looked at him and gasped. That emaciated, aged, bearded wretch with the twisted head and the neck bruised by the harness was none other than his old companion, his renegade brother, the brother who, like a child, craved miracles and could not bear sunlight—John a Capello himself!

"Brother!" Francis exclaimed. "Dear brother!"

The slave did not reply. Tears flooded his face but he stood motionless, afraid lest by the slightest gesture he might rouse the wrath of his masters. The Sultan watched them both with a quizzical smile.

"I see that you know each other," he said. "So much the better. This man is my slave, dervish. He will accompany you as a guide, then he will take you to the Franks' outposts and return to me. Here is my sign. It will open all gates before you. You may go now."

# 10.

## The Mystery of the Sphinx

THE RUINS OF THE ANCIENT CITY OF HELIOPOLIS, OF WHICH CAIRO, THE present capital of the Sultan, was once but a miserable suburb, stretched far and wide in a shapeless heap of rubble. Not a single building had remained standing. All that was left was a double row of obelisks, pointing upright to the sky like the raised fingers of Earth, a double row that stretched into space and led nowhere. The great temple of Amon which they had been erected to adorn lay in ruins; the gods Isida, Osiris and Ra were forgotten. At the very end of this long avenue of stone giants rose a tree, a gnarled and twisted sycamore tree. It was almost as old as the obelisks themselves, sparsely covered with leaves and surrounded with a mass of roots which seemed to push out of the ground, unable to find room in the overcrowded soil. In a hollow of these gnarled roots, his back leaning against the coarse bark of the trunk, sat Francis staring in front of him, lost in thought. The net of branches stretched over his head like a dark, woven tent. The limbs seemed so stout in their great age that one might surmise they had not changed since the days when the Salvation of the world reposed here. For this was the holy sycamore tree called the Tree of the Virgin. And as he gazed upon it Francis suddenly realized that nothing prevented him now from going to the Holy Land. In a short while he would be there, and with his own eyes would behold the places where the Holy Family not only chanced to rest, as here, but lived, worked and suffered. How much accumulated grace must continue to dwell there! How the soul would breathe it in! Not a particle of the great miracle of Redemption could have been lost, and the treasure of merits beyond comprehension still hung over the earth, invisible to the eye. One could draw and draw from it, and it would not diminish ever.

"How wonderful is the history of the world," he said with conviction.

The words were addressed to the Sultan's slave, once called John a Capello, who sat huddled nearby. John gave a start and lifted his eyes. "It is horrible. Horrible and accursed," he replied.

Francis caressed his shaggy, wasted head. "It all depends from what point of view we look at it; that of our weakness and actions or that of God's mercy. Give vent to your bitterness, brother. Tell me all that has happened to you since I saw you last."

"I would rather not tell," muttered John sullenly. "When I left you I let myself be persuaded by the Devil. For surely that man must have been the Devil. You, on the other hand, asked too much. Maybe I wouldn't have left you if things had been different. . . . You told us always to rejoice and admire everything when all around us was so drab and poor and common! Do you still forbid the brethren to possess anything, to keep provisions? Do you still make them lead a homeless, vagrant life?"

"How could I change it, brother, when Christ ordered us to live in this way—and He won't change His words!"

"And did they all remain?"

"And many others joined. There are more than five hundred of us now."

"Strange. Strange indeed. . . . It was so hard . . . And worst of all was the monotony. . . . And also that you never allowed us to talk of any miracles. . . . Nor would you show them. . . . Oh, don't interrupt me, Francis! You do work miracles! Have you not bewitched the Sultan? You can bewitch anyone. It seems incredible that a Christian should have gone to Cairo and departed not only alive but bearing the Sultan's seal, the Sultan's 'firman,' as they call it. It is but seldom they give it to anyone. It gives you limitless power. With it you can go into any city and to the Emir or the Khedi, their chief magistrates, and demand anything you please! To be handed over the city, the treasury, the slaves, anything—and they must obey! And you were given that seal! You could go and order all Christian prisoners captured in the Third Crusade who are working now on the construction of the El Sultan Kalaum mosque in Cairo to be set free. . . . You will do it, won't you, Francis?"

"I will not. I would be abusing the Sultan's trust. I can only go back to him and beg him to release them."

"But you won't order me to . . . ?"

John peered anxiously into Francis' face. Francis smiled. "Were you very unhappy here?"

"It was Hell! Hell! God, what a Hell!"

"Then you won't remain in it . . . And now tell me more. Did none of the children survive? Couldn't some still be found?"

"Do not remind me of the children. It was I, I who urged them to go . . . It was to me they cried for help! Four galleys sank. The one on which I was escaped. Would to God the sea had swallowed it like the rest! We were put ashore. . . . The traders who were already awaiting us there fell at once to wrangling and fighting, inasmuch as the emissaries of the Old Man of the Mountains, who had handsomely paid the Venetians in advance, screamed that all the boys belonged to him and the others insisted they be shared. They fought with each other; tugged at the children. The children cried. That night several of them tried to escape. They were caught and cruelly beaten. Little Marita, from fear, jumped into the sea and drowned . . . At last they were divided and taken away . . . I stood there till the very last. They cried: 'Where is the Angel Gabriel? Why doesn't he come?' I will never forget those cries . . . I know not what became of them afterwards. . . . If they are still alive, they must be somewhere far away, where no one save God can find them . . . Why has God allowed it to happen? Why didn't He save them? I am damned, Francis, for I have lost faith in God's justice!"

"Come, brother, you yourself contributed to their misfortune, and now you blame God?"

"Why did He allow it? I am damned," sobbed John.

"All of us deserve to be damned but God's mercy watches over us. . . . And wherever those children may be, God is with them . . ."

"If I could only forget! Now, again, I can hardly believe I shall at last be free. I would rather we did not go anywhere, but proceed straight to Damietta. I tremble lest the Sultan changes his mind and, seeing I don't return, sends his men in pursuit . . ."

"I shall go back in your stead, so never fear, he won't pursue us."

"You, in my stead?"

"One of us must, of course, come back. You have suffered enough, brother. You deserve to be free."

"I don't want you to remain in my stead!" shouted John. "Why can't we both go back to Damietta?"

"Because the Sultan has put his trust in us."

"He did it deliberately. I saw how he smiled. The devil!"

"The more reason why we must not succumb to temptation."

"But you cannot remain. What would the brethren do without you? You are needed. . . . And I? I, too, cannot remain . . . I can't. If you only knew! The degradation, the squalor, the incessant work! I would soon go mad."

"Therefore you must not go back, brother. Do not worry about me. The brethren will manage. I have fared too well in this world, it is time I suffer a little for Our Lord. I shall learn the language and tell the people about Him. . . . A man can be useful and happy anywhere. . . ."

John burst into loud sobs like a child. "I don't want it! Let us both go back!"

"You know yourself it is impossible. No use talking about it any more. Come, let us drink some more from the spring of the Most Blessed Virgin. After that I would like to go yonder and take a look at those great pyramids of which the king's astrologer told me once. It seems next to them stands the figure of the Sphinx called the Enigma of the Earth."

"I have seen it many times," returned John, indifferent and wretched. "Big as a mountain; the Arabs call him Abu-Hol, the Father of Horror. It seems demons carved it and demons dwell in it. It must be true. It smiles as though it scoffed at everything. Only Satan can smile that way. I used to pass it while dragging stones with the others and each time the burden seemed heavier, the brace cut deeper in the flesh. I used to turn away my head to avoid the sight . . ." He broke off and in a sudden burst of despair shouted: "I don't want to stay! I will not stay!"

"I told you already you shan't . . ."

"But I cannot accept it at such price. . . ."

"The price is small, and I, as you see, do not take it to heart at all. Why should I dread slavery when I do not fear purgatory that is no doubt awaiting me?"

But John would not be soothed and when, after washing themselves at the spring, they set out for Gizeh, he dragged behind, weighted down by his thoughts. Francis constantly turned to him inquiring eagerly of this and that, but John replied in monosyllables, not aware of what he was saying. He kept fingering the Sultan's firman, for Francis had entrusted to him the precious sign, abhorring its very touch. "You keep it now," he had said. "Later, I shall ask brother Illuminatus who probably will go with me to Jerusalem, to carry it for me."

The firman consisted of a tasseled piece of green silk rope clasped in the middle by a golden seal.

"I ought to bolt with it," thought John, "and do as I please. I could go back to the camp loaded with riches or free the prisoners. Francis is out of his head; he always was. I would be a fool to consider him. I would be a fool not to use the firman for my own good, and the good of others. If I turn around he surely will not try to chase me. He will just stop and gaze . . . He will gaze . . . No, I won't be able to bear that gaze of his. Better wait till he falls asleep. He probably sleeps as of old—a deep, untroubled slumber."

So his thoughts ran, while dusk gathered all around. The sun had set, the moon not yet risen. At last there came a moment of complete darkness and silence. There was no sound except from the howling jackals in the shrubs. Along with the darkness chill had fallen upon the world and only the sand that sifted softly under foot still retained the heat of the day and warmed their bare feet.

"I shall bolt," decided John. "Nothing will happen to Francis anyway. He will continue to smile in that way he has, even in captivity. If they beat him or abuse him he will say it is all right—he does not deserve aught else. Don't I know him? And anyway as soon as he finds a way to make himself understood, he will beguile them all. Who knows whether even that cruel old brute Mahmud, the overseer, won't change under his influence? But what will the brothers do without him? What will they say when they see me return instead of Francis? But how will they know? Who will tell them? Not I. . . ." But what if the Sultan should release Francis in spite of his escape and he and Francis should meet in Damietta? Sure thing that Francis would stretch out his hands and call out as friendly as ever: "Brother!" No, no, the very thought was unbearable. . . . Oh, why should there be so many complications? Why couldn't they simply return to Damietta together?

He repeated the last question aloud. Francis stopped and faced him. "Because it would be dishonest!"

"One need not be honest with pagans and enemies."

"Who told you so? One must always be honest with anyone. God commands us to."

"How often even the best among men use stealth to attain some good end?"

"I assure you they won't attain it in this case. Our Lord admits no evil means. There is only one way, the straight one."

John was about to disagree when suddenly he remembered the time Robert stole a denarius from his father and Nicholas praised him for it, insisting no means were bad when the end itself was good. So he kept his peace.

"Do you consider it a sin when one tries to escape from captivity?"

"Not at all. Probaby I would do it myself. But not if I promised I wouldn't."

They continued on their way. The moon rose, big and red. Slowly it turned from red to gold and flooded the sky with light. Francis stopped abruptly. "Is that he?"

"Yes, it is he," replied John, involuntarily lowering his voice. "The Father of Horror."

The mighty slopes of the pyramids seemed to draw back, their granite surface shimmering in the moonlight, and against their background rose the stone face unlike any other in the world. The desert sand had covered it almost to the neck, the line of its back was barely perceptible under the dune.

"They say," whispered John, "that under the sand he is complete: breast, paws and all . . . The wind had buried him in sand. . . . It is awesome to stand here, for at times it seems he will speak up. . . . No one can understand his words but men die at the very thought he may address them. . . . Let us go away. . . . Look, there are the pyramids . . . ! And these ruts here! It is we, the prisoners, who made them when dragging stones from that third one. Almost fifty years ago Sultan Ottoman wanted to tear them down. He started with the smallest one. A thousand men worked for eight months. They tore down such heaps of stones that one could not see the world for them. The Sultan arrived and seeing this was pleased, till he lifted his head and peered. Lo and behold! the pyramid stood as it always stood, only a little scratched at one side . . . do you see that crevice? That's it. The Sultan felt ashamed and ordered work stopped. As for the stones they tore down at the time, they are hewn and smooth, so we must drag them to Cairo to be used as building material. . . . Let us go, it is awesome to stand here . . ."

"On the contrary, I think it's beautiful here," Francis retorted. "I would not depart so soon. We have to stop for the night anyway. Why not here?"

"Francis!" John exclaimed alarmed, "believe me! Any Moslem would rather spend the night on the Rock of the Cranes than here!"

"What is the Rock of Cranes?"

"Across the Nile in the daytime you can see it from here. It is called Gebel al-Fair. There is a crevice in it where demons dwell, just as in this Sphinx. Once a year cranes, herons and storks from all over the country gather upon that rock. They circle around it waiting and croaking till the crevice swallows one bird. Then the rest fly away, released. People dread to pass by Gebel al-Fair at night. But for all that they would prefer to spend the night in that crevice than here in the shadow of the Father of Horror!"

"The Moslems, poor things, are bound to be frightened, but we are not. Our sister stars shine so beautifully over our heads! The divine presence covers us like a tent. Why, brother, there is no spot in this world where a Christian need feel lonely!"

"Listening to you," John remarked with a sneer, "one might think there was no Satan in the world."

"Oh, he is here all right. He prowls everywhere. Only he cannot accomplish anything where Divine protection stands watch."

Ignoring his companion's fears and objections Francis chose a hollow in the sand and both lay down in it huddling close to each other, for the night had grown acutely cold. Despite the closeness of their bodies their thoughts were dissimilar and far apart. John mused about the problems of captivity. Francis did not detach his eyes from the Sphinx that looked over them. Sphinx. . . . What a strange word . . . The astrologer had said it meant a mystery or an enigma. And truly he looked as if he knew something no one else did. The moon sailed across the sky, lengthening and shortening the shadows upon the stony face, and one could easily imagine that the giant was alive and about to speak.

"He is waiting for something," thought Francis. "He lifts his head and peers watchfully. He smiles because he knows that whatever he is waiting for will come. But what is he waiting for . . . ? The Moslems say that demons made him and he himself is a demon . . ." A blue clad feminine figure with the Child in her arms passed over these sands many centuries ago. Maybe it was her return the face of stone awaited? For was she not to beg and obtain salvation for all . . . ?

Salvation for all! . . . Nature would once more become sacred and pure even as it was before the fall. Nature. . . . Was it not Nature that smiled with lips of stone, gazing into space over the desert? And did it not smile just because it knew of its future liberation and was awaiting it? Only a pagan could call the Sphinx a demon or the work of a demon. Demon meant nothing but struggle and unrest, and the Sphinx breathed peace. . . . No, he was no demon but the core of Earth, Nature itself, defiled by the sin of man, abused, enslaved yet smiling in its sense of its inherent, immortal sacredness. And the mystery of the Sphinx—why, it was the conviction of ultimate salvation!

And Francis was filled with overwhelming joy. It swelled in him, till he could no longer contain it. Unable to utter a word he stretched his hands toward the stone giant with a deep sense of brotherhood and common hope.

John, startled by the gesture, lifted his head and gasped. For suddenly it seemed to him that the smile of that good brother Francis was the reflection of the omniscient smile of the Sphinx. . . .

"Look! You can already see our men from here," said Francis, serene as ever. "Those tents belong to the men of Sir Simon de Joinville who are standing watch this month. The army is quartered in the town but some troops are always stationed here to keep an eye on the country. . . . Farewell, brother. May Our Lord guard you and grant you peace. If you see brother Illuminatus and brother Caesar give them my love and tell them I ask them to continue to work even as they do now. They are doing a great deal of good, much more than I, who lately have been only roving about . . . Brother Illuminatus has talked himself hoarse preaching. . . ."

"I can well imagine how they will welcome me," muttered John sullenly.

"How else can they welcome you save like a brother? God be with you!"

"Don't go away yet," shouted John, clutching desperately at his hand. He became lost in contemplation of the tents that shone white a little way off, on the pennants fluttering in the wind . . . Yes, here were

Christians, Latins . . . In town, he would surely find his countrymen, men from Italy . . . A few more steps and he would no longer be a slave but a free man. And Francis? "Don't go away yet," he repeated. "I can't. . . . Listen! You are cruel. You are torturing me! You must understand that I can neither reject nor accept your offer! Oh, how I suffer . . . !"

"My brother," whispered Francis gently, "don't worry over me. I am happy . . ."

But John no longer could control himself.

"Happy?" he almost screamed. "I know! You are always happy! I dread you . . . you tempter . . . I saw last night how you smiled just like the Sphinx and stretched your hands to that stone devil . . . You are terrible in that love of yours for everything . . You are inexorable . . . There is nothing you would not demand of a man, as though it were a trifle . . . ! You would turn the world upside down!"

"Brother of mine . . . Why, I neither want nor demand anything. What am I? The most miserable of the Lord's servants, chaff, a blade of grass. . . . It is He who calls you, it is His love that is inexorable . . ."

"Am I to remain a slave and not return there, to my own kind?" sobbed John.

"Not at all. I tell you, go. I am happy. Perhaps I will be able to atone for some of my sins; to lessen the penance that awaits me after death. . . . It's a great favor to be able to forestall death which can pluck us and fling us before God's judgment before we are ready. . . ."

John kept silently staring at the ground. "I shall go!" he said at last. "I shall go. I will not be a slave."

"You are right. Go in peace."

"Stop! Wait! And the Holy Land? Won't you go to the Holy Land?"

"No. Probably I don't deserve to see it. Don't worry about me any more, brother . . ."

"I can't help it! Don't go away! You will set off at peace with yourself and I . . . I . . . How am I going to live?"

"Then let us pray together . . ."

They knelt side by side . . . From the camp de Joinville's men at arms watched curiously the strange doings of two tattered tramps . . .

"Has the slave I sent with the Christian dervish returned?" inquired Sultan al-Kamil the next day.

"No, Oh Ruler of the Faithful. Shall we send a pursuit?"

"No."

The Sultan put his hands under his head and stared at the vivid pattern of the mosaic which covered the ceiling. "I expected," he thought, "this man would prove to be different from the rest. He seemed different. I was wrong. All men are alike, no matter what their faith. Men are but cattle, contemptible cattle. I was wrong. What do you want?" he inquired sharply of a servant who had slipped in timidly.

"Oh Ruler of the Faithful, I only wanted to tell you that the slave about whom you were pleased to ask has returned a while ago and has gone to work with the rest."

"Allah akhbar. You can go away!"

# 11.

## History Repeats Itself

CARDINAL PELAGIUS GAZED AT FRANCIS INCREDULOUSLY. HE WAS DISpleased, as he always was when something had occurred without his knowledge. "You went to the Sultan without my leave?" he commented sullenly.

"I did not think I needed leave, Reverend Legate. What do I matter? I did not go as an envoy. Not even as a messenger. I just went."

"The idea itself was not bad," conceded the Cardinal, "but I would have preferred if someone else had gone in your place. Somebody more impressive, a better speaker, somebody who could present our faith better than you. He would have made a totally different impression upon the heathen."

"That's true," admitted Francis ruefully. "It did not occur to me."

"Of course it did not. I understand and I am not angry. I know what one can ask of men. It would be asking too much of your mind, brother. What a pity, though, one of our theologians did not go instead. . . . Still, what's done is done. So you spoke with the Sultan himself?"

"Yes, Reverend Legate. I did."

"And what did he seem like to you?"

"He seemed a good man."

"Good?" The Legate's voice swelled with indignation. "Why, the man is a heathen!"

"Maybe Our Lord will permit that he will not remain one. And as a man he is truly good."

"So you got to know him that well? What did you talk about?"

"I besought him to embrace our faith."

Although the Cardinal did not lack courage he was so astonished by this simple statement that for a while he remained speechless. "You besought him to . . . And they did not fall upon you?"

"No. The Sultan even gave me his seal, which brother Illuminatus
319

carries now in his bosom. With that I can go in the Sultan's land where-ever I please. In fact I came here to ask leave to go to Jerusalem."

"You want to go now? All by yourself? Wouldn't you rather wait a few weeks till we all go there in triumph and take possession? . . ."

"May Our Lord free the Holy Land as soon as possible, but I will not wait. What need will there be of me on the day of triumph? I would rather go and worship at Our Lord's tomb now, when it's still forlorn, and when, maybe, no one prays there . . ."

"Do as you please. Do as you please. I do not object . . . God be with you . . . Wait . . . wait a moment. . . ."

Francis, who was about to depart, stopped short. The Cardinal rubbed his brow as though he had forgotten what he meant to say. He was sorry now he had detained his visitor. The presence of Francis always filled him with strangely mixed feelings: he felt pity for the simple-minded fellow and yet, somehow, the man disturbed him. He felt the need of speaking of something, of explaining something to him. This strange urge had grown even stronger now that he heard Francis was about to depart. But as to what he wanted to say—he knew not. Francis continued to stand by the door gazing at him with friendly, expectant eyes.

"Why did you go to the Sultan?" asked the Legate; he had to say something.

"I wanted the war to end and people to stop killing each other. You, Reverend Legate, would not listen to me, so I went to the Sultan . . ."

"Oh! So that was the reason? I remember now how sorry you were for those who perished in Damietta. It can't be helped. People think me a hard-hearted man. It is not so. My heart is not hard but I know how to keep my eyes fixed upon the purpose I've set for myself and let no trifles interfere with it. Anything is permissible as long at it serves that distant and glorious end."

"Oh no! It is not!" protested Francis with spirit.

"What do you mean, it is not?" The League frowned. "Are you going to contradict me? You?"

"I will, Reverend Legate. For it is not as though it did not matter what means we use to attain our ends. Indeed, it matters greatly, because whether we attain the end or not depends on Our Lord, while the choice of means is left to us, and is therefore our own merit or fault . . ."

"Bah!" The Cardinal gave a shrug. "What's the sense of arguing with you? What do you know? Go if you want to, and God be with you!"

Francis kissed the Cardinal's hand and noiselessly stole out of the room. At the door he passed Jean de Brienne who was just coming in, a frown on his face.

"I have bad news," de Brienne announced from the threshold.

"And I have excellent news!" retorted the Cardinal with spirit. "It is strange indeed! Everybody is constantly trying to frighten me even though everything goes for the best! You look darkly upon the world, messer knight. I have positive proof that within a few days the Sultan will send a new mission, accepting our terms."

"May God grant it! For I have just received word from Sir Ibelin whom I left in charge in Acre. He writes that until a while ago the Moslems were hastily tearing down the walls of Jerusalem and other cities as though making ready to depart. Some even say they tore down the castle on Mount Tabor, that fierce castle against which the Hungarian Crusade collapsed! So there was great rejoicing among the Christian population which still remains in the land for they saw in it a sure sign the Sultan was about to abandon the Holy Land. The Moslems, on the other hand, lamented and left Palestine in droves, selling out their entire possessions. More than a thousand Moslem families, it seems, departed from Jerusalem alone. They sold out houses and possessions for next to nothing and left. That is how it was till a while back. But a few weeks ago, it seems, something made them change their minds. They stopped destroying the walls and the Moslems returned. They took back the houses they had sold to the Christians and are acting fiercer than ever so that our people hardly dare to draw breath . . . Just as of old, and Ibelin is worried . . ."

The Cardinal contemptuously shrugged his shoulders. "Rumors, rumors, of no concern to us. Listen to my news; that fool from Assisi, Francis whom you no doubt know, set out, without saying a word to anyone, to pay a visit to the Sultan. . . . Yes, the Sultan himself . . . al-Kamil. . . . And he pressed him to embrace the Holy Faith . . . Pressed the Sultan, mind you!"

"Incredible! Did they cut him to pieces?"

"They did not! That's just it. They did not! The Sultan conversed with him in a friendly manner and finally gave him his firman, with which the good fellow can travel anywhere, even to Damascus. He was here a moment ago. He wants to go to Jerusalem."

"And Your Grace reckons that the reason for the Sultan's kindness was . . ."

"What else could it be but the desire to make contact with us to win our favor? We know Francis: he surely did not dazzle the Sultan, nei·· ther by his oratory nor by his brains, nor by his looks . . . The poor little fellow has the mentality of a child. Al-Kamil, no doubt, wanted him upon his return to praise his magnanimity before us . . . That's why he let him go and gave him his seal to boot. Mind my words, in a few days a new mission will appear . . ."

"May God grant it," repeated de Brienne once more. "What Your Grace says is a great comfort to me, because Ibelin . . ." Unconsciously he unfolded the letter he had brought along. His eyes ran over the lines with concentrated attention. In the latter part of the message the old lord of Beyrouth wrote: "Princess Isabelle, God be praised, is faring well. I had the honor of seeing her yesterday. She sits already upright in her cradle. She is the living image of her late mother, our good and un-forgettable Queen."

"The living image of her mother. . . ." It occurred to Jean it would be painful to have her always before his eyes. And at the same time he felt a new emotion awakening in his heart for that almost unknown little being who sat upright in her cradle.

He thought of it and kept his peace. So did the Cardinal. He had no child to think of but he was still under the spell of the man of whom a while before he had said that he had the mentality of a child. When speaking of Francis he deliberately emphasized his lack of knowledge, his simple-mindedness and at the same time he could not rid himself of the feeling that there was something important he must discuss with him, ask him about. For some inexplicable reason it suddenly seemed to him that the argument as to whether the end justified all means or not was a problem of paramount importance which must be settled; more important in fact than anything that was happening around him, even the possibility of new peace offer. These were strange thoughts indeed and the Cardinal felt ashamed of them. It must be either the climate or the illness he had undergone that affected him this way. It was fortunate no one was aware of these symptoms of weakness, so ill-befitting a leader. . . .

De Brienne was first to recover. "I will avail myself of Francis' jour-ney to Jerusalem," he said, "and bid him to make sure how it was with that tearing down of walls. For all his simplicity he can find out that much. After all Ibelin has not seen it with his own eyes, only heard it at fourth or fifth hand. Where can I find him?"

"That I don't know," admitted the Cardinal. "Francis has no regular abode. He lives like a bird on a branch. Ask the scullions—they are sure to know. They love him and his sermons. But hurry for he is likely to depart any day."

Jean did not tarry. He dispatched squires in every direction. He asked knights of his suite, in case they chanced to meet Francis of Assisi to be sure and stop him. The first one to run into Francis was Gerard d'Avesnes. He had not met him before, and as the entire camp knew already of his visit to the Sultan Sir Gerard eyed him with curiosity.

"His Majesty the King wants to see you before you leave, as it seems you are going to Jerusalem . . ."

"With the help of Our Lord."

"I hear you were in Cairo. How big would you say is the Sultan's army? Has he great forces by his side? More mounted men or troops on foot? Are they levied or mercenaries? How are they stationed?"

Francis began to laugh. "Sir knight, no use asking me such things. I saw on my way many mounted men and men on foot, too, who it seemed, knew nothing of Our Lord. But how was I to tell what regiments they belonged to or how many of them there were?"

"The King wants you to pay more heed to such things in Jerusalem. It is very important to us."

"But how can one heed in Jerusalem anything else save Our Lord's Sepulchre? What does anything matter compared with the site of His Passion?"

D'Avesnes sighed, confused, though he did not know why. "Do as you please," he said. "May I ask you a favor? You will surely be in Acre and on Mount Carmel. At the foot of the mountain on a rocky promontory a castle is being built. They call it the Pilgrim's Castle. It was I who founded it, I who began the work. . . . To defend the Holy Land. . . . I fear lest now that I am away the work be discontinued . . ." He drew his palm over his brow and went on: "I have that castle very much at heart for I intended it as a gift for the Most Sacred Virgin in return for mercy upon a doomed soul . . ."

"How do you know it is doomed?" Francis was scandalized.

"Because the unfortunate one took her own life . . . My wife, that's who it was. . . . She is forever in my mind and I suffer agonies at the thought of her tribulations . . . They say even prayer is of no avail to those who committed suicide—that they are lost beyond redemption. If this be true, I shall go mad. . . ."

"They are not lost," Francis replied, "or at least, we have no way of knowing. It would be a great sin to presume upon divine justice. Thoughts are faster than action and surely it often happens that while the body perishes the frightened thoughts soar in prayer to God and obtain forgiveness."

"Amen," said d'Avesnes. "God bless you for those words."

"One thing is sure," continued Francis with unwonted gravity. "Neither in life nor in death will man escape God or himself. And the hardest judgment is one's own. But God's mercy is as great as the universe and every man will find in it the grace he needs . . . I will find out about your castle, brother knight."

Far away in Ruthenia, of which hardly anyone had heard, Genghis Khan's armies had burnt Kiev, the city of the golden gates.

The Egyptian summer had withered the Crusaders. This was their second summer here. The third year of their stay on the Nile had begun. The Genoans and other trading folks were by now comfortably settled in Damietta and had turned it into their own trading post. Since Egypt was richer and more enterprising than the looted and devastated Byzantium, the Venetians, the once proud conquerors of the Greeks, turned green with envy. Of the Crusaders' forces, led by Cardinal Pelagius, less than a half remained. They crumbled like grain that stands too long in stacks unthreshed. Strife, illness, and above all the ease with which they could return home by the galleys that sailed back and forth continually were responsible for the depletion. One by one the warriors vanished into thin air. The greatest outcry arose when the Teutonic Order of the Holy Virgin Mary of Jerusalem departed for Acre. For a long time they had intended to move to Europe and it was generally believed they meant to do it now. To make matters worse, rumors were rampant that the Sultan's brothers al-Ashraf of Edessa and al-Musaan of Damascus were already on their way to the long awaited rescue of Egypt. Meanwhile the mission the Legate had forecast failed to appear.

Things being as they were de Brienne advised the Cardinal to gather great stores of food in Damietta (he had strengthened the walls of the fortress so that by now they were impregnable) and to prepare for a long siege. At the same time the Christian Lords should be asked for reinforcements, particularly the untrustworthy Emperor Frederick II who, though he had vowed several years before to take the Cross, had so far not fulfilled his pledge. Cardinal Pelagius agreed that the Emperor be pressed but would not hear of retiring to the stronghold. His stubborn, domineering nature foresaw the course of events as they might best suit his own temperament.

"We have been standing here long enough to no good end," he insisted. "We must strike at the Sultan and take Cairo."

"To take Cairo," de Brienne replied, "we would need five times as many troops as we have. Before setting out we must secure our rear, leave a strong garrison in Damietta, establish a line of supplies. How many troops will this leave for the attack? How many times will the Sultan's forces outnumber ours, particularly if he receives reinforcements? Your Grace, take the advice of an old and seasoned soldier! In the stronghold we are absolutely safe; no power can move us from there. We can wait in safety till the emperor comes or the Holy Father sends us help. We will not let them cut us off from the sea so they won't take us by hunger. Let us wait. If we accomplish the conquest of Egypt in twenty years it still will be soon enough!"

Strange to say, the Podesta of Genoa, Bartholomeo Doria, was of the same opinion. But ever since Doria's view did not bear out his own the Cardinal no longer trusted him. "The Sultan would not have twice sent his envoys," he insisted, "if he did not feel we had him in our hands. What was certain then is just as certain today."

"Unfortunately, Your Grace, things were different then. Then Islam trembled before the onslaught of the Mongols and the Sultan's brothers expected help from Egypt—not Egypt from them. The golden bird has flown from our hands—no use recalling past mistakes. This summer is not like the last one. The same leaf never falls twice."

It was not wise to remind the Cardinal of a mistake for which at heart he was beginning to be sorry himself. The Legate's black eyes flashed; he pressed his thin lips and his chin shot out. "You crow like a raven," he said with contempt. "Listening to you I wonder who is talking, a Sultan's ally or a coward?"

White as a sheet Jean sprang to his feet. "What's that? Did I hear aright?"

"You heard me. I stand by my words."

"By God! You. . . . Your Grace . . . were it not for the garb you wear . . . were it not for the Holy Father. . . . Never mind. I'll stand it and won't say a word. And I'll never set my foot here again. This is the last time. I say we have lost the Holy Sepulchre! We have lost it forever! Now we are marching to our own doom. We are on our way to another Hattin! I have pleaded with you even as Raymond of Tripoli pleaded with Lusinian, and like him in vain. We shall perish just as they did. God help the Holy Sepulchre!"

He went out, bursting with rage and grief. He kicked the door so that it nearly fell off its hinges. He leaped on his horse and galloped off, straight ahead, neither knowing nor caring where. He prodded his mount so that blood dripped to the ground; he tore at the reins. A coward . . . The Sultan's ally. . . . Certain doom . . . And to think that it was he who was to be the leader, he, he alone, not that red peacock stuffed with insolence and vainglory. . . .

And why wasn't he? The horse groaned and panted. Bloody foam dribbled from his mouth and flanks. Jean slowed down and turned back towards town. He must not think. He must not think. He must not remind himself. . . .

Cardinal Pelagius sat motionless, from the corner of his eyes watching the door that swung for a long time after Jean's violent departure. He felt he shouldn't have lost his temper. He knew as well as anyone else that de Brienne was neither a coward nor a friend of the Moslems. Were it possible to erase the insult, he would gladly do so. But words once uttered cannot be erased; they can only be withdrawn, and of that the Cardinal of Albano did not feel capable.

Besides, his old grudge against all knights, the grandees, as he contemptuously called them, was too deeply rooted in his soul to be overcome by reason. He was firmly convinced that he was doing the right thing whenever he acted against the Barons' advice. He likewise believed that he could manage without de Brienne's assistance. God would help him, God would inspire his decisions, God would direct everything just as He had done so far. By a happy coincidence God always wanted the same things he did.

De Brienne kept his word and did not leave his own camp. When the elder knights came to ask him to dissuade the Cardinal from undertaking the madcap campaign, he replied: "He called me a traitor and a coward. I did all I could when I did not run him through with my sword. Don't ask me more!"

Panting with rage, they admitted their King was right. A true knight could not forget such an offense. And realizing that the campaign as planned would lead them to their doom, they prepared for it in silence, stout and determined. A man dies but once. They should all die but the Legate's pride would be punished.

For the present the Legate was full of good cheer. With boundless energy he attended personally to everything, issued orders, supervised preparations. He did not call a council. And so upon his own responsibility, at his orders the troops left Damietta in the last week of July.

The troops set out. They moved up the triangle which had Cairo for its apex and Damietta for its base, while the Nile on the right and the lake Menzarch and the arm of the Nile called Bar-el-Sagil on the left formed its sides. The Cardinal was pleased with this position. The enemy would not attack their flanks. The valley was full of foodstuffs and crops; therefore the army took only a week's provisions so as not to delay their progress by too many carts.

The sun, the foe's ally, beat down mercilessly so that the armor burned at the touch. Dust rose in columns and obscured the sky. In silence, in the heat, the army moved on. One day, two days, three. No enemy in sight. In fact, no one in sight. Sometimes fleeting silhouettes of Bedouins would appear on the horizon and disappear again before the Franks had time to come near.

"The Sultan's first outposts," scoffed the Cardinal. "I fear it will not come to a battle after all. They won't dare to try their strength with us. We shall occupy Cairo without a fight . . ."

Emptiness. An immense emptiness that oppressed the soul. Even the fellahs had disappeared and the immemorial water-wheels no longer creaked and drew the water of the Nile to pour into ditches. Clumsily built, filthy Arab villages stood empty and deserted. The inhabitants had left. Only Egyptian deities in greater number than ever stared indifferently at the passing troops. Columns shaped like rolled papyri or open lotus blooms supported granite beams. Under the granite bearer stood mysteriously smiling figures. They turned around, peered with elongated eyes, wrung or stretched their hands as though in warning.

At last the troops reached the deserted empty Sharamshah where the

Cardinal ordered a two-days' stop. The elder knights held council in a tent.

"The fact that the enemy retreats," said Walter de Nemours, "is a sure sign they are preparing a trap. The further south we proceed the more easily we can be cut off from Damietta and our fleet. It would be pure madness to go on!"

All agreed, nodding their heads. Old warriors, they knew the craftiness of war; they had often used it themselves. Their unfailing soldiers' instinct told them they were walking into a trap. And despite their rancor towards the Legate they wanted to save themselves.

And so once more they turned to Jean de Brienne. He was the only man who could and had a right to speak for the knights. He had been leader; he had replaced the Legate during the latter's illness. All successes so far were due to him. The Cardinal could not ignore his advice. It was true he had offended him grievously but here the most important thing was at stake, the victory or defeat of the whole Crusade. De Brienne must swallow his pride and explain to that crimson madman that he could not push the army any further. If he wanted to fight let him dig himself in here in Sharamshah and wait.

De Brienne reluctantly agreed. He appeared before the Cardinal, angry, ruffled, swollen with rancor. They faced each other like two mortal enemies. Under such circumstances the conversation was bound to be brief.

"We will conquer Egypt now or never!" bellowed the Cardinal. "I will not rest till I overtake the Sultan and force him to give battle. Tomorrow men and horses can rest. Day after tomorrow, at dawn, we are off!"

"At least there will be no doubt in the future as to who lost the campaign," retorted de Brienne coldly and left.

The Lord of Cesarea awaited him anxiously.

"Nothing to be done," Jean replied to the mute question of his eyes. "Day after tomorrow we are off to Hattin."

"Where . . . ?"

"Hattin. Don't you remember? Don't you understand?"

Yes, the knight understood now. He asked no more. They strode in silence while before their eyes rose the accursed saddle of a hill, overflowing with blood, the grave in which the kingdom of Jerusalem had been buried thirty-three years before.

# 12.

## The Wrath of the Father of Rivers

THE STIFF MORTAL REMAINS, THAT LOOKED LIKE A LARVAE IN ITS COCOON and haunted the minds of the astrologer Jacob Pochard, the secretary Scholasticus and the scholar Matteo Pesaro, had not yet been unwrapped nor revealed its secret. For although the trio of explorers returned to the tomb on the day following their discovery of the mummy lying in its double coffin, they ran into unexpected difficulties. Their previous visit had attracted the attention of Copts who lived nearby. Black and taciturn, they dared not forbid the strangers to enter the mastaba, but they surrounded the savants with unceasing watchfulness, crowding upon their heels into the painted chambers of rock and with hostile eyes following every one of their movements.

There were two reasons for this suspicion. The Copts, whose name, according to some, was derived from the city of Coptos in Thebaid, according to others from the Greek word "kopto"—circumcised—or the likewise Greek word "Aigyphios"—Egyptians—considered themselves the sole descendants of the people of the Pharaohs. They did not accept the name of Egypt once imposed on their land by Greece, and continued to call it Kemet or Black Land. The awareness of their great heritage did not lift them from the degradation in which they lived. They were barbaric and ignorant. They thoughtlessly destroyed the most beautiful monuments. Greed was their chief characteristic. Of their glorious past they retained only one thing—a fear of upsetting the peace of the dead.

For thousands of years their forefathers had considered respect for the bodies of the dead as the cornerstone of their religion. They had carved passages and chambers in rock, drilled wells and tunnels, a maze of inclines and spiral corridors running up and down. Those ingenious labyrinths, inexplicable though they seemed, had but one purpose: to drive away any possible desecrator of the tombs, to deceive his steps, detour him from the way so he would not reach the tomb proper—that small, narrow chamber in which the mummy rested. To defile a mummy! The consequences of such a crime would be terrible; indeed, they might fall upon the whole country. For didn't the dead, thanks to magic formulas, have the power to assume any form at will? An outraged spirit could avenge itself, avenge itself horribly and obstinately. Woe to the man who risks the vengeance of the dead!

And so ignorant fellahs who understood nothing else, who used as grinding stones segments of pillars covered with most beautiful hieroglyphics, lived in an instinctive fear of the wrath of mummies. They never touched them themselves and would not allow anyone else to do so. The dead strike out blindly. The Latins would leave and the poor native population would have to answer for their deeds.

The second reason was equally important. For a long time now there had persisted among the Copt population the belief that only a part of the treasures concealed in the tombs and pyramids had been looted by the Bedouins and other plunderers. By virtue of a special power with which mummies were endowed the most precious objects had sunk into the ground or turned into stones, and thus had been concealed from the intruders' eyes. But if one knew the proper words the spell could be broken and the gold recovered.

"We don't know that formula and we are not seeking gold," the three explorers protested with complete sincerity as soon as they found out what their unbidden companions had in mind.

The silent throng shook their heads, suspicious and doubtful. "Then why did you come here for the third time? The Latins boast of their learning. You must know how to recover the gold?"

"No, we don't."

"The words of the charm are written upon these walls. But the key to the scripture is lost. If you find it we will allow you to take a part of the gold. It seems one must fumigate the walls with herbs. But we don't know how many times and what herbs to use. Haven't you really heard of it?"

They assured them they had not. The crowd, disappointed, grew indignant. "Then out with you and don't come back. You don't know how to find gold and we won't suffer you to touch the dead. Begone!"

Their hearts heavy, the three friends departed. But not for long. Curiosity once awakened will not be put to sleep again. They returned the next night. Without any light lest it might attract attention, they entered the tomb, groping in the dark. They were so absorbed by their consuming eagerness that it never occurred to them few knights could have equaled their courage. Knowing by heart where the sarcophagus stood they found the coffins and took the mummy, lifting it upon their shoulders. They fled like thieves, pursued by their own shadows, while the jackals howled behind. At dawn they covered the mummy with sugar cane, tied it up into a neat bundle and hired a man with a donkey who agreed to take the sheaf to town. The cane was presumably to be used for scientific experiments. So far so good. It was not till they began to drag the sheaf into the Cardinal's palace to the quarters occupied by Scholasticus that they ran into trouble. The entire court ran out to ask what they were doing and of what use the herb may be? Brother Philip, deeming it was some new and different kind of reed, picked out the longest shafts and chewed them thoroughly, the trio trembling lest he uncover the real contents of the sheaf. The astrologer turned pale, the scholar red. The secretary desperately tried to put on a good face. Suddenly the angry voice of the Cardinal drew everybody's attention away from the bundle.

"What does this assemblage mean?" the Legate inquired. "Ah, here is Scholasticus. At last! I have urgent letters, but the secretary roams about God knows where. I have already forbidden it several times. It seems my words and the obedience due to your superiors means nothing to you. This is the last warning! You are not to leave my chamber without my consent. What are these reeds? This is not a stable!"

"We picked them under particularly favorable astrological auspices," interposed the astrologer with spirit. "They will make a powerful and effective medicament."

"I will denounce you if you touch it without me," muttered Scholasticus to his friends and dejectedly followed the Cardinal. The danger for the present at least had passed. The precious, mysterious booty disappeared in the box in which the astrologer packed his instruments. Secured by a padlock it could wait for a more propitious moment.

But they had no luck, those first European Egyptologists. The propitious moment was not to come. Instead came the order to march upon Cairo. To be sure it did not concern the astrologer and the scholar whom no one had need of in wartime, but Scholasticus was obliged to accompany the Cardinal. Finally all three set out; they did not want to part and besides the very word "Cairo" meant pyramids, the Sphinx and other unknown and mysterious wonders. Although the number of carts that were to follow the army was limited they managed not only to find room for themselves but even take their box along. They did not think it safe to leave it in Damietta. What if it occurred to a servant to peek inside? Besides, no telling how long they would be gone? Maybe they would stay in Cairo for good?

Unperturbed by the future course of the war of which they knew and understood nothing, the trio took advantage of the stop in Sharamshah to set out on their usual explorations. Less than two miles from the encampment, right on the bank of the Nile, rose the familiar oblique surfaces of pylons denoting the presence of a temple. They decided to visit it.

"The Bedouins will catch you," warned Jean d'Arcy, who was in charge of the watch around the camp.

"But there is no one in sight."

"No, but for all that they may be lying in wait anywhere, even in yonder bushes. Accursed country! Did you notice how the river has risen although it has not rained for six months?"

"Last year it swelled just like that, and there is no telling why."

"Go if you like," continued d'Arcy, "only let me warn you if anything befalls you, I will not come to your rescue. To be sure it would stand us in good stead to send a scouting party and find out how far and with how many forces the Sultan stands, but as long as Messire Legate gave no orders to do it . . . be it so!"

His voice was heavy with bitterness and rancor but the three friends paid no attention. They had grown indifferent to everything. The Cardinal would again be furious with his secretary for bolting without leave. No matter! The demon of knowledge held them in his sway. They must see! They must know! Nothing could stop them. Hastily they set out from camp.

The little of the self-preservation instinct they had left made them stop on top of a hillock. Attentively they scrutinized the country. The emptiness and silence which for the last few days had surrounded their march still continued. The countryside seemed dead. Water-wheels did not turn, sweeps, called "shaduf," even more primitive than the water-wheels and more widely in use here up the Nile, did not creak. Only the swollen river roared.

"I see people over there," said the scholar, pointing.

"Oh, across the river. They don't matter as far as we are concerned. I wonder what they are doing?"

"It looks as though they are filling the ditches."

"Here, look! All filled up! And there, and yonder! Dammed with stones, closed!"

Having lived for two years in Egypt they knew by now that the fertility and the very life of the country depended upon those countless ditches so painstakingly filled with water. Therefore they were astonished to see that the mouth of each ditch had been filled with stones. And of all times now when the river rose and foamed impatiently!

"God knows why they did it," the secretary shrugged his shoulders. "Anyway it is their business. Why should we worry?"

At a brisk pace they started in the direction of the temple. Nearby stood a small Copt monastery which they had not noticed before. Like all buildings of this sort it was clumsily fashioned out of clay, straw and manure, and because of its form strongly resembled a beehive or wasp nest.

"Those accursed rams will again be treading on our heels," sighed the astrologer who nurtured a deep grudge against all Copts.

"Still they are Christians. We will go there and ask whether there are no Moslems around."

"Sure, they will tell you. The underhanded beasts!"

"If we go smartly about it they will," Matteo Pesaro assured them. They turned toward the monastery, only to find that like the rest of the country it was deserted. Empty desolation stared from the dark, malodorous cells. Only flies, those noisome Egyptian flies, buzzed in a sunbeam.

"They took fright of us. My . . . my . . ." Scholasticus wagged his head.

"And why? Around Damietta they remained peacefully all the while, and still do, and never think of fleeing."

"No doubt the Moslems must have told them some yarn about how fierce we were."

"Hush! Something is stirring in there."

Indeed, the monastery was not completely deserted. Someone was rummaging in a dark hole, someone who cleared his throat, spat, shuffled his feet. At last he came out—an old stooped monk. His eyes were sore and red; they looked like two gaping wounds. A half-grey, half-black shaggy beard reached to his waist. He was dragging behind him a bundle of cloth and was about to hoist it upon his back when he caught sight of the strangers and stopped short, eyeing them suspiciously.

"Christ is Our Lord," Scholasticus hastened to say in Greek.

The ancient returned the greeting, mumbling it without enthusiasm. His eyes shifted restlessly as though in fear.

"Why is the monastery empty? Where are all the brethren? Are there no Sultan's troops in the vicinity?" the secretary continued to inquire.

"I don't know, I don't know," croaked the ancient hurriedly. "I only saw those who were closing the sluices . . . They have left now . . ." For a second he stared at the visitors, then he lifted both arms, dropped the bundle and cried as though in terror: "They closed the sluices! They closed the canals! And they left."

"Where are the other brethren?" Scholasticus insisted.

"How were they to remain when the canals are closed? I too am going away and you must flee. Hurry! Hurry!"

"But you said yourself the pagans have already left."

The old man did not reply. He picked up the bag, threw it on his back and started toward the exit. Then once more he turned to them: "Go, tell your people that the canals are closed!"

"As soon as we defeat the Sultan our men will repair the ditches," Scholasticus assured him proudly. "Have no fear. We want to take a look at this ruin by the river. Probably some temple. Do you know to whom it was consecrated?"

"To the Goddess Nephtis . . . the pagan goddess of death," replied the ancient sullenly and was gone. He hobbled as fast as he could, bent in two under his load. The trio did not linger, either. They were but a hundred paces from the object of their trip.

They were conscious of a pleasant coolness upon their perspiring faces. For a long while they stood still in the darkness before their eyes got used to the murk and were able to distinguish anything. The scholar took out a previously prepared lint from his bosom and painstakingly struck fire. A tiny flame sprang up.

The walls of the first vestibule were lined with glazed tiles. They had never seen such glazing before; it was as smooth and polished as ice, blue, green and grey in hue. Upon this background appeared hunting scenes, birds soaring over rushes, gazelles and lions. Each tile was fastened to the wall by a thin copper wire. From the vestibule a narrow stone doorway led into the temple proper. Its walls were completely covered with paintings and a multicolored swarm of inscriptions. The usual procession of gods with heads of hippopotami, cats or cows repeated its familiar ritual gestures. The goddess of the temple whom the old monk called the goddess of death, Nephtis, several times larger in stature, presided over the procession.

The savants peered closely at the inscriptions, their noses almost touching the walls, moved their fingers over cavities, searched for reoccurring images.

"Master Jacob," Scholasticus whispered with feeling, "I think if I could only stay here longer, I would be able to trace this alphabet! If I could only stay! For these are not simple pictures as we reckoned at first. They surely stand for sounds corresponding to letters. If we heard but one word in its proper sound, we would have a sure clue. That old man said the temple belongs to the Goddess Nephtis. She must be that big one, topping over the rest. Her name is sure to be repeated here God knows how many times! If we only could find it. Nephtis. Nephtis. . . ."

"Nephtis, it seems, means death . . . What in their minds could stand for death?"

"I assure you, master, that this is a sound character, not a picture one. Although who knows? Here for instance you have an owl and here too . . ."

"Maybe it's an owl or then maybe it isn't. Maybe some other bird. Besides, we don't know whether an owl signified death to them. Among the Greeks it was the symbol of wisdom . . ."

"Death. . . . Death. . . . Nephtis. . . . Nephtis . . ." muttered the astrologer, his nose moving along the wall. "Oh, if we could only stay here longer!"

"Someone is knocking at the wall!" Matteo exclaimed with sudden apprehension.

All three lifted their heads and listened. The painted figures seemed to narrow their eyes as though listening too. A rhythmic pounding muffled by the thickness of the walls came to their ears, monotonous, insistent.

"Likely a branch is knocking against the wall," suggested the astrologer. They returned to their exploration.

"An owl . . . though perhaps it is not an owl . . . maybe a hawk . . . There are a lot of hawks here in Egypt . . . both living and dead . . ."

"Something rustles," Matteo lifted his head again, and in a tone of utter amazement he added: "Water! How did water get in here?"

Water was pouring through the doorway, tumbling over the steps, yellow and foaming, almost breathless. It did not spread at once upon the dry dust-covered floor but ran hither and yon in narrow rivulets as if exploring the corners. But soon new rivulets followed and gradually the whole surface turned dark. Humid spots turned into shining mirrors. Little cascades tumbled down the steps.

"Let us flee!" cried the secretary, who was first to recover. They leaped toward the stairs and struggled up the steps. The water though shallow was rapid, and pushed them back, nearly knocking them off their feet. Clutching the granite doorway they made their way to the exit and stood petrified. . . .

Instead of the previous plain they saw a huge swollen lake. It seemed to stretch from mountain to mountain, from the Libyan desert to the Sahara. Only groves of trees and roof-tops rose like islands above the water. The nearby monastery was already half submerged. Its round roofs trembled as though about to collapse. Palms desperately shook their plumes of leaves above the water. The roar of waves drowned all sounds.

"Let's barricade the entrance," screamed Matteo, drawing back into the building. Slipping, tumbling down with the rushing water they descended the stairs. Yes, barricade the entrance but with what? None of the stones would budge. Three men were not enough to move such weight. It was in vain they strained and pushed and pulled till their hands bled and their lungs burst for lack of breath. And the water continued to rise and roar with ever-growing vehemence.

"It won't rise much higher," exclaimed Scholasticus with sudden hope. "Look! Here on the wall there are marks left by the previous floods. It won't rise higher!"

But a few moments later the water had covered the highest marks and inexorably continued to rise. Already it reached above their knees, to the hips, to the waist . . . Desperately holding each other by the hands, their backs leaning against the wall over which goddess Nephtis presided, they stared with eyes blinded by terror at the world of unknown, leering deities slowly sinking with them into the water.

The ranks of Crusaders pressed in panic. There was not a single man among them who had not seen a flood before. Streams of rain pour from the sky, thunder roars, low overhead the wind rolls heavy blue-black clouds pregnant with storm and rain. The rivers grow fierce, swell, foam. In wild fury they overflow the banks, push, roll, sweep anything they find on their way, destroy villages and towns. That was flood. But what they saw now was unlike any flood. What they saw now could have happened only in Egypt, that land of dreadful miracles, where Moses scourged the recalcitrant Pharaoh with plagues, where he drowned the heathen army in a previously dry sea. Some unknown sorcerers must have learned Moses' magic and had passed it on to their posterity which was now avenging themselves upon the Christians.

It did not rain; there was no storm nor gale. An invariably serene sky spread over their heads and in the sky hung a scorching, dazzling sun. The distant mountains shimmered just as they always did, neither rosy nor blue nor grey. The desert, visible on both sides, remained tawny, like a lion's back. Then where did the water come from? That water which in its magnitude reminded them of Noah's flood; that water which had turned the valley into a yellow, turbid sea? The tumultuous waves carried tufts of grass, floating islands torn off from the shore somewhere in Upper Egypt. The current swept behind them long, weird-looking weeds and rushes. Small monkeys desperately clutching at branches whimpered like children. Down came trunks of uprooted trees and palms loaded with fruit. Hippopotami carried down by the current roared in fear and tried to cut across and climb ashore. Among the hippopotami floated crocodiles looking from a distance like tree trunks. Far, far away, invisible to the human eye, men stood on the high banks. They looked with despair, for here was the Father of Rivers carrying its life-giving annual gift of moisture and fertile mire, and yet, at the Sultan's orders all the ditches and canals distributing the water to reservoirs had been closed and the whole force of the river was rushing uselessly toward the Delta to vanish in the sea. Such were the

Sultan's orders; the Sultan's will was the will of the Prophet; this year would be a year of famine. Famine would mow the people down but the water would drown the impudent and proud Franks. Great is the name of the Prophet!

The crowded ranks of Crusaders stared stupefied. Water surrounded on three sides the elongated hilltop upon which they had set camp. Below Sharamshah the swollen, roaring Nile and its arm, Bar-al-Sagir, joined in one wide sea. A narrow crest winding toward the south was all that connected the encampment with the land.

Amidst silent, dumb-stricken rows the Legate on horseback flew like a red flame. "Onward!" he shouted, "onward! There is nothing else we can do!"

As to that there was no doubt. They had no alternative. The water roared, the narrow strip of land was growing narrower with every passing minute. The ground under their feet already was sodden.

In all haste the troops made ready to set out. The carts would have to be abandoned. The Cardinal ordered the contents checked; all provisions to be distributed among the men; the more valuable or indispensable objects to be taken along.

"What do we do with the chest of Messer Astrologer?" a servant inquired of brother Philip, the chaplain.

"How am I to know what is in that chest? Why doesn't Messer Astrologer take care of it himself? He is not here, nor Messer Scholasticus either . . . Saint Patron! Could it be they've gone off again and the flood got them?"

"What about the chest?" inquired the servant.

"I don't know, I don't know. . . . I reckon we will have to leave it. Surely we wouldn't take it on horseback. His Grace said not to take anything. Just look what is inside."

Distressed and weary, brother Philip went off to attend to his own duties. The servant pried the lid open. It sprang back. He looked inside and gasped. "Good Lord! What's that horror?"

He moved it; it was light. He touched it; it was hard. Strange! It looked like a man swaddled in cloth. Well, he might as well see what was inside. He tried with his knife. Too blunt. He sharpened the blade on a stone and began to rip the wrapping painstakingly. "Jesus Christ!" he suddenly screamed in horror. He dropped the knife and ran.

"What is the man screaming about?" wondered brother Philip, stepping out of his tent. "Look at him run!"

Curiously he leaned over the open chest and at once his face turned ash-grey. With a muffled squeak he fled as fast as the servant. Once in his tent he fell upon his knees and tried to pray. But there was no time for prayer. The bugles had begun to blare. He must in all haste finish the packing of the sacred vessels. Oh God! Oh Great God!

In site of the bugles the curious surged from every direction. The servant, his teeth still chattering, had already had time to spread the news that in one of the Legate's carts, in the astrologer's chest, lay an accursed heathen corpse. It lay there just as though it were alive, staring you straight in the face. Must be a ghost! Oh Saint Martyrs! A ghost! What was to he done with it now? The best thing to do would be to burn it so it could not pursue the army and bring calamity upon them. But there was no time to start a fire. If at least the reverend chaplain sprinkled it with holy water, and pronounced the exorcism over it!

But brother Philip would not hear of it. He fled as fast as he could, pressing the chalice to his breast. Besides, there really was no time. The bugles blared more insistently than ever. The men fell in ranks. Two soldiers mounted each horse unhitched from the carts. Each knight took a squire behind him. Those for whom there were no horses were to follow on foot as best they could. The mounted troops started at a gallop. The Legate as well as all the knights were convinced that the Sultan had been caught unaware by the flood just as they had been and hoped to surprise and overcome him by a sudden attack. If only they could strike at him soon enough!

Two hours had not elapsed when nothing remained upon the hilltop surrounded with ever-mounting water, save deserted carts, abandoned tents and the open chest in which the corpse of a man who had died thousands of years before stared into the same sky he had known when he was alive.

The Crusaders' progress did not last long. No more than two leagues beyond Sharamshah a high wall surmounted by turrets barred their way. It ran across the entire crest, from the swollen waters of the Nile to those of Bar-al-Sagir. That wall, those turrets were the Sultan's surprise; the Sultan had prepared for them; they were the fruit of his supposed idleness—the fortress erected in the course of the last six months and proudly called Mausurah—Victorious.

True, it could not compete with the ramparts and bastions of Damietta; it was not impregnable. Still in order to overcome it one must possess battering rams, catapults, ladders, Greek fire. Above all one must have a well-supplied army and time. The Crusaders had neither. Hungry horses, hungry men, no way of getting supplies. In their hands nothing but naked swords. At their back—water.

No, they were in no position to break through. A man might as well try to overcome a lion with a stick!

The walls had so unexpectedly risen before them, they would not at first believe their own eyes. They had heard that in those nearby deserts strange images would at times deceive the human eye, images of non-existent towns or groves. Maybe this stronghold which no one had seen or heard of before was likewise a deception and would dissolve into a mist as soon as they drew near?

But no, it did not dissolve. It burst forth, instead, with a hail of arrows. The road was closed. The Legate, inexperienced leader that he was, had failed to send out scouting parties or spies, and de Brienne in his stubborn refusal to give him advice had not reminded him of this essential precaution. And so they stood now facing the unconquerable obstacle of the wall, while on both sides water continued to rise. The air was heavy with the stench of fish, mire and sultry humidity. Hunger was beginning to tell. The knights remained silent but the rabble became vociferous. They roared and bellowed like the waves. They rebelled against the leaders. "They were dragging a heathen ghost about," some shouted, "bringing divine wrath down upon us Christians! They kept it in a cart to use it for witchcraft. Because of those loathsome artifices we shall all perish now!" "A heathen corpse nothing," replied others. "God is punishing us because the innocent children were forgotten! Instead of recovering the Holy Land, we remained here, nobody knows why or for whom! We wanted Egypt, instead! That's why God wants to drown us, even as those innocents were drowned."

For the first time since the beginning of the campaign the Legate summoned the knights for a council. They came reluctantly, for what was there to talk about? It was the Legate who had brought them to this plight; let him take the consequences now. Nevertheless, they looked with grudging admiration at the Cardinal who still had not broken down. His voice still retained its masterful ring; he issued orders like a leader.

"We shall send," he said, "a mission to Sultan al-Kamil. As between good knights let him give us battle, win who may."

The idea was good and in spite of their rancor the knights unanimously agreed. Anyway, there was no other way out. Sir Simon de Joinville and Sir Aymar de Layron of Cesarea rode off toward the stronghold blowing their bugles to show they came as emissaries.

They returned sooner than expected. The Sultan was not in Cairo as they all had thought, but here, close by, beyond the wall. He had an innumerable multitude of troops with him, for both his brothers had arrived with strong forces.

"They led us in state across the whole camp to the Sultan's pavilion," recounted de Layron. "There were three of them, Sultans, sitting inside, al-Kamil in the middle. We delivered our message and he laughed. 'I will give you the answer,' he said, 'you gave my emissary when I asked for peace: "Come not again to me with like speech!" And when we insisted he grew wroth and shouted: 'I will not waste my soldiers when the crocodiles will eat your corpses anyway!' Then we bowed and left. . . ."

The crocodiles would eat them! Indeed, the accursed heathen was right!

The army turned back in the same way it had come. Without stopping they passed the encampment they had abandoned in the morning. They continued straight toward the water. For another thought had flashed through the Legate's mind. Perhaps Bartholomeo Doria, the Podesta, realizing their plight, would bring the fleet closer. They might get on board even if they had to swim. . . .

Reality seemed to bear out his hope, for a multitude of sails had come into sight. Our fleet! Our fleet! Sinking in the quagmire, then wading into water, men ran, made signs, stretched their arms . . . Alas! It was not the Crusaders' fleet! Those were the Sultan's galleys. Taking advantage of the high water level they had come here from the Meusalah lake to cut the invaders' retreat. There was no longer any way out, no possibility of rescue.

The army of Cardinal Pelagius, more than twelve thousand men, was lost, irrevocably, shamefully doomed. Less lucky than their unfortunate sires at Hattin, they had not even the consolation of dying sword in hand, in an honorable though uneven battle. Weak from hunger they stood knee-deep in water. Some lay down in the mire. They no longer cared; the sooner they died, the better.

The rest, painfully dragging their feet out of the morass, for the third time proceeded toward the camp. Most of the horses bogged down, exhausted. The soldiers cut their throats at once, dragging the meat to drier spots. Right on their heels crawled crocodiles; the big lizards were climbing out of the water in ever-growing numbers. No doubt they knew these men were meant for their fodder. They were becoming aggressive too, and would not be driven away. Over every horse-carcass hungry men and hungry beasts fought a pitched battle. Very soon now, the Sultan's wish would come true.

Like a horde of spectres spattered with mud the knights entered the abandoned camp. Here everything remained as they had left it. The tents, the carts and the open chest.

At the Cardinal's entreaties de Nemours and d'Arcy set out once more to plead with the Sultan. A dreadful thing it was to go thus, on foot, like penitents under the scorching sun. They promptly returned. These were the Sultan's words: "I will not let the Franks go unless their supreme commander appears in person before me to beg mercy."

De Nemours and d'Arcy, after giving account of their brief mission, stretched upon the naked ground, exhausted. The parched, heathen cadaver preserved intact through devil's artifices, continued to lie on the brow of the hill and leered at them all.

The Cardinal left his tent and proceeded to the tent of the King of Jerusalem. The distance was less than a hundred steps but what an effort it cost him to cross it! Each step weighed him down like a load, each aged him years. How much pride he must trample down, how cruelly break his own spirit! The Legate walked slowly. At last he entered the tent. He found Jean seated upon the ground, his chin cupped in his hands. Despair and hunger gnawed at the King. Lustreless, dull eyes looked up at the Cardinal. Jean felt no surprise at his coming, he was no longer surprised at anything. He motioned the visitor to a stool and continued to sit in a stupor.

"Do you know," inquired Pelagius, "what the Sultan replied?"

De Brienne nodded his head to signify he knew.

"I came . . . I came to ask you . . . " He swallowed hard and finished: ". . . to go in my stead to the Sultan."

"I am not the commander," retorted Jean.

"It is no easy thing for me to implore. . . . I implore you . . ."

"The Sultan wants to speak with the leader. I am not the leader. If I were, instead of waiting here to die, we would be the masters of Jerusalem long since! I will not go. I'll die, for die I must. But I neither need nor will abase myself. Why doesn't Your Grace go yourself?"

The Cardinal hid his face in his hands. "The Lord's hands have broken my pride," he moaned. "I've humbled myself to the dust, to the ground . . . Nothing remains of me . . . and nothing can abase me any more. . . ."

"Then why deliberate?" Jean said rudely. "Why ponder? Go!"

"What of my spiritual dignity?" cried Pelagius in despair. "Even if I would I cannot divest myself of the garb I wear . . . It is part of me . . . I cannot cease to be a Cardinal and the Holy Father's Legate. In my person Christ's Church will abase itself before Mahomet . . . "

"How many times," retorted Jean bitterly, "how many times, oblivious of your high spiritual dignity, have you comported yourself, Sir, like a proud and insolent man, moved neither by the love of your neighbors nor by the Church's teaching? How many times did we hear that the end justified all means and that temporal power is the foundation of the Church's strength? How many times have you humiliated us all, never once thinking of the charity that Our Lord commands?"

"I have sinned . . . I am guilty. . . . But you . . . a Christian . . . have regard for the Church!"

And before Jean had time to stop him, he fell prostrate at his feet, grabbed a handful of dust and threw it on his head. De Brienne gave a start. It seemed to him a rock had crashed, a crimson rock. Against his will he felt awed, as one is awed at the sight of something tumbling down that by its very nature seems unmovable.

"Rise, Your Grace," he said, "people are looking!"

"I will not rise till you take pity. Let the people see. They have looked upon my pride, let them look upon my contrition and chastisement. What am I? Nothing. . . . But the Church . . . the Church. . . ."

Without a word Jean rose to his feet and stalked out of the tent. His thoughts were in turmoil. No, he would not go! He would not think of going. What? Go and let the Sultan jeer at him? Not he! Let the man who was to blame go. . . . The Church? The Church was at stake . . . If they insulted Jean they would insult a knight . . . If they insulted

Pelagius they would insult the Pope's Legate. . . . He, Jean, was a Christian . . . It was his duty to protect the honor of the Church . . . Still he would not go! Never! Best of all let no one go, neither the Legate nor himself . . . Why should they abase themselves? It would be useless anyway. . . . The Sultan would spare the Crusaders' lives but at what price? He might demand that they bow to the Prophet or invent some other infamy to which death, even a death as miserable as the one which awaited them here, would be preferable. No! Let no one go! . . . Let them grit their teeth and die!

He glanced around and saw a throng of hungry, mud-covered men who stared at him with horror-stricken, pleading eyes. The sun above beat unbearably upon them. Swarms of flies tormented those who tried to lie down. And the water still continued to rise. Twelve thousand men were here. Twelve thousand men condemned to death. They would die one by one as those others in Damietta had died. Only those in Damietta had dried up and these would rot. They were already beginning to rot alive. None would be spared and dying they would curse their leaders, who for the sake of their pride would not clutch at the last straw.

"It is not me they will curse," Jean consoled himself. "I am not to blame." And suddenly incredible horror smote at his heart. You are not to blame? Then who? Whom had the Holy Father wanted to appoint commander? For whom had he waited? Why aren't you leading the Crusade, instead of that other stubborn, proud man? Indeed you and you alone are to blame. . . .

With terrible clarity the events of the last few years rose before his eyes. That easy, beautiful life led according to the troubadours' teaching . . . Oh! that accursed poison of poetry which would have people believe that the love of two people was supreme law! How well he remembered those lofty principles quoted from the Code of Amour:

"Matrimony can be no obstacle to lovers. . . . Love is above all law!" On the strength of these principles, convinced that he was a free man and could do as he pleased, he had neglected his duty and his vow. And that neglect had caught up with him today. It was that neglect and not the corpse in the astrologer's chest which was the true ghost and would bring them all to their doom. . . . Contrary to what the troubadours might say life had stern and hard laws which no one could break with impunity. A sin against these laws had wrought a chain of consequences which would drag behind him now all through his life and beyond his life, too. De Brienne would be long in his grave and the consequences of his guilt would still go on and on bringing curses upon the memory of the guilty man.

He returned to his tent. The Cardinal, his face concealed in his garb, still sat on the floor. Something stirred in Jean's heart. Suddenly he felt overcome with pity for the man. He helped him to his feet and seated him upon a stool.

"Trouble yourself no more, Your Grace. I am as much to blame as you are. I shall go to the Sultan at once . . ."

Hastily he snatched away his hand which the Legate had grasped and was trying to kiss.

The multicolored pavilion exceeded in magnificence anything oriental fables might conceive. It was not a tent at all but a portable palace with four turrets and seventy-seven chambers, separated by silk curtains covered with exquisite embroideries. In the main central hall, the back and front walls of which had been pinned back so that the air might circulate more freely, sat Sultan al-Kamil with his two brothers al-Muzaam, Sultan of Damascus, Syria and Palestine, and al-Ashraf, Sultan of Mesopotamia and Edessa on either side. They sat cross-legged with huge gem-covered turbans on their heads, motionless and grave. Behind them slaves noiselessly fluttered fans of feathers. Jean came on foot in his everyday coat of mail and leather jerkin which Willfried had cleaned of mud as well as he could. Ten knights followed him. Their faces were pale, their brows drawn in a grim frown. They stepped as though treading upon live coals. When they drew near, Jean approached the Sultan of Egypt and without a word handed him his sword, hilt forward.

"Keep your sword, King," said al-Kamil in Latin with great dignity, "and be seated by our side."

Jean with a sigh of relief retained his sword and took a seat between the Sultan of Egypt and the Sultan of Damascus. Like a noisome fly the thought buzzed in his brain that this was the same al-Muzaam who had torn down the walls of Jerusalem and the stronghold of Mount Tabor, getting ready at his brothers' bidding to surrender the Holy Land to the Franks. He smothered the howl that rose in his soul at the very thought and began to speak without quite knowing what it was he said. Something about twelve thousand men condemned to death. . . .

"It was not I who condemned them," said the Sultan. "You ask me for mercy when the blood of those who died at Damietta cries to be avenged!"

"Those in Damietta could have surrendered even as we surrender." The Sultan's nostrils dilated with pride.

"They could but they did not choose to."

A long oppressive silence fell over the room. Jean with his sleeve wiped perspiration from his brow. "Truly," he thought, "I am draining the cup of humiliation and bitterness to the last drop. Nothing worse can ever happen to me." And again he began to speak of the flood which none surely could have foreseen . . . of the fact that it would not be seemly for a knight to take advantage of a calamity to defeat his foe.

Al-Kamil gave him a startled glance. "It is more than two years you are in Egypt and you don't know yet that the Father of Rivers always overflows at this time of year. This is no calamity, but the normal course of things . . ."

There was nothing Jean could answer and he bent his head in silence. He couldn't think why he still remained here and why he had come anyway. Black slaves brought in low tables loaded with food, richly flavored with spices. Golden goblets with wine, crystal dishes with sherbets. The Sultan did the honors, but his guest stared in front of him. He saw a piteous encampment upon sodden tufts of grass, the camp of moribunds doomed to starvation. . . . The Sultan by offering him food was plainly showing he would do harm neither to him, Jean, nor to his knights, for whoever broke bread under a Moslem roof was thereafter considered a guest and a friend. . . . But what about those others, those others in the camp.

The slaves refilled the goblets. Beautiful young lads entered the room and began to dance before the masters. Musicians and singers followed. A magnificent banquet, indeed.

One of the singers stepped forward. Bibars, the commander in chief of the Sultan's forces, said something, just a few words. The singer strummed upon a weird, clangorous instrument and began to sing.

"The face of time lit up. The faces of the infidels darkened and withered like leaves in the heat . . . Their souls turned to ashes, their hearts dropped, Satan renounced them. All infidels of the Frankland gathered at Damietta. They had but one thought, one will, one desire—to overcome the Prophet. They crossed the sea, mounted upon vessels as though they were chargers. Where are they today? Ask the hoofs of our mounts which can trample upon them. Allah has shown his justice. Can that which should be at the bottom remain on top?"

Jean de Brienne and his companions did not understand the Arab words of the song, but from the displeasure written upon al-Kamil's face, from Bibars' cruel smile and the amused glances the Sultan's brothers exchanged, they could guess what the song was about and the sherbet stuck in their throats.

Enough of this game! They must find out whether they would obtain mercy or suffer humiliation in vain. Looking straight into the Sultan's face Jean said: "There are twelve thousand men out there who want nothing but to be allowed to return to their own country . . ."

Al-Kamil remained silent.

"Why did they come here, then?" snarled al-Ashraf.

"They came to reconquer the Holy Land which above all else is dear to our hearts," replied Jean.

"I offered to return it twice. You would not take it. It was not the Holy Land you were after but Egypt's wealth!"

Silence. Jean must take a sip of wine to cover up the howl that again rose from his soul. The Sultan had a right to speak as he did, indeed as he had!

Al-Kamil spoke again. "Listen to my words, King! I have vowed by the Prophet's road-weary sandals that none of you Franks shall leave this land alive. And I would have kept my vow. It would have availed you nothing to humble yourself before me. But a while ago a man came here from your camp. . . . Did you hear of it?"

"Yes, I did," replied Jean, startled. "I know he came without telling anyone about it in our camp and then returned. A monk. They call him Francis."

"Is he a man of mark among you?"

"He is but a poor man without any influence. How could he be a man of mark? Most of our people look upon him as a half-wit. To be sure our Holy Father, the Pope of Rome, holds him in great esteem. . . ."

"I, likewise, hold him in great esteem," Al-Kamil said gravely. "Where is he now?"

"He went to the Holy Land, thanks to the leave you gave him."

"I would see him again someday. Anyway remember, King, that only for his sake, for the sake of the one and only Christian whose deeds do not belie his faith, I am ready to spare your lives. Only because of him!

I want him to remember me well. Therefore I shall let go free not only you but all my Christian prisoners. You can take them all with you. I have enough slaves here."

Jean bowed his head in silence. The dour Turk, Bibars, stirred impatiently. He had read in the giaour's face that the Franks had found mercy and seethed at the thought.

"Such is my will, Bibars," repeated the Sultan emphatically. "The infidels may leave." Again he turned to Jean. "In a few days the water will recede. When it does, you may leave. As for food I shall order to have it sent to you today. Allah is great!"

"Allah is great!" echoed his brothers, bowing their heads.

# 13.

## The Right to Live

JEAN DE BRIENNE RODE SLOWLY, PAYING NO HEED TO THE ANGRY SHOUTS, laments and imprecations of the street mobs. The Sultan had given the Crusaders two weeks to leave Damietta and clear out of Egypt. It was a terrible blow to the settlers who, at Cardinal Pelagius' summons, had come in droves from Europe. Genoan merchants were particularly indignant. Some, in fact, had already entered into secret negotiations in order to win the Sultan's favor. They were ready to turn Moslem if only they were allowed to remain. Others, more honest or less enterprising, wrung their hands in despair. Women wailed. They had been brought here, children and chattel, and now they must flee. What would they go back to? What would become of them? As always in such cases the mob had to find someone on whom to pin the blame. The Cardinal, now an old, broken man, no longer appeared in public. He never left the deck of his galley from which the crimson draperies had been removed. Clad in pentitent's garb the once so proud Legate was spending day after day in prayer, weeping and writing to the Holy Father letters full of self-accusation. He had handed over the command to Jean de Brienne. It was Jean de Brienne who directed the evacuation of the city, the departure of the civilians and troops. It was he, too, who had to listen to all the fervent imprecations and curses.

Behind him, Willfried rode, his teeth set. It was plain his fingers itched for the sword. The King, however, remained impassive as though the insults never reached his consciousness, as indeed they didn't. His sorrows were too deep for that. What curse could be worse than memory, memory of past failings and the thought of what might have happened if only one had acted differently? These were the ghosts which haunted Jean day and night. Wherever he went, whatever he did, he saw before his eyes the picture of the Holy Land already recovered, saved, and then

349

lost again. Lost forever. No use expecting a new miracle, another Children's Crusade to set human hearts afire. The same miracles did not happen twice. Neither would the combination of favorable circumstances which had marked this Crusade occur again . . .

Harassed and weary he was going to the only human being to whom he could open his heart—to Blanche. He had not seen her for a long time, since his return from Sharamshah only once, and even then for but a short while and in front of other people. He had missed her lately. For were they not united by a strong bond, if not of past love, at least of guilt shared in common?

Like the Legate, the Countess of Champagne had already moved on board her galley. Unlike the Legate, however, she was neither broken nor repentant. Indeed she grieved over the ignoble outcome of the expedition, but deep in her heart she still believed the disaster had little to do with Jean and herself. They both were alive, that was all that mattered. They still could look forward to a better future.

Sustained by this secret hope she had neither aged nor changed as much as Jean. True, her skin was no longer as smooth as it had been three years before. Nevertheless she still remained a beautiful, hot-blooded woman. At the sight of her lover her eyes shone, a deep blush, like a young maiden's, covered her face.

Her lover! Jean, parched and gaunt, smiled indulgently. Strange though . . . her beauty, instead of filling him with rapture, seemed to shock him. He had come here to seek sympathy, to pour out his heart and confide his grief. He was dismayed to realize that she expected confidences of a very different kind. As of old, he still was her entire world. Uneasily, he began to speak of indifferent matters. Of the astrologer Jacob Pochard who had disappeared without a trace. He must have drowned. . . .

"The Count will be much grieved," said Blanche. "He always said there was no better astrologer anywhere, even in Paris."

"Perhaps it is better that he disappeared," remarked Jean, "for the rabble was dead set against him. He would have perished anyway. An altogether strange story that was. The Legate's secretary, Scholasticus, your astrologer and a scholar who was hanging around my court got together and were forever roaming the country in search of all sorts of pagan ruins and inscriptions. The Legate upbraided his secretary and threatened to dismiss him. No use! You might think they were possessed by the Devil. Nor was that all. They dragged out a pagan corpse from somewhere and kept it in a chest. They brought it along to Sharamshah!"

"It must have stank," Blanche made a wry face.

"No. The cadaver was so parched it could have lain there a thousand years, and for that matter probably had. They call them mummies here. When the flood trapped us, the men opened the chest, saw the carcass and began to scream that we were carrying a ghost around; that it was because of it the flood came. . . . They would have torn the astrologer to shreds if he had shown himself then. But by that time he was probably already facing God's judgment."

"Maybe they were right in saying that the ghost brought the flood? Our chaplain was always suspicious of the astrologer."

"I thought so myself at first, but later the Sultan told me that the flood was a normal occurrence here; it comes every year."

He broke off, his brows drawn in a painful frown. She guessed he had been stung by the memory of his visit to the Sultan and the humiliation he had suffered there.

"You went there to save the others," she whispered with warm tenderness. "You sacrificed yourself for their sake. Everyone knows that if your own life had been at stake you would not have stirred a finger to save it. I would have lost you. What luck those others were there, too!"

"I was not thinking about that," he replied. "I was thinking of Master Pochard who is already facing God's judgment. It occurred to me that I, too, shall someday stand before it. It is no easy thought."

She threw a startled glance at him. Never before had she heard such words from Jean's lips. "I don't see why. Whatever happened was no fault of yours."

"Not mine? On the contrary, Blanche. It was all my own fault."

She flinched at the grief which quivered in his voice. "I don't see in what you are to blame?"

Without a word Jean looked at her for a long while. He looked at her face, her neck, her eyes . . . the same features, the same face which used to charm him, stir him so . . . Blanche was still the same. Why had he changed so much? "I don't see in what way you are to blame?" she repeated.

"In what way? It was because of me that the Holy Land was lost. It was I who urged you to leave your husband. In my mad love for you I neglected to obtain the command over the expedition. It was because of me that Marie died. Her death weighs on my conscience."

She listened petrified. "We had a right to do it," she insisted.

"That's what I used to think, too . . . once. Today I don't believe there is any special law for love and lovers. There is but one law: God's law. And a stern law it is."

Blanche pressed her lips. Who had said it before? Almost the same words! Oh, yes, she remembered now: William Divini, that droll troubadour who first interceded for their love and later became a monk and besought her to return to Troyes and renounce her happiness. She had pushed him angrily away . . . the fool . . . the madman. How vividly she recalled the scene, he sitting on the ground clutching his head in both hands. How ridiculous he had looked in that baggy frock he wore. That once elegant, brilliant, charming Divini . . . And now Jean, her stout knight, was repeating his words.

And just as she had done then, she rebelled now. "That is exactly what the troubadour Divini told me after he turned monk," she said with sarcasm.

"Divini, too?" Jean said with surprise. "People, it seems, follow many ways to reach the same truth. For this is the truth."

She continued to resist with desperate stubbornness. "We are free. And we love each other."

"We are not free. Oh, if I had only known it before! Jerusalem would be free; the Holy Sepulchre in our hands. My name would live forever as the name of the man who helped to restore freedom to the holy places. But now this will never happen . . ."

"It was not your fault the war was lost!"

He made a despondent gesture. "What good will it do me that people blame the Legate, that wretched man against whom I no longer bear a grudge or harbor ill will? I know I am guilty . . . and nothing can silence that conviction . . ."

"But we loved each other," she exclaimed in despair. To her the words were the answer to everything; they explained, they justified, they absolved. . . . We loved each other! Was it not enough for him?

"We loved each other," the knight echoed her words. "And what of it? I still love today. I love you as I love myself; you are a part of me, the most essential part. If I were to lose you I would suffer just as if I lost an arm or a leg. . . ." He paused, then in a low voice, he added: "But it sometimes happens a man will say, 'Would God I had no arm or leg rather than do as I have done.' "

She staggered, caught herself, and stood staring at him wide-eyed. Already he repented his words.

"You are in no way to blame," he said softly. "Were it not for me you would have remained in Troyes. You would have led a peaceful life there to this day . . ."

"That was no life," she whispered in a hollow voice.

"And what has your existence here been, in the last two years?"

He rose and wearily began to pace the deck. She followed him with her eyes, girding herself for the next encounter. Suddenly he stopped in front of her. "Don't you think you had better return there?"

She quivered. Didn't he want her any more? Didn't he love her?

"Indeed I love you, Blanche, but in a different way. How could I help loving you? You are the only human being with whom I can talk in all sincerity. My one and only friend. You and I have grown into one being. When you leave I shall remain terribly alone. And still I tell you: Go back! It is the right thing to do!"

"Never! My husband—and everyone else—would think you've grown weary of me; that you sent me away!"

"Do you still care what people may say? I don't, Blanche. We are no longer young, you and I! It is time we thought of our responsibilities."

"I don't want to think of anything but you and me! You are as ridiculous as that troubadour monk whom old age rendered saintly and fearful of sin. Maybe," she added maliciously, "you are afraid that I will demand the sort of love from you for which you feel too old?"

Suffering must have ploughed his soul through and through, for her words did not seem to goad him. "No, Blanche," he replied calmly, "I am only afraid of responsibility. Of responsibility for the lives we lead. Do you see what I mean?"

She did not want to see. Stubbornly she shook her beautiful head. She clung desperately to life and love, unable to grasp anything beyond.

"I love you more than you love me. That's why such thoughts never occur to me!"

"That I don't know," he confessed, "I can't tell. One thing is certain, though. I care as much for you as I care for myself. I think of both of us. God knows it won't be easy for me to remain alone . . ." Again he paused, faltered and almost unconsciously added: "But it is not easy to be with you, either."

Her cheeks flushed. "Then why did you come here? Go away!"

"I do not want to go away and leave you grieved and angry. Won't you understand me, my dear love?"

"I am not your dear love. I used to be once, long ago. I was happy then. I used to say: I'll face damnation, only let me be with him a year, a day, even an hour! That wish has been fulfilled. You were mine. Nothing existed for you, save myself. You had no misgiving or fear of sin in those days. That was happiness. No, I don't complain. Let it be. I am ready."

He glanced at her horrified. "What are you talking about? What are you thinking about, Blanche?"

She burst into laughter that sounded like sobbing. "Nothing. I thought how happy we used to be. Remember how we would stroll at night to the foot of Mount Carmel? That was what I was thinking about. And also that I will not accept your law, your stern law. Never! I did not ask to be born; why must I assume responsibilities? Why should I live in bondage, scale imaginary mountains? I won't!"

"I, too, do not know why," he admitted, "but I realize it must be done. Some great order, some chain in which you and I are but links, requires it."

"I won't," she repeated, putting all her vitality and passion in the protest. "I won't!"

Proudly she shook her head and rising, leaned against the railing without looking at him. The flood had receded, the Nile flowed in its normal bed. Its banks, robbed of all greenness, were covered with thick, grey, malodorous mud. Above sea gulls circled, screaming rapaciously. She glanced at them while her hand touched her breast. She sighed, relieved. It was there, the little linen bag, sewed to the lining of her dress. She had gone to get it from the witch Margot during a stormy, evil night. She had thought to remove another woman who stood in her way. It was there. She had not lost it. Its time had come, at last. The herbs were pulverized, to be sure, but they had not lost their potency. . . .

"Goodbye, Jean," she said over her shoulder.

There was something in her voice that made him look up. He went up to her and grasped the hand she held against her breast as though concealing something.

"I will go, if you want me to, but I'll still come back tomorrow. I shall not let you leave, till we see eye to eye in this, Blanche! How could we two part in grief?"

With her whole body she clung to him.

"I loved you dearly, Jean."

"Good God!" he exclaimed, "you don't know how I loved you!"

She drew back a step.

"I am glad you admit that you loved me . . . once."

"Please, Blanche, don't. . . . You know very well what I meant."

"Yes, yes, of course. So you are leaving? Yes . . . surely you've stayed here long enough. You might forget some duty again!"

"Blanche!" There was such heartfelt reproach in his voice that she almost burst into tears.

"I am sorry," she whispered. "Go, now. When you return tomorrow, I shall be calm. I promise, I will not argue. . . ."

"Goodbye, then . Until tomorrow."

He wanted to come nearer, to put his arms around her, but she pushed him away with an impatient gesture, her eyes stubbornly fixed on the water.

"No use irritating her now," he thought. "I'll come back tomorrow and I'll convince her. . . . She is bound to understand . . ." He beckoned to his oarsmen to bring the boat around, and left.

When Thibault burst into his chamber pale, confused, unable to utter a word, Jean motioned him to be still. There was no need for him to speak; de Brienne already knew. He had guessed at once. Was it not obvious? Could it have ended otherwise? In that second he realized he had known it since yesterday, that it was precisely this news he expected. Blanche was dead! Dead! It did not matter whether she had jumped into the sea like the wife of Gerard d'Avesnes, taken poison, or stabbed herself with a dagger. What difference did it make? The truth, the horrible truth was that Blanche was dead . . . and it was he, de Brienne, who was guilty of her death.

Through a strange association of ideas he suddenly remembered how once in the Sultan's palace he had felt he was insured against misfortune, for nothing worse than what he had already been through could ever happen to him. How wrong he had been! He had reckoned without that one thing, worst, most painful of all, which he himself had brought about. It was he who was the real slayer, not Blanche. How could he have gone away yesterday leaving her as she was? He recalled now, word by word, everything they had said; her irritation, her rebellion, then that sudden, feigned indifference. It must have been then that she had made up her mind. And he had not guessed. He had gone off, secretly relieved, with a promise to return the next day. "You will find me calm," she had said. And she had kept her word. Her beautiful body, desperately craving caresses and passion, had grown calm forever, but what had become of her proud, defiant soul, of Blanche herself? Was she doomed, as d'Avesnes believed of those who committed suicide? Oh, how horrible to think of it! D'Avesnes had said that at times he was on the verge of losing his mind, and yet d'Avesnes was in no way to blame for his wife's death. While he, de Brienne . . . de Brienne had abandoned her. He had thought more of himself than of Blanche. . . .

"But surely in our dispute it was I who was right," he tried to argue with himself. "You were right," his conscience replied, "but at the same time you were weary of her. Your indifference did not spring from fear of God alone. You left her forlorn, desperate, not caring to what thoughts she might fall prey. You did not care enough to remember that Satan prowls incessantly around those who are left alone in their despair. . . ."

He lifted his head, suddenly aware that Thibault had been speaking to him for a long while. The lad had not changed much. He had remained the meek, awkward, inept youth born to be a minstrel, not a knight. His stay in the Holy Land and in Egypt had left no mark upon him, save for a sunburned skin and freckles on his nose and cheeks. He belonged to those colorless people whom history passes by without touching or caring whether their lot is good or bad. . . .

In a whining voice he was recounting: ". . . Last night she called me and talked for a long time and somehow differently than she used to. 'I guess you will go back to your father, Thibault,' she said. 'Probably you are tired of being a warrior.' I was mighty glad because she had never even allowed me to mention our return. 'When shall we go back, mother?' I asked. And she said: 'Whenever you want.' That's what she really said: 'Whenever you want.' "

He repeated it twice in a tone of utter amazement, for so far no one, and his mother least of all, ever paid the slightest attention to what he might or might not want.

". . . She said: 'Whenever you want,' and she kissed me . . . And then she added: 'Go back to your father, son.' And she left me. I could not even go to sleep, I was so surprised. . . . I wondered what had happened. Was mother going to enter a convent, or what? And she must

have had a premonition of her death, poor mother. . . . I fell fast asleep
toward morning, and then Genevieve burst in screaming . . ."

"Was she already dead then?" whispered de Brienne.

"All cold and stiff," replied Thibault, wiping his eyes. "What had
happened? To die like that without Holy Sacrament, without a priest!
What will the chaplain say? What will father say? And she did not
fulfil her vow, either. She did not go to Jerusalem."

"She did not fulfil her vows," repeated Jean like an echo.

"And she always seemed so hale!" Thibault continued to lament.
"Hale and strong. Do you know, uncle, that when we took a stroll I
would grow tired sooner than she? Nothing ever ailed her. What happened to her? My God! What happened?" His mouth quivered like
a child's. "And, uncle, you don't know, but the worst is . . . they . . .
that is Genevieve . . . say such dreadful things . . . I don't understand
. . . I can't believe it . . . Genevieve says that mother . . . that she
. . . took poison herself . . . Uncle!"

"That's impossible," said de Brienne with an effort. "What could have
put such an idea in Genevieve's head?"

"Of course, it is impossible, isn't it? I think something must have
stung her. Maybe a spider. I have heard of spiders here that will make
people die at once . . . Or maybe she met a basilisk somewhere? They
say you can come across them too. That's what I told Genevieve and
I was very angry with her, but do you know what she said? 'Your uncle,
the King of Jerusalem, will surely know why her ladyship has done it!'
Uncle!"

The ceiling was crashing about de Brienne's head. With an effort he
mastered himself and replied calmly: "The wench must be mad. Likely
she is out of her mind with grief. I know how devoted to your mother
she was. I will talk to her myself and find what she meant!"

"But that's impossible!" sobbed Thibault. "It would be too dreadful!"

"Calm yourself, lad. Your mother was a good, God-fearing woman.
She would never commit such a folly. You were right. It must have
been a spider or a basilisk."

"Yes, yes! Surely."

"And as for Genevieve I shall speak to her myself," added de Brienne,
while in his heart he thought: "Again and again that chain of consequences. When and where will it end?"

# 14.

## The Watch of the Holy Land

THE MAGNIFICENT BASILICA BUILT BY BALDWIN I, WHICH COVERED THE Holy Sepulchre with its vast dome, stood neglected and forlorn. At the entrance a handful of Moslem soldiers played dice to pass the time. In order to enter the church, one had to pay them a stiff admission fee; the amount varying according to the fortunes of the game and the sentry's mood. By paying the fee one gained access to the Shrine but no assurance of remaining there unmolested. Whenever the infrequent Christians who had enough money to pay the tribute and enough courage to brave the risk, would remain too long at prayer before the ruined and ravaged Holy Sepulchre, the Moslem watchmen would noisily rush in, stamp their feet and threaten the worshipers—or even defile the Tomb under their very eyes. During the time when it was reported that Palestine would be handed over to the Franks, and the Moslems hastily departed from Jerusalem, the insolence of the watchmen was much subdued. They ceased to lock the door, no longer slept on the Stone of Anointment and even tried to win the good graces of the Christians. This respite, however, was short-lived, and the recent news of the defeat of the Franks had even increased their old contempt and hatred.

Terror stricken, Christians once more went into hiding, disappearing from the surface of Jerusalem's life in a desperate attempt not to attract attention. They had but one purpose, one concern: not to provoke new persecutions and massacres. Often weeks went by when no one knelt before the Holy Sepulchre and there was not a single taper to lift the gloom.

This was the state of things Francis and brother Illuminatus found upon their arrival at Jerusalem. The Sultan's firman which brother Illuminatus showed whenever the need arose opened all doors to them. It also opened the portals of the Shrine. From inside came a draft of

358

stifling, musty air. Their feet stumbled upon the broken, uneven floor. Not a trace remained of the innumerable gifts and offerings which once used to cover the Holy Sepulchre like a film of gold. Not a lamp, not a chandelier. The tombstones of the Jerusalem kings were battered and chipped. Of all the mementos only one remained—from the vault swung a dusty bunch of arrows which one of the Jerusalem patriarchs hung after the ruthless knights of the Joannites Order had shot them at priests on their way to church. This, the only trace that remained of the Franks, was proof of that fratricide which would not even stop at the Shrine's door.

The side chapels were piled high with rubble and litter. Broken fragments of monuments and statues lay in the way. But the rocky bed carved in solid stone upon which God's Body had rested and the stone which the angel had rolled aside on the Day of Resurrection had not been damaged. It was to these that the two pilgrims rushed with tears. They embraced the gray, rough stone with the same feeling with which a storm-tossed sailor might greet a blessed harbor. For was this not indeed the only secure and safe harbor, the final aim toward which man, whether aware of it or not, strains all through life?

They prayed for a long time, but not too long, for they must tend and clean the church. The sentry looked on in surprise but dared not interfere, assuming that these two dervishes must no doubt have the right to run the place since they were so bold about it. And so they carried out the rubbish and washed the filth-covered walls. Francis recalled how once he had restored the ruined church of St. Damian. "Could I have expected in those days," he said, "that Our Lord would bestow such grace upon me and let me sweep His Own Tomb? Oh, brother! How lucky we are!"

After putting everything in order as best as they could they went out and began to roam through the city in search of Christians. Except for the Lazarist brethren who did not hide at all, the task proved a difficult one. Many Christians preferred to pretend they were Moslems rather than own to their own faith. Francis shamed them for that faintheartedness and urged them to show more courage.

"If you will not avow Our Lord," he would say, "how can you expect Him to avow you? But if you stoutly put your courage in Him he will remember you in the days of tribulation. Just look at the Lazarist brethren, how fearlessly they fulfil their duties?"

"The Lazarists tend to the lepers," they would reply, "therefore they are always needed. And even so, just ask how many of them have been murdered? We have seen enough blood, enough tears. All we want now is to live in peace."

"Better no peace in life and eternal peace and happiness after death, than the other way around," Francis insisted, and little by little he brought people back to church. Many a Christian who was already wearing a turban now came once more to worship the Crucified openly.

Besides tending the Temple of the Sepulchre the two brothers spent long hours in prayer on the Mount of Olives, in the Refectory and the Church of the Holy Virgin's Sleep, and in Elizabeth's small house far up in the mountains where Mary had visited her. Thus wandering from place to place they trod everywhere; they went among the ruins of antique churches built by the Empress Helena and later destroyed by the Persians, as well as among those of the new, magnificent monumental temples which Baldwin I and his successors had built to last for ages and which the Moslems had destroyed. The ground was strewn with shattered statues, capitols and pillars; stone lay upon stone, merging into the rocky landscape which likewise seemed like a ruin, the ruin of the world. They looked upon the rubble, their hearts wrung with grief. For those ruined shrines were the product of a tremendous creative impulse and might. They had been erected by the pride of the conquerors who had come here from afar, had wandered for years across foreign, hostile lands and at the cost of superhuman sacrifices had at last achieved their goal; they had liberated the Holy Land, driven the Saracens away. In the rapture of their triumph they had thought themselves invincible, they were convinced no one could ever dispossess them again. Lavishly they built church upon church to bear witness to their armed power, to prove their unassailable claim. Not a hundred years had gone by and what remained of those men and their monuments? Nothing but ruins and a handful of debased Christians who hardly differed from the Egyptian Copts! So this was what rank upon rank of armored men at arms had achieved? Was that the end to which ardor, faith and incredible valor had served?

"Brother, Brother! How short-lived are all human endeavors," sighed Francis.

Nowhere, however, did they spend as much time or were they as happy and at ease as in Bethlehem. There was less destruction here, for the Basilica of the Nativity, founded by the pious Empress Helena, was the only church in Palestine which had not been destroyed by the Persians in the old days, nor recently by the Moslems. Chosroes had spared it because of the mosaics which adorned it. The homage of the Wise Men from the East and the magnificent robes of the Magi, scintillating with color and gold, were reproduced with such accuracy that they softened the heart of the wanton destroyer. Perhaps the same reason had checked the Moslems; anyhow the Basilica had escaped destruction. Only the huge Roman arch at its entrance had been walled up save for a low passage right above the ground, through which worshipers slipped in like foxes into their holes. This had been made by the Christians themselves in order to prevent the Saracens from bursting into the church on horseback and trampling the praying throngs, as they had so often done before.

Inside four rows of pillars of yellow marble divided the Basilica into five naves. Upon the pillars the Crusaders of the First Holy War had carved their signatures. Rushing into the Church with Tancred at their head they had cut them joyously, using their daggers for chisels and their steel gauntlets for hammers. Francis, enamored of the knightly legends, read the glorious names with admiration and awe and was deeply moved by the innumerable anonymous crosses—the signatures of those Crusaders who did not know the art of letters.

That was above the ground; the splendors of the mosaics, the long naves divided by pillars and the inscriptions. Underneath lay the grotto, the heart and reason of the Shrine's existence. A few worn stone steps led down to it. Small, semi-circular, partly a genuine cavern and partly carved out in the rock to serve as shelter for the herds, it had remained as it had been then. The Crusaders, with that sense of greatness so characteristic of them, did not change its simple, stern dignity. The stone trough for watering the herds, in which the Holy Virgin had laid the Child, stood as in olden times by the wall. Till lately, right above the trough, a small gold altar had stood, the one and only adornment of the grotto. From it, on Feast Days, the Patriarch was wont to read the Holy Mass. But as it was wrought of pure gold the Moslems took it away.

Now one might easily imagine that nothing had happened in the world since the day when shepherds ran here at night attracted by the light that radiated from the place. Never and nowhere had Francis felt the joy of living as deeply as he did here. When he lay prostrated upon the ground, when he pressed his head to the stone trough with the full realization that the Lord, centuries before, had lain in it as a feeble and mortal child, so that men, sinful and weak, might become God's children, he was overcome with such love and rapture that his soul felt as though it would burst asunder. He was beyond himself. Weeping, laughing, he repeated in anguish: "Enough, O Lord, enough! I can't stand more!" Then again he would burst forth with incoherent words, like the words of a song. Unborn hymns sprang from his lips, until at last the good brother Illuminatus would look at him in alarm and try to sober him, to call him back to reality and to his duties.

Of duties there were many. Though reluctant at first, the Christians of Jerusalem had let themselves be drawn by Francis' example and his heart-warming words. He had acquired among them not only friends but companions, as well as a new flock of Brothers Minor. They came mostly from among the members of the knightly order of Lazarite brothers, the only order which had stuck to its post in the Holy Land after the downfall of the kingdom of Jerusalem. In truth, it was nothing new for the Lazarites to live in constant peril of their lives. That most venerable and oldest of all the Palestine orders was founded at the time of Emperor Heraclius and had existed without interruption and carried on its good works ever since. Empires had collapsed but the Lazarite brothers as always continued to tend their sick. Political upheavals, days of glory or calamity did not affect the devotion with which they fulfilled their duties. In particular they tended those whom the world fears and despises, those whom God himself had marked for life—the lepers.

The loyal and heroic Lazarite brethren were ready more than anyone else to welcome and understand Francis, and so he had about him a group of friends who shared his thoughts and feelings; he had the Holy Sepulchre and Bethlehem and he was happy beyond words. Of course neither he nor his brothers could rebuild the ruined churches but at least they could preserve the ruins and keep them clean. They could keep a light burning in front of the Tomb and adorn the Holy Place with palm leaves; they could bring big, scented violets which grew on Mount Olivet or small pink anemones. The grim Moslem watchmen had grown used to have the gay little pauper and his friends around. They paid no more attention to them than one pays to twittering birds. Besides Francis was always so friendly, he so gladly relinquished to them whatever food he had begged for himself! The Sultan's firman sewed under the fold of brother Illuminatus' cloak had become frayed, faded, the seal was almost erased. No one could have recognized in it the precious and powerful sign of the Sultan's favor. And anyhow they did not need it. Much to Francis' satisfaction they had not shown it to anyone for a long time now.

And so Francis was happy and would gladly have remained in the Holy Land for the rest of his life. Admittedly God was present everywhere. Here, however, the Divine presence seemed more palpable, accessible, easier to understand. The fact that His feet had left marks upon the stones, that His voice had rung among those walls, that in the shadows of these trees He had feared and wept like a man, made Him more close, and if possible dearer than ever. And it often seemed to the praying Francis that Bethlehem and Golgotha, the stone trough and the wooden cross, were two pillars of the firmament, two pivots upon which rested the meaning of the whole universe. The beginning and the end of everything.

That was how matters stood with Francis when one day he was astonished to see before him in Arab garb John a Capello, the Sultan's slave with whom he had parted at the gates of Damietta. Francis, who had often thought of him with great tenderness, was overcome with joy.

"Little brother!" he shouted, stretching both his hands toward him.

John smiled. He remembered how in the course of that agonizing struggle he had imagined that Francis would greet him precisely thus. Only what would have seemed unbearable had he come as a culprit, now became the source of sweet joy.

"I put this on to deceive the sentries," he said, taking off the turban. "I speak Arabic so fluently no one would question me. I am no longer a slave, either. I am free. The Sultan turned all of us free when he released the troops trapped in the Delta."

"God bless that good Sultan! How did it happen? Do tell me!"

"It happened because of you, Francis. It is to you and no one else we owe our freedom. The Sultan told the King of Jerusalem—and mind you many people heard him—that he would release the troops and us on account of the only Christian he had ever met. It could be only you. . . ."

"I?" exclaimed Francis and guffawed with laughter, "I? Come, brother, don't make fun of me. I would be truly sorry for the Sultan if he had not beheld a better Christian. No, no, he must have met some saintly hermit. That convinced him. What luck! How kind is Our Lord! But how did it happen, little brother, that you did not go back home?"

"I wanted to see you first," John a Capello replied. "I knew you were in Jerusalem so I went to Acre and waited there. At first I was a little afraid of coming here alone, it was like going back into the lion's jaws. Surely he won't stay there forever, I thought, and on his way back he must pass through Acre. I would probably be still waiting there to this day, were it not that brother Pietro arrived from Italy to fetch you. So I took my courage in both hands and here I am."

"Brother Pietro came to fetch me? Why? What has happened?"

"He would not tell me. He said he would tell you alone. He did not trust me, and no wonder. He knows I ran away from you; he even saw me once with that devil of Nicholas and the Venetians. So he only begged and implored me to bring you to Acre soon, for whatever he had to say was important, most important. . . ."

"I shall start at once," said Francis with a sigh. "I was so happy here, at the feet of Our Lord. I forgot about those others, my most beloved brethren. . . . Shame on me! Whatever could have happened? I must go. . . ."

The very same day he made ready to depart. With tears in his eyes he took leave of brother Illuminatus and his companions. "You shall remain, my little brothers," he said. "And probably I shall never come to you again for this is a far journey indeed. It is with a heavy heart I part with you but I must go back to those other dear friends of mine. . . . And so remain in peace, may God be with you, and be sure to guard the Holy Sepulchre. . . . I appoint you the Watch of the Holy Land. I pray and command you, let nothing ever deter you from this watch. You must go on living here, even as you do now, unarmed . . . No one will guard or protect you save God. On Him alone you must rely. Never strive for any other protection. And you must nurture the same goodwill and charity toward all, be they Christians or heathens, be they Arabs or Turks, good or bad. Serve and help every one of them. And should anyone want to defile the Holy Sepulchre beg him not to do it, for the love of Christ. And should he ignore your pleas, lie down beside the Tomb and say: 'Kill us; destroy our flesh; but we implore you do not touch Our Lord!' And I am sure that if you only act this way

Our Lord will spare you and your watch by His side will last as long as it pleases Him to preserve His Sepulchre upon the earth. I am quite certain of it. And as your superior and my deputy I appoint this brother John who has just arrived. . . ."

"Me?" exclaimed the ex-slave, horrified. "Not me! I am going back with you!"

"Brother," replied Francis, giving him a tender smile, "brother, whom can I appoint but you? You are the most precious for you are tried and true. Whom can I trust more than you, who has won such a glorious victory over your own self?"

"But I wanted to go back to our own land!"

"Is this not our most beloved land? You must stay and direct the brothers. You know the language, you will teach it to the rest and you will all be able to tell the people of Our Lord and His kindness. When they hear of it and see your good deeds they will be converted, I am sure. You will win souls for Heaven. Just think, brother, how wonderfully the Lord has arranged it all. And now let us kneel and for the last time pray together. . . Our Father. . . ."

Although Francis was impatient to hear why he was being summoned home, he discovered on his arrival at Acre that he would have to be patient. Pietro Cani had gone out to observe the town and was not to be found anywhere; he would not be back till the next morning. Francis rested by the roadside. Willfried, who happened to pass, saw him and recognized him. It was through him that de Brienne learned the news when late that night he returned from a ride.

"Does Your Majesty remember that brother in Egypt who went to see the Sultan and then went to Jerusalem? He is here. . . ."

"Francis of Assisi? Bring him here at once . . ."

"Maybe tomorrow, Sire. It's late . . ."

"Tonight I said."

Willfried ran in search of Francis while de Brienne slowly dragged himself to his chamber. He felt dead tired, not so much because of his laborious day, as at prospect of the night, which he knew would be as most of his nights had been—long and sleepless. On the surface life went on pretty much as it had in the first years of his reign. As of old he ruled a strip of the shore, no larger than a half of the Count of Champagne's domains and pompously called the Kingdom of Jerusalem. He ruled the strip with wisdom, honesty and sagacity. On the part of the Barons and the Masters of the Knightly Orders he did not encounter the obstacles with which his predecessors had had to struggle. He was held in general esteem and respect. His child, the little Princess Isabelle fared well. On the surface nothing had changed for the worse in the last few years. Nothing that would account for the growing melancholy of the King.

State affairs took up most of his day. In the evening he would mount his horse and ride off, by himself. He could not bear anybody's company on those trips and he would not come back till nightfall. The older knights, displeased by this habit, often reminded him of the danger to which he was exposing himself and the State by thus risking an ambush. He would only smile at these remonstrances and assure them that death mowed down only those who were afraid of it.

Tonight he had returned from Mount Carmel, a frequent goal of these solitary expeditions. From its summit one could see all of Galilee with Mount Tabor. Below upon the rocky spur rose Gerard d'Avesnes' foundation, the Pilgrim's Castle. The memory of the moments he had spent there with Blanche were oddly associated with the grim silhouette of the fort erected to win mercy for a woman who had committed suicide. "What shall I build to save you, my poor love?" thought de Brienne, riding slowly along the walls. When such musings seized him there was no use even to think of sleep on his return. He would go to bed to get rid of Willfried and his valets, but as soon as they had fallen asleep in the adjoining chamber he would rise and begin to pace the floor. He paced it incessantly, to and fro, as though driven by some invisible force. Sometimes he would stop in front of the window and gaze at the roofs shining below in the moonlight. Thus he had stood once, seeking with his eyes the roof of the hospitium in which Blanche had stopped on her arrival. The window was low, the sill barely reached to his knees. One of the Jerusalem kings, Henry of Champagne, had fallen out of a similar window and killed himself on the flagstones of the yard below. "I always wondered," thought de Brienne, "how a knight could lose his balance and come to such a miserable fall, and yet I've fallen from an even greater height . . ." He resumed his pacing and stood thus for hours. He trod noiselessly so as not to attract the servants' attention, but the traces of those nightly wanderings began with time to show on the worn carpet. The even path which ran through it gave Willfried the idea that the King must be going on a pilgrimage in his way. Probably to Jerusalem . . . That manner of fulfilling a pilgrimage vow was indeed often used. . . . "It is not far to Jerusalem from here. He would have gotten there long since. Why is he still walking and walking? He must have vowed to go to Rome!"

When Francis entered with that serene smile of his, de Brienne's first impression was that he had not changed at all. He was always the same. Slight, grey and joyous. The realization gave the King a jolt. The last few years had brought so many changes and bitter blows; he himself had changed so completely, that unconsciously he had come to believe that time could not have left anyone unaffected. Deep in his heart he felt a shadow of a ridiculous grudge. For a while they looked at each other in silence.

"You are coming from Jerusalem, brother," said de Brienne at last. "Tell me what did you see there? In what condition is the Holy Sepulchre?"

"The Tomb of Our Lord is intact, only the basilica over it has been ruined. All the churches in the Holy Land have been destroyed, and just to look at these ruins wrings your heart. Not a single one remains, save the Shrine of the Nativity in Bethlehem."

De Brienne sighed heavily and began to pace the chamber. "I don't know why," he confessed, "in the old days those things did not affect me so much as now. . . . I lived here and ruled, yet somehow I accepted the fact that the Holy Land belonged to the Moslems. I had other cares. Now, I am bowed down by the thought of it. It wrings my heart to think that the holy places remain neglected and ill-fated."

"Not completely neglected," Francis exclaimed, "for I left a goodly garrison which will neither fail nor surrender!"

"You left what?" asked de Brienne, thinking he had not heard right.

"A garrison . . . A handful of Brothers Minor who joined me there. At present there are but ten of them, but God willing, their number will increase by and by. It is they who will guard and protect the Holy Sepulchre."

De Brienne shrugged his shoulders indulgently.

"Much they would accomplish, those brethren of yours! The Moslems will disperse them to the wind!"

"They will not," Francis said with conviction. "They will stay. Do not worry over the Holy Sepulchre, Sire. It is not deserted, Oh, no!"

"But you said yourself the temple over it is sacked and ruined."

"Our Lord cares nothing for splendor, only for human love. The Brothers Minor will love Him as much as they can. Their prayers will replace the dome."

"I still can't believe they will hold out," sighed de Brienne.

"They will hold out for no one will wish them ill. Only a weapon challenges a weapon, and might challenges might, while that which cares not for worldly protection is the safest and lasts the longest. . . ."

"You have an answer to everything," remarked de Brienne. "Maybe you could explain to me some things that trouble me sorely . . . Life is not easy for me. . . . I live in torment."

"The first time I saw you, Sire, you were in sore torment, too. . . ."

"The first time?" de Brienne mused. "Where was that? Oh yes, I remember, I saw you swinging on a board . . ."

"That was not the first time. To be sure I remember that swinging, too. I behaved most unseemly then and was ashamed of it for a long time afterwards. But we had met before. You, Sire, could not see me, but I marked you well. It was in a hostelry, near Rome. You were on your way to the Holy Father to obtain the Jerusalem crown, and I and my companions were also going our way to the Holy Father to get His approval of our Rule . . ."

De Brienne rubbed his forehead. Vaguely he remembered the torment of those days. He was going against his will, forced, rebellious, repeating at each step his childish "I don't want" and yet continuing his way. Gradually, he recalled the night spent at the inn, the smell of sheep cheese and herbs, the windows open to the dark blue chill of the night, a group of men around a fire below. He remembered now how annoyed he was by the laughter and loud conversation of the louts. An abyss separated him from those people. He, the knight, tomorrow a King and they, the lowly rabble. And today he looked with something akin to humility at the lout he had then resented so; looked to him for help and consolation. In what lay the secret of the serenity and clearness of that strange man? It seemed to de Brienne that if he only could gain possession of it he would understand the real meaning of life. That meaning revealed itself to him at times, appeared for a second, only to vanish again. Indeed, he had realized the necessity of law, that stern law of which he had spoken to Blanche in their last conversation, but why this law should be joyous and blessed, he knew not.

"I saw you through the window," Francis went on. "You walked about vehemently, throwing your head and arms about. I thought then, 'How this knight suffers! How I'd like to help him.'"

"Then help me now. I suffer far more today than I did then. I am not an evil man nor a murderer at heart, yet so many crimes weigh upon my conscience that the thought fills me with terror. The last is the worst; a certain woman, whom I brought to sin, died by her own hand . . . I told her we had no right to go on sinning and she rebelled and cried: 'Why not? We are free!' I could not explain to her why, and . . . I did not save her!"

"The thing to do was to show her love and indulgence as one does to a child, for only a child would not see why. Only a child will say: 'I prefer to crawl rather than to walk, for it is very hard to learn to stand upright.' If an ox puts its head into the yoke it will plow the soil which in turn will bear grain. But if the ox were to roam as it pleases the field would lie waste and would not bear its crop. Our Lord has created us to achieve great and glorious things, but we cannot achieve them without effort."

"When one listens to you, everything seems too simple," smiled de Brienne. "Yet in reality this eternal constraint under which we live breaks a man."

"Why break, Sire? It releases him."

"Releases him? . . . I don't know . . . I must consider. . . . It is getting late . . . You are surely tired, brother. . . . Time you had some rest . . . But promise me you will not leave before you see me once more . . . I would like to continue this conversation and ask you . . . ask you. . . ."

"I will come, indeed," promised Francis. "May Our Lord's peace be with you, Sire."

After he left, de Brienne stood for a long while motionless. And suddenly he felt that his restless, desperate pacing had brought him to his goal; that he had arrived. The goal was here . . . right here . . . where but a moment ago Francis had stood.

Pietro Cani wept for joy. Almost at once he took Francis to a secluded corner of the courtyard where they could talk freely. "I came for you," whispered Pietro, "because . . ."

"Why do you whisper?" laughed Francis, "surely we are not conniving at treason?"

"That's true," admitted Pietro. "It's from habit, I guess. We are not used any more to speak openly and loudly. So, as I was about to tell you, I came here sent by the brethren Angel, Leo, Bernard, Juniper and the rest of our old crowd."

"And by brother Elias, surely?"

"Oh no! Brother Elias does not know at all I am here. He thinks I went to France as he ordered me to."

Francis' eyes opened wide with astonishment. "How could you do such things, little brother? Why, it's dishonest! Against all the commands!"

"What else could I do?" sighed Cani. "Brother Elias would surely not let me go and you would continue to know nothing . . ."

"He would not let you? Why?"

"He prefers that you remain far away until . . . until . . . Oh, Francis! What luck I found you! Don't be surprised, I can't tell you everything at once . . . There is such a lot of it. . . . By and by I'll tell you everything . . . Things have changed a lot with us . . . We, the old ones, get together and weep and pray God that you may return . . . before it is too late . . ."

"But what has happened, brother? Speak plainly! I don't understand anything! What became of the Order? Have you been deprived of the right to preach?"

"Oh, no! On the contrary! We have every sort of right and privilege and support. The Order has grown a lot . . . There are more than three thousand of us now . . . Three thousand, Francis! Our brethren have gone out to every country . . ."

"Are there any in Poland?" Francis interrupted.

"In Poland?" repeated Pietro surprised. "I don't know . . . I think not . . . Why do you ask about Poland?"

"I've heard about it from a certain knight. . . . If there are no brothers of ours there, I shall send some as soon as I get back . . . Go on . . . So there are so many of you . . . Why, that's wonderful!"

"We are a very powerful Order," Pietro continued, "and all other congregations envy us. We have a school where our novices are taught, and soon we will have an academy in Bologna. Brother Pietro Stacia organized it . . . We also have four beautiful stone monasteries . . ."

Francis leaped to his feet. "What? An academy? Monasteries? Are you jesting, brother?"

"I am not jesting at all. It's true!"

"But that's not allowed! It is against the Rule!"

"For the time being there is no Rule. It got lost . . ."

Francis turned pale. His eyes flashed. "Lost? Our Rule? Brother Leo, my lamb to whom I entrusted the Rule? Lost it?"

"Oh, no! Brother Leo would never lose the Rule. It's a long time since it was in his care. Brother Elias took it away. And then he told us it got lost. Now they are preparing a new rule, somewhat different. So you see, Francis, wasn't I right to come, even though by stealth? You must return to us before they compose the new Rule and obtain the Holy Father's approval . . ."

Francis burst into tears. "Our Rule! Signed by the Holy Father Innocent! Our beloved little Rule based on the words of Our Lord! They lost it! They lost it!" He wiped his eyes and with a sudden flash of anger turned on Pietro. "Surely, every single one of you must have remembered its words! Why didn't you go to brother Elias and kneel before him and recite it altogether and beg him to write it down word by word?"

"And wouldn't he have welcomed us, though! You seem to think, Francis, that things are still as they used to be in your times. Brother Elias is stern. A great mind he surely is. The Holy Father himself often asks his advice, but he is stern. Brothers fear him. Fear and obey. I tell you they obey him more than you. . . . Sometimes he is even too stern. . . . He will not let anyone join our Order. First you must pass a test and prove you've led an honest life. . . . A while ago a heretic came to us, a Catharus, who once, it seems, talked with you. He said that ever since that conversation he felt uneasy with himself and something was driving him, driving so hard, he had to come. . . . Brother Elias would not take him . . . 'We need no unclean men, here,' he said. 'Who has once defiled his soul with heresy, will find no room among us . . .'"

Francis hid his face in his hands. Tears dribbled through his fingers.

"How dreadful!" he stammered out. "It's all just the opposite of . . ! My poor heretic! Perhaps I'll be able to find him again. . . ."

"Brother Rufin and brother Gilles have completely withdrawn from the world. They live in hermitages. They have achieved great saintliness. Often we fain would follow their example but we remember how you always urged us not to think of our own salvation alone and not to draw away from the people. So we just knock about in the midst of the new Order. At times we gather in the home of Madonna Giacobbe di Settesoli, the wife of Sir Graciani Frangipani. Remember? You used to call her brother Giacobbe. She is very much devoted to you and always remembers what you said and urges us to do as you taught us. . . . Whenever we are there we talk all the time about you . . ."

"And brother Juniper? My beloved brother Juniper?"

"Brother Elias does not call him his beloved. He dislikes him. Do you want me to tell you what happened to brother Juniper lately? In Viterbo some brigand or thief who was to be hanged broke lose and hid, and the Castellane's men searched for him everywhere. Just then they came upon brother Juniper who by his looks reminded them of the man. So they tied him with ropes and brought him before the judge. The judge asked: 'Did you do so and so?' And Juniper said: 'Not that I remember, but I am quite capable of doing even worse things than that.' So they convicted him and led him to the gallows. He said nothing. A crowd gathered as it always does at an execution, and some recognized him. There was a great outcry. 'Brother Juniper!' they yelled. 'They want to hang brother Juniper! Brother Juniper!' The judges got worried. 'Are you brother Juniper?' they asked. 'I am.' The Castellane got very angry. 'A minute longer and you would hang! Why didn't you talk up?' So Juniper said: 'Messire Castellane! I deserve punishment for I constantly offend Our Lord. And had you hanged me that poor wretch who probably fears death more than I do would have been spared. And I beg and implore you, Messire Castellane, either pardon him or hang me!' And so they pardoned. . . ."

"My beloved brother Juniper!" exclaimed Francis through his tears.

"He is always like that. Never minds anything. During the last feasts the sexton told him to watch the altar of our new church in Assisi. A rich altar it is . . . has silver bells all around! Beautiful bells. So brother Juniper knelt in prayer, when all at once some poor woman came to him and asked for alms. He had nothing to give so he took one of those silver bells and gave it to her. She went away. Well, the sexton returned and began to scream. He ran to brother Elias himself to complain. In came brother Elias and all the superiors, and all of them fell upon Juniper: 'How did he dare? And who does he think he is? And it was God's property and for God's glory . . .' So Juniper said: 'That woman was in sore need of them, and here they were of no use except for magnificence and vainglory.' My! How brother Elias upbraided him then!"

"He upbraided him! He upbraided him because he did as he should have done! O God! Merciful God! I had expected anything but not that. . . . And our guardians, Cardinal Colonna and Cardinal Ugolino. . . . Why didn't you turn to them for help?"

"Cardinal Colonna is ailing and Cardinal Ugolino we went to see several times. He comforted us and soothed us but frankly did not help at all. He explained that this was—how did he put it? Oh, yes, that this was the normal course of life. That it was one thing when there were only twelve of us, personally chosen by you, and another when there are three thousand. . . . That they, the Cardinals, knew from the very first that the original Rule could not be maintained because of human frailty . . . That a big crowd like the present one consists of all sorts of men who must be held by discipline and order. . . . And that education was necessary. And that even with a monastery and books one could live in your way, according to the Gospel. . . ."

"No, no, one can't! Even if you own the smallest thing, you are tied down and cannot freely follow Our Lord."

"That's what we told him, but he would not have it. He gave us such mighty reasons . . . There was no way to refute them. At least we couldn't. You might. Still, sometimes it seems even to me, that in some way he was right. Oh, Francis, don't cry so! You see, it was altogether different when you had but twelve of us, and we wandered about together, slept together, prayed together and knew each other like one family. . . . And you were always with us. It is not the same! Then and now. Just think, three thousand . . . ! Why, there is hardly anyone you know in such a crowd. . . . Maybe what I say is stupid, for I am an ignorant man. Surely I would not dare to open my mouth in front of our present superiors, but with you it's different. But I well remember what the Cardinal said; that when a work grows to be very big it cannot retain the first ardor it had at the beginning. . . . But that the reflection of that initial glow remains and that our Order, although not quite the same as you had imagined, is still quite different from all other Orders and will accomplish a lot of good. . . . We wept with grief at these words and told him we wanted everything to remain just as it was, but the Cardinal said: 'A river cannot stand still nor flow upstream.' . . . After that conversation we told ourselves: 'Perhaps Francis can still help,' and so I came. . . ."

Francis did not say anything and continued to weep. He was shaken, almost broken. In his naïve confidence he had believed that the brethren would continue without him just as though he were around. He had thought that it was enough to set people on the right path to make them follow it. He was so certain of his work, so confident and serene. And here he was learning that not only was everything going on contrary to his principles, not only his Rule, his beloved Rule had been lost, but that a man as wise, kind and sincerely devoted as Cardinal Ugolino called those changes the natural course of events! This was the calamity to Francis; that he accepted them calmly and consoled the brethren that it could not be otherwise.

Then he, Francis, was nothing but a dreamer and his work not fit to survive? So people could not live strictly according to the teaching of the Gospel? In his pride and vanity he had thought that he was preaching what God wanted, that out of the Brothers Minor he would create an army which would change the world. All that was but a delusion, and maybe even a sinful one?

Nothing remained of his beautiful dreams.

Never before had he given in to sorrow, which he considered a sin and a "Babylonian" disease. This time, however, grief overcame him and he wept as though nothing could ever console him. He did not want even to return with Pietro. What for? The Lord had turned away from him. Why should he look upon his work, twisted, warped, when he could not restore it anyway?

Sobs shook his thin shoulder blades. Pietro Cani did not say anything, just looked at him with compassion. Suddenly Francis lifted his head.

"And sister Clara?" he inquired. "Has she likewise. . . ."

"Indeed, no! With the sisters everything is as it used to be. Sister Clara has not lost her Rule and will not relinquish it even by as much as a hair. 'Francis wanted it so,' she says, and nothing can change her mind. The Holy Father wanted to give the sisters a bulla which would provide them with some means of subsistence, and threaten with anathema anyone who would harm them or rob them of anything. She refused. Through Bishop Guido she implored the Holy Father to abandon his plan. But the Bishop too was of the opinion that the bulla was necessary, that the saintly maidens could not live like birds, exposed to every evil. So Clara set out for Rome in person. And she came to the Holy Father and fell at his feet and implored him with tears to allow the sisters to live according to the first Rule. And she told him she would not rise till he granted her this favor. So the Holy Father said: 'My daughter, no one has ever begged me for wealth and honors as you beg for poverty and want. Be it as you wish . . .' And he gave her the privilege of Absolute Poverty. And she returned carrying this privilege, jubilant. She, always so grave, laughed all the way, it seems. . . ."

Francis sat up, wiped his eyes and stared avidly at the speaker. "I knew sister Clara would not fail . . ." he whispered.

"Fail? Not sister Clara! It's so pleasant among them. . . . Everyone in the neighborhood blesses the sisters, for they come to everyone's help. What do they need a bulla for? No one will harm them! Their number has grown too . . . And all worship sister Clara and say she is a saint . . . And she has under her window a little plot which she calls her garden. She plants there three kinds of flowers: lilies, roses and violets. And how they bloom! As though angels tended them. There are nowhere such flowers as in sister Clara's garden. The Bishop asked her once why didn't she ever plant any others but those three? And do you know what she told him? That lilies were the Holy Virgin, and roses the love of Jesus Christ and violets were you, Francis, . . . And that she did not want any other flowers . . ."

"Did she really say so?"

"Truly she did. And those violets smell so good, people stop when they go by to take a whiff of them . . ."

Tears once more welled up in Francis' eyes but now they were tears of joy. So something of his work had remained in its original form! The holy and joyous poverty, the keystone of his life work, had still survived! Suddenly he felt comforted as though the breeze had brought a whiff of the violets of which brother Pietro had just told him. He felt deeply ashamed of his recent despair. He had blasphemed by thinking that Our Lord had turned away from him. How miserable and ungrateful he was! How far from sister Clara's strength and steadfastness. . . .

He smiled through his tears at Pietro Cani. In a voice that was once more brisk and joyous he called: "Then let us go back, brother! God willing, not all of our sowing is lost!"